Rome in the Fourth Century A.D.

*For Alden and Agnes Rollins
Parents and Friends*

Rome in the Fourth Century A.D.

An Annotated Bibliography with Historical Overview

by
Alden Rollins

McFarland & Company, Inc., Publishers
Jefferson, North Carolina, and London

British Library Cataloguing-in-Publication data are available

Library of Congress Cataloguing-in-Publication Data

Rollins, Alden M., 1946–
    Rome in the fourth century A.D. : an annotated bibliography with historical overview / by Alden Rollins.
    p. cm.
    Includes index.
    ISBN 0-89950-624-0 (lib. bdg. : 50# alk. paper) ∞
    1. Rome–History–Empire, 284-476–Bibliography. I. Title.
II. Title: Rome in the 4th century A.D.
Z2340.R653   1991
[DG311]
016.937'06–dc20   91-52762
                                                                        CIP

©1991 Alden M. Rollins. All rights reserved

Manufactured in the United States of America

McFarland & Company, Inc., Publishers
  Box 611, Jefferson, North Carolina 28640

Table of Contents

Preface	vii
Introduction	xi
I. General and Miscellaneous Works	1
II. Politics and Government	18
III. Military Matters	75
IV. Literature and Education	92
V. Monetary Matters	133
VI. Economy, Technology, Science, and Medicine	139
VII. Society and Art	151
VIII. Foreign Affairs and Barbarians	181
IX. Religion and Philosophy	194
X. Christianity	225
XI. Church and State	280
Appendix I. Final Entries	303
Index	311

Preface

Organizers of history have never agreed on what to call the fourth century Roman empire. Its transitional and diverse nature makes it a suitable candidate for at least four traditional identities: ancient, medieval, Byzantine, and early Christian history. Until recently the fourth century was seldom considered a territory of its own. Consequently it is a task of major proportions for the student to find and sample the full spectrum of the rich and rewarding literature that is available.

My hope is that this bibliography will ease the burden of research and suggest the possibilities for more investigation. This work encompasses twentieth century literature in English through 1988, and includes articles, books, dissertations, conference papers, a few novels, and an appendix of material identified in 1989 and 1990. Of course there is and will be much more in a field of study that is at last coming into its own. Computerized systems can be helpful in reaching the literature: an example is the *Arts and Humanities Citation Index*. But there is no substitute yet for browsing such traditional sources of new knowledge as *l'Annee Philologique, Byzantinische Zeitschrift*, and the American Historical Association's *Recently Published Articles*.

The following points may help in the appreciation of the boundaries of the present effort:

1. Those who can work in foreign languages will be unhappy with the English language limitation. But all is not lost. The literature included here references the important European studies in footnotes and bibliographies. The average American student with an interest in the Roman empire can feel safe using the material in English, in which language some of the very best research on later Rome is now being written.

2. As a general principle I have not given preference to literature whose purpose was overwhelmingly to use the fourth century as a vehicle to explain the disasters of the fifth. It would be perverse to suggest that the fourth century was, in modern parlance, a positive experience for everyone who lived through it. On the other hand, by the standards of the ancient world, it was not an unsuccessful period all around, and it is too limiting to see it as a disaster waiting to happen. Fortunately, most scholars of the period now accept this point of view.

3. The annotations are idiosyncratic, and are slanted towards emphasizing that aspect of the piece under consideration which relates to the fourth century. The remarks often presuppose a working knowledge of the fourth century. A person new to the period may find it helpful to have at hand the *Oxford Classical Dictionary,* 2nd ed. (1970), or a similar reference book. Generally, but not dogmatically, there are more substantive remarks for the periodical literature than for the books. Usually for books there are scholarly reviews available, written by people more prepared to give appropriate analysis and professional judgment, and I have appended the English language review citations as often as possible. Where I have read the review, I have indicated by a (+) or a (-) whether it was generally favorable or unfavorable. Occasionally there is a (++-) or a (--+), indicating the slant of the review while noting that there were positive or negative remarks of importance. For lack of access a few items remain without annotations. If they seemed relevant I included them anyway.

4. This was not an exercise in collecting primary source material in translation. Some things have been included that have interesting commentary on the fourth century. The student will find most needs for primary sources satisfied through such well known collections as the *Loeb Classics* or the *Nicene and Post Nicene Fathers of the Christian Church.* Also, Bruce MacBain has compiled a most helpful annotated bibliography of source material for late antiquity in English translation; it covers the translated literature through 1980. Please see (535) under "Literature and Education."

5. Every age has its borderland, its gray area separating it from a different age, its individuals and institutions which have one foot firmly planted in one period and the other planted firmly in another. Without being narrow about dates I have tried to gather in the literature covering from the time of Diocletian (284-305) to the death of Theodosius I in 395. Endings are more difficult than beginnings. It is certainly easy to dither over the end of the fourth century, the end, really, of a united Roman empire whose character was undergoing a dramatic change but which was still strongly related to the Rome and the Roman world of the first century. The year 395 seems good as a symbolic moment. In that year Theodosius I died and Augustine became a priest of the Christian church: secular and religious events of significance in dividing one era from another. But I have included some literature that goes slightly beyond 395 when it seemed relevant. Individuals whose lives considerably overlapped both the fourth and fifth centuries were taken case by case. If their formative experiences were in the fourth century, they were included. Augustine is an interesting case, and the literature is overwhelming. The Augustine we remember is the great fifth century bishop and theologian. But there was a very different and equally interesting fourth century Augustine, the young and ambitious provincial, seeking his fortune at the great imperial centers of power, Rome and Milan, watching for patrons to give him preference for good jobs, sniffing and tasting the exciting religious brews of the late fourth century before the world was conclusively Christian or the Roman state clearly in peril. This is the Augustine emphasized here.

6. Christianity became a large feature of this bibliography. This was not at first my intention, but it became quickly evident that to scale it down would be untrue to the overwhelming fact that Christianity was becoming a central feature of the Roman experience, even for those conservative contemporaries who pretended that it did not exist. Gibbon had it right in seeing the triumph of a rather fanatical brand of Christianity as the biggest story of the time, and so the large section given the movement overall seems appropriate here.

7. The introductory essay is an impression of an age. Naturally one tries to get things right, but especially to the

ancient world the words of Henry Ward Beecher apply: "No man will ever succeed in so reproducing an age long past that it shall seem to the beholder as it did to those who lived in it." (*Life of Jesus, the Christ,* pt.1 [N.Y., 1872],134). Some events and dates cited as factual may be under dispute in scholarly footnotes. The fourth century is better documented than most of the ancient world, but the gaps are very frustrating for the modern historian who wants certainty in his facts and a kind of scientific proof of his theories. There is much that modern techniques can and will do to focus our picture of ancient times; but in the end we may have to be happy with general impressions, distant echoes, and beautiful mosaics shimmering and tantalizing on the edge of the historian's universe of inquiry.

I should like to extend a general thanks to the people of the following institutions who made this effort possible: the University of Alaska Anchorage, the UAA Library, the State of Alaska's generous interlibrary loan system, and the libraries at the University of Hawaii, the University of California Berkeley, and San Diego State University. My special thanks to Alden Rollins Sr. and Dr. William Jacobs who did such careful and constructuve proofreading.

A. Rollins
Anchorage, Alaska
12 July 1990

Introduction: Roma Perpetua

The fourth century . . . The Roman government . . . The military . . . The economy . . . Religion . . . Barbarism . . . Summary

The Roman empire was perpetually rising and falling. This was true not only in the actual world of events but in the minds of men as well. Historians who find it rising will find the proofs of their thesis, as will those who find it falling. So did contemporaries. Proofs are less scarce than perspective.

The fourth century Roman empire needs to be liberated from its future. In the fifth century, the central government suffered political and military reverses of a magnitude sufficient to become known as the fall of the Roman empire, an accurate expression in reference to the western provinces anyway. These events threw all the peoples of Europe into turmoil and cast two long shadows: one into the future where the effects were real and unpleasant, and the other into the past, which became a quarry for historians and others seeking causes of the collapse.

Historians from the fifth century to our time brought the fourth century under severe scrutiny as the main source for later disasters. With this attitude it became easy to conclude that the period from Diocletian to Theodosius I was bad all around. Nor were earlier centuries immune from this narrow scrutiny: one eminent 20th century historian saw the collapse of Rome prefigured in classical Athens. But the fourth century emerged as the most popular villain. Once this was settled it only remained to sort out all the malevolence and determine the direct and the indirect, the immediate and the profound causes, of later tragedy. Sometimes a discriminating researcher would allow good features of the age to emerge, as would apologists for obvious successes like Christianity. But a more common attitude was blanket condemnation, the finding of darkness, oppression, and misery everywhere: a system moving swiftly to its inevitable and deservedly ignominious end.

The recent emergence of the fourth century from this unhappy fate is one of the most remarkable transformations in historical studies. Rescued from characterizations as the degenerate end of the ancient world, the inauspicious start of the dark ages, or of the stultifying Byzantine period, the period from AD 284 to 395 now can be studied individually, on its own terms, accepted as an interesting feature of the historical landscape, worthy of sensitive and serious treatment, even of appreciation.

The old facts do not go away. They are modified by new ones, and transformed by a more probing and receptive attitude towards their context. New impressions, even new sympathies, emerge. The new thinking may one day merge into a grand new synthesis on the scale of a Gibbon, but for now readers and researchers will be busy working with new building blocks and sweeping away old intellectual debris. In any event, certain fundamental subjects of inquiry remain as fixed as the Colosseum, and to some of these we now turn as organizational points for the new thinking.

* * *

For any great state there are essentials that must exist at some level of good health for survival: a central government that has a sense of direction and the will to enforce it, a persistent military presence in the geopolitical theater, and a functioning economy to sustain the expenses of governing. Beyond these there are less tangible features which may all the same be decisive. There are general attitudes and moral commitments about life and its meaning, which for the later empire may conveniently be filed under religion; then there is another phenomenon of great frustration to modern historians but which the ancients accepted as a natural part of the landscape of life: *fortuna*. We may call it luck: strange, unexpected interventions that often made all the difference, for good or bad.

Introduction

The Roman state was at all times both splendid and degenerate, good and bad, powerful and weak, dignified and barbaric, humanitarian and criminal. At any period of Roman history both the best and the worst of mankind were on display in the government; in the imperial period both were often on display in the same emperor. Governments, however, rarely survive or fail solely on the basis of goodness or badness, and this was certainly so in the Roman experience. In the end, it came down to a question of whether the central government had enough power of certain kinds to enforce its will when challenged on its fundamental interests, and for the fourth century the answer was yes.

The Roman government was often corrupt, inefficient, muddled, extravagant, wasteful, ineffective, unpredictable, and brutal. It was all of these things even by the standards of the time, and its many failings were often noted. But these unpleasant features were commonplace in the ancient world, and not unknown in our own, even among successful governments. It is necessary to keep them in perspective, remembering that a government's many failings are not always or even regularly the same as government failure. This point emerges most vividly in the person of the ruler.

The Roman government was usually dictatorial in character, or at best authoritarian, from the time of Augustus if not earlier. This was so despite the polite fictions, often given a semblance of reality, of constitutional restraint; and the many de facto freedoms of the Roman population resulted more from government weakness than intent. Therefore the character of the ruler counted for much, and in this sense the ancient habit of dividing good times and bad times by rulers, rather than more abstract criteria such as economic conditions, was appropriate and accurate.

What was the character of fourth century rulers? In general they were a vigorous lot, filled with a sense of mission that carried them beyond personal ambition or self-indulgence. Their courts were opulent, at least when they were settled in their capital cities, which was in fact rare; but there was always a kind of military restraint and discipline that kept personal indulgence in check. The family lives of the rulers were quiet and conventional, with a few explosive exceptions.

By comparison the Caesars of the first century lived in sinks of iniquity.

Personal flaws could spill over into government. Some emperors had bad tempers, or bad health, thus paving the way for acts of cruelty or blind reckless indulgence of power at the expense of innocent people, sometimes later regretted, sometimes not. Valentinian I fed his victims to his two pet bears; Theodosius I, when in bad humor, gave orders that shocked even hardened contemporaries. More often acts of cruelty were political moves and though lamented were often understood as policy and explained away as such. An example is Constantius II's complicity in the murder of his father's brothers in 337. Diocletian reportedly eliminated his imperial predecessor with his own hands. In these matters, Christian and pagan emperors were of a piece.

But mostly the emperors were men of business, concerned to keep the empire theirs and Roman. Their origins were well removed from the sophisticated and cynical thoughts of the old city of Rome: largely they were provincials and their belief in the eternal destiny of the empire was simple and sincere. They were all Roman patriots, and had no intention of presiding over the decline and fall of the Roman world. Although for the most part products of a military environment, the emperors did not have it in mind to be oppressive. Many did not forget their humble origins and were rather more sensitive to the needs of the poor than their upper class predecessors of the second century. Valentinian I even appointed Defenders of the Poor in major cities. But as military types, they wanted to put things right: everything and everyone orderly and in place. Where they saw, or thought they saw, chaos, they moved ruthlessly, though often unsuccessfully, to bring Roman order, as they understood it. As conservatives, they mostly had it in mind to restore old conditions. This was certainly Diocletian's hope. The irony of course is that the innovations used to restore a lost past intermingled instead with current conditions to generate a new Roman empire.

The emperors were at great pains to keep the government in shape. They wanted to mold it into an effective tax-collecting machine to bring in the funds necessary to keep up appearances and to maintain the military. But there was also a sincere effort to make the government fair, even to the humble. The emperors, and many of their advisors who often were themselves hardly more than jumped up peasants, were well aware that the rich got away with things while the poor carried the load. Diocletian's government and tax reforms were intended to put things right by making everybody, including the formerly privileged Italian Romans, pay a fair share, and by giving all a fighting chance at Roman justice by making the law known and uniform. It was an uphill fight: a growing bureaucracy mocked many of these efforts and the emperors had to wink at many flaws. But it can be argued without embarrassment that in the midst of a muddled and corrupt system there were imperial efforts to be decent. Beyond this there were many other ways in which humane gestures could succeed. Family connections, influence at court, religious brotherhoods, judicious use of gifts: all these and more were ways by which the system could be bent in favor of the interests even of the humble. Sometimes divine powers from the unseen world stepped in to give a hand. In any event, the people of the Mediterranean were used to capriciousness in both nature and in government, and very likely did not feel more oppressed than did their ancestors under the early Caesars.

The much touted rigidity and inflexibility of the highly bureaucratized government needs some qualification. The Roman world in the fourth century was creative and energetic. It was very hard to get a concensus on anything, from art to barbarian policy. In this bewildering arena, the emperors cajoled, demanded, begged, marched, ordered, and generally intervened any way they could through the army and the bureaucracy to maintain Roman power. The central authority had many things to do, or at least many that it wanted to do, and for this it needed big government. The Romans were fanatics for upholding traditional practices and for keeping up forms for their own sake, but they were not beyond imaginative efforts and creative responses, especially if these could be rationalized as upholding traditional values. The fact of the matter is that the government was a hotbed of innovation and experimentation. Bureaucratic organization, lines of authority, titles, dress codes, employment standards, rituals, and so on, changed at a rapid pace. Constantine was a notorious innovator, and was much criticized for it by traditionalists. But everyone, from the emperor down, tinkered when necessary. Stultifying rigidity was not a characteristic of this period.

The guiding principle and the most memorable characteristic of the Roman government in the fourth century was not its traditional features, its corruption, or its heavy handedness, but its clumsy, costly, and eventually successful search for a new identity. This search was encompassed, in traditional Roman fashion, under the theme of "restoration." The comfort of this psychology of returning to a better age should not obscure the fact that the Roman government, along with all its peoples, was in uncharted waters, facing new religions, new barbarians, new thoughts, shifting centers of economic and cultural power. What, in short, was it to be a Roman in a world far removed from that of the first Caesars?

This question found its most practical political expression in the search for a capital city which could be both the symbol and the citadel of Roman power and culture. For much of the fourth century the emperors were like pilgrims searching for the New Jerusalem. They and their courts seemed constantly on the move. In this they were often responding to civil conflict or barbarian troubles. But they were also looking for cities where they could be both at home and in Rome. Names like Nicomedia, Antioch, Sirmium, Trier, Thessalonika, and Milan came and went among the favored places of the mighty.

Rome on the Tiber had naturally the strongest claims, and these were neither relinquished nor challenged. No emperor, no matter how daring, considered for a moment challenging Rome's position as capital of the world. Nevertheless Rome was abandoned. It is not so much the creation of Constantinople but the abandonment of Rome as the working capital of the empire that symbolizes the movement towards a new Roman order. What happened? All the modern fussing about Rome's unstrategic location will not do. It was after from this place, strategic or not, that the empire had been conquered, and it was from here that the civilized world had been ruled for centuries. The city was complete, well appointed, heavily fortified, wealthy, experienced, and full of entertainments. Nor was Constantinople, the eventual successor capital, the perfect location. The water supply was bad, and its geographical location, although in many respects favorable, required a vast investment to make it secure from both land and sea attacks. Nor were the great Eastern cities like Alexandria or Antioch pleased to have a great new rival city competing for food and prestige. Not least, all the emperors except Julian were from the Latin rather than the Greek world, and a huge Latin speaking population had to be bribed or enticed to the new site, making Constantinople all the more unpopular in its Greek setting. Some eastern rhetoricians could not bear even to pronounce its name, referring to it obliquely when required to at all. Libanius once referred to it as the "city in Thrace, which runs to fat on the sweat of other cities" (Or.1.279; see entry 253).

Essentially all the huffing and puffing about finding a permanent seat of power for the central government was a choice which the emperor and his followers had to make between the old and the new. The old, represented by Rome, was always an enticing, compelling image. The gleaming marbles, bronzes, and gold, the traditional art so full of dignity and authority, the charmed lives of the ancient senatorial families, who always knew how to put on a good display when the emperor came home: all this was there for the asking. And many emperors asked. Constantine gave Rome a real try in the early years of his reign, and spent large sums on new buildings and improvements. Maxentius before him had ruled from the palace of the Caesars, and the Praetorian Guard and the Senate had once again been at the center of affairs. All the major emperors of the century put in an appearance. And yet, despite its appeal, Rome was doomed to compete with Constantinople, which by the end of the century was being commonly referred to as the second capital or the second Rome. The fact was the emperors found Rome a foreign and alien place, rather in the way that many U. S. presidents find Washington. Rome was a closed society to many of them, and its lingering republican traditions were not much to their taste either, nor was its overwhelming paganism very congenial to serious Christian emperors. But mostly they were just lost in the ancient culture of the city, and they did not have the education and manners that would make them successful in high society. Diocletian finally visited the city late in his reign, and had plans to stay there for a long time; but this sincere Roman patriot found the city too much for his simple tastes, and left in a hurry. The famous visit of Constantius II in 357 was perhaps more telling. The historian Ammianus relates that the emperor had a wonderful time, and no doubt he did. He stood in awe, gazing at the sights. He was entertained. He made gifts to the city. And then he left, never to return. It all rather reads like the account of an important tourist, in the style of the visits of Roman Senators to Egypt in the first century. The fact emerged at every imperial visit that Rome was not in tune with the rhythm of the times, and its leading families had no intention of meeting the new leaders of the Roman world half way in culture, in religion, or in modernizing their skills for participation in the new styles of government and thought. The old city could represent the past, but it could never quite capture the spirit of the new present. In any event, it was no longer this city, or even Italy, which was the driving force behind the imperial mission. In this it was eclipsed by a notion that it helped create, the notion of Rome as a universal ideal of government and indeed of life, rather than one city with an empire: hence a new Latin word, *Romania*, which appeared on record for the first time in the mid-fourth century. This word conveyed the sense that all the lands under the emperor's writ were as Roman as any other part, and that somehow the Roman state was evolving into something different from earlier times under the rule of the old city. In this sense the new word symbolized a release from the past without a rejection of it. Therefore the emperors could build a new capital in Constantinople, a new Rome as much like the old one as they wished to make it, updating it where necessary to make it more congenial to the religious, political, and cultural tastes of the new age of *Romania*.

* * *

The Romans did not separate the armed forces from the civil government in the fashion to which late twentieth century westerners are accustomed.   To them the entire power structure commanded by the emperor was an armed camp, and technically all fourth century government employees were known as soldiers. Like the government the military was often muddled and corrupt. But the Romans could always put armies into the field far superior to anything the barbarian tribes could offer, and when properly trained and led the Roman forces were usually able to carry the day. Disasters such as Adrianople were exceptional. Even in the ruinous Persian campaign under Julian, resulting in the first loss of territory in half a century, the Roman army was not defeated in the field.

The most innovative emperors like Diocletian and Constantine made many changes in the military configuration. There were the usual complaints. The enlarged army cost too much. It was not deployed properly. There were too many barbarians hired. Soldiers became too involved in local politics. The military draft was unfair and ham-handed: the rich could buy their way out, and the poor served disproportionately. The soldiers were brave when harassing civilians, but ran away when confronting the barbarians.

Most of the complaints were not new. But some did have a greater legitimacy in the sense that the military system was larger than before and its faults were the more noticeable. Many of the traditional accusations against the innovations of Constantine were first advanced by pagan historians of the fifth and sixth centuries who found an opportunity both to investigate the causes of the collapse of the western empire and to discredit the first Christian emperor.

Despite the criticisms and its actual failures, the Roman military was capable in the fourth century of defending the interests of the state, and regularly did so. The least agreeable aspect of government policy, the use of the military to settle political disputes among contending emperors, was a general waste. Aurelius Victor, a contemporary, remarks in his history that enough men were lost at the Battle of Mursa, when Constantius II defeated the usurper Magnentius, to defeat and conquer the barbarians. Fortunately, however, most civil strife was managed without severe bloodshed. Besides, there was a tendency by the end of the fourth century to use mercenary barbarians to settle Roman conflicts: a cynical practice applauded by the Christian historian Orosius, who with perverse practicality applauded the wisdom of shedding barbarian blood rather than Christian over political matters.

A more serious charge was that barbarians were being hired to do all Rome's military work, and were ruining discipline. As long as the armies were controlled by Roman officers there seems to have been little danger. Barbarian recruits were content to mix with other soldiers, learn a little Latin, and take home regular pay. When entire armies became barbarian, including their commanders, things were indeed in danger of getting out of control: a point recognized and acted upon in the fifth century with more success in the eastern empire than in the western.

When armies failed, Roman technology and strategic planning might carry the day. An example is Adrianople in 378, when the Goths killed an emperor and decimated an important field army. This was a serious loss, and left all of Thrace vulnerable to barbarian raiding parties. But the celebrations of the Goths were short-lived, and the fruits of their victory a mirage. Adrianople gave a violent jolt to the armed forces of the Roman world, but the defense system did not collapse. On the contrary, the Romans quickly proved themselves able to protect their vital interests, much to the frustration of the barbarians, who had hoped to gain something substantive from their surprising victory. While the hungry barbarians looked for an easy city to sack, the interim government at Constantinople labored to neutralize the barbarian success on the field. Domnica, widow of the emperor Valens, helped organize city defenses. A military commander, with the support of the local senate, arranged for the massacre of all the Gothic military trainees in Asia Minor, thus in one brutal afternoon removing the fear of an internal rising in support of their victorious brethren in Thrace. Troops were swiftly moved in from the Asian provinces; among them were the Saracens and their queen Mavia, who demoralized the Goths before Constantinople by riding wildly out of the gates of the city and drinking the blood of the wounded. The city of Adrianople itself, so close to the Roman defeat and housing the imperial treasure chest of Valens, gathered in many of the surviving Roman troops and held off the Goths. In fact, the Goths, being unprepared for seige warfare, took no city of any consequence. The grain supplies and the state factories of Thrace were secure behind city walls. Great imperial armies still threatened the Goths from the west, and even in Thrace the Romans were able to field small but troublesome armed units. The Romans controlled the sea in front of the Goths and the Danube behind them. The barbarians were hemmed in and hungry. All in all, Adrianople was among the least accommodating victories in history.

Much has been made of the influence of Adrianople in establishing the primacy of cavalry in warfare. A judgment by a gifted late nineteenth century English undergraduate student, Charles Oman, that Adrianople marked the end of infantry and the rise of cavalry as the predominant force in military units for the next thousand years, has echoed through the textbooks to our own time, and has taken on the aura of absolute truth. It is an example in history of a hypothesis repeated so often that it takes on a life of its own, beyond question, beyond doubt. It has come to represent one of the most important developments of the fourth century. But contemporaries knew nothing of it, and for a good reason. The circumstances at Adrianople did not suggest it as a fruitful line of inquiry. Both sides had cavalry, and both had infantry. The Romans were unfortunate in that their cavalry deserted: the Goths were fortunate in that their cavalry, which had not been kept close to the main force, showed up in time to make a difference, hemming the Roman infantry into a bad spot. The only lesson the Romans could infer was that cavalry was not of much value when it deserted. They could also see that cavalry could make a difference in some circumstances. But this they already knew. A military author, Vegetius, writing after Adrianople, was all for restoring the traditional strength of the ancient legions, primarily infantry units with cavalry attachments. He was an intelligent observer of the contemporary military situation, and offered no judgment parallel to that of Charles Oman. In fact, both barbarians and Romans relied on infantry as their primary force for the duration of the military contest between them in the fourth and fifth centuries.

* * *

The economy of the Roman world was primitive but resilient. Its wealth was largely drawn from agriculture. Most people in every province either worked the land or had investments involving its produce. Good land was highly prized, and the wealthy always kept most of their capital in land. The great cities derived much of their income from land investments. The church increasingly in the fourth century became a great landowner, and derived ever larger shares of its revenues from this source. Beyond this, there was a modest amount of industrial activity, occasionally on a large scale especially if related to government contracts, but mostly of the cottage variety. There was a robust commerce in goods and services from one end of the empire to the other, for both the government and for the wealthy. Most people, being poor or of restrained means, obtained everything they needed in life from their immediate surroundings, making therefore most trade modest and local in character.

In peaceful conditions, and when the government was not excessive in its demands, the Mediterranean economy overall was a success; and under the umbrella of one government there was a considerable cross fertilization of creative entrepreneurial energies. Even in the deteriorating political conditions of the fifth century, the Mediterranean economy chugged along, reluctant to change old and successful patterns despite the collapse of political unity.

The Roman government is often regarded as a burden on the empire's economy, but it may be more helpful to see it as a participant and to a limited extent a leader in economic direction through its patronage and through its distribution of tax revenues. In one sense it encouraged economic growth by the transfer of surplus wealth to the frontier provinces, which in turn bought goods and services from the older and more sophisticated centers of enterprise and production. The political division between east and west after 400, followed by the loss of control of the western Mediterranean to the Vandals, was a serious blow to this activity.

The tax system of the state is often said to have been a drain on the economy. No doubt it was corrupt, and there was an irresistible temptation to raise taxes when the government was growing rapidly in the fourth century. There was some hardship, and marginal lands were often abandoned if they did not produce enough wealth to pay their way. On the other hand, the tax system introduced under Diocletian was more balanced and attempted to spread taxes equitably. Diocletian knocked down many privileges and reached deeper into the pockets of those who had hitherto been lightly touched. Naturally there was much complaining. For instance, Italy became at last a province like all the others, and had to pay taxes in the same way. This did not sit well with the original Romans, who expected special treatment; but the howls of protest could not mask the fact that the Italians were capable of paying their share, and that in a world where everyone could now be a Roman, it was unlikely that one geographic region should forever have privileges based on the events of four centuries earlier. The tax burden increased in the fourth century, but so did the wealth of the empire, at least in the first half of the century. In many areas, government expenditure promoted considerable economic growth, and the historian is hard pressed to find any area where, except in anomalous conditions, the tax burden was so horrific as to destroy the economic infrastructure. There was often tax relief in time of famine, or when productivity was destroyed by barbarian invasions.

The most serious complaining about excessive taxation came from the western provinces in the fifth century, and should not be confused with earlier circumstances. This may indirectly reflect an unhappy consequence of the political split between east and west after the time of Theodosius I: the tax revenues of the east were no longer being spent to shore up western defenses. The western provinces were neither impoverished nor without resources, but the economic powerhouse of the empire had always been in the east, and the loss of revenues was a severe blow. Trying quickly to make up this loss just at a time of increased pressure on the frontiers may have caused hardship and an eclipse of economic development. In a regrettable political decision, the western government in the late fourth century permitted the great landed nobles to collect taxes and forward the revenues to the central government. In the absence of central supervision, the inevitable happened: the nobles tended to collect more than they should, keep more than they should, and forward less than they should to central government. The timing for this experiment could not have been worse, and made its contribution to the weakening of conditions generally in the western world. Nevertheless, the west was never impotent, and as late as the 460s a vigorous emperor like Marjorian could raise armies, bring in revenues, and make the imperial standard a force to be reckoned with again, presiding though he did over a reduced but not yet ruined economic field.

* * *

Gibbon had the focus right when he spoke of the triumph of religion and barbarism. Through this conceptual structure we can see most vividly the transformation of the Roman world from its cultural base in Greece and its power base in Italy, to the new world in which power was fragmented from one end of the Mediterranean to the other and in which to be Roman was to be a member of a universal religious movement rather than of a political order. Gibbon had something else right too: he had the perspective to see these transformations over many centuries, recognizing the glacial movement of change in the ancient world, which came grudgingly after a number of military, political, and cultural shocks.

Of all the miracles in the early Christian church the greatest was the conversion of the emperor Constantine. Other miracles showed a greater spiritual dimension, but through this one event the earthly church was catapulted overnight from the defeat and dissension of Diocletian's persecution to the status of an imperial organization, protected and promoted by the head of the Roman state. In this setting one can appreciate the story in Eusebius of the tears and awe in the reception hall of the palace at Nicaea when the bejewelled and purple robed Constantine kissed the empty eye sockets of those who had recently been persecuted and tortured. In the murky world of Roman religious developments, so full of syncretistic and contradictory features, the persecution on the one hand and the sudden elevation on the other lent both a separateness and an aura of prestige and power to the Christian sect that could hardly fail to impress. All of this fed the ego of the Christians who already carried with them the feeling of uniqueness. Something else worked for the Christians at this critical moment: their emperor patron was a success. Over a long reign of thirty years Constantine conquered all his rivals and died in bed. In the Roman world, this was success on the scale of Augustus or Alexander the Great.

Behind every great emperor there was a great god. This was a guiding principle of thought for millions in the confusing religious milieu of the age. By the later third century Christianity had softened its claims of uniqueness and edged toward the mainstream. But the persecution under Diocletian shattered the fragile bridges to the pagan world, and under Constantine the church ironically did not find it necessary to rebuild them, although the emperor seems to have had this in mind. Instead it was placed above the other religions, and could from there nurture its ancient dream of uniqueness, superiority, and, finally, conquest. For a religion already possessed of the notion that there was only one truth, of which it was the divinely appointed guardian, this was heady stuff.

As the Christian movement increased in power, prestige, and wealth, there arose new problems. To a large extent the fourth century churches were engaged in a period of self-definition, expressed through councils and creeds. The overwhelming problem was to relate the Christian message to the world, and to make a home for the Christian churches, the purveyors of the message in the world, without becoming absorbed and lost in the strong Greco-Roman undercurrent. There was a temptation on all ecclesiastical levels to go native. The great Arian heresy, so troublesome from the time of Constantine to Theodosius, had underlying it an effort to bring theology into line with neo-Platonic thought. This may not be what Arius himself had in mind, but others soon moved in that direction. The orthodox correctly saw that giving way to the seductive arguments of Arianism and later neo-Arianism on the relationship of God the Father to Christ the Son would open the way for pagan attitudes regarding the hierarchical structure of the gods. The Christian message could not be compromised no matter how compelling the ingenious arguments of Greek philosophy or the other kinds of persuasion available to the many more or less Arian emperors, who were anxious to make Christianity as palatable to everyone as possible. In the end the Christian churches carried a great deal of the cultural baggage of the Roman world into later centuries, including Greek philosophy and Roman law and government. The papal ceremonies of our own time were lifted in essence from the ceremonial ambience of the fourth century emperors. But much of the uniqueness of Christianity was saved, often at the expense of good relations with pagans and Jews.

In the midst of all the turmoil about defining its message and place in the world, the Christian movement inevitably confronted the Roman government, but now from the inside rather than the outside. In the Roman world it was a premise accepted without question that good government, or at any rate successful government, depended on the favor if the divinities. "Our State is sustained more by religion than by official duties and physical toil and sweat," said Constantius II towards the end of his reign (CTH, Parr, 16.2.16). This was not a sentiment exclusive to the fourth century. The remark might as easily have been made in the time of Augustus: the basic sentiment that getting right with the gods was essential for the success of the state was a typically Roman point of view at all times. In the fourth century there was a considerable dispute about which gods the Romans needed to get right with, which helped intensify the quest and give it more publicity, but the underlying feature was the same.

But when Christianity became a state religion, and finally the only state religion, was the Christian church ready to give the Roman government the wholehearted support that the old pagan cults once had? The ecclesiastical leaders were of two minds. A strong faction, inspired by Eusebius, Bishop of Caesarea, was absolutely ready to embrace the partly Christianized Roman government of Constantine and his successors as God's special gift to the church, as protector and indeed as a reflection on earth of the heavenly government: Constantine, for example, being God's reflection on earth, and the imperial court being a reflection of the heavenly powers, the angels, saints, and so on, up to God. This highly developed and polished political theology flourished in the east. It was an agreeable pattern of thought to the Greek mind, fixed on Plato's image of earthly things as a reflection or shadow of divine concepts, and eventually it triumphed in the inseparable symbiosis of the Byzantine state and Greek Orthodox Church.

The west was not without its proponents of this view, and in the first blush of goodwill between church and state under Constantine everyone was willing to feed from the generosity of the imperial treasury, resulting in beautiful churches and rich bishops everywhere. Nevertheless, the movement to keep the church at some distance from the state derived its strength from the western Mediterranean. It found its most eloquent spokesman in Augustine, whose mature views may be consulted in the *City of God,* where the famous theme of the two cities, spiritual and earthly, is developed. Augustine was at pains not to bring the two cities together, as Eusebius was, but rather to keep them well apart. The heavenly city is reflected on earth in the church, not state and church hand in hand. Augustine taught that the church could, and may one day have to, get along without Rome. He was content to live in the Roman empire, but could imagine life without it. This view had much currency among the spiritually inclined in the fifth century. The great aristocrat Paulinus of Nola remarked that if the barbarians could not be used to save Rome, they must at all costs be brought into the service of the church. To come to this conclusion, the thinking mind of the Roman world had made a great voyage indeed.

The only pagan emperor after Constantine was Julian. This competent prince was a terrifying surprise to the church. Athanasius might remark that he was a small cloud that would soon pass, but others were reminded how fragile the victory of the church in the empire was, and how quickly gains might be reversed and lost. In the event Athanasius was right. Julian passed from the scene in a couple of years, and much of his pro-pagan legislation was reversed. The lesson, however, was not lost, and the Christian drive to dominate and drive out all opposition was intensified. Toward the end of the century, there arose a great debate over the Altar of Victory in the Senate House in Rome. It had been there since the time of Augustus, and the rituals involving it had become associated with the continuing success of the government. Some powerful Christians, however, were having none of this, and wanted the pagan altar removed. When the distinguished senator Symmachus told the emperor that there were many ways to the truth, Ambrose, Bishop of Milan, impressed upon the emperor that there was only ONE way, no other. Although even at the Christian court of Milan there was much sympathy for the Roman senator's point of view, the bishop prevailed. In a world dominated by symbols, this triumph carried a profound message.

At last, the orthodox church had everything it could hope for in an earthly prince in the person of the very catholic emperor Theodosius, who at the end of the fourth century condemned and abolished all forms of religious expression that did not conform to the rather narrow set of premises and principles that by now had attached themselves to the church. In this sense, the arrival in the east of Theodosius in 379 as a replacement for the dead Valens was a far more important consequence of the battle of Adrianople than its immediate military result. What Gibbon condemned in the triumph of religion was not Christianity but the triumph of religious fanaticism, expressed through a form of Christianity that was intolerant, exclusive, and self-centered.

In this context there were two aspects of the church's triumph that were unhelpful, but not fatal, to the fortunes of the Roman state. First, the church throughout the empire enticed talented men and women of good families into ecclesiastical service, which was a loss to state administration, and perhaps to the military. Second, and more important, the triumph of the church in the state resulted in the loss of enthusiastic support for the state of untold thousands of influential people from important and well connected families, whether pagan or Jewish. They continued to pay their taxes, of course, but they were proscribed from serving the state in civil or military matters. All this was very inopportune and portentous just when the state needed the broadest base of support it could command in the perilous conditions of the fifth century. Nevertheless, the support of the church for the state government provided a strength of its own. Although all in all it may successfully be argued that a more tolerant religious perspective may have retained the sympathies of more of its citizens, the Roman state was partially compensated through the firm convictions of its Christian supporters, who were pleased to wed the Roman empire with their march towards spiritual conquest and who never lost sight of Rome as an essential participant in the church's earthly success.

* * *

    The barbarians were the proximate cause of the collapse of the Roman state in the fifth century. This is beyond dispute. Historians have expended a great deal of energy dissecting and analyzing the barbarian tribes of the fourth and fifth centuries, looking for the sources of their strength. Roman writers too participated in this exercise: Ammianus appreciated that the Huns would be a force to be reckoned with, and in his history gave a lengthy aside on their habits and organization. Always these exercises worked with two premises: the barbarians were strong, and the Romans were weak. And the big question was why. The results have often been profound and invaluable studies of the Roman and barbarian worlds, but the accepted premises have forced good work into narrow frameworks. Here rests the source of many misunderstandings about the later empire. It is at this point that the question of perspective needs to be raised, and the basic condition of vulnerability of all extended empires. Here Gibbon has something else to teach us when he reminds us that we should wonder less at the fall of Rome and more that it subsisted so long. The more prescient Romans were not unmindful of the precarious state of things, and a shrewd observer like Tacitus, writing centuries before the fall of the empire, could remark that the safety of the Romans rested in keeping the barbarians at each others' throats.

    Frontier barbarians were an endless source of irritation to the Romans, rather in the way illegal immigrants are to the United States: they were forever infiltrating the borders, and required constant attention. Like the Americans, the Romans were of two minds about these strangers pressing to participate. One mind wanted to clear them from the empire, remove them from all employment, and strictly patrol the frontiers. In the years after Adrianople, this attitude enjoyed a revival in some circles, but when the time came some decades later to implement the plan, the results were incomplete, frustrating, and irritating for everyone. The other mind was more attuned to the value of these strangers in the midst: they could fill the ranks of the army, they could serve in the great households of the nobility and of other lesser Roman families, they could till the fields, they could be educated, they could be taught Latin, receive higher religion, and in the fullness of time they could become Roman citizens, no matter how they had originally entered the empire. Aurelius Victor, an amateur historian writing in the middle of the fourth century, remarked that Rome had grown and prospered through the constant influx of barbarians.

The barbarians themselves, insofar as we can know their thoughts through the Roman sources, saw the empire as an endless opportunity for wealth easily gained, for employment, and for a general frame of reference with which to associate themselves or from which to dissociate themselves. Barbarian leaders were often uncertain in their own minds the type of relationship they wished to have with the empire, but there was a general sense that it was or should be a part of their world and that the emperor was the mightiest king in a great but nebulous political structure whose hierarchical arrangement of power somehow included them, perhaps eventually as Roman military commanders.

The great Roman defeat at Adrianople in 378 has traditionally been seen as a turning point in the relations of barbarians and Romans. There is truth in this, although contemporaries did not see the same causes or consequences of this event as modern historians, who have often been dazzled by the Roman loss on the battlefield to the distraction of appreciating its more profound results in the Roman world. The defeat was expensive and inconvenient, and it resulted in a nightmare for the people of Thrace, but Roman power was not seriously eclipsed except in the immediate environs of the barbarian victory. The Romans read significance into the event, usually of a religious kind involving punishment by God or the gods for some wrongdoing or other; but they did not expect the collapse of their empire, although a few pessimists were always available to say so on any disastrous occasion. Moreover, the Gothic hordes were there in the first place not because they were strong but because they were weak: they were escaping their own defeats at the hands of the Huns, and had at first come into the empire with the emperor's permission, although things soon got out of hand. In the end, the question was not what the barbarians would do with their victory, but what the Romans would do with their defeat. Here is the real key to later events, and the key to barbarian relations with Rome in the fifth century.

In the wake of the defeat and death of Valens, the last of the Arian emperors, the remaining western emperor chose a new colleague, Theodosius, whose first order of business was to stabilize the Balkans and settle the religious commitments of his government. After a brief period of toleration, he pursued a vigorous policy of making Catholic Christianity the state religion and the absolute standard for good citizenship, for government service, and of course for salvation. This in fact was the most profound result of Adrianople for the subsequent history of the empire as a cultural and civilizing force. But all this could be settled over the length of Theodosius' reign. The more immediate problem was to decide what to do about the tens of thousands of barbarians milling about mischievously between Greece and the Danube. In his eastern court Theodosius discovered two schools of thought on the barbarians. One faction sought to eliminate them entirely, seeing no circumstances in which these foreigners could be useful in the Roman state, except as slave labor. Another faction had a quite different view, one with seductive appeal especially in the immediate circumstances. Its most eloquent and persistent spokesman was the famous rhetorician Themistius, who for many years had pressed his arguments. The emperor, he said, who saw the barbarians as his subjects was truly the emperor of the world, but the emperor who merely bashed them at every chance was only emperor of the Romans. The barbarians needed to be drawn into the Roman political system, so they might be tamed for the mutual benefit of all. They would neither be defeated permanently nor go away. Warring with them time after time was expensive: the blood and treasure of the empire was wasted on the fruitless effort to destroy them. And in the present situation Themistius was unhappy at the prospect of higher taxes and thousands of Roman deaths in order to drive the Goths from the Balkans. He counseled moderation and compromise, predicting that the tribes would be pleased and honored to be accepted as subjects of the emperor.

Theodosius was ready to be pursuaded, ready to be the great philosopher king of whom Themistius dreamed, and he had some pursuasive reasons of his own. He campaigned in Thrace for a few years after Adrianople, not without success; but there were setbacks and the work was tedious and expensive. Moreover, distractions in Thrace kept him away from other things he wanted to do, such as settle his dynasty firmly in control of the empire and work on the religious settlement. He also knew that the Gothic tribes entered the Roman world in the first place because their own confederation beyond the Danube had been destroyed by the Huns, a savage people whom the Romans did not wish to face alone - or at all, if they could get the Goths to do it instead.

In 382 Theodosius signed a treaty with the Goths, in which the barbarians pledged loyalty to the empire or at least to the emperor in return for which they received land and various subsidies: a not altogether unprecedented arrangement, except that Goths were now on Roman territory and, most risky of all, were permitted to stay together under their own chieftains. At the time it did not seem a bad deal all around, and the agreement stuck until the death of the emperor. With a little luck it might have ended happily, as one supposes Munich might have: Hitler might have died, the barbarians might really have settled into a new life with happy consequences for all. Alas, no, and a regrettable train of events insensibly led to the most shocking event of the early fifth century, the sack of Rome itself, followed by various Roman efforts to sort things out, a task not without hope of success, but at last thwarted in the western arena under the combined attacks of Vandals and Huns and other inconveniences.

* * *

What does weakness or strength count for when neither guarantees the fates of empires? Was not the French empire of 1810, or the British empire of 1939, or the German empire of 1914 invincible? Were they not all gone a few years later? Was not the Austrian empire a pathetic and unlikely survivor of the Napoleanic wars? Was it not a dominant power after the Congress of Vienna, and was it not doing reasonably well nearly a hundred years after that, despite continuing predictions of its imminent collapse? In the 1640s the Spanish empire was universally considered a terminal case. A hundred years later it was flourishing in a way entirely beyond the expectations of contemporaries.

All great empires are over-extended and vulnerable. This is a condition of their existence, and the length of their survival may depend less on profound matters than on luck of the draw. And then too there are illusion, theatrics, and the Commanding Presence. Of course there must be some degree of brute strength: a functioning and not completely archaic economy, a sentient government, an ability to project some strength through a military structure, and so on. But much has to do with perceptions and traditional patterns of behavior built up over time, and in this sense the longer an empire survives the better its chances are of surviving longer still. The Romans added a new dimension to this principle by surviving as a great state for so long, for being a part of the landscape for so long, that even after the fall, the barbarians and Romans could not face the void and patched up illusionary Roman empires that survived under one name or other until the time of Napoleon.

Our historians must go on mining the rich quarry of the Roman empire. They must go on looking for profound and proximate causes of this or that. We are all enriched by learning more and more about the experiences of those who have gone before us, and the intellectual constructs we develop to give our knowledge order and meaning are as important as the simple facts. But our initial inquiries must be as untainted by our knowledge of what followed as we can make them. Historical inquiry will always be more productive, balanced, and honest with the words of Maitland in mind: "It is very hard to remember that events now long in the past were once in the future." And nowhere is this maxim more relevant than in considering the Roman empire toward the end of its long life.

I. General and Miscellaneous Works

Includes general regional studies. General church histories are under "Christianity," or "Church and State."

1. *The Age of Diocletian: A Symposium*, December 14-16, 1951. Moderated by Sterling A. Callisen, New York: The Metropolitan Museum of Art, 1953. Includes six essays. The first, "The Historical Pattern," by Casper J. Kraemer, summarizes the reign of Diocletian and makes comparisons with the United States. There is included an interesting portrait of Diocletian done in 1935 as part of a WPA project. Next, Eberhard F. Bruck, "Law in a Changing World," says that Diocletian did everything he could to preserve "the pure Roman law of classical times" (p.19), and that his goal was to help unite the empire by standardizing private and constitutional law everywhere. In "Price Controls and Wages," William L. Westermann discusses Diocletian's price edict, and makes comparisons with the U.S. Office of Price Stabilization in the early 1950s. Erwin R. Goodenough's "Religious Aspirations" is analyzed separately. In "Books and the Crisis," Gilbert Highet reviews the literature of the age, in which he mostly hears "angry cries, loud declamation, wails of pain and roars of rage, insults and groans and shouts of defiance" (p.49). This is colorful stuff, but some of his judgments would not hold up to current scholarly scrutiny: for instance, his view that the *Historia Augusta* "was apparently written by half-wits and edited by an idiot" (p.58). In the final essay, "Art in Transition," Rhys Carpenter contrasts and compares developments in the visual arts and architecture, including some parallels with modern art.

2. **Baldwin, Barry.** "Late Antiquity: A Review Article." *Echos du Monde Classique/Classical Views* 28 (1984): 57-68. Reprinted in his *Studies on Greek and Roman History and Literature*, pp. 562-572. Amsterdam: J. G. Gieben, 1985. In the context of a review of four books, Baldwin notes the astonishing proliferation of interest in the later Roman period.

3. **Baldwin, Barry.** "Some Addenda to the Prosopography of the Later Roman Empire." *Historia* 25 (1976): 118-121; 31 (1982): 97-111.

4. **Baldwin, Barry.** *Studies on Late Roman and Byzantine History, Literature and Language.* London Studies in Classical Philology, 12. Amsterdam: J. C. Gieben, 1984. The essays relevant to the fourth century are listed individually.

5. **Baynes, Norman H.** *Byzantine Studies and Other Essays.* London: The Athlone Press, 1955; reprint ed., Westport, Conn.: Greenwood Press, 1974. The relevant larger essays are analyzed individually. This anthology also contains excerpts from some of Baynes' book reviews, which include interesting remarks on the campaigns of Valentinian I, Lactantius' literary efforts, Ambrose, Julian, Symmachus, Athanasius, Diocletian and Mithraism, and the *Historia Augusta.*

6. **Bowder, Diana, ed.** *Who Was Who in the Roman World 753 B.C.-A.D. 476.* Oxford: Phaidon, 1980. Heavily illustrated.

7. **Bradshaw, Gillian.** *The Beacon at Alexandria.* Boston: Houghton Mifflin, 1986. Fiction set in the time of Valens and Valentinian. Not a bad read for a dark and stormy night. The author consulted Ammianus Marcellinus, although her library apparently was only able to supply her with the 1863 edition of C. D. Yonge, long since superceded by the Rolfe translation in the Loeb Classics.

8. **Brock, Sebastion P.** *Syriac Perspectives on Late Antiquity.* London: Variorum Reprints, 1984. The relevant essays are identified individually in this bibliography.

9. **Brown, Peter.** "The Later Roman Empire." *Economic History Review (Essays in Bibliography and Criticism,* 56) 20 (1967): 327-343. Reprinted in his *Religion and Society in the Age of Augustine,* pp. 46-73. New York: Harper and Row, 1972. In a fine tribute to *The Later Roman Empire, 284-602,* by A. H. M. Jones, Brown offers an interesting perspective on the fourth century empire as one which had successfully survived the crisis of the third century, and was blinded by its success to many of the challenges of the fourth century: "The Byzantine Empire of the early Middle Ages, a state chastened by bitter experience, is infinitely superior in this respect to the omnipotent and obtuse collosus of the fourth century." And there is much more, in a very provocative article.

10. **Brown, Peter.** *The Making of Late Antiquity.* Cambridge, Mass. and London: Harvard University Press, 1978. Continuity and change: both features apply in the late Roman world. Brown offers a helpful frame of mind when trying to sort it all out: ". . . the changes that came about in Late Antiquity can best be seen as a redistribution and a reorchestration of components that had already existed for centuries in the Mediterranean world" (p.8). Brown is largely interested in religious change, and works over the second and third centuries to find for the fourth century a shift in spiritual power from temples and holy places to individuals, holy men, who brought the divine to earth, and through whose persons the divine worked, and in whose bodies even after death divine power lingered. These friends of God, who usually included Christian ascetics but could even embrace an emperor such as Constantine, were emerging as the new heroes of the Roman world. E. D. Hunt, *Classical Review* 31 (1981): 255-256 (+); D. B. Nagle, *The History Teacher* 13 (1980): 302-303 (+).

11. **Brown, Peter.** *Society and the Holy in Late Antiquity.* Berkeley and Los Angeles: University of California Press; London: Faber and Faber, 1982. An anthology of thirteen articles, reviews, and lectures, of which the following are most relevant to the fourth century: "In Gibbon's Shade," which

reintroduces the relevance of Gibbon to late Roman studies; "The Last Pagan Emperor: Robert Browning's The Emperor Julian," where Brown takes the opportunity to show that Julian was not an anomaly in his own age; "The Rise and Function of the Holy Man in Late Antiquity," discussed elsewhere; "Town, Village and Holy Man: The Case of Syria," where we are advised to break the classical-colored spectacles through which we look at change in the late empire, especially in the large areas which had always been beyond Greco-Roman culture; "Eastern and Western Christendom in Late Antiquity: A Parting of the Ways," in which we learn that Greek and Roman cultures were not by themselves hostile to each other, and that outside forces and differing views on the locus of holy power forced the split; and "The View from the Precipice," in which Brown advises us to push later centuries of Christian art out of our minds if we wish to appreciate the earlier art. R. A. Markus, *Times Literary Supplement* (October 22, 1982): 1157 (+); J. duQ. Adams, *Speculum* 59 (1984): 373-376 (+).

12. Brown, Peter. *The World of Late Antiquity.* London: Thames and Hudson; New York: Harcourt Brace Jovanovich, 1971.   Among the most formidable surveys of the later Roman period to emerge in recent decades, this book should also be one of the most stimulating adventures into another thought-world that a student could undertake. It is the excitement of the age that really comes through: excitement over new experiments in religion, government, styles of life, and so on.   Brown encourages the attitude of seeing transformation rather than only decline and fall. Through this approach a more profound understanding can flourish regarding changes in the later Roman period. Averil Cameron, *English Historical Review* 88 (1973): 116-117 (++-); R. A. Markus, *History* (February 1973): 74-75 (+).

13. Browning, Robert. "The Late Roman Empire." In *The Encyclopedia of Ancient Civilizations*, pp. 260-269.   Edited by Arthur Cotterell.   New York: Mayflower Books, 1980.

14. *The Cambridge Ancient History.* 12 vols. Cambridge: At the University Press, 1923-1939. Vol. 12: *The*

Imperial Crisis and Recovery A. D. 193-324. The chapters on the age of Diocletian and Constantine are beginning to show their age in some particular respects, but they constitute still an informed and compelling narrative of a decisive and colorful period of Roman history.

15. ***The Cambridge Medieval History.*** 8 vols. New York: MacMillan Co., 1911-1936. Vol. I: *The Christian Roman Empire and the Foundation of the Teutonic Kingdoms.* This volume covers the fourth and fifth centuries, and after the passage of many decades is still a standard reference. The historical technicians of our own time may have much improved the bases of our knowledge of the fourth century; but the essays of such historical artists as Baynes and Gwatkin will always be an impressive and informative read, suffused as they are by much sound learning and a generous perspective on the variety of the human experience.

16. Christ, Karl. *The Romans: An Introduction to Their History and Civilisation.* Translated by Christopher Holme. Berkeley: University of California Press, 1984. A significant feature of this informed general history of Rome is that a large section is devoted to the later empire, thus making the fourth century an integral part of the history of Rome, an uncommon feature in texts of this sort generally.

17. ***Civilization of the Ancient Mediterranean: Greece and Rome.*** 3 vols. Edited by Michael Grant and Rachel Kitzinger. New York: Charles Scribners' Sons, 1988. From the introduction: "The eighty-eight contributors have written ninety-seven essays on the geography of the area, the physical appearance of its inhabitants, their politics and religions, their languages, arts, and technologies, their social and economic activities, and their personal lives " (p.xxv). The list of contributors is a who's who of scholars in Greek and Roman studies; the essays usually represent a very current knowledge of the subject areas, and the quality of the writing is high, although the limits of space often seem to have induced some superficiality of treatment. The three volumes are well worth a browse for information on the late empire, although this material is relatively a small part of the whole.

18. **Cleary, Simon Esmonde.** "The End of Roman Britain." *History Today* 38 (December 1988): 35-40. Magnus Maximus, a military usurper who left his station in Britain to try his luck as a Roman emperor and who perished in the effort after defeat in battle against Theodosius I, is the central focus of Cleary's look at fourth century Britain and its relationship with the Roman world.

19. **Cornell, T. and Matthews, J.** *Atlas of the Roman World.* New York: Facts on File; Oxford: Phaidon Press, 1982. Includes a good section of narrative, maps, and illustrations on the later empire.

20. **De Ste.-Croix, Geoffrey C. M.** *The Class Struggle in the Ancient Greek World from the Archaic Age to the Arab Conquest.* London: Duckworth; Ithaca, N. Y.: Cornell University Press, 1981. A book so powerfully well-informed that even the most devoutly anti-Marxist scholars will readily forgive, or at least overlook, the Marxist approach. The title is a bit of a misnomer: so much of the book is devoted to the Roman empire that all Roman scholars must consult it. The extraordinary footnotes alone would justify publication. The fourth century is richly although not lovingly treated. P. A. Brunt, *Journal of Roman Studies* 72 (1982): 158-163 ("[the author] is not . . . one who thinks that history is a record of what the few have achieved and not also of what millions have suffered. Herein lies the value of the book."); R. Browning, *Past and Present* #100 (August 1983): 147-156 (+); J. A. Crook, *The Classical Review* 33 (1983): 71-72 (+); O. Murray, *New Statesman* 105 (January 7, 1983):24-25 (+); W. E. Higgins, *American Historical Review* 87 (1982): 1369-1370 (+); T. D. Barnes, *Phoenix* 36 (1982) 363-366 (+); K. R. Bradley, *American Journal of Philology* 103 (1982): 347-350 (+).

21. **Downey, Glanville.** *Antioch in the Age of Theodosius the Great.* Norman: University of Oklahoma, 1962. This is

THE book for those who want Antioch in the fourth century. For more, see the author's *A History of Antioch in Syria from Seleucus to the Arab Conquest* (22); for both more than *AATG* and less than *HASSAC*, see the author's *Ancient Antioch* (c.1963). The treatments of such important fourth century personalities as Julian and Libanius are most helpful.

22. **Downey, Glanville.** *A History of Antioch in Syria from Seleucus to the Arab Conquest.* Princeton, N. J.: Princeton Unviersity Press, 1961. The treatment of Antioch in the fourth century is outstanding and fundamental. The many pages on Julian and Antioch are necessary reading. The sources get full treatment. A more popular treatment is the author's *Ancient Antioch* (1963). T. A. Brady, *American Historical Review* 67 (October 1961): 94-95 (+); A. F. Norman, *Journal of Roman Studies* 52 (1962): 261-262 (+).

23. **Downey, Glanville.** *The Late Roman Empire.* New York: Holt, Rinehart and Winston, 1969. This useful introduction covers from the time of Diocletian to the death of Justinian in 565. Occasional factual errors. Good bibliographical notes.

24. **Finley, M. I.** *Aspects of Antiquity: Discoveries and Controversies.* London: Chatto and Windus; New York: The Viking Press, 1968. There are fifteen essays, nearly all having appeared elsewhere first. Two have value to the student of the fourth century: "The Emperor Diocletian," pp. 143-152; and "Manpower and the Fall of Rome," pp. 153-161. The latter is a compact version of a review article from the *Journal of Roman Studies* (1958): 156-164, in which Finley delivered a powerful and perhaps decisive blow against Boak's arguments about manpower shortages in the later empire.

25. **Frend, W. H. C.** *Town and Country in the Early Christian Centuries.* London: Variorum Reprints, 1980. The relevant sections of this anthology are analyzed separately in this bibliography.

26. **Grant, Michael.** *The Fall of the Roman Empire; a Reappraisal.* Radnor, Penn.: Annenberg School Press, 1976. The theme is "disastrous disunities." Everything was wrong and everyone was against everyone in the later Roman empire. Grant's eloquence and all the pretty pictures make the theme seem refreshing and new, but in fact it's old wine in new bottles.   P. Brown, *New York Review of Books* 23 (April 15, 1976): 14-18 (-).

27. **Groh, D.** "Galilee and the Eastern Roman Empire in Late Antiquity." *Explor* 3 (1977): 78-93.

28. **Hawkes, S. C. and Dunning, G. C.** "Soldiers and Settlers in Britain, Fourth to Fifth Century." *Medieval Archaeology* 5 (1970): 1-70.

29. **Haywood, Richard M.** *The Myth of Rome's Fall.* New York: Thomas Y. Crowell Co., 1958.   Haywood is an antidote to the gloom and doom approaches to the fourth century. He puts the spotlight on all the best features of the age, including perhaps some that were not really there.   A. Momigliano, *Journal of Roman Studies* 49 (1959): 211 ("For a moment the title made me hope for some revolutionary thesis. Perhaps Professor Haywood was going to deny that Rome fell. Alas, nothing else in the book suggests that the author would ever deny the obvious or go beyond it.");   M. L. W. Laistner, *American Historical Review* 64 (July 1959): 985-986 (-).

30. **Hodges, R.** "Aspects of the Decline and Fall of the Roman Empire." *Journal of Roman Archaeology* 1 (1988): 215-222.

31. **Hohfelder, Robert L.,** ed. *City, Town, and Countryside in the Early Byzantine Era.* Byzantine Series, 1. Boulder: East European Monographs; New York: Distributed by Columbia University Press, 1982.   Collection of nine essays, covering the third to the sixth centuries in the Eastern Mediterranean and the Balkans.   S. MacCormack, *American Historical Review* 89 (1984): 744-745 (+).

32. **James, Jamie.** "New Ways of Looking for the Past." *Discover* 7 (September 1986): 64-75.   The great earthquake of A. D. 365 (or perhaps 363), described by Ammianus Marcellinus, flattened the city of Kourion on Cyprus. Now the Americans are at work there, applying the techniques of the New Archaeology and revealing "a snapshot of life in the late Roman Empire" (p. 66).

33. **Johnson, Stephen.** *Later Roman Britain.* New York: Charles Scribner's Sons, 1980.   The first three chapters have to do with Britain in the later empire; the last three have to do with the Anglo-Saxon intrusion. Defense is a predominant theme of the book, properly reflecting the major preoccupation of a frontier territory. The maps are especially helpful.   C. Wells, *American Historical Review* 87 (1982): 161-162; Casey, *Britannia* 13 (1982): 435-436.

34. **Johnston, Alan.** "A Fourth Century Graffito from the Kerameikos." *Mitteilungen des Deutschen Archaeologischen Instituts. Arbeitung (Athens)* 100 (1985): 293-307.

35. **Jones, A. H. M.** "The Decline and Fall of the Roman Empire." *History* 40 (October 1955): 209-226.   Jones summarizes weaknesses of the Roman world, but cautions against magnifying them all out of proportion to their relevance to the fall of the empire in the west.

36. **Jones, A. H. M.** *The Decline of the Ancient World.* New York: Holt, Rinehart and Winston, 1966.   A condensed version of Jones' magnum opus, *The Later Roman Empire, 284-602.* There was decline, but it was neither universal nor uniform. And it was not enough to bring down the empire. The barbarians did that.   J. A. Crook, *Journal of Roman Studies* 58 (1968): 251-253 (+).

37. **Jones, A. H. M.** *The Later Roman Empire, 284-602: A Social Economic and Administrative Survey.* 2 vols. Norman: University of Oklahoma Press; 4 vols., Oxford: Basil Blackwell and Mott, 1964.   This is a work so important that it must

always be at the side of the student of the fourth century. It is a classic and it is essential. It has been heavily reviewed, of course, and almost all the reviews are favorable; but they also offer a number of corrections and criticisms that are useful supplementary material. The review by Peter Brown is especially compelling as a discussion of the conceptual strengths and weaknesses of the work.   J. Alsop, *New Yorker* 41 (August 28, 1965): 114-120 (+); E. J. Bickerman, *American Historical Review* 70 (1965): 750-751 (++-); F. M. Heichelheim, *Journal of Roman Studies* 55 (1965): 250-253 (++-); P. Brown, *Economic History Review* 20 (1967): 327-343 (+); M. Hammond, *Speculum* 42 (1967): 168-172 (+); M. McGuire, *Catholic Historical Review* 53 (1967): 251-154; *Times Literary Supplement* #3279 (December 31, 1964): 1173- (+); J. M. Wallace-Hadrill, *English Historical Review* 80 (1965): 785-790 (+).

38.   **Jones, A. H. M., Martindale, J. R. and Morris, J**. *The Prosopography of the Later Roman Empire. Vol. I: A. D. 260-395.* Cambridge: University Press, 1971.   The is THE who's who of late Roman personalities. Though impressive, it is not free of serious flaws. Consult the reviews for cautions and corrections.   A. R. Birley, *Journal of Roman Studies* 62 (1972): 185-186; T. D. Barnes, *Phoenix* 26 (1972): 140-182 (-); G. W. Bowersock, *American Journal of Philology* 97 (1976): 84-86 (-).

39.   **Jones, A. H. M.** "Thoughts on the Decline of the Roman Empire." *Bulletin de la Societe d'Archeologie d'Alexandrie* 43 (1975): 43-52.   Jones succinctly reviews the internal weaknesses of the later empire, but pins the fall squarely on the shoulders of the northern barbarians, Persians, and finally Arabs.

40.   **Kaegi, Walter E**. *Army, Society and Religion in Byzantium*. London: Variorum Reprints, 1982.   Reprints of separately published papers, many relevant to the fourth century. These are listed elsewhere.

41. **Keay, Simon J.** *Roman Spain.* Exploring the Roman World, 2. Berkeley: University of California Press, 1988. Chapter 8, "Hispania During the Late Empire," may be of some interest. The focus of the narrative is on the decline of towns, the rise of great country estates, the restoration of Roman administrative control after the late third century, and the growth of Christianity. Handsomely illustrated.

42. **Krautheimer, Richard.** *Rome: Profile of a City, 312-1308.* Princeton, N. J.: Princeton University Press, 1980. Krautheimer is especially good on the fourth century period, whose architecture, especially in its social and political context, he has studied extensively. R. Brentano, *Speculum* 56 (July 1981): 622-625 (+).

43. **Laing, LLoyd and Laing, Jennifer.** "Scottish and Irish Metalwork and the *'Conspiratio barbarica.'*" *Proceedings. Society of Antiquaries of Scotland* 116 (1986): 211-221. The barbarian activity here has to do with incursions into Britain in the middle of the fourth century.

44. **Lieberman, S.** "Palestine in the Third and Fourth Centuries." *Jewish Quarterly Review* 36 (1946): 329-370.

45. **Liebeschuetz, J. H. W.** *Antioch: City and Imperial Administration in the Later Roman Empire.* Oxford: The Clarendon Press, 1972. Antioch in the fourth century. Libanius has a large coverage at the start of the book. B. Levick, *Journal of Roman Studies* 63 (1973): 270-271 ("No student of city administration, of the political, cultural and economic life of the later Empire, or (to a lesser extent) of its language and law, can afford to neglect it.").

46. **MacMullen, Ramsay.** *Corruption and the Decline of Rome.* New Haven: Yale University Press, 1988. MacMullen is no soft touch for decline theories. He takes a very skeptical view of most of them, and discovers instead that the later Roman empire was healthy enough in most respects - or, at least, not more unhealthy than in many previous centuries - to maintain itself. The wealth and

institutions of the empire were sufficient to defend and maintain it if properly used. Nevertheless, after a careful probe of each region of the empire, he does see a greater trend of internal weakness in the west: "The decline of the Roman empire was a decline only of its younger part" (p. 35). There was, moreover, a menace that plagued the whole system. This was the privatization of power, the tendency of great magnates, political leaders, and military leaders, to identify their personal interests with public service, and later, especially after, say, 350, to let their personal interests overwhelm every other public consideration. In practical terms, this meant corruption and chaos at high levels of government; it meant, worst of all, a deterioration in the military forces just when their strength and ability were needed more than ever. MacMullen sees and laments "the will of a great empire dissolving in the uncontrolled impulses of private enterprise" (p.197). This is a fascinating read, richly documented, full of the color and flavor of late Roman life at all levels of society.

47. Marasovic, Tomislav. *Diocletian's Palace.* Translated by Sonia Weld-Bicanic. Belgrade: NOLIT, 1982. There is a 1967 edition. Also, there are 1968, 1970, and 1972 reports on Diocletian's palace by Jerko and/or Marasovic.

48. Mazzarino, S. *The End of the Ancient World.* Translated by G. Holmes. London: Faber and Faber, 1966. Perhaps most helpful is Mazzarino's long consideration of what decline meant at different times and places. He finds problems in the later Roman state, but no universal decadence. J. A. Crook, *Journal of Roman Studies* 58 (1968): 251-253 (+-).

49. Millar, Fergus. "Italy and the Roman Empire: Augustus to Constantine." *Phoenix* 40 (1986): 295-318. Millar addresses "in what ways the functioning of the Roman state may have affected the economic and social history of Italy" (p. 296). For the fourth century, Millar works with such new developments as the introduction of direct taxes, the movement of the imperial court and army to Milan, the loss of revenue to the cities through the granting of immunities to local aristocrats who had imperial appointments, and changes in the number and functions of governors and judges who represented the central government in Italy. In a very important section, Millar disputes the "established doctrine" that the central government under the Constantine family confiscated city lands. Millar says these public lands were improperly requisitioned by private individuals, and that legislation under Julian attempted to restore these lands to enhance city revenues.

50. **Mirkovic, M.** "Sirmium: Its History from the 1. Century to 582 A. D." *Sirmium* 1 (1971): 5ff. Sirmium was a strategically significant place in the fourth century, and frequented by the emperors of that time.

51. **Popovic, Vladislav.** "A Survey of the Topography and Urban Organization of Sirmium in the Late Empire." In *Sirmium I. Archaeological Investigation in Sirmium Pannonia,* pp. 119-133. Edited by V. Popovic and E. L. Ochsenschlager. Belgrade: Archaeological Institute, 1971.

52. **Potter, Timothy W.** *Roman Italy.* Berkeley: University of California Press, 1987. An archaeological tour of Italy. The relevant chapter is "Later Roman Italy and the Rise of Christianity." Sometimes literary sources have mislead us, and archaeology can set the record straight. For the later empire, archaeology shows us something worth remembering: many people and many parts of Italy went about life as usual, surviving or ignoring religious changes, civil wars, barbarians, and so on.

53. **Reynolds, Joyce M**. "The Cities of Cyrenaica in Decline." In *Themes de recherches sur les villes antiques d'Occident*, pp. 53-58. Published under the direction of P.-M. Duval and Ed. Frezouls. Paris: Editions du Centre National de la recherche scientifique, 1977.

54. **Rouge, Jean.** *Ships and Fleets of the Ancient Mediterranean.* Translated from the French by Susan Frazer.

Middleton, Conn.: Wesleyan University Press, 1981. Includes some information on the fourth century empire. E. N. Luttwak, *American Historical Review* 87 (1982): 1368-1369 (+).

55. **Rubin, Zeev.** "The Mediterranean and the Dilemma of the Roman Empire in Late Antiquity." *Mediterranean Historical Review* 1 (1986): 13-62. Although there is not much in here on the fourth century, Rubin does offer a broad perspective on a dilemma of the empire: how to keep its western provinces in order and the Persians at bay at the same time.

56. **Russell, Kenneth W.** "The Earthquake of May 19 A. D. 363." *Bulletin of the American Schools of Oriental Research* 238 (1980): 47-62. Russell reviews the historical and archaeological evidence to get a sense of the effects of the great 363 earthquake on Palestine.

57. **Salzman, M. R.** "New Evidence for the Dating of the Calendar at Santa Maria Maggiore in Rome." *Transactions of the American Philological Association* 111 (1981): 215-227. A large but deteriorated fresco calendar discovered in 1966 is certainly Roman, but from what period? An Italian scholar dated the remains to A. D. 299/332 and 354, but Salzman pushes the date back to A. D. 176-224/275.

58. **Salzman, M. R.** "Studies on the Calendar of 354." Ph. D dissertation, Bryn Mawr College, 1981.

59. **Soren, David.** "The Day the World Ended at Kourion: Reconstructing an Ancient Earthquake." *National Geographic* 174 (July 1988): 30-53. Kourion is becoming to the fourth century Roman empire what Pompeii is to the first century empire: a provincial city brought to a halt by a natural disaster, now an important look at how people really lived. Soren's work continues, and his judgment is that "Kourion's ruins promise to yield the most complete picture yet of life in the late Roman Empire as well as a rare chance to study an

General and Miscellaneous Works   15

ancient population in its original context" (p. 53)   Heavily illustrated.

60. **Thompson, Homer A.** "Athenian Twilight: A. D. 267-600." *Journal of Roman Studies* 49 (1959): 61-72.   The extensive devastation in Athens in A. D. 267 by the northern barbarians called Heruli left a permanent scar on the appearance and life of the city in the fourth century.

61. **Velkov, Velizar.** *Cities in Thrace and Dacia in Late Antiquity.* Amsterdam: A. M. Hakkert, 1977.   The importance of the Balkans to the fourth century is underscored by this important piece of Bulgarian scholarship.   The vital military factories alone in the prosperous cities of the region give one pause to think why the emperor would permit tens of thousands of barbarians into the region in 376; but, after all, they were supposed to be settled in the countryside and along the frontier, where they could guard against a new horror: the Huns. Velkov stresses the continuity of cities and of life in the countryside despite the upheavals of the time. He covers the period from the late third century to the end of the sixth century, and includes lots of valuable information on most aspects of life and government.

62. **Velkov, Velizar.** "Thrace and Lower Moesia During the Roman and Late Roman Epoch." *Klio* 63 (no.2, 1981): 473-483.   A convenient outline of the history of this strategically important area through the sixth century.   Velkov offers an interesting statistic: forty percent of the armaments industry of the eastern empire was in the diocese of Thrace in the fourth century.

63. **Vidal, Gore.** *Julian, a Novel.*   Boston: Little, Brown, 1964.   Light reading for late night recreation.   Where's the movie?

64. **Vogt, Joseph.** *The Decline of Rome.* Translated by J. Sondheimer.   London: Weidenfeld and Nicholson, 1967. Covering the period from the Severi to the fall of the empire in the west, Vogt gives a balanced, measured, informed analysis.

There is a tendency to see the best in Christianity and the barbarians, and there is an emphasis on the western empire. See especially Chapter 2, "The Monarchy, the Christian Church and Ruling Society in the Fourth Century," pp. 87-176.   W. H. C. Frend, *English Historical Review* 84 (1969): 376 (+-); R. Browning, *Journal of Roman Studies* 59 (1969): 272-274 (+).

65.   Wacher, J. S.   "Yorkshire Towns in the Fourth Century." In *Soldier and Civilian in Roman Yorkshire*, pp. 165-177. Edited by R. M. Butler. Leicester: Leicester University Press, 1971.   In the "fluid conditions obtaining in the fourth century," a small town's character could change a lot in a short time, says Wacher, making it hard to generalize.   Wacher is largely involved with sifting the evidence for military versus civilian orientations at various sites.

66.   Walbank, F. W. *The Decline of the Roman Empire in the West.* London: The Cobbett Press, 1946; revised ed., Toronto: University of Toronto Press, 1969.   Walbank identifies a long, long economic decline, with the fourth century naturally having a lot of attention, although the third century overshadows it. Slavery and technical stagnation figure prominently as factors of decline.   R. L. Hohlfelder, *Rocky Mountain Social Science Journal* 9 (1972): 117-121 (+-); A. H. M. Jones, *Journal of Roman Studies* 38 (1948): 149-150 (+-).

67.   Warmington, Brian H. *The North African Provinces from Diocletian to the Vandal Conquest.* New York and Cambridge: Cambridge University Press, 1954; reprint ed., Westport, Conn.: Greenwood Press, 1971.   This is a good introduction to the administration, the military, the cities and the countryside, the Romans versus native elements, and the Donatist movement in fourth century Africa.   W. H. C. Frend, *Journal of Roman Studies* 45 (1955): 203-204 (++-); A. R. Burn, *History* 40 (1955): 120 (+).

68.   Weitzmann, Kurt, ed. *Late Classical and Medieval Studies in Honor of Albert Mathias Friend, Jr.* Princeton, N. J.: Princeton University Press, 1955.   Relevant essays from this anthology are analyzed individually.

69. White, Lynn, ed. *The Transformation of the Roman World: Gibbon's Problem After Two Centuries.* Berkeley and Los Angeles: University of California Press, 1966. Nine essays, plus an introduction and a conclusion. The focus is more or less the obsolescence of Gibbon in many respects. There is incidentally some material on the fourth century, but perhaps not enough to give a ringing endorsement to the book as an important item on the fourth century student's reading list. R. Browning, *Journal of Roman Studies* 59 (1969): 272-274 (+-); W. H. C. Frend, *English Historical Review* 84 (1969): 140-141 (+-)

70. Wightman, Edith M. *Gallia Belgica.* London: Batsford; Berkeley: University of California Press, 1985. The emphasis is on social and economic developments of northern Gaul. Wightman offers a healthy section on the fourth century, when imperial interests in the area were often represented by the emperor himself who now maintained an imperial center at Trier. R. Van Dam, *American Historical Review* 91 (1986): 894 (+); J. H. Humphrey, *Archaeology* 40 (January 1987): 71-72 (+-); G. Herring, *Journal of Roman Studies* 77 (1987): 238-239 (+).

71. Wightman, Edith M. "North-eastern Gaul in Late Antiquity, the Testimony of Settlement Patterns in an Age of Transition." *Berichten van de Rijksdienst voor Oudheidkundig Bodemonderzoek* 28 (1978): 241-250.

72. Wightman, Edith M. *Roman Trier and the Treveri.* London: Hart-Davis, 1970. Includes much information on fourth century Trier, a frequent seat of the emperors. J. C. Mann, *Journal of Roman Studies* 61 (1971): 294 (+).

II. Politics and Government

Includes Roman law and most literature on the emperors. But see also "Church and State," where for instance there is a great deal of material on Constantine I.

73. Alfoldi, Andras. *A Conflict of Ideas in the Late Roman Empire: The Clash Between the Senate and Valentinian I.* Translated by Harold Mattingly. Oxford: Clarendon Press, 1952; Westport, Conn.: Greenwood press, 1979. Alfoldi sees black and white: the Senate is black and Valentinian is white. Much of value but caution is advised. J. Seaver, *American Historical Review* 58 (1952-53): 83-84 (+-); F. Cramer, *Speculum* 28 (1953): 128-131 (+-); N. Baynes, *Journal of Roman Studies* 43 (1953): 169-170 (+-).

74. Alfoldy, Andras. "A Few Notes on the Foundation of Constantinople." *Journal of Roman Studies* 37 (1947): 10-16. Through the use of coins and medallions, Alfoldy speaks of Constantine's gradual abandonment of old Rome as effective captial of the new Christianized government and the increasing attraction of the new city on the Bosporus, Constantinople, as a reflection of the old capital but without all the pagan baggage: "Thus Constantine left Rome as the 'museum' of the great national past. . . [A]t the same time, he made of his new capital the Rome of the Christian world" (p. 15).

75. Andersen, Thomas B. "*Patrocinium* : the Concept of Personal Protection and Dependence in the Later Roman Empire and the Early Middle Ages." Ph. D. dissertation, Fordham University, 1974. As the central government demanded more and gave less, so rose the power of the local patron who could offer protection and service. This development was especially pronounced in the fifth century west, but was picking up momentum in the late fourth century.

76. Anderson, J. G. C. "The Genesis of Diocletian's Provincial Reorganisation." *Journal of Roman Studies* 22 (1932): 24-32. Anderson adduces evidence to show that Diocletian's administrative and military reforms often had precedents going back into the middle third century, and that while there were definite trends, there was no wholesale restructuring of provincial government, but a gradual one depending on circumstances.

77. Anderson, Richard L. "The Rise and Fall of Middle-Class Loyalty to the Roman Empire: A Social Study of Velleius Paterculus and Ammianus Marcellinus." Ph. D. dissertation, University of California Berkeley, 1962. Ammianus is seen to be a champion of upper middle class rights against both the aristocratic elements and the central government.

78. Arce, J. "Constantius II Sarmaticus and Persicus: A Reply." *Zeitschrift des Deutschen Palastina-Vereins* 57 (1984): 225-229. The reply is to Timothy Barnes, "Two Victory Titles . . . " (103).

79. Arnheim, Michael T. W. *The Senatorial Aristocracy in the Later Roman Empire*. Oxford: Clarendon Press, 1972. All in all, the great aristocratic families of the west did well in the fourth century, consolidating and expanding their vast wealth, and moving into influential government posts, especially after Valentinian I. S. J. Simon, *American Historical Review* 78 (1973):1029-1030 (+); J. W. Eadie, *American Journal of Philology* 96 (1975); 93-96 (+-).

80. Arnheim, Michael T. W. "Vicars in the Later Roman Empire." *Historia* 19 (1970): 593-606. Arnheim discusses titles and their significance for fourth century administrators known commonly to us as vicars.

81. Athanassiadi-Fowden, Polymnia. *Julian and Hellenism: An Intellectual Biography.* New York and London: Oxford University Press, 1981. In this treatment, Julian is usually photographed on his better side. But there is rich documentation and at least not a total denial of Julian's faults. The same for Hellenism. G. W. Bowersock, *American Historical Review* 88 (1983): 90-91 ("an air of hagiography"); Averil Cameron, *Times Literary Supplement* (February 26, 1982): 206 ("oscillates between praise and irritation"); S. Runciman, *History Today* 32 (1982): 56 (+).

82. Austin, N. J. E. "Constantine and Crispus, A. D. 326." *Acta Classica* (Capetown) 23 (1980): 133-138. "[Austin] . . . attempts to break some new ground in proposing that the usual explanation of treason, adultery or palace plots do not meet the circumstances depicted by what evidence is available, but rather that Crispus was detected in the use of magic, and had his position and activities misrepresented to Constantine" (p. 133). In fact, the evidence on Constantine's talented first son is too insignificant to admit of any final conclusions. The incidents leading to his death are forever shrouded in mystery. See P. Guthrie, "The Execution of Crispus," *Phoenix* 20 (1966), 325-331, for another view (198).

83. Austin, N. J. E. "Julian at Ctesiphon: A Fresh Look at Ammianus' Account." *Athenaeum* 50 (1972): 301-309. "This paper attemps to rehabilitate Ammianus by showing how different aspects of his account on this occasion are by no means wrong or incompatible, nor do they fail to explain Julian's strategic aims" (p. 301).

84. Austin, N. J. E. "A Usurper's Claim to Legitimacy: Procopius in A. D. 365/366." *Rivista Storica dell' Antichita* 2 (1972): 187-194. "Procopius' usurpation claimed to be legal on the grounds of his relationship to Constantine, and of his designation as successor by Julian; he exploited his claim through the coinage and by surrounding himself with personnel connected with the house of Constantine. His propaganda effort justifying his claims influenced contemporary writers much more than that of the legitimate Valens" (p. 194).

85. Avery, William T. "The *adoratio purpurae* and the Importance of the Imperial Purple in the Fourth Century of the Christian Era." *Memoirs of the American Academy in Rome* 17 (1940): 66-80. The act of kissing the hem of the emperor's purple robe had great symbolic significance in the fourth century as a sign of obeisance and acceptance of the entire order of government as arranged, or at least preserved, by the chief executive. Culling the ancient literature, and with a special emphasis on Ammianus Marcellinus, Avery traces the introduction of the ceremony to Diocletian, relates it to Roman antecedents rather than Persian, and discusses the ramifications and use of this powerful symbolic act along with the concept of the purple robe generally in the politics of the age.

86. Bagnall, R. S., et al. *Consuls of the Later Roman Empire, 284-541.* Atlanta, Ga.: Scholars Press, 1987. Published for the American Philological Association, *Consuls* brings together all the evidence to give some coherence and stability to the long list of consuls upon which depends much of the dating for events in late antiquity. J. Harries and M. Whitby, *Classical Review* 39 (1989: 90-92 (+-).

87. Baldwin, Barry. "The *Caesares* of Julian." *Klio* 60 (1978): 449-466. Reproduced in *Studies on Late Roman and Byzantine History, Literature and Language*, pp. 171-188. Amsterdam: J. C. Geiben, 1984. "The *Caesares* brings together many points from Julian's other writings. Its purpose is propaganda. Julian wanted to reassure his audience that a single emperor could combine the virtues of predecessors in both military and civilian matters" (p. 466).

88. Baldwin, Barry. "The Career of Oribasius." *Acta Classica* 18 (1975): 85-97. Reproduced in *Studies on Late Roman and Byzantine History, Literature and Language*, pp. 157-169. Amsterdam: J. C. Geiben, 1984. Baldwin tells all there is to know about Oribasius, a doctor who was a close friend of the emperor Julian, and who after Julian's death (and after a period of eclipse) had an interesting life in the limelight until at least the end of the fourth century.

89. Baldwin, Barry. "Jordanes on Eugenius: Some Further Possibilities." *Antichthon* 11 (1977): 120-121. Reproduced in his *Studies on Late Roman and Byzantine History, Literature and Language*, pp. 119-120. Amsterdam: J. C. Gieben, 1984. More on the historian Jordanes' bungling regarding the usurper Eugenius. See also Brian Croke (168), "Jordanes' Understanding of the Usurpation of Eugenius," *Antichthon* 9 (1975), 81-83.

90. Barnes, Timothy D. "An Anachronism in Claudian." *Historia* 27 (1978): 498-499. Events surrounding the rebellion of Gildo, 397-398.

91. Barnes, Timothy D. "The Career of Abinnaeus." *Phoenix* 39 (1985): 368-374. Barnes reviews the chronology and events of the career of Abinnaeus, who under Constantius II held a military command in Egypt and some of whose correspondence survives. See also H. I. Bell et al (111).

92. Barnes, Timothy D. "Constans and Gratian in Rome." *Harvard Studies in Classical Philology* 79 (1975): 325-333. Rome was not often the working capital of the empire in the fourth century, but it remained a ceremonial capital, and there certainly was no better setting for a display of imperial splendor. Barnes lists the imperial visits to Rome in the fourth century, observing that many occurred after a civil war or a political crisis. He ends with an interesting aside on some primary source material for the age.

93. Barnes, Timothy D. "The Conversion of Constantine." *Classical Views* 4 (1985): 371-391. There was no sudden conversion of Constantine in 312. He was already, and had been for some time, a Christian sympathizer and a patron and protector of the Christian Church. In 312 he confirmed this role publicly, perhaps encouraged by political developments. Barnes offers interesting information on political developments of the early fourth century, on the events of 312 when Constantine won in Italy, and on the famous Speech to the Saints (*Oratio ad Sanctos*), which Barnes considers a genuine work of Constantine.

94. **Barnes, Timothy D**. "Himerius and the Fourth Century." *Classical Philology* 82 (1987): 206-225. "The general picture that emerges is a disappointing and depressing one of an academic who attempted to achieve political prominence by attaching himself to Julian, then suffered disgrace (though not complete disaster) when Julian failed so spectacularly and the Roman Empire again became officially Christian" (p. 224).

95. **Barnes, Timothy D.** "The Historical Setting of Prudentius' *Contra Symmachum.*" *American Journal of Philology* 97 (1976): 373-386. Barnes argues that the *Contra Symmachum* was written in 402 to answer pagan arguments that the abandonment of the old ways in favor of Christianity led to disasters like Alaric's invasion of Italy.

96. **Barnes, Timothy D.** "Imperial Chronology, A. D. 337-350." *Phoenix* 34 (1980): 160-166. Barnes traces the movements of the emperors Constantinus, Constantius, and Constans,

97. **Barnes, Timothy D and Vander Spoel, J.** "Julian on the Sons of Fausta." *Phoenix* 38 (1984): 175-176. In a panegyric on Constantius, the emperor's cousin Julian offered some remarks on Constans, Constantinus, as well as Constantius, which are discussed.

98. **Barnes, Timothy D.** *The New Empire of Diocletian and Constantine.* Cambridge, Mass.: Harvard University Press, 1982. This is Barnes' companion volume to his *Constantine and Eusebius* (1306), and is a kind of statistical abstract of the Roman Empire in the first quarter of the fourth century. Essential. T. Africa, *American Historical Review* 88 (1983): 660 (+).

99. Barnes, Timothy D. "Proconsuls of Africa, 337-392." *Phoenix* 39 (1985): 144-153.

100. Barnes, Timothy D. "Proconsuls of Africa: Corrigenda." *Phoenix* 39 (1985): 273-274.

101. Barnes, Timothy D. "Synesius in Constantinople." *Greek, Roman, and Byzantine Studies* 27 (1986): 93-112. Barnes analyzes the political literature from the pen of Synesius, written while he was living in Constantinople from 397 to 400 representing the interests of his city and of the upper middle class conservative view of how the empire should be run.

102. Barnes, Timothy D. "Two Senators under Constantine." *Journal of Roman Studies* 65 (1975): 40-49. A prosopographical look at two senators, using evidence from an unlikely source: a contemporary handbook of astrology.

103. Barnes, Timothy D. "Two Victory Titles of Constantius." *Zeitschrift fur Papyrologie und Epigraphik* 52 (1983): 229-235. Barnes reviews a debate about when Constantius II took certain victory titles. On the debate hinges some chronology about events involving Constantius' military campaigns. For more, see J. Arce (78).

104. Barnes, Timothy D. "The Unity of the Verona List." *Zeitschrift fur Papyrologie und Epigraphik* 16 (1975): 275-278. Barnes disputes the view of scholars such as Bury and A. H. M. Jones that the Verona list of early fourth century provinces is a homogeneous piece.

105. Barnes, Timothy D. "The Victims of Rufinus." *Classical Quarterly* 34 (1984): 227-230. Barnes has a look at the poet Claudian's *In Rufinum* and learns that the poet has respected the chronology of events during the ministry of Rufinus in the 390s.

106. Barrow, R. H. *Prefect and Emperor: The Relationes of Symmachus A. D. 384.* Oxford: Clarendon Press, 1973.

R. S. O. Tomlin, *Journal of Roman Studies* 65 (1975): 203-204 ("Barnes has done English late Roman studies a great service by translating the *relationes* with almost complete accuracy." Then follows a series of corrections and criticisms of other parts of the book.)

107. Baynes, Norman H. "The Death of Julian the Apostate in a Christian Legend." *Journal of Roman Studies* 27 (1937): 22-29. The historians Sozomen and Faustus of Byzantium (late fourth century, according to Baynes) and other sources are worked to show the evolution of an early Christian legend about the death of Julian which had its origins in Antioch shortly after his death in 363.

108. Baynes, Norman H. "The Early Life of Julian the Apostate." *Journal of Hellenic Studies* 45 (1925): 251-254. Baynes re-works the chronology for Julian in the 330s and 340s.

109. Baynes, Norman H. "Two Notes on the Reforms of Diocletian and Constantine." *Journal of Roman Studies* 15 (1925): 195-208. Reprinted in his *Byzantine Studies and other Essays*, pp. 173-185. London: Athlone Press, 1955; Westport, Conn.: Greenwood Press, 1974. The first note has to do with Gallienus and the gradual elimination of senators from military leadership and from governorships; the second has to do with army reforms under Diocletian and Constantine, with Baynes taking the now unpopular view that Diocletian created a permanent mobile field army.

110. Beck, Hans-Georg. "Constantinople: The Rise of a New Capital in the East." In *Age of Spirituality: A Symposium*, pp. 29-37. Edited by Kurt Weitzmann. New York: Metropolitan Museum of Art, in Association with Princeton University Press, 1980. Constantinople was not an instant success. In the fourth century, it was not favored by all the emperors, and it was deeply resented as an unnecessary upstart by the older cities of the east. Nevertheless, a great deal of money and attention were lavished on it, and by the end of the century it was established as the permanent home of the imperial court, a religious center next in importance to Rome, and the most populous city of the empire next to Rome. Its success was by then assured. Beck tells the story in rich detail.

111. Bell, H. I., Martin, V., Turner, E. G., and van Berchem, D., eds. *The Abinnaeus Archive: Papers of a Roman Officer in the Reign of Constantius II.* Oxford: Clarendon Press, 1962. Translations of fourth century Greek and Latin papyri from the sands of Egypt.

112. Bellinger, Alfred R. "Diocletian's Farewell." In *Late Classical and Mediaeval Studies in Honor of Albert Mathias Friend, Jr.*, pp. 1-6. Edited by Kurt Weitzmann. Princeton, N. J.: Princeton University Press, 1955. Bellinger discusses coins issued to commemorate the abdication of Diocletian and Maximian in 305.

113. Bird, H. W. "Diocletian and the Deaths of Carus, Numerian and Carinus." *Latomus* 35 (1976): 123-132. Bird reviews the circumstances of the deaths of the three emperors just preceding Diocletian, and finds the fingerprints of Diocletian everywhere.

114. Bird, H. W. "Eutropius: His Life and Career." *Classical Views* 7 (1988): 51-60. Bird sorts out what we can and cannot know about the high court official Eutropius, and finds a man who served the emperors from Constantius II to Theodosius I with honesty and shrewdness. Bird adduces much incidental information about government and governing personalities in the second half of the fourth century.

115. Blockley, R. C. "The Coded Message in Ammianus Marcellinus 18.6." *Classical Views* 5 (1986): 63-65. Blockley sees a strong hint of fabrication in this passage of Ammianus, which has to do with a message smuggled out of Persia to the emperor Constantius II, advising him in code about Persian troop movements.

116. Blockley, R. C. "Constantius Gallus and Julian as Caesars of Constantius II." *Latomus* 31 (1972): 433-468.

Blockley tries to moderate and balance the unfavorable report of Gallus found in Ammianus. The true cause of Gallus' fall is revealed: "Gallus' real crime, in the Emperor's eyes, was not his savagery or his condemnation of the curials, but that he has acted in an area where he had no competence, the civil jurisdiction" (p. 464). In fact, both Gallus and Julian followed a pattern as Caesars: "Both were appointed Caesars for military purposes; both found themselves drawn into civil affairs; both were suspected by the Emperor and slandered by his officials. In both cases, when the Caesar has shown an inclination to interfere in civil affairs Constantius decided to act against him" (p. 465). Blockley includes an interesting discussion on the position of the Caesar generally in the Tetrarchic system as developed by Diocletian.

117. Blockley, R. C. "Constantius II and His Generals." In *Studies in Latin Literature and Roman History*, pp. 467-486. Vol. II. Edited by Carl Deroux. Collection Latomus, 168. Brussels: Latomus, 1980. Blockley sifts through the evidence to find a political pattern, rather than mere matters of weak or strong personalities, in the difficulties Constantius experienced with his generals. Instead of seeing Constantius as a weak and suspicious person, as the sources encourage us to do, it is more instructive to see that he was working to "strike a balance between the centralizing tendencies of the central authority (which included himself) and the localist interests of the military and the provinces" (p. 472). But Diocletian proved right in the end. The conditions of the fourth century seemed to require multiple emperors who would respond more directly to local interests: hence Valens and Valentinian, and even more paired emperors after them.

118. Blockley, R. C. "The Date of the 'Barbarian Conspiracy.' " *Britannia* 11 (1980): 223-225. Blockley disputes Roger Tomlin's (*Britannia* 5 [1974], 303-309) chronology regarding the campaign of Theodosius to restore the British frontier in the late 360s.

119. Blockley, R. C. "The Panegyric of Claudius Mamertinus on the Emperor Julian." *American Journal of*

Philology 93 (1972): 437-450. Mamertinus is an important source on Julian, but he was very pro-Julian and must be used with caution. The speech was delivered in January of 362, and Blockley shows that certain omissions on religious and military matters point up the bias. There is a discussion of the relation of Ammianus Marcellinus to Mamertinus, and of the trials of Chalcedon, by which representatives of the previous regime of Constantius II were condemned.

120. Boak, Arthur E. R. *The Master of the Offices in the Later Roman and Byzantine Empires.* New York: Macmillan, 1919; New York: Johnson Reprint Corp., 1972. Originally issued as V. 14 of University of Michigan Studies; later reprinted in Boak's *Two Studies in Later Roman and Byzantine Administration* (124).

121. Boak, Arthur E. R. "The Role of Policy in the Fall of the Roman Empire." *Michigan Alumnus Quarterly Review* 56 (1950): 281-284. The argument here is that political policy of the fourth century government favored the eastern half of the empire, leaving the west pretty much on its own. The premise is that the west was generally less wealthy, less developed than the east, and that a lot of western talent ended up in the eastern court.

122. Boak, Arthur E. R. "Roman Magistri in the Civil and Military Service of the Empire." *Harvard Studies in Classical Philology* 26 (1915): 73-164. Boak reviews the entire history of the use of the term *magister* in the Roman government. The majority of the material relates to the later empire.

123. Boak, Arthur E. R. "*Tessarii* and *Quadrarii* as Village Officials in Egypt of the Fourth Century." In *Studies in Roman Economic and Social History in Honor of Allan Chester Johnson*, pp. 322-335. Edited by P. R. Coleman-Norton, Princeton, N. J.: Princeton University Press, 1951. With papyri from the desert Boak reveals information on the functions of village officials.

124. Boak, Arthur E. R. and Dunlap, James E. *Two Studies in Later Roman and Byzantine Administration.* New York: Macmillan Co.; London: Macmillan and Co., 1924. Contents: pt. 1: "The Master of the Offices in the Later Roman and Byzantine Empire," by Boak; pt. 2: "The Office of the Grand Chamberlain in the Later Roman and Byzantine Empire," by Dunlap.

125. Boer, William den. "The Emperor Silvanus and His Army." *Acta Classica* 3 (1960): 105-109. Boer reconstructs the circumstances and events of the twenty-eight day reign of the usurper Silvanus in 355.

126. Boer, William den. "Two Letters from the Corpus Iulianeum." *Vigiliae Christianae* 16 (1962): 179-197. Boer argues for the authenticity of two letters, one from Gallus to Julian, the other from Julian to the Jews.

127. Born, Lester K. "The Perfect Prince According to the Latin Panegyrists." *American Journal of Philology* 55 (1934): 20-35. Mostly fourth century speeches are sifted for information on how the emperor was expected to conduct himself in office.

128. Bowder, Diana. *The Age of Constantine and Julian.* London: Elek, 1978. There is good use of non-literary evidence to illuminate this exciting age, plus an excellent selection of photographs. Bowder's extensive treatment of religious developments is a good reminder that Christians and pagans were not always, in fact rarely, at each other's throats, even though there was plenty of mutual dislike. E. D. Hunt, *Classical Review* 30 (1980): 100-102 (+-); T. E. Gregory, *American Historical Review* 85 (1980): 608 (-); R. Browning, *Times Literary Supplement* (November 3, 1978): 1282 (+).

129. Bowersock, G. W. "The Emperor Julian on His Predecessors." *Yale Classical Studies* 27 (1982): 159-172. One of Julian's better known writings, the *Caesares*, is seen to offer "an unusual perspective on fourth-century traditions about earlier emperors" (p. 160), as well as Julian's own view of the Roman past, which was very limited. Fundamentally, says Bowersock, the piece is highly personal and reveals more about the author and his views than it does about the Roman emperors.

130. Bowersock, G. W. "The Imperial Cult: Perceptions and Persistence." In *Jewish and Christian Self-Definition.* Vol. 3: *Self-Definition in the Graeco-Roman World*, pp. 171-182. Edited by B. F. Meyer and E. P. Sanders. London: SCM Press, 1982. Bowersock shows how the imperial cult prospered under Christian emperors. With some sanitizing, such as the removal of sacrifices, the cult could be imported into a Christian milieu and given characteristics that made it very agreeable indeed both religiously and politically.

131. Bowersock, G. W. *Julian the Apostate.* Cambridge, Mass.: Harvard University Press, 1978. This is essential reading on Julian. Scholarly response to the book has been favorable, and negative remarks have mostly centered around the brevity of treatment of some aspects of Julian's life. W. E. Kaegi, *American Historical Review* 84 (1979): 130 (+); J. Matthews, *Times Literary Supplement* (November 3, 1978): 1283 (+-).

132. Bowersock, G. W. "Mavia, Queen of the Saracens." In *Studien zur Antiken Sozialgeschichte: Festschrift Friedrich Vittinghoff*, pp. 477-495. Edited by Werner Eck, Hartmut Galsterer, and Hartmut Wolff. Cologne: Bohlau, 1980. The story of a fourth century Arabian Christian Queen, who after troubling the Romans for some years became an ally and sent warriors to the protection of Constantinople after the defeat of Valens at Adrianople in 378. The sources are carefully reviewed.

133. Bowman, Alan K. "Two Notes." *Bulletin of the American Society of Papyrologists* 21 (1984): 33-38. Note one: a revolt of two Egyptian towns in the 290s; note two: market taxes at Oxyrhynchus.

134. **Bradbury, Scott.** "The Date of Julian's Letter to Themistius." *Greek, Roman, and Byzantine Studies* 28 (1987): 235-251. After a full review of the scholarly arguments, and a review of the relevant primary sources, with some interesting information on Themistius' public service, Bradbury concludes that "Julian composed the Letter to Themistius soon after his elevation to the rank of caesar on 6 November 355, either in late 355 or in early 356" (p. 251).

135. **Breebaart, A. B.** "Aspects of the Divorce Between East and West in the 4th Century." In *Actes du VIIe Congres de la Federation Internationale des Associations d'Etudes Classiques*, v. 2, pp. 9-22. Budapest: Akadeniai Kiado, 1984. Breebaart discusses forces tending towards division: the two ways of being Roman, symbolized in the two capitals, Rome and Constantinople; the independent tendencies of local magnates; problems of communication; the contribution of religious controversy; and so on.

136. **Brock, Sebastian P.** "The Rebuilding of the Temple under Julian, a New Source." *Palestine Exploration Quarterly* 108 (1976): 103-107. A source which Brock traces to about 400 offers new information on the abortive rebuilding of the temple in Jerusalem during the time of Julian.

137. **Browning, Robert.** *The Emperor Julian*. Berkeley and Los Angeles: University of California Press, 1976. This would be an excellent beginning for a student with an interest in Julian, a figure so compelling and complex that interpretations of him are bound to be prolific. Browning is informed and unfanatical, which leads to a reasonable and sympathetic narrative. R. O. Edbrooke, *American Journal of Philology* 98 (1977): 316-318 (+-); J. W. Halporn, *Classical Journal* 72 (1977): 365-367 (++-); R. M. Grant, *Church History* 45 (1976): 524 (+).

138. **Browning, Robert.** "The Riot of A. D. 387 in Antioch. The Role of the Theatrical Claques in the Later Empire." *Journal of Roman Studies* 42 (1952): 13-20. Reprinted in his *Studies on Byzantine History, Literature and*

Education. London: Variorum Reprints, 1977. This is the best documented riot in a late Roman city, and Browning takes the opportunity "to examine in detail one case which shows how the ever more crushing burden of the Empire in its decline was stimulating the growth of new forms of organized resistance among the mass of the people, in the great cities as well as the countryside" (p.20).

139. Bruce, Lorne D. "Diocletian, the Proconsul Iulianus and the Manichaeans." In *Studies in Latin Literature and Roman History,* pp. 336-347. Vol. 3. Edited by Carl Deroux. Collection Latomus, 180. Brussels: Latomus, 1983. Bruce dates the anti-Manichaean legislation of Diocletian to 31 March 297, and explains the political context, insofar as it can be inferred from the evidence.

140. Bruun, Patrick. "The Battle of the Milvian Bridge: The Date Reconsidered." *Hermes* 88 (1960): 361-370. Bruun says it may be 311 rather than the traditional 312.

141. Bruun, Patrick. "Constantine's Change of Dies Imperii." *Arctos* 9 (1975): 11-29.

142. Bruun, Patrick. "Constantine's *Dies Imperii* and *Quinquennalia* in the Light of the Early Solidi of Trier." *Numismatic Chronicle* 9 (1969): 177-209.

143. Bruun, Patrick. "The Disappearance of Sol from the Coins of Constantine." *Arctos* 2 (1958): 15-37. Bruun finds the latest Sol coin in 321.

144. Bruun, Patrick. "From Polis to Metropolis: Notes on Thessalonica in the Administration of the Late Roman Empire." *Opuscula Romana* 15 (1985): 7-16. Bruun studies the coins struck at Thessalonica from 284 to 368 for information on the importance of that city politically and administratively.

145. Bruun, Patrick. "Notes on the Transmission of Imperial Images in Late Antiquity." In *Studia Romana in Honorem Petri Krarup,* pp. 122-131. Edited by Karen Ascani and others. Odense: Odense University Press, 1976. Concentrating on the first quarter of the fourth century, Bruun considers the political dimension behind the protocol of delivering imperial images around the empire and behind the way in which portraits were configured.

146. Bruun, Patrick. "Roman Imperial Administration as Mirrored in the IV Century Coinage." *Eranos* 60 (1962): 93-100. Bruun defines the concept of the travelling mint to mean that in the fourth century gold minting travelled but not the mint itself: the models of reverses and portraits were on the road with the emperor, but these were handed over to the local mints to be struck. Bruun concentrates on the Constantinian period, using coin types to indicate political changes and imperial itineraries.

147. Bruun, Patrick. *Studies in Constantinian Chronology.* Numismatic Notes and Monographs, 146. New York: American Numismatic Society, 1961. Through coins, important events from the time of Constantine, such as the Battle of the Milvian Bridge and the dating of laws in the Theodosian Code, are reconsidered. The dating of the Milvian Bridge to 311 instead of 312 is further considered in Bruun (140).

148. Burch, Vacher. *Myth and Constantine the Great.* London: Oxford University Press, 1927.

149. Burns, J. H., ed. *The Cambridge History of Medieval Political Thought, c. 350-c. 1450.* New York: Cambridge University Press, 1988. Although not primarily concerned with the Roman world, this book's initial essays by Henry Chadwick, John Procope, P. G. Stein, D. M. Nicol, R. A. Markus, and P. D. King, offer in varying degrees so much of interest regarding religion, law, and political theory in reference to the late fourth century empire, that the student would be well advised to browse at length. The essays in general are so beautifully crafted and so well informed that the reader may have difficulty stopping at just the Roman material.

150. Burns, Thomas S. "The Battle of Adrianople: A Reconsideration." *Historia* 22 (1973): 336-345. The importance of Adrianople derived more from the political results than from supposed tactical or technical innovations of the barbarians on the field of battle. The decision that the Romans took in 382 to grant a treaty permitting a barbarian nation under its own leaders to settle in Roman provinces was the important result of Adrianople.

151. Bury, J. B. "The Constitution of the Later Roman Empire." In *Selected Essays of J. B. Bury,* pp. 99-125. Edited by Harold Temperley. Cambridge: University Press, 1930.

152. Bury, J. B. "The Provincial List of Verona," *Journal of Roman Studies* 13 (1923): 127-151. In Bury's view, the Verona List "reflected a provincial division of the Empire which as a whole existed only for a few years from A. D. 308 at the earliest to A. D. 315" (p. 146).

153. Cameron, Alan. *Claudian: Poetry and Propaganda at the Court of Honorius.* Oxford: Clarendon Press, 1970. Although strictly speaking the court poetry of Claudian covers events outside the scope of this bibliography, the man himself was very much a product of the fourth century. Cameron gives a good profile of Claudian as a well educated man of the age, who happened also to be a genius at poetry, a talent he used in the service of a western Roman government facing political and military crises whose eventual outcomes made the fifth century so different from the fourth. J. Martin, *American Journal of Philology* 95 (1974): 82-84 (+); J. W. Eadie, *Classical World* 65 (September 1971): 29 (+); *Times Literary Supplement* (December 18, 1970): 1488 (+).

154. Cameron, Alan. "Gratian's Repudiation of the Pontifical Robe." *Journal of Roman Studies* 58 (1968): 96-99. Cameron argues that Gratian repudiated the title Pontifex Maximus in 383, not 382 or 379 as others have argued.

155. Cameron, Alan. "Theodosius the Great and the Regency of Stilicho." *Harvard Studies in Classical Philology*

73 (1969): 247-280. "I shall be arguing in this paper that Stilicho's appointment as regent of Honorius was not a deathbed wish of Theodosius, but a decision both taken and made public some little while before he fell fatally ill. I do not believe that Stilicho was ever appointed regent of Arcadius - at least not in any significant sense of the word" (p. 247)

156. **Cameron, Alan.** "An Unknown General." *Classical Philology* 83 (1988): 149-150. A coin hoard reveals the career of a high-ranking soldier from the time of Diocletian.

157. **Cameron, Averil M.** "Agathias and Cedrenus on Julian." *Journal of Roman Studies* 53 (1963): 91-94. This is an interesting discussion, based on a reported visit of Julian to the Delphic oracle before the Persian war, of the problems of working with the primary sources, some of which are primary and taken seriously only by virtue of the absence of anything better.

158. **Cameron, Averil M.** "Constantinus Christianus" [review article]. *Journal of Roman Studies* 73 (1983): 184-190. In the context of a review of T. D. Barnes' two books on Constantine, Cameron gives a helpful analysis of many problems involved when dealing with the career of the first Christian emperor.

159. **Casey, P. J.** "Carausius and Allectus - Rulers in Gaul?" *Britannia* 8 (1977): 283-301. Casey reviews political and military developments in Britain and northern Gaul during the 290s, with much help from coin hoards.

160. **Chalmers, Walter R.** "Eunapius, Ammianus Marcellinus and Zosimus on Julian's Persian Expedition." *Classical Quarterly* 10 (1960): 152-160. Chalmers shakes down the primary sources to find out who consulted whom for information on Julian and the Persians.

161. **Charlesworth, M. P.** "Imperial Deportment: Two Texts and Some Questions." *Journal of Roman Studies* 37 (1947): 34-38. Charlesworth links the public deportment of

the fourth century emperors with Persian antecedents. The texts are Xenophon and Ammianus Marcellinus.

162. Cosenza, Mario E. *Official Positions After the Time of Constantine.* Lancaster, Pa.: New Era Printing Co., 1905. Based on the author's Ph. D dissertation, of the same year and title, at Columbia.

163. Coster, Charles H. *Late Roman Studies.* Cambridge: Harvard University Press, 1968. Most of these reprinted essays do not have much to do with the fourth century, but there is one on Paulinus of Nola, and two on Synesius of Cyrene, both fourth century types who lived long enough to face fifth century problems. Alan Cameron, *American Journal of Philology* 90 (1969): 124-127 (+-).

164. Coster, Charles H. "Synesius, a *Curialis* of the Time of the Emperor Arcadius." *Byzantion* 15 (1940-41): 10-38. Reprinted in his *Late Roman Studies*, pp. 145-182. Cambridge: Harvard University Press, 1968. Synesius bridged the fourth and fifth centuries in many ways. He was a bishop with a classsical outlook on things. But most of all he was a *curialis*, a class under pressure but certainly not ruined in the fourth century. This class still had vigor and infuence at court. Synesius travelled to Constantinople and made a pitch for restoration of the second century ideals of government and for a military machine free of barbarians. "At the end of the fourth century we find a *curialis* who is still hoping for the return of a Marcus Aurelius to the throne" (p.25).

165. Cristo, Stuart. "A Judicial Event in the Urban Prefecture of Symmachus." *Latomus* 36 (1977): 688-693. A little case of intrigue in the bureaucracy of the city of Rome sheds light on how the late Roman administration worked in reality.

166. Cristo, Stuart. "Quintus Aurelius Symmachus: A Political and Social Biography." Ph. D. dissertation, Fordham University, 1974. While recognizing Symmachus' importance as an influential patron and representative of the old Roman order, Cristo does not find much of importance or relevance to the Roman state generally in his political career.

167. **Croke, Brian.** "Arbogast and the Death of Valentinian III." *Historia* 25 (1976): 235-244.   Croke says the young emperor probably committed suicide. Full citations are provided for the relevant literature on a question whose answer was as uncertain then as it is now.

168. **Croke, Brian.** "Jordanes' Understanding of the Usurpation of Eugenius." *Antichthon* 9 (1975): 81-83. Poor Jordanes. His bungled treatment of Eugenius, who is confused with Gratian, is severely handled by Croke, who has little use for Jordanes as an historian.

169. **De Ste-Croix, Geoffrey E. M.**   "Suffragium: From Vote to Patronage." *British Journal of Sociology* 5 (1954): 33-48.   By the fourth century, *suffragium* referred to the influence of great men, rather than the vote of a sovereign people. Even in the church it meant "intercession."

170. **Del Tredici, Kelly Luise.** "Three Historiographical Problems in the Ancient Sources for the Reign of Constantius II (337-361)." Ph. D. dissertation, Fordham University, 1982. Del Tredici concludes that Constantius participated in or permitted the massacre of his relatives in 337, that the Caesar Gallus was largely responsible for his own downfall in 354, and that the Caesar Julian promoted himself to Augustus in 360 but was not prompted to do so by abuse from Constantius.

171. **Di Maio, Michael.** "Zonaras' Account of the New-Flavian Emperors: A Commentary." Ph. D. dissertation, University of Missouri, 1977.   Part I is a translation of Epitome 12.32-13.13 (A. D. 305-363). Di Maio discusses exhaustively all the sources and compares them for all the incidents in the lives of the new-Flavians. The footnotes are mines of information. Statistical questions receive full treatment. All in all, this is a valuable reference tool for events of the first half of the fourth century.

172. Di Maio, Michael. "Zonaras, Julian, and Philostorgios on the Death of the Emperor Constantine I." *Greek Orthodox Theological Review* 26 (no. 1-2, 1981): 118-124.

173. Dirks, Carolyn. "The Historical Value of Pacatus' Panegyric upon Theodosius I (with Special Reference to the Usurpation of Magnus Maximus)." M. A. thesis, Carleton University, 1976. Dirks says that Pacatus, while he adds much to our knowledge of Magnus, must be used with caution because of prejudices and the requirements of the political situation of the moment.

174. Dornier, A. "The Province of Valentia." *Britannia* 13 (1982): 253-260. This province was created in the fourth century, and the incentive was military. The territory covered north and central Wales, with a command center at Chester.

175. Downey, Glanville. "The Emperor Julian and the Schools." *Classical Journal* 53 (1957): 97-103. In his effort to save the Roman state from the misdirection of his uncle Constantine and his immediate successors, Julian had great ambitions for promoting the new, improved paganism in the schools. He wanted only teachers who were true believers in the old ways - i.e., sincere only need apply. That, in Julian's view, left Christians out of teaching positions. In fact, Julian, like many other conservatives, considered the total package of Hellenic culture the essential feature of the Roman empire. No gods, no empire. Downey tells the story, with lengthy quotations from Julian's laws regarding educational reform.

176. Downey, Glanville. "A Study of the Comites Orientis and the Consulares Syriae." Ph. D. dissertation, Princeton University, 1939.

177. Drinkwater, John F. "The Pagan Background: Constantius II's Secret Service and the Survival and the Usurpation of Julian the Apostate." In *Studies in Latin Literature and Roman History,* pp. 348-387. V. 3. Edited by Carl Deroux. Brussels: Latomus, 1983. Drinkwater dismisses the notion of a "pagan underground" gravitating to the young prince Julian in the 350s as the pagan political hope of the future. Then Drinkwater gives a new perspective on the "secret service" of the central government, showing how divided, amateurish, and often unsuccessful and incompetent were the paid informants of Constantius' reign. Finally, Drinkwater reviews in detail the conditions and events leading to the usurpation of Julian, who is portrayed as seeing his survival and military successes in the late 350s as Fate, thus leading easily to a belief that he should and would also be the master of the empire.

178. Dunlap, James E. *The Office of the Chamberlain in the Later Roman and Byzantine Empire.* New York: Macmillan Co., 1924. An elaboration of his doctoral thesis.

179. Dvornik, Francis. "The Emperor Julian's 'Reactionary' Ideas on Kingship." In *Late Classical and Mediaeval Studies in Honor of Albert Mathias Friend, Jr.*, pp. 71-81. Edited by Kurt Weitzmann. Princeton, N. J.: Princeton University Press, 1955. Julian's political philosophy, and particularly his ideas on the head of state, were inspired more by the Roman republic and principate than by the inheritance from the Hellenistic kingdoms of the east.

180. Eadie, John W. "City and Countryside in Late Roman Pannonia: The *Regio Sirmiensis.*" In *City, Town and Countryside in the Early Byzantine Era*, pp. 25-42. Edited by Robert L. Hohlfelder. New York: Columbia University Press, 1982. Eadie looks at developments from 375 to 441 that resulted in Roman abandonment of Pannonia, and the effects upon the civilian population.

181. Edbrooke, Robert Owen, Jr. "The Visit of Constantius II to Rome in 357 and Its Effect on the Pagan Roman Senatorial Aristocracy." *American Journal of Philology* 97 (1976): 40 -61. Edbrooke disputes a popular scholarly thesis that there was an important reconciliation between Christian emperor and pagan aristocrats in 357 when Constantius spent a month in Rome being imperial and admiring the ancient monuments. He finds little evidence that the great aristocratic families were better off after than before the event. They retained about what they had before: "their estates, their influence in the city of Rome and environs, and whatever was recognized of their prestige based on past traditions, wealth, and service" (p. 61).

182. Ehrhardt, Arnold. "The First Two Years of the Emperor Theodosius I." *Journal of Ecclesiastical History* 15 (April 1964): 1-17.   Ehrhardt says we must focus on the compelling need to stabilize the military situation in the Balkans after the disaster at Adrianople if we are to understand Theodosius' religious and other activities in 379-380.

183. Ehrhardt, Arnold. "Some Aspects of Constantine's Legislation." *Studia Patristica (Texte und Untersuchungen,* 64; Berlin 1957) 2: 114-121.   This is an interesting look at the way laws were issued, and how they were modified within the bureaucracy once they were beyond the emperor's personal control.   Ehrhardt even finds "a pagan fifth column in Constantine's chancellery" (p. 120), which worked to suppress some pro-Christian legislation and to modify other laws.

184. Eichholz, D. E. "Constantius Chlorus' Invasion of Britain." *Journal of Roman Studies* 43 (1953): 41-48.   The entire campaign of 296 is reviewed, taking into account all the sources and modern interpretations of what happened.

185. Elliott, T. G. "Constantine's Conversion: Do We Really Need It?" *Phoenix* 41 (1987): 420-438.   "[Elliott] conclude[s] that there is no reliable contemporary evidence for a conversion of Constantine" (p. 433).   Why?   Because Constantine was a Christian, more or less, all his life, and so was his father, more or less.   A fascinating argument, reviewing all the evidence in a new way. If Elliot's argument prevails in the future, the fourth century will have to relinquish its most famous event. The conversion will become among the greatest non-events in history. Stay tuned.

Politics and Government 41

186. **Field, L. L.** "Liberty, Dominion, and the Two Swords: On the Origins of Western Political Theology (180-398)." Ph. D. dissertation, University of California, Los Angeles, 1985.

187. **Firth, John B.** *Constantine the Great: The Reorganisation of the Empire and the Triumph of the Church.* New York: Putnam's, 1905; Freeport, N. Y.: Books for Libraries Press, 1971. *Nation* 81 (August 10, 1905): 128 (+); *Athenaeum* 1 (May 27, 1905): 649 (+-).

188. **Frank, Richard I.** "*Commendabiles* in Ammianus." *American Journal of Philology* 88 (1967): 309-318. Frank sees in the new fourth century use of the word *commendabiles* a reflection of the distinction and even hostility between the civilian upper classes who traditionally ruled the empire (partly based on hereditary rights and through connections) and the new military elite which to a large extent governed the empire after Constantius II. These new military types also ruled partly through heredity and partly through connections, and the word *commendabilis* was used to indicate the military way of becoming prominent.

189. **Frank, Richard I.** "*Scholae Palatinae:* The Palace Guards of the Later Roman Empire." Ph. D. dissertation, University of California Berkeley, 1965.

190. **Frank, Richard I.** *Scholae Palatinae: The Palace Guards of the Later Roman Empire.* Rome: American Academy, 1969. The palace guards are studied as agents of an absolute monarch and through him participants of some significance in the political flow of power. A. H. M. Jones, *Journal of Roman Studies* 60 (1970): 227-229 ("The author has collected a great deal of interesting material but often interprets it wrongly"); E. S. Gruen, *American Historical Review* 75 (1970): 1085-1086 (+).

191. **Gleason, Maud W.** "Festive Satire: Julian's *Misopogon* and the New Year at Antioch." *Journal of Roman Studies* 76 (1986): 106-119. Historians have often thought Julian's *Misopogon* a strange piece of satire to come from an

emperor's pen, perhaps indicative of a slightly deranged mind, certainly not the usual kind of official document to be posted outside the imperial palace in Antioch, as we are told it was. But contemporaries did not think it strange, and Gleason shows how this criticism of the Antiochenes was a sort of imperial participation in a local satirical holiday, and in any event was "not without precedent as a method of imperial chastisement" (p. 108).

192. Goffart, W. A. "Did Julian Combat Venal '*Suffragium*'? A Note on *CTh* 2.29.1." *Classical Philology* 65 (1970): 145-151.   Julian did not like influence-peddling because of its potential for abuse, but he did not abolish it. He tried to regulate it, as his predecessors had, with the object of seeing to it that both parties received some good from the transaction. Goffart reminds us not to see the selling of offices and influence through our eyes, and to remember that influence-peddling was not a unique feature of the late empire. It was a regular feature of Roman life going back for many centuries. The new feature of the late empire may have been the noble effort of the government to encourage merit as the basis of promotion and rewards, and the effort to implement this principle.

193. Goffart, Walter. "Rome, Constantinople, and the Barbarians." *American Historical Review* 86 (1981): 275-306.   Government decisions taken in the late fourth century led to the loss of provinces in the fifth. In a fascinating conceptualization, Goffart sees the central government responding to two forces: internal conflicts and external threats. The government cared for neither, but saw the unending stream of usurpers from the western Roman armies as a greater threat to the imperial government and ruling dynasty than the barbarians, whose leaders never sought to make themselves emperors and were often brought under the influence of the government. There was a tendency therefore to let the western armies of Gaul and Britain run down, and to permit the settlement of the less threatening barbarian tribes.

Politics and Government

194. Grant, Michael. *The Roman Emperors: A Biographical Guide to the Rulers of Imperial Romes, 31 BC-AD 476.* New York: Scribner's; London: Weidenfeld and Nicolson, 1985. Helpful outlines for those who want the basics on each fourth century ruler, except Eugenius, who does not rate his own entry although he is mentioned under Theodosius I. R. Seager, *Times Literary Supplement* (August 30, 1985): 957; R. Lenardon, *Library Journal* 110 (November 15, 1985): 90 (+-).

195. Graves, David A. "Consistorium Domini: Imperial Councils of State in the Later Roman Empire." Ph. D. dissertation, The City University of New York, 1973. Graves considers the development of the council of ministers of state from the time of Diocletian. Never independent and always basically reflecting the policies of an active emperor, it was nevertheless important as an administrative and ceremonial operation, advising, co-ordinating, arguing over policy.

196. Grierson, Philip. "The Roman Law of Counterfeiting." In *Essays in Roman Coinage Presented to Harold Mattingly*, pp. 240-261. Edited by R. A. G. Carson and C. H. V. Sutherland. Oxford: University Press, 1956. Over half the article pertains to the fourth century, when the written law was brutal but does not appear to have been literally applied in average cases.

197. Grigg, Robert. "Constantine the Great and the Cult without Images." *Viator* 8 (1977): 1-32. Grigg disputes the view that sees Constantine associated with the introduction of images into the basilicas. On the contrary, Constantine rejected the use of images, partly for Christain reasons, partly not to antagonize pagans, who were still the majority of his subjects.

198. Guthrie, P. "The Execution of Crispus." *Phoenix* 20 (1966): 325-331. Crispus was the brilliant first son of Constantine, executed suddenly at the age of 23. His problem: he was illegitimate. By now Constantine had legitimate heirs.

Therefore, curtains for Crispus. See Austin (82) for another view of this mysterious episode the meager evidence for which precludes a definitive study.

199. Hardy, B. C. "The Emperor Julian and His School Law." *Church History* 37 (1968): 131-143. "The school law . . . is far more easily explained as ancillary to Julian's conservative political vision than . . . a persecutory contrivance of malice and hate" (p. 138). The law forbad Christian teachers in the public classrooms of the empire. Julian was not really a persecutor, but he did wish to restore the spirit as well as the privileges of Hellenism. He did not see how the religion of the Christian teachers would permit them to be an effective symbol of Greek culture in its entirety. "The emphasis on cultural renewal, rather than religious persecution, permits not only a friendlier image of Julian but a more consistent one as well" (p. 143).

200. Harries, Jill. "The Roman Imperial Quaestor from Constantine to Theodosius II." *Journal of Roman Studies* 78 (1988): 148-172. The quaestor was an evolving position in the fourth century, largely centering on legal matters and on special ambassadorial missions for the emperor. In the course of her discussion of the evolution of the quaestor's functions, Harries offers some interesting information on the development of the centralized law codes of the Roman state and of the central bureaucracy at the higher administrative levels. Finally, there is an appendix of known quaestors from 354 to 438.

201. Head, Constance. *The Emperor Julian.* Boston: Twayne Publishers, 1976. A beginner's Julian.

202. Hind, J. G. F. "The British 'Provinces' of Valentia and Orcades." *Historia* 24 (1975): 101-111. Hind re-reads the source material, especially in Ammianus, to discover that Valentia was really a new and, as it proved, temporary name for the diocese of Britain in the time of Valentinian and Valens. Orcades refers to the Orkney Islands, which were not really a province apart from the imagination of a poet like Claudian.

203. Holsapple, Lloyd B. *Constantine the Great.* New York: Sheed, 1942. Generously sympathetic, with an emphasis on religious developments. C. B. Coleman, *American Historical Review* 48 (1943): 770 (+); A. R. Bellinger, *Saturday Review of Literature* 26 (February 20, 1943): 21 (-).

204. Honore, Tony. *Emperors and Lawyers.* London: Duckworth, 1981. The workings of the legal system under Diocletian are discussed in Chapter 4.

205. Hopkins, Keith. *Conquerors and Slaves.* New York: Cambridge University Press, 1978. Chapter IV, "The Political Power of Eunuchs," will be useful to students of the fourth century. Z. Stewart, *American Historical Review* 85 (1980): 97-98 (+-).

206. Hopkins, Keith. "Eunuchs in Politics in the Later Roman Empire." *Proceedings of the Cambridge Philological Society* 189 (1963): 62-80. Eunuchs were an integral part of the complex system of politics in the later empire. Hopkins sees this from the time of Diocletian, and investigates political shifts and balances in the eastern empire to explain why eunuchs consistently held so much power in the central government and what they did with this power.

207. Hughes, Richard Van V., Jr. "The Government of Constantius II." Ph. D. dissertation, University of California Berkeley, [?].

208. Ison, D. "The Constantinian *Oration to the Saints* - Authorship and Background." Ph. D. dissertation, King's College, London, 1985.

209. Jones, A. H. M. "Collegiate Prefectures." *Journal of Roman Studies* 54 (1964): 78-89. Jones is unhappy with the notion that holding of the office of praetorian prefect by two persons as colleagues was common in the late empire. "Collegiate prefectures are an invention of modern scholars," he says. Jones has appended a useful table of praetorian prefects from 337 to 408 for the four prefectures of Gaul, Italy, Illyricum, and the Orient.

210. Jones, A. H. M. "The Roman Civil Service (Clerical and Sub-clerical Grades)." *Journal of Roman Studies* 39 (1949): 38-55.   Jones covers the civil service from the Republic to the early Byzantine period.

211. Jones, David. "The Altar of Victory: The Late Roman Empire and the Christian Faith." *History Today* 20 (April 1970): 255-262.   Jones reviews the conflicts of the old versus the new religious order in the western empire in the late fourth century, giving a full journalistic flair to the important symbolic event "when Symmachus and Ambrose, the urbane pagan orator and the unscrupulous zealous priest, fought at the court of a boy emperor over the restitution of the revenues of the Roman priesthood and over the restoration of the altar of Victory to its place in the Curia in Rome" (p. 262).

212. Jones, David. "The Emperor Theodosius." *History Today* 21 (1970): 619-627.   Helpful biographical sketch of the career of the famous emperor whose family rose from disgrace at the end of the reign of Valentinian I to dominate the entire empire at the end of the fourth century.

213. Kaegi, Walter E. "The Emperor Julian's Assessment of the Significance and Function of History." *Proceedings of the American Philosophical Society* 108 (1964): 29-38. Reprinted in his *Army, Society and Religion in Byzantium,* Part I. London: Variorum Reprints, 1982.   "In sum, Julian deeply respected the study of history. He was persuaded that this discipline offered an important avenue to truth, served as a good guide to the formation of character, contributed to wise decisions and provided a stimulating challenge to achieve noble deeds" (p. 38).

214. Kaegi, Walter E. "The Emperor Julian at Naissus." *L'Antiquite Classique* 44 (1975): 161-171.   Reprinted in his

Army, Society and Religion in Byzantium, Part III. London: Variorum Reprints, 1982.

215. **Kaegi, Walter E.** "Research on Julian the Apostate, 1945-1964." *Classical World* 58 (1965): 229-238. A very helpful annotated bibliography of scholarly Julian studies. Includes non-English literature.

216. **Kajava, Mika.** "Some Remarks on the Name and Origin of Helena Augusta." *Arctos* 19 (1985): 41-54.

217. **Kazhdan, A.** "'Constantine Imaginaire.' Byzantine Legends of the Ninth Century About Constantine the Great." *Byzantion* 57 (1987): 196-250.

218. **Kent, J. P. C.** "The Office of Comes Sacrarum Largitionum." Ph. D. dissertation, University of London, 1951.

219. **King, C. E.** "The *Sacrae Largitiones:* Revenues, Expenditure and the Production of Coin." In *Imperial Revenue, Expenditure and Monetary Policy in the Fourth Century A. D.*, pp. 141-173. Edited by C. E. King. Oxford: B. A. R., 1980. King offers a helpful outline of the Roman tax system in the fourth century, as well as a look at the evolution of the mint and the coinage.

220. **King, N. Q.** *There's Such Divinity Doth Hedge a King: Studies in Ruler Cult and the Religion of Sacral Monarchy in Some Late Fourth Century Byzantine Monuments.* Edinburgh: Nelson, for the University of Ghana, 1960. Features of Egyptian, Persian, Jewish, Hellenistic, Roman and Christian cultures are adduced to bring understanding to the origins of fourth century Roman monarchy.

221. **Kojeve, Alexandre.** "The Emperor Julian and His Art of Writing." In *Ancients and Moderns: Essays on the Tradition of Political Philosophy in Honor of Leo Strauss*, pp. 95-113. Edited by Joseph Cropsey. New York: Basic Books, 1964. An imaginative reconstruction of Julian as an athiest

who only supported paganism because it posed no threat to philosophical inquiry unadorned and unhindered by theology.

222. Kopecek, Thomas A. "Curial Displacements and Flight in Later Fourth Century Cappadocia." *Historia* 23 (1974): 319-342. With the help of the writings of Basil of Caesarea and Gregory Nazianzus, Kopecek sorts out the how and why of curials escaping their traditional civic and imperial duties.

223. Krautheimer, Richard. *Three Christian Capitals: Topography and Politics.* Berkeley: University of California Press, 1983. Krautheimer finds political meaning in the topography of Christian churches in Rome, Constantinople, and Milan in the fourth century. In Rome, for instance, Constantine built monuments for the new religion far from the old pagan centers to avoid unnecessary friction with the pagan Senatorial class. A fascinating study. G. Armstrong, *American Historical Review* 90 (1985): 399 (+); W. E. Kleinbauer, *Catholic Historical Review* 71 (1985): 584-587 (+).

224. Larsen, Jakob A. O. "The Position of Provincial Assemblies in the Government and Society of the Late Roman Empire." *Classical Philology* 29 (1934): 209-220. Although different in character from their predecessors, provincial assemblies were still active institutions in the fourth and even fifth centuries. Larsen studies their role and composition.

225. Leedom, Joe W. "Constantius II: Three Revisions." *Byzantion* 48 (1978): 132-145. In an effort to rehabilitate Constantius, based on a revising of three traditionally accepted stories, Leedom finds inadequate evidence to conclude that Constantius killed his relatives after his father's death, considers that his semi-Arianism was political and an effort to promote unity rather than religious fanaticism, and that his Persian policy was prudent, given other geopolitical factors.

226. Lenox-Conyngham, Andrew. "The Topography of the Basilica Conflict of A. D. 385/6 in Milan." *Historia* 31 (1982): 353-363. This is a tale of Catholics versus Arians, the imperial court versus Ambrose bishop of Milan, city versus soldier: a quintessential late fourth century story if ever there was one. L.-C. tries to sort out the stage settings.

227. Levine, Neil A. S. "The *Caesares* of Julian: An Historical Study." Ph. D. dissertation, Columbia University, 1968. Levine gives a thorough airing to the sources and possible sources for the *Caesares*, and considers the historical situation that inspired and informed the work.

228. Levy, Harry L. "Claudian's *In Rufinum* and an Epistle of Saint Jerome." *American Journal of Philology* 69 (Baltimore, 1948): 62-68. The political events of A. D. 395 are the background for Levy's thesis of a literary connection between the court poet Claudian and the writings of Jerome.

229. Levy, Harry L. *The Invectice in Rufinum of Claudius Claudianus.* Edited with Introduction and Textual Commentary. New York: W. F. Humphrey Press, Inc., 1935. Levy has appendices and notes that help make the text useful in discovering the politics of a divided empire in the 390s. J. W. Pearce, *Journal of Roman Studies* 26 (1936): 134-135 (++-).

230. Lieu, Samuel N. C. *The Emperor Julian: Panegyric and Polemic.* Translated Texts for Historians, Greek Series, v.1. Liverpool: Liverpool University Press, 1986. Translations of important source material on Julian: Claudius Mamertinus, "A Speech of Thanks to the Emperor Julian"; John Chrysostom, "Homily of St. Babylas, against Julian and the Pagans xiv-xix"; and Ephrem the Syrian, "Hymns against Julian." Includes prefatory material, full commentary, large bibliography. J. Paterson, *Greece and Rome* 34 (1987): 224 (+).

231. Linder, Amnon. "The Myth of Constantine the Great in the West: Sources and Hagiographic Commemoration." *Studi Medievali* 16 (1975): 48-95.

232. L'Orange, H. P. "The Adventus Ceremony and the Slaying of Pentheus as Represented in Two Mosaics of about A.

232. L'Orange, H. P. "The Adventus Ceremony and the Slaying of Pentheus as Represented in Two Mosaics of about A. D. 300." In *Late Classical Studies in Honor of Albert Mathias Friend, Jr.*, pp. 7-14. Edited by Kurt Weitzmann. Princeton, N. J.: Princeton University Press, 1955. Interesting information on the ceremony of receiving an emperor in the fourth century.

233. MacCormack, Sabine. "Change and Continuity in Late Antiquity: The Ceremony of *Adventus*." *Historia* 21 (1972): 721-752. The ceremonial arrival of emperors in late antiquity was an event full of symbolic meaning for all the participants. MacCormack shows the metamorphosis of this ancient vehicle of political affirmation in the changing circumstances of the fourth century, especially in religion.

234. MacMullen, Ramsay. *Constantine.* New York: Dial Press, 1969. Lively, informed, provocative without being outrageous: all that one might expect of MacMullen. Constantine emerges as an innovator and a pivotal figure, yet operating within the constraints of centuries of tradition. His conversion to Christianity is shown to be sincere based on a common attitude of the age: the desire to be in with the strongest divinity, rather than a search for a moral code. Good illustrations, good maps. Chapter 1 has a memorable description of the pomp and circumstance of the imperial court. W. Sinnigen, *American Historical Review* 75 (1970): 1431 (+); G. Downey, *American Journal of Philology* 91 (1970): 384 (+).

235. MacMullen, Ramsay. "Imperial Bureaucrats in the Roman Provinces." *Harvard Studies in Classical Philology* 68 (1964): 305-316. MacMullen writes here of the lower-level bureaucrats of the late empire. These people were well-positioned to be intermediaries between local populations and the higher officials of the state; and they were positioned to prosper both at the expense of the locals and of the central government. But they also represented something else: "The world they lived in was threatened by a general collapse, and upon this threat the strength of the preserver of order was founded. The greater the threat, the greater the prestige and authority of strong central government. On this prestige even a modest civil servant could draw inexhaustibly, to assert his weight in society" (p. 312). There is incidentally some useful information on how soldiers and civilian bureaucrats dressed.

236. MacMullen, Ramsay. "Judicial Savagery in the Roman Empire." *Chiron* 16 (1986): 147-166. In this depressing article, MacMullen follows the spiraling incidence of judicial violence in the later empire. Not that things were lots better in the early empire. But they were a little better. Gruesome stuff.

237. MacMullen, Ramsay. "More Government, Less Power: The Case of the Decline of Rome." *Ancient Society, Resources for Teachers* (North Ryde, N.S.W., Australia, Macquarie University) 13 (1983): 98-107. Bribery and corruption in the army and the bureaucracy made a contribution to the decline of governmental effectiveness.

238. MacMullen, Ramsay. "Roman Bureaucratese." *Traditio* 18 (1962): 364-378. "The machinery of the state was clogged not only by corruption, and red tape, and triplicate copies, but by the nature of governmental language" (p. 377), says MacMullen, who provides rich examples of inflated and sometimes unintelligible language from the bureaucracy. Absolute emperors could be almost reduced to impotence when the bureaucracy fumbled (sometimes on purpose) communications between the palace and the provinces. One cannot help thinking of Washington, D. C.

239. MacMullen, Ramsay. *Roman Government's Response to Crisis A. D. 235-337.* New Haven: Yale University Press, 1976. Refusing to become enmeshed in the decline and fall syndrome, MacMullen looks at how the imperial government responded to the difficulties of the third century, at first in a kind of ad hoc way, and then in a more systematic and informed way under Diocletian and Constantine, when circumstances were perhaps more conducive to an orderly reflection on immediate past lessons. There are chapters on propaganda, intelligence, law, money, taxes, supplies and services, and the military. J. C. Mann, *Journal of Roman Studies* 69 (1979): 190-191 (+-)

240. MacMullen, Ramsay. "Two Notes on Imperial Properties." *Athenaeum* (Pavia) 54 (1976): 19-36. In his colorful investigative reporting style, MacMullen discusses how the emperors dispersed some of their vast holdings of land and things (MacMullen identifies these categories of distribution: free gifts, enforced gifts, gifts to groups and institutions, sales), and where the emperors stayed on their travels (wherever they wanted, but as often as possible in their own palaces). A large share of the material MacMullen uses is from the fourth century.

241. Maguinness, W. S. "Eumenius of Autun." *Greece and Rome* 21 (1952): 97-103. Eumenius was private secretary to Constantius I, later head of the academy at Autun. He delivered a speech in A. D. 298 (which survives in the *Panegyrici Latini*), thanking the emperor for restoration work at Autun, which had been sacked in 269. Maguinness reviews the speech and reflects on the circumstances of its delivery.

242. Malley, William J. "The *Contra Julianum* of St. Cyril of Alexandria and St. Peter Canisius." *Theological Studies* 25 (1964): 70-74. A discussion of primary sources pertaining to Julian and his *Contra Galilicos.*

243. Martindale, J. R. "Note on the Consuls of 381 and 382." *Historia* 16 (1967): 254-256. A prosopographical profile of the consuls, two of whom were closely connected with the family of Theodosius I.

244. Mathisen, Ralph W. "Patricians as Diplomats in Late Antiquity." *Byzantinische Zeitschrift* 79 (1986): 35-49. The old title of patrician was revived by Constantine I, but was now honorary and bestowed upon individuals for life. Mathisen studies in detail the use of patricians as diplomats in the fourth, fifth and sixth centuries.

Politics and Government

245. Matthews, John F. "The Family and Supporters of the Emperor in Western Society in the Age of Theodosius." Ph. D. dissertation, Oxford University, 1970.

246. Matthews, John F. "Gallic Supporters of Theodosius." *Latomus* 30 (1971): 1073-1099. Reprinted in his *Political Life and Culture in Late Roman Society*, Ch. IX. London: Variorum Reprints, 1985. The Gauls who followed Theodosius' court all over the empire tended to settle back home when their time in the imperial limelight was over. There in Gaul they gave continuing impetus to family traditions of leadership in local matters of government and culture, an increasingly important effort in the fifth century when the central government was collapsing around them.

247. Matthews, John F. "The Historical Setting of the 'Carmen contra Paganos' (Cod. Lat. Par. 8084)." *Historia* 19 (1970): 464-479. Reprinted in his *Political Life and Culture in Late Roman Society*, Ch. VII. London: Variorum Reprints, 1985. Matthews discusses the poem "Carmen" in its context: the pagan revival during the time of the usurper Eugenius in 393-394.

248. Matthews, John F. "Macsen, Maximus, and Constantine." *The Welsh Historical Review* 11 (1983): 431-448. Reprinted in his *Political Life and Culture in Late Roman Society*, Ch. XII. London: Variorum Reprints, 1985. Matthews takes an ancient Welsh story, "The Dream of Macsen," and considers the influence on it of fourth and early fifth century Roman political events, especially the rise of the emperor Maximus, who had strong British connections.

249. Matthews, John F. "A Pious Supporter of Theodosius I: Maternus Cynegius and His Family." *Journal of Theological Studies* 18 (1967): 438-446. Cynegius was from Spain, and served as a high official in the eastern empire, where as an orthodox and rather fanatical Christian, he became the bane of pagans through repressions and destruction of temples in the 380s. Matthews discusses what we can learn about and from this example of the new ruling party under Theodosius I.

250. Matthews, John F. *Political Life and Culture in Late Roman Society.* London: Variorum Reprints, 1985. Reprints of twelve studies that Matthews did between 1967 and 1983. The relevant ones are analyzed individually.

251. Matthews, John F. Review of *La Politica Gotica di Teodosio nella Pubblicista del Suo Tempo,* by Massimiliano Pavan. *Journal of Roman Studies* 56 (1966): 245-246. Matthews gives a succinct discussion of the decisions having to be made, and the options discussed by contemporaries, in the aftermath of the Roman defeat at Adrianople in 378.

252. Matthews, John F. "Symmachus and the *magister militum* Theodosius." *Historia* 20 (1971): 122-128. Reprinted in his *Political Life and Culture in Late Roman Society*, Ch. X. London: Variorum Reprints, 1985. A look at the relations between a prominent senator and a leading military man in the late fourth century.

253. Matthews, John F. *Western Aristocracies and the Imperial Court, A. D. 364-425.* Oxford: Clarendon Press, 1975. Before the collapse of the western imperial frontier in the fifth century, the great senatorial aristocracy was on the move ahead of the barbarians and had done much to recapture power in the central government, lost to them since the late third century. The full dimensions of this movement, taking into account private and public interests, changes in religion, and so on, are explored with great subtlety and care by Matthews. This is one of the most important books in English on the whole milieu of the dynamic elements of western society in the late fourth and early fifth centuries. F. M. Clover, *Classical Philology* 71 (1976): 269-273 ("penetrating and exciting," although the conclusions are "slightly misleading"); W. Goffart, *English Historical Review* 91 (1976): 351-354 (+); P. Wormald, *Journal of Roman Studies* 66 (1976): 217-226.

254. **Mattingly, Harold.** "The Clash of the Coinages Circa 270-296." In *Studies in Roman Economic and Social History*, pp. 275-289. Edited by Paul R. Coleman-Norton. Princeton, N. J.: Princeton University Press, 1951; Freeport, N. Y.: Books for Libraries Press, 1969. Coin reforms were accepted reluctantly in the western provinces even after the reunification under a central government during the time of Aurelian, cemented in the time of Diocletian. Mattingly sees symbolized in this rejection of new government money the economic troubles of western provinces where many felt that the central government did not have solutions.

255. **McCormick, Michael.** *Eternal Victory: Triumphal Rulership in Late Antiquity, Byzantium, and the Early Medieval West.* Cambridge: University Press, 1986. The emperor had to be seen to be victorious, and the Roman empire had to be confirmed as eternally victorious. Hence the importance of victory celebrations. There were other relevant propaganda devices, but this was the best, says McCormick: "Above all - and this constitutes the central theme of this study - triumphal ceremonial, propaganda and public display celebrated and confirmed the victorious rulership of the emperor" (p. 5). In the fourth century there was "an extraordinary resurgence in the frequency and import of imperial victory festivals" (p. 35). There was an especially strong acceleration after Adrianople in 378, when the government needed to restore confidence through military successes of any kind. McCormick takes the story into the tenth century. R. I. Frank, *Choice* 24 (July 1987): 1687 (+); D. J. Constantetos, *Church History* 57 (1988): 221-222 (+); R. Van Dam, *American Historical Review* 93 (1988): 1028-1029 (+).

256. **McCoy, Marsha B.** "Corruption in the Western Empire: The Career of Sextus Petronius Probus." *Ancient World* 11 (August 1985): 101-106. The sources about Probus, a great late fourth century aristocrat, are contradictory: some praise his virtues, some condemn his corruption in government. No problem, says McCoy, who reconciles the sources to show that "Probus was indeed corrupt, but also that he amassed great wealth and power by means of his corruption, and that he

used his ill-gotten gains to ward off criticism and buy himself respectability" (p.101).

257. McGeachy, John A., Jr. "Quintus Aurelius Symmachus and the Senatorial Aristocracy of the West." Ph. D. dissertation, University of Chicago, 1942.

258. Mierow, Herbert E. *The Roman Provincial Governor as He Appears in the Digest and Code of Justinian.* Colorado Springs, Co.: Colorado College, 1926. An interesting composite, carefully outlined, of the executive and judicial duties of the late Roman governor, as that office had developed since the time of Diocletian.

259. Millar, Fergus. *The Emperor in the Roman World (31 BC-AD 337).* London: Duckworth; New York: Cornell University Press, 1977. "The emperor was what the emperor did" (p. 6). This is the fundamental thesis and the most often quoted epigram of this large book, and sums up the "complex and undefinable nature of the developed monarchy" (p. 619). But of course what the emperor did was largely in response to the inherited cultural, economic and political baggage which the Roman state carried around and which in its essentials was little changed from the time of Augustus to Constantine. Millar therefore notes the considerable extent to which Diocletian and Constantine worked within the traditional concepts of what an emperor's powers were and how they were discharged, despite changes in the theatrics of the office. Millar treats the emperor only in relation to civil things; the emperor's military capacity is left undiscussed. P. Garnsey, *English Historical Review* 93 (1978): 377-378 (+); K. R. Bradley, *Gnomen* 51 (1979): 258-263 (+); K. Hopkins, *Journal of Roman Studies* 68 (1978): 178-186 (-); T. R. S. Broughton, *American Journal of Philology* 99 (1978): 530-534 (+).

260. Millar, Fergus. "Empire and City, Augustus to Julian: Obligations, Excuses and Status." *Journal of Roman Studies* 73 (1983): 251-278. The central government and the cities became competitors for revenues available from the tax base. As the central government grew in power, so did its command of resources increase. At the same time, the government did not wish to ruin the cities, and there was uncertainty especially in the fourth century as to how much of their traditional revenues the cities should have and how much they should give up.

261. Millar, Fergus. "The *Privita* from Diocletian to Theodosius: Documentary Evidence." In *Imperial Revenue, Expenditure and Monetary Policy in the Fourth Century A. D.,* pp. 125-140. Edited by C. E. King. Oxford: B. A. R., 1980. Millar discusses "one of the frameworks within which the state, in the person of the emperor and his agents, acquired landed or movable property, disposed of it by way of *beneficia,* administered what it kept, and exploited it for revenues in cash or kind" (p.125). There is an appendix of primary sources that refer to the *privita*.

262. Minor, Clifford E. "Brigand, Insurrectionist and Separatist Movements in the Later Roman Empire." Ph. D. dissertation, University of Washington, 1971.

263. Monks, George R. "The Administration of the Privy Purse: An Enquiry into Official Corruption and the Fall of the Roman Empire." *Speculum* 32 (1957): 748-779. Monks sees a direct relationship between corruption in government and the collapse of the empire in the west. The east was saved by timely reforms. Includes fourth century material.

264. Monks, George R. "The Office of Count of the Privy Purse in the Late Roman Empire." Ph. D. dissertation, University of Michigan, 1938.

265. Mudd, Mary M. "Aspects of the Internal Government of the Later Roman Empire in the Reign of Constantius II, A. D. 337-361." Ph. D. dissertation, Rutgers University, 1984. Mudd sees Constantius as a concerned administrator who sought stability and prosperity for his empire, but who in his Arianizing religious policy was repressive and arbitrary towards pagans, Jews and non-Arian Christians.

266. Murray, Alexander. "Peter Brown and the Shadow of Constantine." *Journal of Roman Studies* 73 (1983): 191-203. In a favorable review of five books by Brown, Murray finds a theme that threads its way, thougn not always visibly, through all the books. This is the Constantinian Problem, which Murray works over in consultation with Brown and which he breaks out into a trinity of related problems - viz., the ecclesio-political one (how the emperor and his earthly empire should relate to the Christian church); "the problem that arises when a small church of underdogs becomes a church of the dominant majority"; and the problem "that arises when capitals are moved nearly nine hundred miles" (p. 192). This framework is a helpful approach to the richness of the Brown books, and incidentally clearly places the origins of some of the most characteristic developments of late antiquity in the fourth century.

267. Negev, A. "The Inscription of the Emperor Julian at Ma 'ayan Barukh." *Israel Exploration Journal* 19 (1969): 170-173.

268. Nicholson, Oliver. "Hercules at the Milvian Bridge: Lactantius, *Divine Institutes* I, 21, 6-9." *Latomus* 43 (1984): 133-142. Lactantius is seen as trying to associate the emperor Maximian, whom he disliked as a violent and brutal persecutor, with human sacrifice. Hercules was the special patron of Maximian in the political ideology of the day.

269. Nicholson, Oliver. "The Wild Man of Tetrarchy: A Divine Companion for the Emperor Galerius." *Byzantion* 54 (1984): 253-275. After his great Persian victory, the ambitious junior emperor Galerius associated himself with the god Dionysius, also known in mythology for conquests in the East. Unfortunately, like most of the ancient gods, Dionysius had rather a racy side too, full of drink and good times. Nicholson describes how Lactantius indirectly took on Galerius in the *Divine Institutes* by a harsh review of the least favorable characteristics of his divine companion, Dionysius.

270. **Nixon, C. E. V.** "Latin Panegyric in the Tetrarchic and Constantinian Period." In *History and Historians in Late Antiquity*, pp. 88-99. Edited by Brian Croke and Alanna M. Emmett. New York: Pergamon Press, 1983. "The late Latin panegyrics are both manifestations of the political and intellectual control of the educated classes by the central government, and an important tool in the process of that political and intellectual control - that is in the education of youth" (p. 97).

271. **Nixon, C. E. V.** "The Panegyric of 307 and Maximian's Visits to Rome." *Phoenix* 35 (1981): 70-76. Was the emperor Maximian in Rome in A. D. 303 to help Diocletian celebrate his vicennalia? Around the answer hinges matters having to do with Diocletian's abdication in 305. Nixon argues against those who say Maximian was not in Rome that year by showing that they have misinterpreted a piece of primary source material.

272. **Nock, Arthur D.** "Deification and Julian." *Journal of Roman Studies* 47 (1957): 114-123. Reprinted in his *Essays on Religion and the Ancient World*, pp. 832-846. V. 2. Cambridge: Harvard University Press, 1972. Nock discusses an expression in Libanius which seems to identify a miracle resulting from a prayer to the deceased emperor Julian. Nock says we should not think it was to be taken in a literal sense. Rather, Libanius was trying to create an atmosphere, a kind of halo, around the memory of his deceased hero, and called upon a rhetorical expression that would be meaningful to a contemporary audience, living in a world full of Christian miracles performed by deceased persons.

273. **Nock, Arthur D.** "The Emperor's Divine *Comes.* "*Journal of Roman Studies* 37 (1947): 102-116. Nock considers the various meanings that could be brought to bear on the concept of the relationship of the emperor to a companion-god.

274. **Novak, David M.** "Constantine and the Senate: An Early Phase of the Christianization of the Roman Aristocracy."

Ancient Society 10 (1979): 271-310. There is dispute in academia as to how well Constantine got on with the conservative Senate of Rome. Novak finds that Constantine managed to engender a fair amount of senatorial support and some senators even opted for the new imperial religion, Christianity. Also, Novak does not consider the pagan opposition as intense as sometimes portrayed.

275. Nulle, Stebelton H. "Julian and the Men of Letters." *Classical Journal* 54 (1959): 257-266. Nulle traces the changing views of Julian in western literature from ancient times to the present.

276. Nulle, Stebelton H. "Julian *Redivivus.*" *Centennial Review* 5 (1961): 320-338. The emperor Julian was condemned as the apostate by the Christian church, but in Renaissance times his memory underwent rehabilitation in Italy, Germany, and most especially in France, where Montaigne pronounced him "a very great and a very uncommon man." Nulle tells the story.

277. O'Flynn, John M. *Generalissimos of the Western Roman Empire.* Edmonton, Alta., Canada: University of Alberta Press, 1983. After A. D. 375, powerful military men, often of barbarian origin, figured greatly in the politics of the western empire. In a balanced and convincing way, O'Flynn studies this important development, which eventually had its impact on the unhappy fate of the empire in the fifth century. R. K. Sherk, *Classical World* 77 (1984): 380-381 (+).

278. Oikonomides, A. N. "Ancient Inscriptions Recording the Restoration of Greco-Roman Shrines by the Emperor Flavius Claudius Julianus (361-363 A. D.)." *Ancient World* 15 (1987): 37-42. Oikonomides adduces inscriptions to show the significant degree of popularity that Julian's restoration efforts enjoyed. It was not for nothing that Christian leaders were beside themselves over the possibilities inherent in the reign of the Apostate.

279. Oost, S. I. "Count Gildo and Theodosius the Great." *Classical Philology* 57 (1962): 27-30. Oost takes the poet Claudian to task, and reinterprets the relations between Gildo the Count of Africa and the emperor in the 380s and 390s. Oost says that Theodosius was not a bungler in this matter, as some modern historians have decided.

280. Pacatus' Panegyric to the Emperor Theodosius. Translated by C. E. V. Nixon. Liverpool: Liverpool University Press, 1987. This is the first English translation of this important speech lauding Theodosius on his defeat of Magnus Maximus. Extensive commentary from the translator. J. Harries, *Classical Review* 38 (1988): 51-52 (+-).

281. Pack, Roger. "Two Sophists and Two Emperors." *Classical Philology* 42 (1947): 17-20. When in 362 the emperor Julian met the sophist Libanius of Antioch, did they both have in mind (and thus acted accordingly) the famous friendship of Marcus Aurelius and Aelius Aristides of two centuries before? Pack thinks so. In a later article, A. F. Norman thinks not ("Philostratus and Libanius," *Classical Philology* 48 (1953) 20-23). Pack respond with another yes in "Julian, Libanius, and Others: A Reply," *Classical Philology* 48 (1953): 173-174; and Norman continues the discussion ("it seems that Pack and I have agreed to disagree") in "Julian and Libanius Again," *Classical Philology* 48 (1953):239.

282. Peachin, Michael. "*Praepositus* or *Procurator* ?" *Historia* 36 (1987): 248-249. Peachin discusses nomenclature in Ammianus regarding officials of the mid-fourth century Roman government.

283. Pearce, J. W. E. "Eugenius and His Eastern Colleagues." *Numismatic Chronicle* 17 (1937): 1-27. Pearce looks at the coins from the time of the emperor Eugenius to see what they might tell as to the political maneuverings between east and west.

284. Pears, Edwin. "The Campaign Against Paganism." *English Historical Review* 24 (1909): 1-17. Pears narrates the events involving the conflict for power between Constantine and Licinius, culminating in the complete victory of Constantine and concomitantly of Christianity, whose God was more than ever associated with victory in the temporal struggles of the Roman state. Pears offers lively descriptions of the famous land and sea battles between the two emperors.

285. Pedersen, Fritz Saaby. *Late Roman Public Professionalism.* Odense University Classical Studies, 9. Odense: University Press, 1976. In this slight revision of his 1974 doctoral dissertation, Pedersen reviews the requirements for late Roman public posts, and finds a wide range of standards for appointment and retention, generally of an informal kind (at least by our standards), and involving many factors such as influence, tradition, family connections, and politics, as well as some education and general competence. Pedersen disputes the common notion that the imperial government was solicitous of public education in order to keep up the supply of good bureaucrats.

286. Pedersen, Fritz Saaby. "On Professional Qualifications for Public Posts in Late Antiquity." *Classica at Mediaevalia* 31 (1970): 161-213. Preliminary studies for his *Late Roman Public Professionalism* (285).

287. Penella, Robert J. "Did a Hilarius Govern Lydia in the Fourth Century A. D.?" *American Journal of Philology* 106 (1985): 509-511. No, he governed the province of Asia, says Penella. Through what is otherwise an unimportant matter, Penella demonstrates the great difficulty involved in getting the true sense of many ancient texts, in this case Eunapius.

288. Pharr, Clyde, trans. and ed. *The Theodosian Code and Novels and the Sirmondian Constitutions: A Translation with Commentary, Glossary and Bibliography.* Princeton, N. J.: Princeton University Press, 1952. The availability of this code in English is more important for the historian and sociologist of the empire than for lawyers, who would be more interested in the Justinian code. The Theodosian Code is both indispensable and dangerous. Containing over 2500 statutes, the code reflects every aspect of life in the fourth century, as well as other periods. But the extent to which it actually regulated life is open to skeptical analysis. It may best be studied as a testament to the way the central government wanted things, and as an indicator of actual trends in Roman society, whose momentum was often beyond firm regulation. H. E. Barnes, *American Journal of Sociology* 58 (1952-1953): 220 (+); M. H. Shepherd, *Church History* 21 (1952): 275-276 (+); M. G. Fisher, *Journal of Roman Studies* 43 (1953): 181-182 (+-); E. Levy, *Speculum* 27 (1952): 412-415 (++-).

289. Pohlsander, H. A. "Crispus: Brilliant Career and Tragic End." *Historia* 33 (1984): 79-106. The first son of Constantine comes under close scrutiny: early life, marriage, career, military activities, art and literature of the age that may relate to him, the circumstances of his death. Primary and secondary sources get full consideration in the text and in footnotes.

290. Rebenich, Stefan. "Gratian, a Son of Theodosius, and the Birth of Galla Placidia." *Historia* 34 (1985): 372-385. "All the evidence speaks for the fact that there was a son of Galla and Theodosius named Gratian who was born in 388, or early 389. The logical consequence is to set Placidia's birth in 392 or 393" (p. 385). Rebenich gives a chronology of relevant events from 387 to 395.

291. Ricciotti, Giuseppe. *Julian the Apostate.* Translated by M. J. Costelloe. Milwaukee: Brace Publishing Co., 1960. A modern Catholic treatment of Julian which is, all in all, sympathetic, not of course to Julian's anti-Christian policy, but rather to the circumstances of his personal life which induced an anti-Christian attitude. There is a generally favorable attitude to many of Julian's fiscal and other secular reforms. M.R.P. McGuire, *Catholic Historical Review* 47 (1961): 31-32 (+).

292. Ridley, R. J. "The Fourth and Fifth Century Civil and Military Hierarchy in Zosimus." *Byzantion* 40 (1970): 91-

104.   Ridley discovers that Zosimus is a reliable and sometimes the only source on high office holders in the later empire. Ridley extracts the names of individuals from Zosimus and lists them by their offices, together with the references in Zosimus.

293. Roberts, C. H. "A Footnote to the Civil War of A. D. 324." *Journal of Egyptian Archaeology* 31 (1945): 113. Roberts discusses a fourth century papyrus letter, published in 1941, which may bear on preparations of the eastern fleet for the final war between Licinius and Constantine.

294.   Rodgers, Barbara Saylor. "Merobaudes and Maximus in Gaul." *Historia* 30 (1981): 82-105.   Rodgers reviews the complex court politics of the 370s and 380s in the west, culminating in the overthrow of the emperor Gratian in 383, and the succession of Maximus with the complicity of Merobaudes.

295. Sasel, J. "The Struggle between Magnentius and Constantius II for Italy and Illyricum." *Ziva Antika* 21 (1971): 205-216.   A detailed narrative of political and military events, from the time of Magnentius' usurpation in 350 to his retreat from Illyricum and Italy into Gaul in 352.

296. Sickle, C. E. van. "Diocletian and the Decline of the Roman Municipalities." *Journal of Roman Studies* 28 (1938): 9-18.   Diocletian increased the financial burden of the curiales on behalf of the state while diminishing their local obligations. "The unhappy middle class, caught between the imperial hammer and the municipal anvil, was crushed" (p. 18).

297. Sickle, C. E. van. "Conservatism and Philosophical Influence in the Reign of Diocletian." *Classical Philology* 27 (1932): 51-58.   "Diocletian was indeed founder of a new order of things; but this fact does not preclude his being a man of conservative temperament. . . . Diolcetian's ideals . . . were largely derived from the great days of the Stoic emperors - Nerva, Trajan, Hadrian, and the Antonines.   Doubtless his understanding of their reigns and policies was imperfect; and he lived in a period when a complete revival of the second-century order of things was impossible. But, as far as circumstances and his own knowledge permitted, he seems to have been guided by the Stoic ideal of ruling for the benefit of his subjects; and he has as good a claim to be considered the last of the 'first citizens' as he does to be called the first of the 'autocrats'" (pp. 57-58).

298. Simpson, W. Douglas. *Julian the Apostate.* Aberdeen: Milne and Hutchinson, 1930. Sympathetic and sometimes emotional appreciation of Julian, who is seen as a tragic figure wedded to a fading past, especially a religious past. Some of the generalizations about the fourth century would not hold up under modern scrutiny. F. A. Christie, *American Historical Review* 36 (1931): 573-574 (++-); M. P. C., *English Historical Review* 48 (1933): 318 (+); H. St. L. B. Moss, *History* 16 (1931): 150-151 (++-); C. E. Stevens, *Journal of Roman Studies* 21 (1931): 135-136 (+-).

299. Sinnigen, William G. *The Officium of the Urban Prefecture during the Later Roman Empire.* Papers and Monographs of the American Academy in Rome, XVII. Rome: American Academy, 1957. Sinnigen describes the organization and function of this important office, responsible for governing the city of Rome and presiding at the Senate. He covers the time from Diocletian to Justinian. Based on his 1954 Ph. D. dissertation at the University of Michigan. L. L. Howe, *American Historical Review* 63 (1958-59): 716-717 (+).

300. Sinnigen, William G. "The Roman Secret Service." *Classical Journal* 57 (1961): 65-72. Although largely concerned with the earlier empire, Sinnigen takes the story of the Roman secret service briefly through late antiquity.

301. Sinnigen, William G. "Three Administrative Changes Ascribed to Constantius II." *American Journal of Philology* 83 (1962): 369-382. Sinnigen disputes the location of certain administrative changes in the time of

Constantius, saying that the evidence is too murky to know for sure, but the time of Constantine seems more likely.

302. Sinnigen, William G. "Two Branches of the Late Roman Secret Service." *American Journal of Philology* 80 (1959): 238-254. Sinnigen discusses the *agentes in rebus* and the *notarii.* Both groups had different historical backgrounds, but were much alike in function by the time of Constantine, and Sinnigen considers them "two interrelated branches of a system which deserves to be called the Late Roman imperial secret service" (p. 254).

303. Sinnigen, William G. "The Vicarius Urbis Romae and the Urban Prefecture." *Historia* 8 (1959): 97-112. Sinnigen sees in this story of confused local government in the fourth century a symbol of the central government's difficulty and ultimate failure in bringing the great urban aristocracy to heel.

304. Smith, John Holland. *Constantine the Great.* New York: Scribner's, 1971. Smith is heavy on maybe, perhaps, probably and must have. These qualifiers are regularly attached to conclusions that have been arrived at after a useful although often tedious sifting of the evidence. There are some interesting although rather strained judgments, but the options are usually advanced for consideration. All in all, this is a useful biography of compromise conclusions, a satisfactory beginning for the student. J.A.S. Evans, *American Historical Review* 77 (1972): 758-759 (+-); R. H. Storch, *Catholic Historical Review* 60 (1974): 122-123 (+-).

305. Smith, R. E. "The Regnal and Tribunician Dates of Maximianus Herculius." *Latomus* 31 (1972): 1059-1071. Smith gives a very technical discussion of the problems regarding the evidence that can be adduced to help in understanding the political relation of Maximian to Diocletian during the stages of their long association as rulers of the Roman state.

306. **Stern, Henry.** "Remarks on the 'Adoratio' under Diocletian." *Journal of the Warburg and Courtauld Institutes* 17 (1954): 184-189. There has been scholarly controversy about the extent to which Diocletian was responsible for a new court protocol which included kissing the hem of his robe, and so on. Stern comes down firmly in support of Diocletian as "the first to have carried out a methodical and lasting reform of court ceremonial based on an entirely new idea of imperial dignity" (p. 189).

307. **Stevens, C. E.** "Magnus Maximus in British History." *Etudes Celtiques* 3 (1938): 86-94. Using sources outside the mainstream of Greek and Roman source material, Stevens reconstructs the career of Magnus Maximus before his bid for the emperorship in 383.

308. **Storch, Rudolph H.** "The 'Absolutist' Theology of Victory: Its Place in the Late Empire." *Classica at Mediaevalia* 29 (1968): 197-206. Storch identifies "A widened theology of victory, involving the suggestion of an invincible emperor, winning eternal and universal Roman victories" (p. 206), as a feature of the later empire.

309. **Sutherland, C. H. V.** "Flexibility in the 'Reformed' Coinage of Diocletian." In *Essays in Roman Coinage Presented to Harold Mattingly*, pp. 174-189. Edited by R. A. G. Carson and C. H. V. Sutherland. New York and London: Oxford University Press, 1956. Examples of the political flexibility of the coins: gold coins tended to have themes and images which would appeal to the upper crust civilians most likely to use them, whereas the silver coins tended to be designed to appeal to the soldiers, in whose hands they were more likely to be found than gold.

310. **Sutherland, C. H. V.** "The Folles of Ticinum, A. D. 305-307." *Numismatic Chronicle* 14 (1954): 68-75. Sutherland discusses the rather amusing efforts of the small mint at Ticinum to keep abreast of the latest political developments in the chaotic college of emperors after the abdication of Diocletian.

311. **Sutherland, C. H. V.** "Some Political Notions in Coin Types Between 294 and 313." *Journal of Roman Studies* 53 (1963): 14-20. Careful study of coin types reflects political changes, almost year by year sometimes, in the empire or in sections of the empire during the Tetrarchy.

312. **Swift, L. J. and Oliver, J. H.** "Constantius on Flavius Philippus." *American Journal of Philology* 83 (1962): 247-264. Swift and Oliver provide the text, translation, and commentary on an imperial letter of praise for a high government official named Philippus which was discovered at Ephesus in 1955. Swift and Oliver date the letter to 344, and conclude that the author was the emperor Constantius II himself, not some bureaucrat.

313. **Sydenham, E.** "The Vicissitudes of Maximian after His Abdication." *Numismatic Chronicle* 14 (1934): 141-167. With the help of the numismatic evidence, Sydenham relates the "strange policy of opportunism" (p. 143) that characterized the efforts of Maximian to regain the imperial power that he had abdicated with Diocletian in 305. Includes a convenient chronology of the years 305 to 310.

314. **Syme, Ronald.** "Danubian and Balkan Emperors." *Historia* 22 (1973): 310-316. With primary sources at hand, Syme ruminates on the origins of late third and early fourth century emperors.

315. **Syme, Ronald.** "Union and Discord." *Acta Antiqua Academiae Scientiarum Hungaricae* 24 (1976): 337-340. Syme reflects informally on features of the fourth century empire that tended to encourage the division between east and west, which became a permanent political reality in the fifth century.

316. **Teall, John L.** "The Age of Constantine: Change and Continuity in Administration and Economy." *Dumbarton Oaks Papers* 21 (1967): 11-36. Calling the later empire "a society in spotty or uneven development" (p. 18), Teall also notes that

it was both "tough and resilient and . . . more fluid and mobile than it had ever been" (p. 19). In this context, Constantine was certainly a busy little bee, and qualifies as an innovator in various ways which Teall discusses; but he does not emerge as a "thoroughgoing revolutionary." Teall's most valuable contribution is to encourage us to get away from looking at the fourth century from the perspective of 476 and all that, and to look at it on its own merits based on developments that had already occurred rather than on those yet to come.

317. Tellegen-Couperus, Olga E. *Testamentary Succession in the Constitutions of Diocletian.* Zutphen, Netherlands: Uitgeverij Terra, 1982.

318. Thomas, G. S. R. "Maximin Daia's Policy and the Edicts of Toleration." *L'Antiquite Classique* 37 (1968): 172-185. Thomas reviews the confusing politics of the period 311-313, when Constantine, Licinius, Maxentius and Maximin Daia jostled for power.

319. Thomas, J. David. "The Date of the Revolt of L. Domitius Domitianus." *Zeitschrift fur Papyrologie und Epigraphik* 22 (1976): 253-279. Egypt in the 290s, when there was a revolt against Diocletian.

320. Thomas, J. David. "The Disappearance of the Dekaprotoi in Egypt." *Bulletin of the American Society of Papyrologists* 11 (1974): 60-68. Administrative changes in Egypt in 302.

321. Thomas, J. David. "A Family Dispute from Karanis and the Revolt of Domitius Domitianus." *Zeitschrift fur Papyrologie und Epigraphik* 24 (1977): 233-243. Thomas dates the revolt of Domitianus to 297/8.

322. Thomas, J. David. "Sabinianus, *Praeses* of Aegyptus Mercuriana?" *Bulletin of the American Society of Papyrologists* 21 (1984): 225-234. Thomas offers some thoughts on the evidence for a Roman governor in one of the small provinces of Egypt in the first quarter of the fourth century.

323, Thomas, J. David. "The Strategus in Fourth Century Egypt." *Chronique d'Egypte* 35 (1960): 262-270. Discussed are the functions and status of the strategus, a local official of curial rank with tax collecting and other responsibilities.

324. Thompson, E. A. "The Emperor Julian's Knowledge of Latin." *Classical Review* 58 (1944): 49-51. Thompson says Julian had a superficial familiarity with Latin and its literature.

325. Thompson, E. A. "Peasant Revolts of Late Roman Gaul and Spain." *Past and Present* 2 (1952): 11-23. Reprinted in *Studies in Ancient Society*, Chap. 14. Edited by M. I. Finley. Boston: Routledge and Kegan Paul, 1974. Thompson outlines the history and aims of the Bacaudae (or Bagaudae), disaffected peasant groups in rebellion against Romans authority and against the social structure in the fourth and fifth centuries.

326. Van Dam, Raymond. "Emperors, Bishops, and Friends in Late Antique Cappadocia." *Journal of Theological Studies* 37 (1986): 53-76. In the time of the emperor Valens there was a lot more than Christianity going on in Roman Cappadocia. Through the activities of Basil, bishop of Caesarea, Van Dam teaches us that traditional politics involving local aristocrats and the central government, and traditional styles of local politics and issues of influence and prestige, were involved in many incidents that later commentators have too often seen as having an exclusive basis in theological disputes. In two appendices the author provides a helpful discussion of the chronology of the emperor's movements from 370 to 372.

327. Vogt, Joseph. "Pagans and Christians in the Family of Constantine the Great." In *Paganism and Christianity in the Fourth Century*, pp. 38-55. Edited by Arnaldo Momigliano. New York: Oxford University Press, 1963. Making his family Christian did not do Constantine much good keeping it unified and in power after his death. Ironically, the last member of the family on the imperial throne was Julian, a pagan by choice partly in reaction to his dislike of the family.

328. Wade, W. V. "Carausius, Restorer of Britain." *Numismatic Chronicle* 12 (1953): 131. A coin makes a contribution to our knowledge of Carausius, ruler of Britain without Diocletian's permission in the 290s.

329. Wahba, M. "Politics by Idolatry or by Reason: The Case of Constantine." In *The 17th International Byzantine Congress: Abstracts of Short Papers*, p. 381. Washington, D. C.; August 3-8, 1986, Dumbarton Oaks/Georgetown University. Baltimore: U. S. National Committee for Byzantine Studies, 1986.

330. Ward, John H. "The 'Notitia Dignitatum.'" *Latomus* 33 (1974): 397-434. Ward discusses dating and internal structure. He gives a very detailed review of all the N. D.'s parts, and concludes that "we have remarkably clear panoramic views of two instants in the life of the Roman Imperial Government - the East in 394 and the West in 430" (p. 434).

331. Wardman, Alan E. "Usurpers and Internal Conflicts in the 4th Century A. D." *Historia* 33 (1984): 220-237. Civil conflict has always been seen as a defect in the life of the Roman empire. Certainly, in all the revisionist activity over the fourth century, it should not now be seen as a good thing. But, as Wardman points out, it had its positive or benign aspects. In the first place, usurpation was a part of the system of change and succession, and a usually brief civil conflict gave or withdrew legitimacy from an emperor and his policies. In the second place, there was not an automatic relationship between Roman civil strife and barbarians flooding in while armies were otherwise engaged. Independent factors were often involved here. Wardman elaborates these and related themes to show that usurpation, while not a feature to be recommended, had a place in the political landscape, rather a like a mountain chain which the traveler accepts as having to be crossed to reach the other side, though he might wish for a plain instead.

332. Warmington, B. H. "The Career of Romanus, Comes Africae." *Byzantinische Zeitschrift* 49 (1956): 55-64. Warmington reviews the controversies surrounding Romanus' response to barbarian invasions of Africa during the time of Valentinian I, and discusses court politics of the time and the defense system of the African provinces.

333. Warmington, B. H. "Virgil, Eusebius of Caesarea and an Imperial Ceremony." In *Studies in Latin Literature and Roman History*, pp. 451-460. Vol. IV. Edited by Carl Deroux. Collection Latomus, 196. Brussels: Latomus, 1986. To describe a scene involving Constantine receiving homage and gifts from distant peoples, Eusebius evokes a passage from Virgil. Although not directly derivative, the Eusebian passage shows the similarity of concern with Virgil to enhance the reputation of the emperor. In an interesting aside, Warmington says that Eusebius, whether he knew directly the passage in Virgil or not, did know Latin.

334. Webb, Diana M. "The Truth about Constantine: History, Hagiography, and Confusion." *Studies in Church History* 17 (1981): 85-102. Stories about the baptism of Constantine and other events of his career took on a life of their own after his death. Webb shows how scholars and researchers of medieval and Renaissance times sorted through the confusion and what conclusions they came to.

335. Webb, H. "The Reign and Coinage of Carausius." *Numismatic Chronicle* 7 (1907): 1-88; 291-338; 373-426.

336. Webster, Graham. "The Possible Effects on Britain of the Fall of Magnentius." In *Rome and Her Northern Provinces*, pp. 240-254. Edited by Brian Hartley and John Wacher. Gloucester (U.K.): Alan Sutton, 1983. Webster presents evidence in support of the thesis that after the fall of the usurper Magnentius in 353, Constantius II went after his rich supporters in Britain and other western provinces with a

Politics and Government 73

vengeance, resulting in changes in the great villas and pagan sites which are reflected in archaeological evidence that may in the past have been incorrectly associated with barbarian raids in the late 360s.

337. Wells, Benjamin W. "Taxation and Bureaucracy in the Declining Empire." *Sewanee Review* 30 (1922): 421-445. A sad portrait of the later Roman empire, which Wells finds a bottomless pit of corruption and despair.

338. Wilkes, J. J. *Diocletian's Palace, Split: Residence of a Retired Roman Emperor.* Sheffield, England: University of Sheffield, 1986. A summary of knowledge about and an interpretation of this famous residence. Chapter One is a useful introduction to the reign of Diocletian. The illustrations are many and important, but the photographs are badly reproduced. J. Humphrey, *American Journal of Archaeology* 91 (1987): 635 (+).

339. Williams, Stephen. *Diocletian and the Roman Recovery.* New York: Methuen, Inc., 1985. This is a first: the first full-scale biography of Diocletian in English. Luckily, it is a good product, comprehensive, sympathetic, well informed, steady, and readable. There are good chapters on all aspects of the reign of this New Deal prince, whose success in so many areas was later overshadowed by his persecution of the new-fangled religion, Christianity, whose adherents survived to blacken his name in literature forever thereafter. E. Luttwak, *American Historical Review* 91 (1986): 640-641 (+); J. Patterson, *Greece and Rome* 32 (1985): 223 (+); N. J. Hackett, *Historian* 49 (1987): 387 (+).

340. Wilson, Edward. "Studies in the Lives of the Sons of Constantine." Ph. D. dissertation, University of British Columbia, 1977. Wilson believes that the sons of Constantine were what they were largely because of their teachers and advisors, rather than heredity or paternal influence.

341. Wistrand, Erik. "A Note on the *Geminus Natalis* of Emperor Maximian." *Eranos* 62 (1964): 131-145. Reprinted in his *Opera Selecta,* pp. 427-441. Stockholm, 1972. Wistrand's investigations of the meaning of a panegyrical phrase relating to the emperor Maximian's birthday leads to the discovery that a Swiss scholar three hundred years ago had resolved the problem. Along the way some interesting tidbits about Maximian and Diocletian and their epoch are mentioned.

III. Military Matters

This section encompasses technical matters as well as campaigns and battles.

342. **Alfoldi, A.** "Cornuti: A Teutonic Contingent in the Service of Constantine." *Dumbarton Oaks Papers* 13 (1959): 171-179. Alfoldi discusses the origins and development in the Roman army of the Cornuti, a unit of barbarian warriors who wore horns on their helmets and who came especially into imperial favor after a decisive role in winning the battle of the Milvian Bridge for Constantine in 312.

343. **Arvites, James A**. "The Military Campaigns of Adrianople." *History Today* 31 (April 1981): 30-35. All the old cliches about Adrianople are dusted off for yet another tour of duty. The battle "totally demolished the army of the Eastern Empire" (p. 35), and "completely revolutionised methods of warfare" (p. 35). Without qualification or explanation, this great battle, fought in 378, is seen to have "directly affected the affairs of the Western provinces during the course of the fifth century" (p. 31). For those uninitiated into the mysteries of Adrianople, the Thomas Burns (150) article would be more enlightening.

344. **Austin, N. J. E.** "Ammianus' Account of the Adrianople Campaign: Some Strategic Observations." *Acta Classica* (Capetown) 15 (1972): 77-83. Through Ammianus' account of the twenty-two months from autumn of 376 to August of 378, Austin identifies and discusses the phases of Roman military strategy in the Balkans while trying to control the Gothic migration over the Danube. Austin also reviews the disaster at Adrianople, giving an analysis of the numbers and giving the emperor Valens a more favorable press than this

unfortunate brother of the great soldier-emperor Valentinian I usually gets.

345. **Austin, N. J. E.** *Ammianus on Warfare: An Investigation into Ammianus' Military Knowledge.* Collection Latomus, 165. Brussels: Latomus, 1979. Austin puts Ammianus in the forefront of ancient military historians: "I have attempted to show this by demonstrating that he possesses an extensive knowledge of the three principal phases of military activity - intelligence, planning and operations - though he is perhaps not quite so good on the operations side compared with the other two " (p. 7). Austin provides incidentally of course a great deal of valuable information and analysis of the military activities of the Roman state in the last half of the fourth century, such as the Adrianople campaign of 378.

346. **Austin, N. J. E.** "Investigations into the Military Knowledge of Ammianus Marcellinus." Ph. D. dissertation, University of London, 1971.

347. **Barnes, Timothy D.** "The Date of Vegetius." *Phoenix* 33 (1979): 254-257. Barnes puts the composition of Vegtius' *De re militari* in the 380s, where it "finds its most appropriate historical niche as part of the debate which the disaster of 378 [Adrianople] initiated" (p. 257).

348. **Barnes, Timothy D.** "Imperial Campaigns, A. D. 285-311." *Phoenix* 30 (1976): 174-193. Barnes shakes down the evidence, such as it is, for the time of Diocletian, and draws some new conclusions on the dating, numbers, and meanings of the military campaigns in this important period of restoration of Roman prestige at home and abroad. The first paragraph has a useful outline of the meager primary source material for the reign of Diocletian.

349. **Berchem, Denis Van.** "On Some Chapters of the *Notitia Dignitatum* Relating to the Defense of Gaul and Britain." *American Journal of Philology* 76 (1955): 138-147. Observations on the constantly evolving military organization

Military Matters

of the late empire in Gaul and Britain. Rigidity was not one of the failings of the later Roman military organization, as a careful reading of the *Notitia* will help show.

350. **Biernacka-Lubanska, M.** *The Roman and Early Byzantine Fortifications of Lower Moesia and Northern Thrace.* Translated by Lorraine Tokarczyk. Bibliotheca antiqua, 17. Wroclaw: Polish Academy of Sciences, 1982.

351. **Bivar, A. D. H.** "Cavalry Equipment and Tactics on the Euphrates Frontier." *Dumbarton Oaks Papers* 26 (1972): 271-291. Contains some fourth century material. The greatest source of innovation in cavalry warfare derived from the nomadic tribes of Central Asia, and one of the great testing grounds was along the Euphrates where the Romans and Persians often clashed.

352. **Bowman, Alan K.** "The Military Occupation of Upper Egypt in the Reign of Diocletian." *Bulletin of the American Society of Papyrologists* 15 (1978): 25-38. Military activity and organization in Egypt in the 290s.

353. **Bushe-Fox, J. P.** "Some Notes on Roman Coast Defences." *Journal of Roman Studies* 22 (1932): 60-72. Late Roman defenses along the coast of Britain.

354. **Butler, R. M.** "The Defences of the Fourth-Century Fortress at York." In *Soldier and Civilian in Roman Yorkshire*, pp. 97-105. Edited by R. M. Butler. Leicester: Leicester University Press, 1971. Butler reviews the evidence to dispel any doubts that the defensive walls and gates of fourth century York were built in the time of Constantine I.

355. **Butler, R. M.** "Late Roman Town Walls in Gaul." *The Archaeological Journal* 116 (1959): 25-50.

356. **Crump, Gary A.** "Ammianus and the Late Roman Army." *Historia* 22 (1973): 91-103. By using information from Ammianus, Crump demonstrates a "vitality and responsiveness in the later Roman army which has hitherto

gone unsuspected" (p. 103). The army was never so tight and rigid as the formal military structure portrayed in official sources such as the *Notitia Dignitatum*. The entire system was indeed huge and cumbersome, but fourth century emperors and military leaders were not shy about tinkering with what was at hand, improvising if necessary according to the needs and conditions of the moment.

357. Crump, Gary A. *Ammianus Marcellinus as a Military Historian*. Wiesbaden: Steiner, 1975. For Ammianus, a former military officer, military matters were of fundamental importance. Crump says that Ammianus reported and grasped strategy very well. He was less secure with tactical matters, although his reporting of key incidents compensated for this deficiency. Crump sees in Ammianus plenty of proof that the later Roman military system was far less rigid that many sources might lead us to believe. Based on Crump's Ph. D. dissertation, University of Illinois, 1969.

358. Davies, R. W. "The Supply of Animals to the Roman Army and the Remount System." *Latomus* 28 (1969): 429-459. Mostly this has to do with horses in the early Roman period. But there is some material from the later period too.

359. *The Defence of the Roman and Byzantine East.* Edited by Philip Freeman and David Kennedy. 2 vols. Oxford: British Archaeological Reports, 1986. The essays relevant to the fourth century are: A. D. H. Lee, "Embassies as Evidence for the Movement of Military Intelligence Between the Roman and Sasanian Empires," pp. 455-461; J. H. W. Liebeshchuetz, "Generals, Federates and Buccelarii in Roman Armies around AD 400," pp. 463-474; S. Lieu, "Captives, Rufugees and Exiles: A Study of Cross-Frontier Civilian Movements and Contacts between Rome snd Persia from Valerian to Jovian," pp. 475-505; C. S. Lightfoot, "Tilli - a Late Roman *Equites* Fort on the Tigris?," pp. 509-529; J. F. Matthews, "Ammianus and the Eastern Frontier in the Fourth Century: A Participants View," pp. 549-564; T. B. Mitford, "A Late Roman Fortress South of Lake Van," pp. 565-573; S. T. Parker, "Retrospective on the Arabian Frontier After a Decade of Research," pp. 633-660; D. N. Riley, "Archaeological Air Photography and the Eastern Limes," pp. 661-676. B. Issac, *Journal of Roman Studies* 78 (1988): 240-241 (+-).

360. Delbruck, Hans. *History of the Art of War Within the Framework of Political History.* Translated by Walter J. Renfroe, Jr. 2 vols. Westport, Conn.: Greenwood Press, 1975-1980. This translation is based on Delbruck's third edition (1921) of his four volume study. These first two volumes have to do with antiquity, and students of the fourth century will find the second volume especially useful. There are, for instance, important discussions of two critical battles: Strasbourg (AD 357), and Adrianople (AD 378).

361. Duncan-Jones, R. P. "Pay and Numbers in Diocletian's Army." *Chiron* 8 (1978): 541-560. Working largely with Egyptian papyri, Duncan-Jones discusses army pay and the size of army units. The process of reducing the size of legions appears to have been under way during Diocletian's time, rather than later as many modern historians, including A. H. M. Jones, have held.

362. Eadie, John W. "The Development of Roman Mailed Cavalry." *Journal of Roman Studies* 57 (1967): 161-173. Mailed cavalry is powerful but clumsy and easily tripped up. The Romans experimented and eventually found it a home in the military system; but it was never quite a success. In the fourth century, Constantine easily defeated the mailed cavalry of Maxentius in 312 by encirclment. Constantius II used it successfully at Mursa in 351; Julian did not find it useful at Strasbourg in 357. Mailed cavalry is not mentioned at Adrianople, but seems to have been reintroduced in the time of Theodosius. Eadie sees the Roman experiment with mailed cavalry ending in failure, but as a good example of Roman willingness to try new things.

363. Ferrill, Arthur. *The Fall of the Roman Empire: The Military Explanation.* New York: Thames and Hudson, 1986. In one respect, this is old wine in new bottles. Considered as a thesis, Ferrill is Vegetius and Zosimus again: the reforms of

Constantine and the general barbarization of the army were bad things to do. This is in contrast to the currently predominant notion that the reforms of Constantine were a good thing, and that change is not necessarily barbarization. Ferrill transcends or modifies his own thesis by making it clear that the fourth century Roman army was still a success and quite up to dealing with the enemy when properly lead and maintained. This is a well informed book and a good one for new students of the military history of the later empire. J. Patterson, *Greece and Rome* 34 (1987): 96-97 (+); S. Williams, *History Today* 36 (August 1986): 59-60 (+).

364. Goodburn, R. and Bartholomew, P., eds. *Aspects of the Notitia Dignitatum.* British Archaeological Reports, Suppl. Series, 15. Oxford: B. A. R., 1976. "Three contributions are devoted to the document itself, one is a general examination of civil and military imperial officials, and the remaining seven explore specific military aspects or provinces" (Harries review, p. 187) J. D. Harries, *Journal of Roman Studies* 67 (1977): 187-188 ("the wide range of this volume in both subject-matter and approach makes it an invaluable aid to understanding of, and research in, more aspects of Late Antiquity than the specialized title alone might suggest").

365. Goodchild, G. "The Roman and Byzantine Limes in Cyrenaica." *Journal of Roman Studies* 43 (1953): 65-76. Goodchild takes a look at the defense system of Cyrenaica at the end of the fourth century.

366. Gordon, C. D. "Vegetius and His Proposed Reforms of the Army." In *Polis and Imperium: Studies in Honor of E. F. Salmon*, pp. 35-55. Edited by J. A. S. Evans. Toronto: Hakkert, 1974. Vegetius, whether he wrote in the late fourth or well into the fifth century (Gordon inclines towards the latter), has a lot to say that is relevant to the structure of the late fourth century army. Gordon gives an unsympathetic look at Vegetius, whom he calls "reactionary and timid" (p. 55).

Military Matters 81

367. Hawkes, S. C. "Soldiers and Settlers in Britain, Fourth to Fifth Century." *Medieval Archaeology* 5 (1961): 1-70.

368. Holder, P. A. *The Roman Army in Britain.* New York: St. Martin's Press, 1982. See pp. 97-103 for the fourth century Roman army in Britain.

369. International Congress of Roman Frontier Studies. 1949- . This series is as elusive as a barbarian raiding party. So far there have been fourteen of these congresses. The ones whose published papers have received bibliographic treatment in the WLN or OCLC databases or which I have found independently are as follows: 1st, 1949 (published by Durham University, 1952); 6th, 1964, held at Bohlau Verlag; 7th, 1967, held at Tel Aviv University; 8th, 1969, at Cardiff, Wales (published by University of Wales, 1974); 9th, 1972, in Mamaia, Romania; 10th, 1974, in Cologne; 11th, 1976, in Szehesbehavar, Hungary (published in 1977); 12th, 1979, at University of Sterling, Scotland (published by B. A. R., 1980); and the 14th, 1986, at Carnuntum [Petronell], Austria. The reader will have to investigate these for late Roman material. One paper from the 11th Congress may suggest the kind of material the researcher may hope to find in the others: B. H. Warmington, "Objectives and Strategy in the Persian War of Constantius II," pp. 509-520.

370. Isaac, Benjamin. "The Meaning of the Terms *Limes* and *Limitanei*." *Journal of Roman Studies* 78 (1988): 125-147. Isaac reviews the changing definitions of these military words from the first to the fifth centuries. Much primary source material is adduced. In the later empire, *limes* "is the formal term used to designate a frontier district under the command of a *dux*," and the *limitanei* were not peasant farmers, but "simply units under the command of a *dux limitis* " (p. 146).

371. Johnson, J. S. "Late Roman Fortifications in the Western Empire: A Study of the Origins and Development of the

Roman Defensive System in the Late 3rd Century and After." Ph. D. dissertation, Oxford University, 1974.

372. Johnson, Stephen. *Late Roman Fortifications.* Totowa, N. J.: Barnes and Noble Books, 1983. An important work, covering the western empire primarily, and heavily illustrated. Johnson does not do much with the army; his emphasis is on forts and walls and road protection. S. S. Frere, *English Historical Review* 101 (1986): 208-209 (+); G. Webster, *American Historical Review* 89 (1984): 743-744 (+).

373. Johnson, Stephen. *The Roman Forts of the Saxon Shore.* London: Paul Elek, 1976.

374. Johnston, D. E., ed. *The Saxon Shore.* C. B. Research Report, 18. London: Council for British Archaeology, 1977. The wonderful thing about this collection of papers is not only that we are brought into the latest thinking on the Saxon shore defense system in the fourth century, but that we are as well given so much useful information about so many aspects of life and of course especially military matters in the later empire. Heavily and nicely illustrated.

375. Kaegi, Walter E. "Constantine's and Julian's Strategies of Strategic Surprise Against the Persians." *Athenaeum* 59 (1981): 209-213. Reprinted in his *Army, Society and Religion in Byzantium*, Part IV. London: Variorum Reprints, 1982.

376. Kaegi, Walter E. "Domestic Military Problems of Julian the Apostate." *Byzantinische Forschungen* 2 (1967): 247-264. Reprinted in his *Army, Society and Religion in Byzantium*, Part II. London: Variorum Reprints, 1982. "Julian's reign found the army volatile in its allegiances (hence his efforts to create a more loyal force through religious tests), prone to voice its many grievances, and so expensive to support that . . . Julian himself feared that Roman resources were insufficient to maintain it" (p. 264). When reading articles on the difficulties of controlling the fourth century army, it is important to remember that during most of the

Military Matters

history of the Roman empire, the army was a large and loud and expensive element of power in the Roman system of government, and required constant attention. In fact, as Kaegi grants, Julian did control his army, "through a combination of flattery, threats, money, and honors" (p. 263). Alexander the Great did not have it much better, though his army was much smaller.

377. Lander, James. *Romans Stone Fortifications: Variation and Change from the First Century A. D. to the Fourth.* Oxford, England: British Archaeological Reports, 1984.

378. Lightfoot, C. S. "Facts and Fiction - the Third Seige of Nisibis (AD 350)." *Historia* 37 (1988): 105-125. Ammianus thought the surrender of Nisibis in 363, as part of a settlement with the Persians, a humiliation without precedent in Roman history. Considering the importance strategically of the city and the fact that it recently had withstood three seiges by the Persians, Ammianus' sentiment can be appreciated. Lightfoot concentrates on the seige of 350, sifting through the evidence to reconstruct the story, and relating it to other events in the empire. There are interesting paragraphs on seige warfare, on the divine powers of the emperor, and on the Christian contribution to the defense of the city.

379. Luttwak, Edward N. *The Grand Strategy of the Roman Empire from the Third Century A. D. to the Third.* Baltimore: Johns Hopkins University Press, 1976. Despite the title, Luttwak in fact takes his discussion briefly to the middle of the fourth century, and breaks off just when things are becoming interesting. Luttwak sees three stages of defense, and it is the third that pertains to our period: "a defense-in-depth based on a combination of static frontier armies and mobile field forces." J. C. Mann, *Journal of Roman Studies* 69 (1979): 175-183 (++-); S. Oost, *History Reviews of New Books* (August 1977): 201 (+); C. M. Wells, *American Journal of Philology* 99 (1978): 527-529 ("A valuable, exciting, and in some ways brilliant book, but flawed. It could have been so much better").

380. MacMullen, Ramsay. "How Big Was the Roman Imperial Army?" *Klio* 62 (1980): 451-460. MacMullen reviews the wildly varying estimates, and concludes that the military system encompassed about 400,000 in the later empire. To MacMullen, however, there are even more interesting features: "first, that the later Roman army suffered such a loss in numbers of well trained, mobile fighting men, who constituted only a minority within a total that was itself little larger than under Septimius Severus; second, that the organization of the army had grown so much more primitive, so that high commanders could not allot troops to new duties or new fronts with much speed or accuracy" (p. 460).

381. MacMullen, Ramsay. "The Roman Emperor's Army Costs." *Latomus* 43 (1984): 571-580. MacMullen advances the interesting thesis that the late Roman army was configured in small clusters near market centers and that the great field armies were stationed in large cities as cost-saving measures.

382. MacMullen, Ramsay. *Soldier and Civilian in the Later Roman Empire.* Cambridge, Mass.: Harvard University Press, 1967. Covering the period from 200 to 400, MacMullen shows the blurring of distinctions between military and civilian functions in the Roman empire as the military increasingly permitted its people to engage in official and unofficial nonmilitary activities, such as being local farmers and patrons and administrators. MacMullen sees this as a bad trend at a time when more than ever soldiers should have been concentrating on soldiering. B. H. Warmington, *Journal of Roman Studies* 54 (1964): 205-206 (+).

383. Maloney, John and Hobley, Brian, eds. *Roman Urban Defences in the West: A Review of Current Research on Urban Defences of the Roman Empire with Special Reference to the Northern Provinces*, Based on Papers Presented to the Conference on Roman Urban Defences, Museum of London, 21-23 March 1980. CBA Research Report, 51. London: Council for British Archaeology, 1983. The studies relevant to the fourth century are: J. Mertens, "Urban Wall-Circuits in Galla

Military Matters

Belgica in the Roman Period," pp. 42-57; Malcolm Todd, "The Aurelianic Wall of Rome and Its Analogues," pp. 58-67; Stephen Johnson, "Late Roman Urban Defences in Europe," pp. 69-76; Brian Hobley, "Roman Urban Defences: A Review of Research in Britain," pp. 78-84; John Maloney, "Recent Work on London's Defences," pp. 96-117; Graham Webster, "The Function and Organization of Late Roman Civil Defences in Britain," pp. 118-120; John Casey, "Imperial Campaigns and 4th Century Defences in Britain," pp. 121-124; R. M. Butler, "The Construction of Urban Defences," pp. 125-129; T. F. C. Blagg, "The Reuse of Monumental Masonry in Late Roman Defensive Walls," pp. 130-135; D. Baatz, "Town Walls and Defensive Weapons," pp. 136-140. Heavily illustrated throughout.

384. Mann, J. C. "Duces and Comites in the 4th Century." In *The Saxon Shore*, pp. 11-15. Edited by D. E. Johnston. London: Council for British Archaeology, 1977. This tightly organized and lucid essay is much more than the title indicates. It is in fact a perfect introduction to the evolution of the Roman military in the fourth century, with an emphasis on the command structure. In a very few paragraphs the author has summarized the best information that recent decades of scholarship offer on this topic.

385. Mann, J. C. "Power, Force and the Frontier of the Empire." *Journal of Roman Studies* 69 (1979): 175-183. Although to a large extent devoted to matters before and beyond the fourth century, there are some valuable paragraphs discussing fourth century military strategy from Diocletian to Stilicho.

386. Martin, K. M. "A Reassessment of the Evidence for the *comes Britanniarum* in the Fourth Century." *Latomus* 28 (1969): 408-428. Martin reviews the military situation in Britain in the second half of the fourth century.

387. Naude, C. P. T. "Battles and Sieges in Ammianus Marcellinus." *Acta Classica* 1 (1958): 92-105. Naude praises the general accuracy of Ammianus in battle and siege descriptions. There is some standardization of description, yes; but that is inevitable in ancient writers.

388. Nischer, E. C. "The Army Reforms of Diocletian and Constantine and Their Modification up to the Time of the Notitia Dignitatum." *Journal of Roman Studies* 13 (1923): 1-55. Diocletian augmented the army and Constantine reorganized it. This is now accepted as commonplace. But when Nischer was writing Mommsen ruled, and it had been his belief that the new fourth century arrangement of mobile field armies and fixed frontier units was the joint creation of Diocletian and Constantine. Nischer provides in this article the basis for subsequent discussion of fourth century army reforms. The main thread is the clear distinction between what happened under Diocletian and what happened under Constantine. Nischer provides plenty of statistical considerations and takes the story down to the time of Stilicho.

389. Nixon, C. E. V. "Coin Circulation and Military Activity in the Vicinity of Sirmium, A.D. 364-378, and the Siscia Mint." *Jahrbuch fur Numismatik und Geldeschichte* 33 (1983): 45-56. Taking advantage of large coin finds of the 1970s, Nixon has the "opportunity of bringing numismatic data to bear on the Pannonian frontier" (p. 46), and concludes that "it is not easy to correlate the literary and epigraphic evidence for the fortification of the Pannonian limes with the numismatic" (p. 54). Along the way to this conclusion, Nixon discusses interesting aspects, mostly military, of the reign of Valentinian I.

390. Oliver, Revilo P. "A Note on the *De Rebus Bellicis.*" *Classical Philology* 50 (1955): 113-118. Oliver discusses some of the artillery of the late Roman army, and says we need to take the author of the *De Rebus* seriously as a military engineer.

391. Oman, Charles W. C. *The Art of War in the Middle Ages, A. D. 378-1515.* Revised and edited by John H. Beeler. Ithica, N. Y.: Cornell University Press, 1953; 1968. In 1884 Oman as an undergraduate at Oxford penned a judgment

Military Matters 87

upon the battle of Adrianople that was to echo through popular and scholarly literature almost uncontested for one hundred years: "The military importance of Adrianople was unmistakable; it was a victory of cavalry over infantry" (p. 4, 1968 ed). Oman's classic little book underwent a number of revisions over the years; but this judgment remained to haunt late empire studies. Recently, however, the significance of Adrianople has undergone revision, and its position as a military watershed has been subject to scrutiny. In 1988 there was this firm response to Oman: "The view that this was the first victory of cavalry over infantry and that it began the period of the predominance of the horseman in military history is mistaken: the Visigoths were infantrymen like the Romans." (E. A. Thompson, "Late Roman Migrations," in *Civilization of the Ancient Mediterranean: Greece and Rome* [Vol I], p. 172. Edited by Michael Grant and Rachel Kitzinger. New York: Charles Scribners' Sons, 1988.)

392. Parker, H. M. D. "The Legions of Diocletian and Constantine." *Journal of Roman Studies* 23 (1933): 175-189. Parker defends Theodor Mommsen's position that the central strategic reserve was first created by Diocletian rather than Constantine.

393. Petrikovits, Harald von. "Fortifications in the North-Western Roman Empire from the Third to the Fifth Centuries A. D." *Journal of Roman Studies* 61 (1971): 178-218. This important discussion indicates a great flurry of building activity from the mid-third century to the time of Valentinian I, who died in 375. The great military and civil fortifications were not only a response to the barbarian incursions, but reflected the new strategies of the late Roman state. The author has appended a long list (and complementary map) of known construction from 260 to 375. Helpful illustrations throughout.

394. Ridley, R. T. "Notes on Julian's Persian Expedition (363)." *Historia* 22 (1973): 317-330. Includes "parallel gospel" arrangement of the relevant sources: Ammianus,

Zosimus, Libanius, Magnus. Ridley discusses various questions regarding Julian's last, doomed military project.

395. Roessel, D. "The Battle of the Milvian Bridge: Another Look at a Historical Problem." In *The 17th International Byzantine Congress: Abstracts of Short Papers,* pp. 295-296. Washington, D. C., August 3-8, 1986, Dumbarton Oaks/Georgetown University. Baltimore: U. S. National Committee for Byzantine Studies, 1986.

396. Scorpan, C. *Limes Scythiae: Topographical and Stratigraphical Research on the Late Roman Fortifications on the Lower Danube.* Oxford, England: British Archaeological Reports, 1980.

397. Simpson, C. J. "Foederati and Laeti in Late Roman Frontier Defence." Ph. D. dissertation, University of Nottingham, 1971. For more on the origins of the concept of *laeti*, see his "Laeti in Northern Gaul . . . ," *Latomus* 36 (1977): 169-170.

398. Sommer, C. Sebastian. *The Military Vici in Roman Britain: Aspects of Their Origins, Their Location and Layout, Administration, Function, and End.* Oxford, England: British Archaeological Reports, 1984.

399. Speidel, Michael P. "*Catafractarii clibanarii* and the Rise of the Later Roman Mailed Cavalry: A Gravestone from Claudiopolis in Bithynia." *Epigraphica Anatolica* 4 (1984): 151-156. Speidel discusses new information on the mailed cavalry of the late empire. Scholars have inclined to think that mailed cavalry was clumsy and not a very successful addition to the Roman military arsenal; but Speidel doubts that it would have been retained in service for such a long time if it had proved consistently useless.

400. Speidel, Michael P. "The Later Roman Field Army and the Guard of the High Empire." *Latomus* 46 (1987): 375-379. Speidel seeks to demonstrate that "the first units of the

Military Matters

uexillationes, the horse of the field army, came from the [praetorian] guard of the High Empire" (p. 375).

401. Speidel, Michael P. "Maxentius and His *Equites Singulares* in the Battle at the Milvian Bridge." *Classical Antiquity* 5 (1986): 253-259. Speidel identifies the defeated and dying Maxentius and the rout of his Horse Guards on the Arch of Constantine, and discusses the last years of the Horse Guards of Rome, whose close association with Maxentius lead to their abolition by Constantine along with that of the Praetorian Guard.

402. Speidel, Michael P. "The Rise of the Later Roman Field Army from the Guard of the High Army." *Latomus* 46 (1987): 375-379. Speidel says that "the question whether Diocletian or Constantine created the Later Roman field army is wrongly put. Neither emperor created it, each merely enlarged it" (p. 379), because it had its origins in the old Praetorian Guard.

403. Speidel, Michael P. *Roman Army Studies.* V. I. Amsterdam: J. C. Gieben, 1984. Thirty-seven papers, written between 1970 and 1983. The ones directly relevant to the late empire are: "A Latin Gravestone of AD 390 from Sebaste/Phrygia," pp. 381-389, which gives information on Roman forces sent to guard the cities of Phrygia against Gothic settlers in the 380s; "Stablesiani: The Raising of New Cavalry Units During the Crisis of the Roman Empire," pp. 391-396, which discusses the creative response to barbarian threats during the time of Gallienus and beyond. A couple of other short papers offer some sidelights on the later Roman army. Some of the other papers offer excellent background material for understanding the origins of the fourth century military system.

404. Speidel, Michael P. "The Roman Road to Dumata (Jawf in Saudi Arabia) and the Frontier Strategy of *Praetensione Colligare*." *Historia* 36 (1987): 213-221. Diocletian's system of outposts and patrols along an important frontier road leading to the Persian Gulf is the subject of investigation in this interesting essay, which includes a helpful map.

405. Thompson, E. A. "Constantine, Constantius II, and the Lower Danube Frontier." *Hermes* 84 (1956): 372-381. Thompson reviews Roman military activities, including building programs and campaigns, along the lower Danube in the first half of the fourth century. He also discusses relations with the Goths, the primary barbarian power in the area.

406. Todd, Malcolm. *The Walls of Rome.* London: Paul Elek, 1978. The Aurelian wall, plus fourth and fifth century improvements: among the most massive projects of antiquity. J. J. Wilkes, *Classical Review* 30 (1980): 169-170 (+).

407. Tomlin, Roger. "The Later Empire, AD 200-450." In *Greece and Rome at War*, pp. 249-261. Edited and largely written by Peter Connolly. Englewood Cliffs, N. J.: Prentice-Hall, Inc., 1981. Good narrative, based on current scholarship, of the military configuration of the later empire. Good illustrations.

408. Tomlin, Roger. "*Seniores-iuniores* in the Late Roman Field Army. *American Journal of Philology* 93 (1972): 253-278. Tomlin considers the matter of junior and senior regiments in the Roman army of the second half of the fourth century, and weaves into his discussion a great deal of useful information on the late Roman military establishment generally.

409. Varady, L. "New Evidences on Some Problems of the Late Roman Military Organization." *Acta Antiqua* 9 (1961): 333-396. Varady deals at length with the following problems: replacement of soldiers in the late Roman aarmy, the paper versus actual strength of units, organizational questions and leadership, the value of the *Notitia Dignitatum* as a source, and morality in the army.

410. Warry, John G. *Warfare in the Classical World: An Illustrated Encyclopedia of Weapons, Warriors, and Warfare in the Ancient Civilizations of Greece and Rome.* New York: St.

Martin's Press, 1980. The final chapters are of some interest to the student of the later empire. A light narrative is accompanied by heavy illustrations, which are in fact the best feature of the book. The diagrams of famous battles, such as Adrianople, are especially helpful. D. G. Chandler, *History Today* 31 (January 1981): 51-52 (+-).

411. Welsby, Derek A. *The Roman Military Defence of the British Provinces in Its Later Phases.* B. A. R. British Series, 101. Oxford: British Archaeological Reports, 1982. By "later phases" is meant the fourth century, plus some introductory material. There is a heavy reliance on archaeological evidence, as might be expected. A good share of the narrative may be considered useful in understanding the late Roman military in general. Lots of fort illustrations.

412. Wilson, D. A. H. "A Declining and Disadvantaged Society and the Implications of Its Military Commitments: The Western Roman Empire in the Second Half of the Fourth Century as Evidenced by Ammianus Marcellinus." M. A. thesis, University of Birmingham, 1979.

IV. Literature and Education

Includes secular historiography generally. Christian literature is primarily to be found under "Christianity." Includes studies on fourth century primary sources, and on fifth and sixth century sources that have relevance to the fourth century. There was no systematic effort to collect primary sources in English translation, which nevertheless are to some extent included depending mostly on the amount of useful commentary they contain. The student may consult the Loeb Classics and the Nice and Post-Nicene Fathers of the Christian Church series to find a significant share of the fourth century primary sources in English. Writings that discuss primary sources material in depth but whose purpose is to elucidate a topic will generally be found under the heading that encompasses the topic.

413. **Adams, J. N.** "On the Authorship of the *Historia Augusta*." *Classical Quarterly* 22 (1972): 186-194. More on this perennial topic. Adams votes for one author.

414. **Archbold, Geoffrey J. D. E.** *A Concordance to the History of Ammianus Marcellinus [microform]*. Toronto: University of Toronto Press, 1980. 49 microfiches.

415. **Aspects of the Notitia Dignitatum.** Papers Presented to the Conference in Oxford, December 13 to 15, 1974. Edited by R. Goodburn and P. Bartholomew. Oxford: British Archaeological Reports, 1976. The *Notitia Dignitatum*, like the *Historia Augusta*, has in recent decades provoked some of the best scholars of the late Roman period to try to come to grips with its meaning and undoubted value as a fundamental primary source. In this important anthology are the following essays: J. C. Mann, "What Was the Notitia Dignitatum for?"; J. J. G. Alexander, "The Illustrated Manuscripts of the Notitia

Dignitatum"; J. P. Wild, "The Gynaecea"; M. M. Roxan, "Pre-Severan Auxilia Named in the Notitia Dignitatum"; J. S. Johnson, "Channel Commands in the Notitia"; M. W. C. Hassall, "Britain in the Notitia"; A. L. F. Rivet, "The Notitia Galliarum: Some Questions"; R. M. Price, "The Limes of Lower Egypt"; J. F. Matthews, "Mauretania in Ammianus and the Notitia"; R. S. O. Tomlin, "Notitia dignitatum omnium, tam civilium quam militarium"; C. E. Stevens, "The Notitia Dignitatum in England."

416. **Astin, Alan E.** "Observations on the *De Rebus Bellicis.*" In *Studies in Latin Literature and Roman History*, pp. 388-439. Vol. 3. Edited by Carl Deroux. Brussels: Latomus, 1983. Astin examines two questions: "whether or not the work shows the author to have been actuated by - or even aware of - a shortage of manpower available for the Roman army; and what was the primary purpose or concept underlying the work as a whole" (p. 389). Astin's answer to the first is, "No"; his answer to the second is that the author, writing between 366 and 374, was largely concerned to restrain imperial expenses and lighten the tax burden. There is much other incidental and useful information on the DRB in this informed essay.

417. **Austin, N. J. E.** "In Support of Ammianus' Veracity." *Historia* 22 (1973): 331-335. Austin defends Ammianus against charges of subordinating truth to art.

418. **Bagnall, R. S., ed.** *Columbia Papyri VII: Fourth Century Documents from Karanis.* Transcribed by R. S. Bagnall and N. Lewis. American Studies in Papyrology, 20. New York: American Society of Papyrologists, 1979.

419. **Baker, Aaron E.** "Eunapius and Zosimus: Problems of Chronology and Composition." Ph. D. dissertation, Brown University, 1987.

420. **Baldwin, Barry.** "Acclamations in the *Historia Augusta.*" *Athenaeum* 69 (1981): 138-149. Reprinted in his *Studies on Late Roman and Byzantine History, Literature and Language*, pp. 33-44. Amsterdam: J. C. Gieben, 1984.

421. Baldwin, Barry. *An Anthology of Later Latin Literature.* London Studies in Classical Philology, 19. Amsterdam: J. C. Gieben, 1987. Baldwin finds late Latin literature "exciting," and offers an interesting selection of mostly secular literature from the second to the seventh centuries as proof. Over a third of the entries relate to the fourth century. In each, Baldwin gives the author or the selection a lively introduction, followed by the literary selection in the original language, with helpful notes in English. Baldwin wisely emphasizes the (to us) obscure, and gives a wide sampling of the kinds of literature available to contemporary audiences. R. P. H. Green, *Classical Review* 39 (1989): 142-143 (+--).

422. Baldwin, Barry. "Ausonius and the *Historia Augusta.*" *Gymnasium* 88 (1981): 438. Reprinted in his *Studies on Late Roman and Byzantine History, Literature and Language,* p. 51. Amsterdam: J. C. Gieben, 1984. More proof, or near proof, that the *Historia Augusta* dates from the late fourth century.

423. Baldwin, Barry. "Catiline in the *Historia Augusta.*" *Parola del Passato* 200 (1981): 315-316. Reprinted in his *Studies on Late Roman and Byzantine History, Literature and Language,* pp. 53-54. Amsterdam: J. C. Gieben, 1984.

424. Baldwin, Barry. "The *De Rebus Bellicis.*" *Eirene* 16 (1978): 23-39. Reprinted in his *Studies on Late Roman and Byzantine History, Literature and Language,* pp. 101-117. Amsterdam: J. C. Gieben, 1984. It is very difficult to date this important piece of source material. Baldwin shows why, then offers the 380s as a good possibility. Regarding authorship, Baldwin inclines towards a "knowledgeable civilian," with a good education, whose native tongue was Latin, which he wrote in a "competent and sometimes adventurous" style.

425. Baldwin, Barry. "Festus the Historian." *Historia* 27 (1978): 197-217. Reprinted in his *Studies on Late Roman and*

Byzantine History, Literature and Language, pp. 79-99. The author pursues the question of who Festus was and what his religious position was, and concludes that less can be known of this mid-fourth century minor historian than some historians would have us believe. Then Baldwin discusses the text of the *Breviorium:* for whom it was meant, sources, style and language.

426. Baldwin, Barry. "Greek Historiography in Late Roman and Early Byzantium." *Hellenika* 33 (No. 1, 1981): 51-65. Reprinted in his *Studies on Late Roman and Byzantine History, Literature and Language*, pp. 191-216. Covering the period 238-565, Baldwin discusses the kinds of history produced and the kinds of historians who produced them. The emphasis is on the lesser known historians whose works are lost, mostly lost, or at least unread.

427. Baldwin, Barry. "Gregory Nazianzus, Ammianus, *scurrae,* and the *Historia Augusta.*" *Gymnasium* 93 (1986): 178-180. Word plays in the *Historia Augusta.*

428. Baldwin, Barry. "Leopards, Roman Soldiers, and the *Historia Augusta.*" *Illinois Classical Studies* 10 (1985): 281-283. Baldwin finds "yet another small link in the chain of details that betrays the fraudulent nature of the *Historia Augusta*" (p. 283).

429. Baldwin, Barry. "Literature and Society in the Later Roman Empire." In *Literary and Artistic Patronage in Ancient Rome*, pp. 67-83. Edited by Barbara K. Gold. Austin: University of Texas Press, 1982. In the ancient world the fortunes of literary culture were in a large way dependent upon government stability. In the stable conditions of the fourth century, literature flourished, although the type and standard of Latin and Greek writings may not be as agreeable to us as the literature from the early empire.

430. Baldwin, Barry. "Some Alleged Greek Sources of the *Historia Augusta.*" *Liverpool Classical Monthly* 4 (1979): 19-23. Reprinted in his *Studies on Late Roman and Byzantine*

History, Literature and Language, pp. 45-49. Amsterdam: J. C. Gieben, 1984.

431. Baldwin, Barry. "Verses in the *Historia Augusta.*" *Bulletin of the Institute of Classical Studies* 25 (1978): 50-59. Reprinted in his *Studies on Late Roman and Byzantine History, Literature and Language*, pp. 23-31. Amsterdam: J. C. Gieben, 1984.

432. Baldwin, Barry. "The *Vita Avidii.*" *Klio* 58 (1976): 101-119. Reprinted in his *Studies on Late Roman and Byzantine History, Literature and Language*, pp. 3-21. Amsterdam: J. C. Gieben, 1984.   More on the *Historia Augusta.*

433. Banchich, Thomas M. "The Date of Eunapius' *Vitae Sophistarum.*" *Greek, Roman and Byzantine Studies* 25 (1984): 185-194.   Banchich picks the autumn or winter of 399 for the composition of the VS.

434. Banchich, Thomas M. "Eunapius and Jerome." *Greek, Roman and Byzantine Studies* 27 (1986): 319-324. "When all things are considered . . . the collective weight of the evidence inclines the balance towards Eunapius as one of Jerome's sources for secular events through 378, and reinforces existing arguments that the portion of the *History* in circulation before the publication of the *Vita sophistarum* culminated in the battle of Adrianople" (p. 324).

435. Banchich, Thomas M. "Eunapius on Libanius' Refusal of a Prefecture." *Phoenix* 39 (1985): 384-386.   Banchich dates the incident ca. 368, and suggests implications for the publication dates of Eunapius' *History.*

436. Banchich, Thomas M. "The Historical Fragments of Eunapius of Sardis."   Ph. D. dissertation, University of New York at Buffalo, 1985.

437. Banchich, Thomas M. "On Goulet's Chronology of Eunapius' Life and Works." *Journal of Hellenic Studies* 107 (1987): 164-167.   In a dispute about mid-fourth century dates, Banchich advances some interesting information on secondary and postsecondary education and students in the later Roman period.

438. Barnard, Sylvia E. "An Historiographical Study of Ammianus Marcellinus." Ph. D.. dissertation, Yale University, 1966. Ammianus does not directly discuss his historical methods, but shows a preference for Heroditus and Livy, and also generally shows more enthusiasm for Greek than Latin literature. Barnard shows his social and economic conservatism, and says that in religion, he could find favor for any orderly religious expression, although he had a preference for the pagan heritage. His large interest was in military matters, on which he wished to write in the grand style of the ancient Greek historians.

439. Barnes, Timothy D. "The *Epitome de Caesaribus* and Its Sources." *Classical Philology* 71 (1976): 258-268. This complex article is a useful example to the student of the difficulties of getting on firm ground with a piece of fourth century source material which is both important to get to know and impossible to get to know with complete satisfaction.

440. Barnes, Timothy D. *The Sources of the Historia Augusta.* Collection Latomus, 155. Brussels: Latomus, 1978. Barnes gives the *Historia Augusta* one author and dates it to the late fourth century, makes an effort to separate fact from fiction in this important but frustrating primary source, and identifies the sources that he believes were used to compose it. R.P.H. Green, *Journal of Roman Studies* 69 (1979): 227-228 (+); R. O. Edbrooke, *American Historical Review* 84 (1979): 434 (+).

441. Baynes, Norman H. *The Historia Augusta: Its Date and Purpose.* Oxford: Clarendon Press, 1926. Baynes argues that the *Historia Augusta* was written in the time of Julian and was sympathetic to the last pagan emperor's cause.

442. Baynes, Norman H. "The *Historia Augusta:* Its Date and Purpose. A Reply to Criticism." *Classical Quarterly* 20

(1928): 166-171. Baynes defends his position that the *Historia Augusta* was written in support of and during the time of Julian.

443. Binns, J. W., ed. *Latin Literature of the Fourth Century.* Boston: Routledge and Kegan Paul, 1974. Includes: "Paganism, Christianity and the Latin Classics in the Fourth Century, " by R. A. Markus; "Decimus Magnus Ausonius: The Poet and His World," by Harold Isbell; "The Letters of Symmachus," by J. F. Matthews; "The Two Worlds of Paulinus of Nola," by W. H. C. Frend; "Claudian," by Alan Cameron; and "Prudentius," by Valerie Edden. J. W. Halporn, *Classical Journal* 72 (1976): 362-365 (-).

444. Bird, Harry. "Eutropius: In Defence of the Senate." *Cahiers des Etudes Anciennes* 20 (1987): 63-72.

445. Bird, H. W. "The Roman Emperors: Eutropius' Perspective." *Ancient History Bulletin* 1 (1987): 139-151. Eutropius wrote his history of Rome for the emperor Valens, and he took the opportunity to instruct him on how to be a good emperor. This mission of course colors his portraits. Eutropius "loathed cruelty, excessive severity, greed and ingratitude. On the other hand he admired military ability, efficient administration, moderation, liberality and civility" (p. 151). He liked emperors who were good to and for the traditional order of things, especially those with a respectful attitude towards the senatorial class.

446. Bird, H. W. *Sextus Aurelius Victor: A Historiographical Study.* Liverpool: F. Cairns, 1984. The life of Aurelius Victor, important imperial bureaucrat and minor historian, spanned the fourth century. He was personally known to and patronized by emperors, and his views on Rome and the world reflected the milieu in which he travelled. Bird provides a most helpful analysis of his writings, which reveal attitudes regarding politics, religion, morality, culture, the Roman state, and so on.

447. **Bird, H. W.** "The Sources of the *De Caesaribus*." *Classical Quarterly* 31 (1981): 457-463. After a review of scholarly opinions and possibilities regarding sources, Bird reminds us that there was a commonly accepted core of information about the history of Rome and its emperors available. "It was presumably from this general pool of information as well as from his recollections (occasionally faulty) of earlier authors and discussions with colleagues and others that Victor rounded out his basic account" (p. 463).

448. **Birley, A. R.** "The Augustan History." In *Latin Biography*, pp. 113-138. Edited by Thomas Dorey. New York: Basic Books; London: Routledge and Kegan Paul, 1967. A general survey of the problems and opportunities inherent in this elusive fourth century history of the emperors.

449. **Blockley, R. C.,** ed. *Ammianus Marcellinus: A Selection, with Introduction, Notes, and Commentary.* Bristol: Bristol Classical Press, 1980. The selections (in Latin) are on the following themes: the revolt of Silvanus, the city of Rome, the emperor Julian, Britain, magic trials at Antioch, and the battle of Adrianople. Students without Latin can use the Rolfe translation in the Loeb Classics. The real value of Blockley is in the well-informed footnotes and the introductory material, where a succinct review of the organization of the fourth century empire and a chronology are useful.

450. **Blockley, R. C.** *Ammianus Marcellinus: A Study of His Historiography and Political Thought.* Brussels: Latomus, 1975. Excellent introduction to the most important of later Roman historians.

451. **Blockley, R. C.** "Dexippus of Athens and Eunapius of Sardis." *Latomus* 30 (1971): 710-715. The late third century historian Dexippus and the late fourth century historian Eunapius, and their relationship, come under review. With only fragments of Eunapius, and even less of Dexippus, Blockley works through to tentative conclusions on the histories they wrote.

452. Blockley, R. C. *The Fragmentary Classicising Historians of the Late Roman Empire: Eunapius, Olympiodorus, Priscus and Malchius.* 2 vols. Liverpool: Francis Cairns, 1981-1983.   Eunapius is the only one whose history covers the fourth century. Volume I discusses each historian and lists the fragments that survive; Volume II brings all the fragments together in translation, with the Greek on the facing pages. Reviews here have only to do with Volume I.   A. B. Breebaart, *Mnemosyne* 37 (1985): 232-235 (+); Averil Cameron, *Classical Review* 33 (1983): 18-20 (+-).

453. Blockley, R. C. "Tacitean Influence upon Ammianus Marcellinus." *Latomus* 32 (1973): 63-78.   Tacitus had a renaissance of popularity in the late fourth century. While not a heavy borrower of expressions, Ammianus does show a more general dependence on Tacitus' style of presentation, the aspects of which Blockley explains. Still, all in all, Tacitus should not be considered a major historiographical influence upon Ammianus.

454. Boer, William den. *Some Minor Roman Historians.* Leiden: E. J. Brill, 1972.   Boer covers Florus, and three fourth century authors: Aurelius Victor ("the writer of fear"), Eutropius ("resigned"), and Festus ("great hopes for the future").   They are as useful, perhaps more so, for the attitudes they give regarding their own age as for the information they give about earlier times.   *Times Literary Supplement* (January 26, 1973): 95 (+).

455. Bonner, S. F. "The Edict of Gratian on the Remuneration of Teachers." *American Journal of Philology* 86 (1965): 113-137.   In a very thorough way, Bonner analyzes the text of the edict of 376 to determine the answers to questions having to do with its geographical application generally, the cities addressed, how and in what form payments were to be made, and how teachers were in fact affected.

456. Booth, Alan D. "The Academic Career of Ausonius." *Phoenix* 36 (1982): 329-343.   The author concentrates on the early career of Ausonius, before he became a high government official under Gratian. The goal of the essay is "to increase knowledge not only about Ausonius but about professorial careers in general and schooling in the later Empire" (p. 329).

457. **Booth, Alan D.** "Elementary and Secondary Education in the Roman Empire." *Florilegium* 1 (1979): 1-14. Booth encourages us to appreciate the diversity and flexibility of educational arrangements in the Roman world. He adduces a fair amount of material from fourth century Gaul, especially Bordeaux.

458. **Booth, Alan D.** "Notes on Ausonius' *Professores.*" *Phoenix* 32 (1978): 235-249. Booth gives a prosopographical treatment to the teachers of fourth century Gaul who appear in Ausonius' epitaphs.

459. **Booth, Alan D.** "On the Date of Eunapius' Coming to Athens." *Ancient History Bulletin* 1 (1987): 14-15. The philosopher/historian Eunapius started his studies in Athens shortly after the death of the emperor Julian, says Booth after an analysis of relevant passages in Eunapius' *Lives of the Philosophers.*

460. **Breebaart, A. B.** "Eunapius of Sardes and the Writing of History." *Mnemosyne* 32 (1979): 360-375. Only 6 or 7% of Eunapius' history covering A.D. 270-404 has survived. Breebaart works with the evidence to discover a historian who is more in the tradition of Plato than of Thucydides. The result is not objectivity as we know it, but Truth as found in the mind of a late Greco-Roman intellectual.

461. **Brock, Sebastion P.** "Greek into Syriac and Syriac into Greek." *Journal of the Syriac Academy III* (1977): 1-17. Reprinted in his *Syriac Perspectives on Late Antiquity*, Chap. II. London: Variorum Reprints, 1984. The thrust of the article is beyond the fourth century, but there is some relevant material showing the flow of Greek material into Syriac after 350.

462. Buck, David F. "Dexippus, Eunapius, Olympiodorus: Continuation and Imitation." *Ancient History Bulletin* 1 (1987): 48-50. Dexippus, who wrote a history of the third century, was followed by Eunapius, who covered the fourth, and he was followed by Olympiodorus, who covered part of the fifth. They picked up where their predecessors had left off; but each had his own style and did not seek to imitate: "Eunapius may have taken Herodian as his model, but Olympiodorus appears to have been idiosyncratic" (p. 50).

463. Buck, David F. "Eunapius of Sardis." Ph. D. dissertation, Oxford University, 1978.

464. Buck, David F. "The Structure of the Lausiac History." *Byzantion* 46 (1976): 292-307. "Although thematic considerations sometimes override strict autobiography, in its broad outline the structure of the *Lausiac History* is based upon the course of Palladius' life . . . " (p. 306). Buck reconstructs the chronology.

465. Bury, J. B. "The Notitia Dignitatum." *Journal of Roman Studies* 10 (1920): 130-154. Bury gives a detailed analysis of the ND that is the basis for much of the 20th century debate on this significant piece of primary source material.

466. Butler, C. "The Dialogus de Vita Chrysostomi and the Historia Lausiaca." *Journal of Theological Studies* 22 (1920-21): 138-155.

467. Calder, W. M. "The Eumeneian Formula." In *Studies Presented to W. H. Buckler*, pp. 15-21. Manchester, England: Manchester University Press, 1926. The Eumenius in question was a famous Gallic rhetorician in the time of Constantine I.

468. The Cambridge History of Classical Literature II: Latin Literature. Edited by E. J. Kenney and W. V. Clausen. New York: Cambridge University Press, 1982.

Part VI, "Later Principate," covers the period from the middle of the third century to the middle of the fifth. All the chapters were written by Robert Browning, with the exception of Chapter 42, "Apuleius," which was located here as an "aesthetic rather than a historical decision on the part of the Editor" (p. xiii). It still grates. Browning covers the fourth century literary figures authoritatively. He has written a particularly thoughtful and succinct introduction to the period generally and its literary orientation. One of the joys of reading in late Roman history is the high level of prose employed by so many historians in the field. This little introductory essay is an especially compelling example. R. G. M. Nisbet, *Journal of Roman Studies* 73 (1983): 175-179 ("Robert Browning has summarized the literature of the late Empire with a clarity and orderliness of method that are not conspicuous in all of the book.")

469. Cameron, Alan. "An Alleged Fragment of Eunapius." *Classical Quarterly* 13 (1963): 232-236. A piece of primary source material on Julian's Persian campaign is not from Eunapius, says Cameron.

470. Cameron, Alan. "The Latin Revival of the Fourth Century." In *Renaissance Before the Renaissance: Cultural Revivals of Late Antiquity and the Middle Ages*, pp. 42-58. Edited by Walter Treadgold. Stanford, Ca.: Stanford University Press, 1984. Cameron stresses that Christians as well as pagans were involved in fourth century literary trends, which evolved from a renewed interest in the writers of the Latin Silver Age of the first century.

471. Cameron, Alan. *Literature and Society in the Early Byzantine World.* London: Variorum Reprints, 1985. The relevant essays from this anthology are treated individually.

472. Cameron, Alan. "Macrobius, Avienus and Avianus." *Classical Quarterly* 17 (1967): 385-399. Cameron ruminates on dates and relationships in the late fourth and early fifth century literary world of the western empire.

473. Cameron, Alan. "Wandering Poets: A Literary Movement in Byzantine Egypt." *Historia* 14 (1965): 470-509. In the fourth and fifth centuries, a prolific school of professional pagan poets from Egypt wandered the empire in search of fame and employment in the great houses, including the emperor's. Cameron discusses the characteristics of the poets, and follows the careers of specific examples, including the most famous, Claudian, whose works were unique for being in Latin, and for having survived for us to read today.

474. Cameron, Averil and Alan. "Christianity and Tradition in the Historiography of the Later Empire." *Classical Quarterly* 14 (1964): 316-328. Historians of the later Roman empire often avoided mentioning Christianity or dealt with it in circumlocutions. The extent of this treatment or non-treatment of Christianity, however, cannot be used to determine the religious sympathies of the writer. The fact of the matter is there was a great reliance on ancient Greek historians for the proper way to write history, and Christianity simply did not fit the ancient scheme of doing history.

475. Chadwick, Nora K. *Poetry and Letters in Early Christian Gaul.* London: Bowes and Bowes, 1955. Although in a few respects not quite up to the minute regarding recent scholarship and new intellectual approaches to the period of time covered, this delightful book is well worth a read or two. The author is warmly sympathetic towards "the great Gaulish officials and bishops, . . . the men of letters and the country gentlemen." Her assessment: "Men brought up like ourselves in the classical tradition, they faced the political and military crisis with a reserve of strength, an ungrudging public spirit, a balanced judgment and an appreciation of literary and spiritual values, which are congenial to the modern mind" (pp. 8-9). Encompassing the later fourth century and the fifth to about 475, Chadwick ably discusses religious, social, political and military developments in the context of her review of literature.

476. **Chalmers, Walter R.** The *Nea Ekdosis* of Eunapius' Histories." *Classical Quarterly* 3 (1953): 165-170. Chalmers says that Eunapius himself was responsible for the second as well as the first edition of his mostly lost *History*, rather than a later figure as some historians have argued.

477. **Charlet, Jean-Louis.** "Aesthetic Trends in Late Latin Poetry (325-410)." *Philologus* 132 (1988): 74-85.

478. **Chimock, E. J.** *A Few Notes on Julian and a Translation of His Public Letters.* London, 1901.

479. **Christensen, Torben.** "The So-called Appendix to Eusebius' *Historia Ecclesiastica* VIII." *Classica et Mediaevalia* 34 (1983): 177-209. Christensen discusses Eusebius' "scissors-and-paste method" of composing his church history, working primarily with material in Eusebius that has to do with the emperors from Diocletian to Constantine.

480. ***The Chronicon Paschale: From the Conversion of Constantine to Heraclius' Victory over Persia.*** Translated by Michael and Mary Whitby. Liverpool: Liverpool University Press, 1987.

481. **Clark, Charles U.** *The Text Tradition of Ammianus Marcellinus.* New Haven: The Author, 1904. This is Clark's Ph.D. dissertation, Yale, 1903. He did the translation of Ammianus in the Loeb Classics.

482. **Courcelle, Pierre P.** *Late Latin Writers and Their Greek Sources.* Translated by Harry E. Wedeck. Cambridge: Harvard University Press, 1969. The dynamic of Hellenic culture and thought was very strong in the late empire, influencing as well as contending with Christianity. Courcelle is mostly concerned with fifth and sixth century thought, but through a review of Macrobius and Jerome, Part I offers an analysis of the condition of pagan and Christian Hellenism at the end of the fourth century.

483. Crees, James H. E. *Claudian as an Historical Authority.* Cambridge: University Press, 1908.

484. Croke, Brian. "The Editing of Symmachus' Letters to Eugenius and Arbogast." *Latomus* 35 (1976): 533-549. Croke sees no reason to think that the letters from Symmachus to the usurper Eugenius were deleted from the published collection.

485. Croke, Brian and Emmett, A. M., eds. *History and Historians in Late Antiquity.* Sydney: Pergamon Press, 1983. Of the fourteen papers here are the most relevant for the fourth century: Brian Croke and Alanna M. Ennett, "Historiography in Late Antiquity: An Overview"; E. A. Judge, "Christian Innovation and its Contemporary Obervers"; John Matthews, "Ammianus' Historical Evolution"; Alanna M. Emmett, "The Digressions in the Lost Books of Ammianus Marcellinus"; N. J. Austin, "Autobiography and History: Some Later Roman Historians and Their Veracity"; R. F. Newbold, "Patterns of Communication and Movement in Ammianus and Gregory of Tours"; C. E. V. Nixon, "Latin Panegyric in the Tetrarchic and Constantinian Period"; G. Maslakov, "The Roman Antiquarian Tradition in Late Antiquity"; Brian Croke, "The Origins of the Christian World Chronicle"; Garry W. Trompf, "The Logic of Retribution in Eusebius of Caesarea"; Roger Scott, "Epilogue: Old and New in Late Antique Historiography." T. D. Barnes, *Classical Review* 35 (1985): 398-399 (+).

486. Davies, J. G. "The *Peregrinatio Egeriae* and the Ascension." *Vigiliae Christianae* 8 (1954): 93-100. Davies considers the dating of the PE, and settles on the late fourth century for this important travel itinerary of a pilgrim to the Holy Land.

487. *De Rebus Bellicis.* Edited by M. W. C. Hassall and R. I. Ireland. Oxford: British Archaeological Reports, 1979. Part I contains essays. The ones directly concerning the DRB and the fourth century are: A. Cameron, "The Date of the Anonymous"; J. J. G. Alexander, "The Illustration of the *de*

Rebus Bellicis "; R. M. Reece, "The Anonymous: A Numismatic Commentary"; J. S. Johnson, "Frontier Policy in the Anonymous"; M. W. C. Hassall, "The Inventions." The Cameron essay (which dates the DRB to ca. 368/9) is reprinted in his *Literature and Society in the Early Byzantine World*, Chap. IX. London: Variorum Reprints, 1985. The remaining essays have an interest apart from the DRB, and are treated separately in this bibliography. Part II is the text itself, in Latin and in English translation by Robert Ireland, with extensive commentary on the text, language, and style.

488. De Rebus Bellicis. A Roman Reformer and Inventor. Translated and edited by E. A. Thompson. New York: Oxford University Press, 1952. Includes a lengthy and informed essay on this remarkable work which proposes various reforms of the Roman state regarding finance, currency, military, administrative, and legal matters. Thompson dates the document to 366-375, and includes the Latin text as well as the English translation. M. Grant, *English Historical Review* 68 (1953): 454 (+).

489. DiMaio, Michael. "The Antiochene Connection: Zonaras, Ammianus Marcellinus and John of Antioch on the Reigns of the Emperors Constantius II and Julian." *Byzantion* 50 (1980): 158-185. DiMaio sorts out the extent to which Zonaras relied on Ammianus and John for information on events of the mid-fourth century.

490. Downey, Glanville. "The Builder of the Original Church of the Apostles at Constantinople, a Contribution to the Criticism of the *Vita Constantini* attributed to Eusebius." *Dumbarton Oaks Papers* 6 (1951): 53-80. Constantine built it, says Downey.

491. Downey, Glanville. "Education and Public Problems as Seen by Themistius." *Transactions of the American Philological Association* 87 (1955): 291-307. Themistius, the great pagan educator and orator, whose influence at the Christian courts of emperors from Constantius II to Theodosius I was remarkable and undimmed even as the court became more

Christian, believed that an updated and enlightened education of classical wisdom ("philosophy") would help solve the problems of the Roman state by producing citizens and leaders who could more clearly see their interests for the long term. A favorite example for Themistius is enlightened treatment of the barbarians. In an address to Theodosius I (Or. 34), Themistius presses the point that the wisdom of the emperor (through philosophical studies) has spared the barbarians and put them to good use, rather than uselessly shedding their blood and spending Roman money to do it: "He who is forever pursuing the contumacious barbarians, makes himself merely the ruler of the Romans; but he who conquers them, and spares them, understands that he is the ruler of mankind" (p. 302).

492. Downey, Glanville. "Education in the Christian Roman Empire: Christian and Pagan Theories under Constantine and His Succesors." *Speculum* 32 (1957): 48-61. Constantine, Eusebius, Lactantius, and Themistius are consulted to get a perspective on educational practices and beliefs in the fourth century.

493. Downey, Glanville. "Themistius' First Oration." *Greek, Roman and Byzantine Studies* 1 (1958): 46-69. English translation of Oration 1, "On Love of Mankind; or, Constantius," dating from about 350. Downey includes background information.

494. Drake, H. A. "When Was the *De Laudibus Constantini* Delivered?" *Historia* 24 (1975): 345-356. The traditional date is 25 July 335. Through a review of internal and external evidence Drake feels able to move the date of Eusebius' speech up to 25 July 336.

495. Eadie, J. W. *The Breviarium of Festus: A Critical Edition with Historical Commentary.* London: Athlone Press, 1967. Festus was *magister memoriae* under Valens, to whom the work was dedicated. It appeared after the Gothic peace (369) and about the time of the Persian war, and seems to have been a guide to eastern provinces and their history for government officials. T.D. Barnes, *Journal of Roman Studies*

58 (1966): 263-265 (+-); Alan Cameron, *Classical Review* 19 (1969): 305-307 (++-).

496. *Egeria: Diary of a Pilgrimage.* Translated and annotated by George E. Gingras. New York: Newman Press, 1970. As well as a fairly literal translation with notes, Gingras provides an extensive bibliography.

497. *Egeria's Travels to the Holy Land.* Translated with supporting documents and notes by John Wilkinson. Revised ed. Jerusalem: Ariel Publishing House; Warminster: Aris and Phillips, 1981. The Wilkinson translation is in a free conversational style. It was first published in 1971 by S. P. C. K.

498. Ehrhardt, C. T. H. R. "Constantinian Documents in Gelasius of Cyzicus' Ecclesiastical History." *Jahrbuch fuer Antike und Christentum* 23 (1980): 48-57. "To summarise, the documents Gelasius brings which purport to derive from the records of the Council of Nicaea are worthless as source material for it, though they may make some contribution to our knowledge of disputes about the Emperor's place in the Church and about correct dogma in the fourth and early fifth centuries" (pp. 56-57).

499. Elliott, Thomas G. *Ammianus Marcellinus and Fourth Century History.* Sarasota: S. Stevens, 1983. This work is an expansion of Elliott's Harvard Ph. D. thesis of 1971, and is largely an exposition of Ammianus with a view to pinning the historian down on the issue of reliability. The introduction has an interesting summary of literature regarding Ammianus' reliability. Elliott himself concludes that the historian was less than impartial and in fact should be seen as a pagan apologist with an anti-Christian tendency. The last chapter has a helpful review of the Balkan problem culminating in the battle of Adrianople in 378. J. M. Alonso-Nunez, *Journal of Roman Studies* 76 (1986): 328 (--+).

500. Emmett, Alanna. "Introductions and Conclusions to Digressions in Ammianus Marcellinus." *Museum Philologum*

Londiniense 5 (1981): 15-33. "From the detailed study of the introduction and conclusions, it is possible to see their positive value. First, they reflect Ammianus' historical ideals and, in particular, the principle on which he built the digressions (for example brevity, truthfulness, and the desire for explanation). Secondly, they are relevant to the structure of the work, for they make clear Ammianus' consciousness of his theme" (p. 33).

501. Eusebius of Caesareae. *The Ecclesiastical History and the Martyrs of Palestine.* Translated by H. J. Lawlor and J. E. L. Oulton. 2 vols. London: S. P. C. K., 1927-28.

502. Field, Larry F. "The Epilogues of Ammianus Marcellinus." Ph. D. dissertation, Johns Hopkins University, 1968. The epilogue technique, reviewing each emperors virtues and vices, is a regular feature in Ammianus. Field reviews this device in the context of ancient historiography.

503. Fitton, James D. "Eunapius and the Idea of the Decline of the Roman Empire in Zosimus." Ph. D. dissertation, McMaster University, 1975.

504. Fletcher, G. B. A. "Stylistic Borrowings and Parallels in Ammianus Marcellinus." *Revue de Philologie* 11 (1937): 377-395. Fletcher inventories Ammianus' echoings of the following Latin authors: Terence, Cicero, Caesar, Sallust, Virgil, Ovid, Livy, Valerius Maximus, Curtius, Seneca, Lucan, Pliny the Elder, Statius, Silius Italicus, Pseudo-Quintilian, Tacitus, Florus, Suetonius, Aulus Gellius, Apuleius, Justin, Ausonius.

505. Glover, Terrot R. *Life and Letters in the Fourth Century.* Cambridge: University Press, 1901; reprint ed., New York: Russell and Russell, 1968. Glover offers lively and informed chapters on the following literary personalities of the age: Ammianus, Julian, Quintus of Smyrna, Ausonius, Symmachus, Macrobius, the early Augustine, Claudian, Prudentius, Sulpicius Severus, Palladas, Synesius, as well as a number of women pilgrims, and a chapter on Greek and

Christian novels. Some of the opinions and material are a bit dated, and his final judgment should induce some caution: ". . . the conclusion is forced upon me when I survey the fourth century, its interests and energies, that the Church had absorbed all that was then vital in the civilized world" (p. 18). J. W. Platner, *American Historical Review* 8 (1902): 105-107 (+).

506. Goffart, Walter. "The Date and Purpose of Vegetius' *De re militari.*" *Traditio* 33 (1977): 65-100. A great point of controversy about Vegetius has been the date of composition of his treatise. Of late there has been a trend to put it in the fourth century. Goffart reviews the literature involved in the dispute, most of it German. He analyzes and disputes all of the arguments for the fourth century, and puts the date of composition in the time of Valentinian III (d.455), where Gibbon placed it two centuries ago.

507. Goffart, Walter. "Zosimus, the First Historian of Rome's Fall." *American Historical Review* 76 (1971): 412-441. Zosimus, writing c. 500, saw himself in a post-Roman world. For him the traditional empire had already fallen. This was not only a political and military fall, but a religious fall as well: a fall from the ancient cults to Christian barbarism. What Zosimus disliked was innovation. He therefore had much to dislike about the fourth century. From him many subsequent historians have received their impressions of that period. Some have essentially passed on the same view through their own words. Gibbon is an example. Goffart has larger concerns than Zosimus' view of the fourth century, but the article in general is important for an appreciation of the intellectual context of Zosimus and his frame of mind regarding the whole of Roman history to his own time. The fourth century has in a sense been held hostage to developments in the fifth and sixth centuries. Seeing the fourth century on its own terms is the corrective action needed.

508. Gradilone, Th. J. "The Text of the Parentalia and Professores of Ausonius." Ph. D. dissertation, Fordham University, 1962.

509. Green, R. P. H. *The Poetry of Paulinus of Nola: A Study in His Latinity.* Collection Latomus, 120. Brussels: Latomus, 1971. Paulinus did his important writing in the fifth century; but he learned his style in the fourth century.

510. Green, Tamara M. "Zosimus, Orosius and Their Traditions: Comparative Studies in Pagan and Christian Historiography." Ph. D. dissertation, New York University, 1974. Both Zosimus and Orosius addressed the fourth century in their historical works; but both saw the same time differently. Green compares and comments.

511. Haarhoff, Theodore J. *Schools of Gaul: A Study of Pagans and Christian Education in the Last Century of the Western Empire.* 2nd ed. Johannesburg: Witwatersrand University Press, 1958. This is basically a photocopy of the original 1920 edition. Haarhoff uses primary sources to the fullest, and he presents an orderly and thorough consideration of educational developments in prmarily the fourth and fifth centuries. In the fourth century at least, the government took a large interest in education, and this is given considerable treatment. H. S. Jones, *History* 6 (1922): 263-264 (+); *Journal of Roman Studies* 9 (1919): 220.

512. Harries, Jill. "Prudentius and Theodosius." *Latomus* 43 (January-March 1984): 69-84. Harries offers dates for some writings of Prudentius which have relevance for the reign of Theodosius I. The *Contra Symmachum* is dated in part to 394 and in part to 402. This contrasts with the more mainstream view of Timothy Barnes (95), who sees this important work as one and indivisible, dating entirely to 402.

513. Hengst, D. den. *The Prefaces in the Historia Augusta.* Amsterdam: Gruner, 1981.

514. Hilten, P. "Critical Notes on the Chronica of Sulpicius Severus." *Traditio* 19 (1963): 447-460.

515. **Holdsworth, Christopher and Wiseman, T. P., eds.** *The Inheritance of Historiography, 350-900.* Exeter Studies in History, 12. Exeter, U. K.: Exeter University, 1986. Essays relevant to the fourth century are individually analyzed. J. M. Alonso-Nunez, *Classical Review* 38 (1988): 160-161 (+).

516. **Honore, Tony.** "Scriptor Historiae Augustae." *Journal of Roman Studies* 77 (1987): 156-176. For twentieth century scholars the *Historia Augusta* has been perhaps both the most tantalizing and frustrating of primary sources from the fourth century. Long debates have swirled around the questions when it was written, by whom it was written, for whom it was written. Honore offers a truly remarkable synthesis which explains everything and around which the debate must now focus: "A pupil of Ausonius, or at any rate a *grammaticus* from Gaul, [the author of the HA] moved to Rome possibly when Symmachus was urban prefect (384-5) and became an official in the urban prefect's office. While there he undertook in 393 or 394 to write biographies of the emperors up to Diocletian, began writing in 394 and completed the HA in 395. The battle of the Frigidus in September 394 and the death of Theodosius I in January 395 required some changes of emphasis as the writing proceeded. . . . [H]is writing combines the learned frivolity of Ausonius with official and political interests acquired in the capital" (p. 156).

517. **Houston, George W.** "A Revisionary Note on Ammianus Marcellinus 14.6.18: When Did the Public Libraries of Ancient Rome Close?" *Library Quarterly* 58 (1988): 258-264. Finding that Ammianus has been misinterpreted to suggest that the public libraries were closed by 380, Houston reviews the contemporary evidence and feels comfortable concluding that the libraries functioned to some degree or other well into the fifth century.

518. **Isidore of Seville.** *History of the Goths, Vandals and Suevi.* Translated from the Latin with an introduction by Guido Donini and Gordon B. Ford, Jr. 2nd rev. ed. Leiden: E. J. Brill, 1970. M. Reydellet, *Latomus* 32 (1973): 439 (-).

519. Jenkins, F. W. "Ammianus Marcellinus' Knowledge and Use of Republican Latin Literature." Ph. D. dissertation, University of Illinois at Urbana-Champaign, 1985.

520. Jenkins, F. W. "Theatrical Metaphors in Ammianus Marcellinus." *Eranos* 85 (1987): 55-63.

521. Jones, A. H. M., ed. *A History of Rome Through the Fifth Century.* Vol. II: *The Empire.* New York: Walker and Co., 1970. This is a particularly useful anthology of translated primary sources because Jones gives heavy coverage to the fourth century. There are documents on the emperors, the senatorial class, the equestrian class, the civil service, the army, the provinces, the cities, taxation, justice, economic affairs, and religion. Another anthology by N. Lewis and M. Reinhold, called *Roman Civilization,* Vol II (1955), is helpful but only goes to the time of Constantine. *Times Literary Supplement* (August 7, 1970): 873 (+).

522. Jones, A. H. M. and Skeat, T. C. "Notes on the Genuineness of the Constantinian Documents in Eusebius' Life of Constantine." *Journal of Ecclesiastical History* 5 (1954): 196-200. An argument used to swirl around the authenticity of the documents quoted by Eusebius. After Jones wrote this article, the anti-authenticity faction was reduced to a whimper. The documents are real.

523. Jonge, Pieter de. *Philological and Historical Commentary on Ammianus Marcellinus.* Groningen, 1935-1982. This massive ongoing project now encompasses books 14 to 19 of Ammianus, whose followers will want to have it nearby. C. J. Simpson, *Phoenix* 32 (1978): 365-366 (-+). (Simpson comments on Book 17.)

524. Jordanes. *The Gothic History of Jordanes.* Translated with an introduction and commentary by Charles C. Mierow. 2nd ed. Princeton, N. J.: Princeton University Press, 1915; New York: Barnes and Noble, 1966.

525. **Kaster, Robert A.** *Guardians of Language: The Grammarian and Society in Late Antiquity.* The Transformation of the Classical Heritage, 11. Berkeley: University of California Press, 1986.

526. **Kaster, Robert A.** "A Reconsideration of 'Gratian's School Law.'" *Hermes* 112 (1984): 100-114. Gratian's edict of 376 has to do with state compensation for teachers in the cities of northern Gaul. Kaster sees the law as a supplement to an already existing system of government subsidies to teachers, about which little is directly known.

527. **Kennedy, George A.** *Greek Rhetoric Under Christian Emperors.* A History of Rhetoric, v. 3. Princton, N. J.: Princeton University Press, 1983. Although Kennedy carries his story to about A. D. 700, he has a heavy emphasis on the fourth century, where he discovers "the greatest Greek orators since Demosthenes" (p. 50): Gregory of Nanzianzus and Synesius of Cyrene. Kennedy shows how the traditional art of rhetoric was adapted to new concerns in the late empire: the survival of Hellenism, the unity of the state in the emperor's person, the advancement of Christianity. A. Kazhdan, *Speculum* 59 (1984): 662-664 (+-); A. Kolp, *Church History* 53 (1984): 233 (+); T. Halton, *Catholic Historical Review* 71 (1985): 578-579 (+-).

528. **Kennedy, Mary J.** *The Literary Work of Ammianus.* Lancaster, Pa.: New Era Printing Company, 1912. This is based on Kennedy's Ph. D. dissertation at the University of Chicago, 1906.

529. **Kenney, E. J.** "The Mosella of Ausonius." *Greece and Rome* 31 (1984): 190-202. Kenney sees the Mosella both as a good poem that conveys what Ausonius actually saw, and as a tribute to Greco-Roman culture and, at least subliminally, to the civilizing mission of Rome and the desirability of man controlling nature.

530. **Lactantius.** *De Mortibus Persecutorum.* Edited and translated by J. L. Creed. Oxford: Clarendon Press, 1984.

531. Laistner, M. L. W. *Christianity and Pagan Culture in the Later Roman Empire.* Ithaca, N. Y.: Cornell University Press, 1951; 1967. In three chapters (originally lectures), Laistner looks at educational processes, first among the pagans, then among the Christians. Laistner works strongly with the theme of reconciliation of pagan culture and Christian religion. There is appended a translation of a delightful little essay by John Chrysostom on how to raise children in the fourth century. Laistner included it partly as an example of the extent to which the culture of the pagan world had suffused the thinking of Christian leaders like Chrysostom. M. M. Deems, *Church History* 20 (September 1951): 92-93 (+); N. H. Baynes, *Journal of Roman Studies* 43 (1953): 188 (+-); M. D., *History* 39 (1954): 135 (+); W. F. McDonald, *Catholic Historical Review* 37 (1952): 441-442 (+-).

532. Levitan, W. "Dancing at the End of the Rope: Optatian Porfyry and the Field of Roman Verse." *Transactions of the American Philological Association* 115 (1985): 245-269. Levitan analyzes the poetry of Publilius Optatianus Porfyrius, who served in government during the time of Constantine.

533. Libanius. *Libanius' Autobiography. (Oration 1).* Greek Text edited with introduction, translation and notes by A. F. Norman. New York: Oxford University Press, 1965.

534. The Life of Pachomius. Translated by Apostolos N. Athanassikis. Missoula, Montana: Scholars Press, 1975. Translated from the Greek, this is the only English version of this important fourth century material on monasticism and one of its founders.

535. MacBain, B. "An Annotated Bibiliography (to 1980) of Sources for Late Antiquity in English Translation." *Byzantine Studies* 10 (1983): 88-109; 223-247. Jeremy Patterson (*Greece and Rome* 32 [April 1985], 96.) tells us that "One day the Later Empire will take its place as a subject suitable for schools and undergraduates. It is an exciting period, vital for the development of Europe and with a wealth of evidence. The breakthrough will come when most of that evidence becomes easily accessible in translation." The breakthrough is happening, and the MacBain bibliography shows the results. Covering the period A. D. 284 to 602 roughly, MacBain has collected an impressive amount of literature now available in English, and has divided it into: I. Sourcebooks and Documents; II. History and Chronicle; III. Literature, General; IV (A. and B.) Christian Literature; and V. Pagan Philosophy and Religion.

536. **MacKail, John W.** "The Last Great Roman Historian." In his *Classical Studies*, pp. 159-187. London: John Murray, 1925. Despite a subtle but finally evanescent racial theory of the decline of the empire, and some outdated theories and now retired facts, there is much of permanent interest and value in this eloquent and often perceptive appreciation of Ammianus and the fourth century.

537. **MacMullen, Ramsay**. "Sfiducia nell'intelletto nel quarto secolo." Translated into Italian by D. Panzieri. *Rivista Storica Italiana* 84 (1972): 5-16. It has to do with the rise of anti-intellectualism in the fourth century. Because it was translated into Italian, there must be an English version around somewhere.

538. **Macrobius.** *The Saturnalia.* Translated with an introduction and notes by Percival V. Davies. New York: Columbia University Press, 1969. A fifth century dialog set in fourth century Rome, the *Saturnalia* can be used only with extreme caution as a source on the fourth century Roman personalities who participate in the conversations. The Romans were great ones for looking back to find better days, but this was common among all the ancients, and even in the troubled late fourth and fifth centuries it was by no means a universal attitude. Says Furius Albinus (3.14.2): "But it must be confessed that with all their abundant virtues those times had their faults as well, some of which have been corrected by the sober habits of our age" (p. 231).

539. **Maenchen-Helfen, O. J.** "The Date of Ammianus Marcellinus' Last Book." *American Journal of Philology* 76

(1955): 384-399. M.-H. declares for the winter of 392/393. Some important primary source material for the late fourth century is discussed at length.

540. Maguinness, W. S. "Locutions and Formulae of the Latin Panegyrists." *Hermathena* 48 (1933): 117-138.

541. Maguinness, W. S. "Some Methods of the Latin Panegyrists." *Hermathena* 47 (1932): 42-61.

542. Malalas, John. *Chronicle*. Translated with commentary by E. M. Jeffreys et al. Melbourne: Australian Association for Byzantine Studies, 1986. Covering from the creation to the time of Justinian, this chronicle informed many, perhaps too many, Byzantine writers on ancient history.

543. Markus, R. A. "Church History and the Early Church Historians." In *The Materials, Sources, and Methods of Ecclesiastical History*, pp. 1-17. Edited by Derek Baker. New York: Barnes and Noble, 1975. Markus considers the fourth and fifth century historians, beginning with Eusebius.

544. Marriott, Ian. "The Authorship of the *Historia Augusta:* Two Computer Studies." *Journal of Roman Studies* 69 (1979): 65-74. The computer says one person wrote the *Historia*.

545. Matthews, John F. "Ammianus Marcellinus." In *Ancient Writers: Greece and Rome (Vol. II)*, pp. 1117-1138. Edited by T. J. Luce. New York: Charles Scribner's Sons, 1982. This is a rich and rewarding essay on a great historian. Matthews downplays the influence of Tacitus, but upgrades the influence of the Latin language and the Roman way of thinking in Ammianus' early life. Matthews cautions against searching too diligently for a "central attitude or preoccupation" in Ammianus; but he does see a general orientation that "lies in his view of law and justice and in the obligation of Roman emperors to respect the public institutions by which law and justice and individual rights are defended" (p. 1132).

546. Matthews, John F. "Ammianus and the Eternity of Rome." In *The Inheritance of Historiography 350-900*, pp. 17-29. Edited by Christopher Holdsworth and T. P. Wiseman. Exeter, U. K.: University of Exeter, 1986. In a rich essay, Matthews advances the theme of Ammianus as a very classical historian, especially through his "emphasis on the autonomy and effectiveness of the human will" (p. 27). Ammianus believed that the legacy of Rome would live forever through those who took up her civilizing mission. "Nowhere is Ammianus more Classical in his perspective . . . than in so connecting the eternity of Rome with the dimension of the human will and human effort" (p. 28).

547. Matthews, John F. "Mauretania in Ammianus and the *Notitia*." In *Aspects of the Notitia Dignitatum*, pp. 157-186. Edited by R. Goodburn and P. Bartholomew. Oxford: British Archaeological Reports, Suppl. Series 15, 1976. Reprinted in his *Political Life and Culture in Late Roman Society*, Ch. XI. London: Variorum Reprints, 1985. Matthews finds an opportunity to judge the accuracy of Ammianus by comparing his account of events in late fourth century Mauretania with other sources, including archaeology. Ammianus emerges with honor.

548. Momigliano, Arnaldo. "The Lonely Historian Ammianus Marcellinus." *Annali della Scuola Normale Superiore di Pisa* 4 (1974): 1393-1407. Reprinted in *Essays in Ancient and Modern Historiography*, pp. 127-140. Edited by A. Momigliano. Oxford: Blackwell, 1977. An interesting portrait of Ammianus, who emerges as a basically conservative person, longing for the better times of old, yet fascinated by and even sympathetic towards new developments of his own time, such as some aspects of Christianity.

549. Momigliano, Arnaldo. "Some Observations on the Origo Gentis Romanae." *Journal of Roman Studies* 48 (1958): 56-73. Momigliano discusses a fourth century anthology of materials on the history of Rome, some of whose parts have survived, including Aurelius Victor's lives of the emperors to A. D. 360.

550. **Momigliano, Arnaldo.** "An Unsolved Problem of Historical Forgery." *Journal of the Warburg and Courtauld Institutes* 17 (1954): 22-46. Reprinted in his *Studies in Historiography*, pp. 143-180. London, 1966. Eschewing any firm conclusions himself, Momigliano gives a vivid, perceptive, and well organized review of *Historia Augusta* theories since the late nineteenth century. This essay should be required reading for those who wish to be introduced to the relevant questions and tentative answers up to the 1950s regarding this strange piece of fourth century literature.

551. **Mosshammer, Alden A.** *The 'Chronicle' of Eusebius and Greek Chronographic Tradition.* Cranbury, N. J.: Bucknell University Press, 1979.

552. **Naude, C. P. T.** "The Date of the Later Books of Ammianus Marcellinus." *American Journal of Ancient History* 9 (1984): 70-94. "The object of the present study is to explore the contemporary historical context in which Ammianus concluded his *History*, on assumption, as a plausible hypothesis, that the late 380s provide such a context" (p. 73) Naude has some important paragraphs on the politics of the 380s.

553. **Naude, C. P. T.** "Fortuna in Ammianus Marcellinus." *Acta Classica* 7 (1964): 70-88. Naude unravels the Greek and Roman strands in Ammianus' historiography to show the various and the predominant uses of the concept of *fortuna* (very roughly meaning "lady luck," in English) in the *Res Gestae*.

554. **Neugebauer, O.** "The Horoscope of Ceionius Rufius Albinus." *American Journal of Philology* 74 (1953): 418-420. Some remarks in support of dating a surviving horoscope to the fourth century.

555. Newbold, R. F. "Perception and Sensory Awareness Among Latin Writers in Late Antiquity." *Classica et Mediaevalia* 33 (1981-1982): 169-190. Newbold poses the following questions: "What justification is there for considering late Latin authors to be more eye oriented than in an earlier period and is there a corresponding decline in tactile awareness and sensitivity? And if there is a shift towards greater eye and/or ear perception, what is it?" (p.172) As he unfolds the answers, Newbold offers some interesting observations, for example: "There was a tendency for the ear dominated world of late antiquity to view the world of the eye as a storehouse of memory cues: books, even written legal contracts, were aide-memoires, not independent documents or repositories of information. Truth was conveyed by the mouth: a man's word was proof: hearing was believing. Important works, to be considered read, had to be memorised and orally re-created" (p. 185).

556. Nixon, C. E. V. "The 'Epiphany' of the Tetrarchs? An Examination of Mamertinus' Panegyric of 291." *Transactions of the American Philological Association* 111 (1981): 157-166. Nixon decides that the panegyric was simply for the birthday of the emperor Maximian in combination with a festival for Hercules. He challenges the interpretations of other historians.

557. Nixon, C. E. V. "An Historiographical Study of the *Caesares* of Sextus Aurelius Victor." Ph. D. dissertation, University of Michigan, 1971.

558. Norman, A. F. "Magnus in Ammianus, Eunapius, and Zosimus: New Evidence." *Classical Quarterly* 7 (1957): 129-133. Norman tries to sort out who used whom among the ancient sources on Julian's Persian campaign.

559. Oberhelman, Steven M. "The *Cursus* in Late Imperial Latin Prose: A Reconsideration of Methodology." *Classical Philology* 83 (1988): 136-149. A lot of nice late Latin literature is stripped nekkid, submitted to a computer, and forced to show its rhythms. See Oberhelman's other articles (with Ralph G. Hall as co-author) for more of the same, viz.: "A New Statistical Analysis of Accentual Prose Rhythms in Imperial Latin Authors, *Classical Philology* 79 (1984): 114-130; "Meter in Accentual Clausulae of Late Imperial Latin Prose, *Classical Philology* 80 (1985): 214-227; "The History and Development of the cursus mixtus in Late Latin Literature," *Classical Philology* 83 (May 1988). There are others, including one by Oberhelman alone on Ammianus: "The Provenance of the Prose Style of Ammianus Marcellinus," *QUCC* n.s. 24 (1988).

560. Orosius. *History Against the Pagans.* Translated by Irving W. Raymond. Columbia University Records of Civilization, Sources and Studies, v. 26. New York: Columbia University Press, 1936.

561. Oulton, J. E. L. "Rufinus' Translation of the Church History of Eusebius." *Journal of Theological Studies* 30 (1928-1929): 150-174. This translation was a free rendering with additions.

562. Owens, E. E. L. "Phraseological Borrowings and Parallels in Ammianus Marcellinus from Earlier Latin Authors." Ph. D. dissertation, University of London, 1958.

563. Palladius. *The Lausiac History.* Translated by R. T. Meyer. Westminster, Md.: Newman Press, 1965.

564. Pauw, D. A. "Ammianus Marcellinus and Ancient Historiography, Biography and Character Portrayal." *Acta Classica* 22 (1979): 115-129. Pauw considers the intellectual background of historical writing in the ancient world, and on this standard concludes that "Although Ammianus is in the first place a *historiographer*, unmistakable elements of *biography* are found in his writings" (p. 129).

565. Pauw, D. A. "Methods of Character Portrayal in the *Res Gestae* of Ammianus Marcellinus." *Acta Classica* 20 (1977): 181-197. Taking Ammianus' treatment of four major characters (Constantius, Julian, Valentinian, Valens) and four secondary ones (Gallus, Jovian, Procopius, and Gratian), Pauw analyzes the techniques that Ammianus used to portray character, and how all this related to Ammianus' main intent, which was to write history rather than biography.

566. **Peachin, Michael.** "The Purpose of Festus' Breviarium." *Mnemosyne* 38 (1985): 158-161.   Peachin says that the *Breviarium* was prepared for Valens before his Persian campaign to show the world the difficulty of wars in the east (in comparison with the relative ease of success of Roman arms in the Mediterranean basin). Thus, if Valens did well, his victory would be the more significant; on the other hand, if he did poorly he would still be "in acceptable company, if not quite the best" (p. 160).

567. **Peebles, Bernard.** *The Poet Prudentius.* New York: McMullen Books, 1951.   Peebles presents an interesting Catholic perspective on the poetry of the fourth century Spanish official Prudentius, who wrote largely on Christian themes. Some of the poetry has historical value for reflecting and responding to contemporary issues, such as the debate over the altar of Victory in the Senate house in Rome during the 380s

568. **Penella, Robert J**. "A Lowly Born Historian of the Late Roman Empire: Some Observations on Aurelius Victor and His *De Caesaribus*." *Thought* 55 (1980): 122-131.   Penella sees Victor as a good example of the mid-fourth century government official who had risen from humble origins and whose objective in writing was to bring attention to himself so that he might rise higher still in government circles.

569. **Plommer, Hugh.** *Vitruvius and Later Roman Building Manuals.* Cambridge: University Press, 1973.   Includes an introduction, text and translation of Cetius Faventinus' *De Diversis Fabricis Architectonicae*, and a commentary. According to Plommer, Faventinus wrote c. 300. He used Vitruvius, but was not a slave to him. He had his own agenda, and wrote to suit the needs of his own time. He, in turn, was used by Palladius a century later.   G. E. Richman, *Journal of Roman Studies* 65 (1975): 222-223 (+).

570. Ridley, R. T. "Eunapius and Zosimus." *Helikon* 9/10 (1969-1979): 574-592.   Zosimus was a heavy user of Eunapius for information on the fourth century, but he did not take his Eunapius hook, line, and sinker. At least, not all the time. Ridley describes in detail the relation between the two historians, and incidentally reviews some fourth century highlights, such as the rise of monks, or events relating to the Roman defeat at Adrianople.

571. Ridley, R. T. "Zosimus the Historian." *Byzantinische Zeitschrift* 65 (1972): 277-302.   Ridley discusses the date of Zosimus' history (early sixth century), his sources, plan and themes (the decline and fall of the Roman empire, or at least the pagan empire), historical causation, styles of dating, his historical judgments, his accuracy (lots of trouble here), and his value. Zosimus' influence is considerable: his treatment of the fourth century still informs the way we look at it too.

572. Roberts, C. H. and Skeat, T. C. *The Birth of the Codex.* New York: Oxford University Press, 1983.   The codex form of making books came into its own in the fourth century through Christian encouragement, but it was not a fourth century creation nor was its practical form appealing to Christians alone. The evidence is such that the full story may always remain fuzzy, but Roberts and Skeat have offered interesting possibilities.   P. J. Parsons, *Classical Review* 37 (1987): 82-84 (+).

573. Rodgers, Barbara S. "Divine Insinuation in the *Panegyrici Latini*." *Historia* 35 (1986): 69-104.   Analysis of panegyrics from the later empire. "There is no system and there never was. There is circumstance, preference, and ambiguity" (p. 99).

574. Rodgers, R. H. *An Introduction to Palladius.* London: University of London, Institute of Classical Studies, 1975. Intricate textual criticism. Not for the beginner. Palladius, in this case, is the fourth century author of agricultural works.

575. **Roselle, Leone R.** "Tacitean Elements in Ammianus Marcellinus." Ph. D. dissertation, Columbia University, 1976.

576. **Rowell, Henry T.** *Ammianus Marcellinus Soldier-Historian of the Late Roman Empire.* Lectures in Memory of Louise Taft Semple. Cincinnati, Ohio: University of Cincinnati, 1964. A friendly and helpful appreciation of Ammianus as a great historian.

577. **Rowell, Henry T.** "The First Mention of Rome in Ammianus' Extant Books and the Nature of the 'History.'" In *Melanges d'archeologie, d'epigraphie et d'histoire offerts a Jerome Carcopino*, pp. 839-848. Paris, 1966.

578. **Rufinus.** *The Epigrams of Rufinus.* Edited with an introduction and commentary by Denys Page. Cambridge Classical Texts and Commentaries, 21. Cambridge: Cambridge University Press, 1978. Page places this person in the fourth century, although he may be first century. Texts in Latin. D. A. Campbell, *Phoenix* 32 (1978): 367-368 (+).

579. **Sacks, Kenneth S.** "The Meaning of Eunapius' History." *History and Theory* 25 (1986): 52-67. Eunapius is shown to be in the mainstream of the Greek style of doing history, expressing classical values, speaking against autocracy and fanticism, bridging the gap between history and biography in a very fourth century way. The focus is not anti-Christian, although there is some of that too.

580. **Saddington, D. B.** "The Function of Education According to Christian Writers of the Latter Part of the Fourth Century A. D." *Acta Classica* 8 (1965): 86-101. Four Christian intellectuals are discussed to indicate the ambiguity with which the traditional pagan classical education of the age was considered. In general, it was thought to be an acceptable part of the educational process, but only in preparation for a higher calling through Christianity.

581. **Salisbury, F. S.** "On the Date of the 'Notitia Dignitatum.'" *Journal of Roman Studies* 17 (1927): 102-106. Salisbury places most of it in the period 378-383.

582. **Scavone, Daniel C.** "Zosimus and His Historical Models." *Greek, Roman and Byzantine Studies* 11 (1970): 57-67. Zosimus' style of historiography reflects standard classical models, but also new trends from the fourth and fifth centuries in the art of writing history.

583. **Schneider, John S.** "The Scope and Content of and Some Reflections upon the Papyri for the Period of Diocletian as Found in the Oxyrhynchus Collection." Ph D. dissertation, University of Wisconsin, 1931.

584. **Seager, Robin.** *Ammianus Marcellinus: Seven Studies in His Language and Thought.* Columbia: University of Missouri Press, 1986. Seager studies the language of Ammianus to find the central themes of his history and to discover the nature of late Roman emperorship. J. Paterson, *Greece and Rome* 34 (1987): 224 (+).

585. **Seager, Robin.** "Some Imperial Virtues in the Latin Prose Panegyrics: The Demands of Propaganda and the Dynamics of Literary Composition," pp. 129-165. In *Papers of the Liverpool Latin Seminar* 4, 1983. Edited by F. Fairns. Liverpool, 1984. Using mostly fourth century material, Seager looks at the tension between political reality and the requirements of rhetoric.

586. **Seagraves, R.** "The Riddle of R. Festus." In *Actes du VIIe Congres International d'Epigraphie Grecque et Latini*, pp. 468-470. Bucharest: Editura Academiei; Paris: Societe d'edition Les Belles Lettres, 1979.

587. **Skeat, T. C., ed.** *Papyri from Panopolis in the Chester Beatty Library Dublin.* Dublin: Hodges, Figgis and Co., 1964. Contains primary source material on Diocletian, especially on the preparations for an imperial visit to Egypt.

588. Starr, Chester G. "Aurelius Victor: Historian of Empire." *American Historical Review* 61 (1956): 574-586. "Aurelius Victor was not a genius, but among the minor historians of the [fourth] century he stands out as a man of unusual stamp. Two of the most interesting aspects of his thought are his picture of the development of the imperial system as an autocracy and his assertion that the Empire was justified primarily by its support of culture" (p. 576). Also, says Starr, Victor represented a voice not often heard in the surviving sources: the thought patterns of "the average educated class" (p. 586).

589. Stertz, Stephen A. "Ammianus Marcellinus' Attitudes toward Earlier Emperors." In *Studies in Latin Literature and Roman History*, pp. 487-514. Edited by Carl Deroux. Collection Latomus, 168 (II). Brussels: Latomus, 1980. Ammianus did not have a pro-senatorial point of view in his analysis of the emperors of his own time; but for earlier emperors he reflected his sources, which for the most part were in the senatorial tradition.

590. Syme, Ronald. *Ammianus and the Historia Augusta.* Oxford: Clarendon Press, 1968. Tackling the murky world of the origins of the *Historia Augusta*, Syme believes that the *HA* used Ammianus, whose history he dates 395/6, and therefore must come later. Alan Cameron, *Journal of Roman Studies* 61 (1971): 255-267 ("subtle and provocative. . . , illuminating and original but not uniformly persuasive, and ultimately not easy to assess"); A. Momigliano, *English Historical Review* 84 (1969): 566-569 (++-); H. W. Benario, *American Journal of Philology* 91 (1970): 482-484 (+).

591. Syme, Ronald. "The Composition of the Historia Augusta: Recent Theories." *Journal of Roman Studies* 62 (1972): 123-133. Written in the late fourth century, but giving largely fictional biographies of emperors from 117 to 284, the *Historia Augusta* excites no end of controversy and interest, because it gives some information on an obscure period of Roman history. Syme again discusses the possibilities.

592. **Syme, Ronald.** *Emperors and Biography: Studies in the Historia Augusta.* Oxford: Clarendon Press, 1971. Syme advances once again his view that the *Historia Augusta,* written in the very late fourth century, is largely fiction and useless to consult on the periods of time that it covers. A. J. Graham, *Journal of Roman Studies* 63 (1973): 259-260 (+-); R. I. Frank, *American Journal of Philology* 94 (1973): 392-395 (+).

593. **Syme, Ronald.** *The Historia Augusta: A Call of Clarity.* Bonn: R. Habelt, 1971. Syme reviews his own arguments, and everyone else's too, on the origins and meaning and value of the *Historia Augusta.* His conclusion: "A work of erudite imposture imbued with literary fantasy presupposes an appropriate milieu and reading public. Where is it to be discovered save in the renascence of letters towards the end of the Fourth Century?" (p.112)

594. **Syme, Ronald.** *Historia Augusta Papers.* Oxford: Clarendon Press; New York: Oxford University Press, 1983. This anthology of papers, mostly from the Bonn Colloquium, is a sequel to Syme's *Ammianus and the Historia Augusta* (1968), *Emperors and Biography* (1971), and *The Historia Augusta: A Call for Clarity* (1971). For those trying to come to grips with the *Historia Augusta,* there is this compelling advice: "Anyone who wants certain facts about the HA will have to distrust manuals (even if recent and reputable); and he will be well advised to go slow on bibliography and the 'literature of the subject'. Instead, read the text" (p. 29). A. T. Kraabel, *Religious Studies Review* 12 (January 1986): 67 (+); *Classical Outlook* 62 (May 1985): 136.

595. **Synesius.** *The Letters of Synesius of Cyrene.* Translated with an introduction and notes by Augustine Fitzgerald. London: Oxford University Press, 1926. Synesius: a fourth century philosopher trying to become a fifth century Christian. One suspects his heart remained in the

fourth century. This volume includes the famous *De Regno*, which elaborates Synesius' political philosophy of emperorship and gives his advice for rejuvenating the Roman state at the end of the fourth century. There is a complementary volume entitled *The Essays and Hymns of Synesius of Cyrene* (1930). N. H. Baynes, *English Historical Review* 42 (1927): 416-418 (+-).

596. Thompson, E. A. "Ammianus Marcellinus." In *Latin Historians*, pp. 143-157. Edited by Thomas A. Dorey. London: Routledge and Kegan Paul; New York: Basic Books, 1966. Convenient and informed outline of the life and literary activity of Ammianus.

597. Thompson, E. A. "The Historical Method of Ammianus Marcellinus." *Hermathena* 59 (1942): 44-66. "The result of our inquiry into Ammianus' historical method then is: (i) The assertion that he used the works of previous historians to a large extent in compiling his extant historical narrative cannot be supported by any evidence in his work or in its relations with other histories. (ii) This assertion is absolutely contrary to what Ammianus himself tells us of his method. (iii) Certain factors in his work tend to bear out his own statements as against the modern theory. . . " (p. 64).

598. Thompson, E. A. *The Historical Work of Ammianus Marcellinus.* New York: Macmillan Co., 1947; reprint ed., Groningen: Bouma's Boekhius, 1969. This is an excellent introduction to Ammianus. Since Thompson, a great deal has been done in Ammianus studies, but this remains a competitive work, and offers a sympathetic and appreciative study of a great Roman historian. There is much excellent background material on the later Roman state. C. U. Clark, *American Historical Review* 53 (1948): 314-315 (+); G. B. A. Fletcher, *Journal of Roman Studies* 39 (1949): 202-203 (++-); M. Hammond, *Speculum* 23 (1948): 150-153 (+).

599. Thorndike, Lynn. "A Roman Astrologer as a Historical Source: Julius Firmicus Maternus." *Classical*

Philology 8 (1913): 415-421. Thorndike looks for social history in the writings of a fourth century astrologer.

600. Vanderspoel, John. "The Fourth Century Philosopher Maximus of Byzantium." *Ancient History Bulletin* 1 (1987): 71-74. Using the Byzantine encyclopedic work called the *Souda*, Vanderspoel discerns what we can know of a number of fourth century intellectuals named Maximus.

601. Victor, Sextus Aurelius. *Brief Imperial Lives (Caesares).* Translated by Edward C. Echols. Exeter, N. H.: Privately Printed, 1962.

602. Victor, Sextus Aurelius. *Liber de Caesaribus.* A translation with introduction and notes by Beverly Turpin Moss. Chapel Hill, North Carolina, 1942. Available on microfilm. This effort was Moss's Ph. D. thesis, done at the University of North Carolina.

603. Warmington, B. H. "Ammianus Marcellinus and the Lies of Metrodorus." *Classical Quarterly* 31 (1981): 464-468. Metrodorus (Ammianus xxv,4,23) says the Persians stole the gifts he was bringing from India to Constantine, who used the incident as further pretext for war against Persia. But Warmington says Eunapius, used by Ammianus as the source for the story, made it all up.

604. Warmington, B. H. "Aspects of Constantinian Propaganda in the Panegyrici Latini." *Transactions of the American Philological Association* 104 (1974): 371-384. Warmington urges "extreme caution in handling the panegyrics" (p. 371), riddled as they are with propaganda in favor of Constantine, and on matters for which there may be no other points of view surviving for our consideration.

605. Warmington, B. H. "The Sources of Some Constantinian Documents in Eusebius' *Ecclesiastical History* and *Life of Constantine.*" In *Papers of the Ninth Oxford Patristics Conference, 1983,* pp. 93-98. *Studia Patristica* 18.1. Edited by E. A. Livingstone. Kalamazoo, 1985.

606. **Wedeck, H. E.** "A Gallery of Roman Schoolmasters in Ausonius." *Classical World (Weekly)* 27 (1934): 137-138. Information on the teachers of fourth century Gaul.

607. **White, Peter.** "The Authorship of the *Historia Augusta*." *Journal of Roman Studies* 57 (1967): 115-133. "This paper is meant to strengthen Hermann Dessan's contention that one man composed the *Historia Augusta*, not six as the collection itself attests" (p. 115).

608. **Wiedemann, Thomas.** "Petitioning a Fourth-Century Emperor: The *De Rebus Bellicis*." *Florilegium* 1 (1979): 140-150. "The petitioner [the author of the DRB] was neither an inventor of genius nor a crank: what he did know was how to package his proposals for financial reform in such a way as to attract the attention of the one man upon whom all decisions depended - the emperor Valentinian" (p. 147). Valentinian I, that is. It was for him, says Wiedemann, that all the military contraptions were added to the petition, along with the handsome illustrations: he liked both.

609. **Wild, P. S.** "Ausonius: A Fourth Century Poet." *Classical Journal* 46 (1951): 373-382. Ausonius was poet, teacher, and high court official, and lived almost from one end of the fourth century to the other. Wild finds much to fault in fourth century rhetoric, poetry, literature in general, nor is Ausonius spared in the general criticism; but he acknowledges the occasional flashes of creativity, as well as more widespread ingenuity, in the work of Ausonius, and likes him as a personality.

610. **Witke, Charles.** *Numen Litterarum: The Old and New in Latin Poetry from Constantine to Gregory the Great.* Leiden and Cologne: E. J. Brill, 1971. Witke studies how the poets of the fourth, fifth and sixth centuries adjusted their art to incorporate the pagan forms of the past to the Christianity of their time, gradually bringing about a Christian literature into which a fair amount of classical culture was absorbed. S. Prete, *Speculum* 48 (1973): 432-434 (+).

611. **Zosimus.** *Historia Nova: The Decline of Rome.* Translated by J. J. Buchanan and H. T. Davis. San Antonio, Texas: Trinity University Press, 1967. Zosimus covers the fourth century in a rather muddled way, but his theme is clear: under Christian emperors the empire started a decline leading to the misfortunes that he could see in his own day, c. 500. Zosimus' theme of decline has colored almost all accounts of the fourth century ever since. This translation is now superceded or at least complemented by the Ridley translation (612).

612. **Zosimus.** *New History.* Translated by Ronald T. Ridley. Byzantia Australiensia, no. 2. Sydney: Australian Association for Byzantine Studies, 1982. Averil Cameron, *Classical Review* 34 (1984): 27-28 (+).

V. Monetary Matters

Many coin studies that elucidate political developments will be found under "Politics and Government." Some related material is also under "Economy, Technology, Science, and Medicine."

613. **Adelson, Howard L.** "Roman Monetary Policy from Diocletian to Heraclius." Ph. D. dissertation, Princeton University, 1952.

614. **Bagnall, Roger S. and Sijpesteijn, P. J.** "Currency in the Fourth Century and the Date of CPR V 26." *Zeitschrift fuer Papyrologie and Epigraphik* 26 (1977): 111-124.

615. **Barrandon, J. N., Callu, P. P., and Brenot, C.** "The Analysis of Constantinian Coins (A.D. 313-340) by Nondestructive Californium 252 Activation Analysis." *Archaeometry* 19 (1977): 173-186.

616. **Bruun, Patrick.** "The Christian Signs on the Coins of Constantine." *Arctos*, n.s.3 (1962): 5-35.

617. **Bruun, Patrick**. "The Consecration Coins of Constantine the Great." *Arctos* 1 (1954): 19-31.

618. **Bruun, Patrick.** "The Constantinian Coinage of Arelate." Ph. D. dissertation, Helsinki, 1953.

619. **Bruun, Patrick.** "Some Dynastic Bronze Coins of Constantine the Great." *Eranos* 53 (1955): 193-198.

620. Callu, J. P. "The Distribution and the Role of the Bronze Coinage from A. D. 348 to 392." In *Imperial Revenue, Expenditure and Monetary Policy in the Fourth Century A. D.*, pp. 95-124. Edited by C. E. King. Oxford: British Archaeological Reports, 1980.

621. Callu, J. P. "Silver Hoards and Emissions from 324 to 392." In *Imperial Revenue, Expenditure and Monetary Policy in the Fourth Century A. D.*, pp. 213-254. Edited by C. E. King. Oxford: British Archaeological Reports, 1980. Callu divides the fourth century into seven periods and within each discusses the silver coin policies of the emperors.

622. Carson, R. A. G. *Principal Coins of the Romans. 3. The Dominate A. D. 294-498.* London: British Museum Publications, 1981.

623. Carson, R. A. G. "Rare Coins of the Late Roman Empire." *British Museum Quarterly* 21 (1957): 44-46. Carson details some interesting coins, mostly fourth century issues, which had recently come to the British Museum.

624. Carson, R. A. G. and Kent, J. P. C. "Constantinian Hoards and Other Studies." *Numismatic Chronicle* (1956): 83-161.

625. Carson, R. A. G. and Kent, J. P. C. *Late Roman Bronze Coinage A. D. 324-498.* London: Spink and Son, 1960.

626. Crawford, Michael H. "Finance, Coinage and Money from the Severans to Constantine." In *Aufstieg und Niedergang der romischen Welt*, pp. 560-593. Vol. II.2. Edited by Hildegard Temporini. Berlin, 1975.

627. Erim, Kenan, Reynolds, Joyce, and Crawford, Michael. "Diocletian's Currency Reform: A New Inscription." *Journal of Roman Studies* 61 (1971): 171-177.

628. Gilliard, Frank D. "Notes on the Coinage of Julian the Apostate." *Journal of Roman Studies* 54 (1964): 135-

141. Gilliard ruminates on several questions relating to coinage or for which coins may have an answer, such as when Julian grew a beard.

629. **Harl, Kenneth W.** "Marks of Value on Tetrarchic Nummi and Diocletian's Monetary Policy." *Phoenix* 39 (1985): 263-270. Harl discusses the purposes of the monetary reforms of Aurelian in 274 and Diocletian in 293.

630. **Hendy, Michael F.** "Mint and Fiscal Administration under Diocletian, His Colleagues and His Successors, A. D. 305-24." *Journal of Roman Studies* 62 (1972): 75-82. Hendy revives an old argument of Mommsen showing a close relation between Diocletian's changes in fiscal administration and coin production. Hendy modifies the Mommsen argument, but still finds the essential connection between the mint system and the new fiscal structure.

631. **Hill, P. V., Kent, J. P. C. and Carson, R. A. G.** *Late Roman Bronze Coinage, A. D. 324-498.* London: Spink and Son, 1960.

632. **Kent, J. P. C.** "Gold Coinage in the Later Roman Empire." In *Essays in Roman Coinage Presented to Harold Mattingly,* pp. 190-204. Edited by R. A. G. Carson and C. H. V. Sutherland. London: Oxford University Press, 1956. Kent discusses "the problem of the administrative organization which underlay the vast structure of the imperial coinage, and which made possible the coherent presentation of official policy together with an adequate supply of ready money" (p. 190). Kent's article encompasses the fourth century, when the empire went on a gold standard that became the basis of the entire financial system and had to be maintained at all costs.

633. **Kent, J. P. C.** "An Introduction to the Coinage of Julian the Apostate." *Numismatic Chronicle* 19 (1959): 109-117.

634. **Kent, J. P. C.** "The Pattern of Bronze Coinage under Constantine I." *Numismatic Coinage* 17 (1957): 16-77.

635. **King, Cathy E.** "The Constantinian Mints 306-313." *American Numismatic Society. Museum Notes* 9 (1960): 117-138.

636. **King, Cathy E., ed.** *Imperial Revenue, Expenditure and Monetary Policy in the Fourth Century A. D.* The Fifth Oxford Symposium on Coinage and Monetary History. Oxford: British Archaeological Reports, 1980.   The English-language essays from this anthology are listed individually.

637. **King, Cathy E.** "Late Roman Silver Hoards in Britain and the Problem of Clipped Siliquae." *British Numismatic Journal* 51 (1981): 5-31.

638. **King, Cathy E.** "The Maxentian Mints." *Numismatic Chronicle* 19 (1959): 47-78.

639. **Mattingly, Harold.** "The Monetary Systems of the Roman Empire from Diocletian to Theodosius I." *Numismatic Chronicle* 6 (1946): 111-119.   Mattingly explores the labyrinth of fourth century monetary reforms, which were many and are not well documented.

640. **Metcalf, W. E.** "The 'Cairo' Hoard of Tetrarchic Folles." *Revue Belge de Numismatique* 120 (1974): 73ff.

641. **Odahl, Charles.** "Constantinian Coin Motifs in Ancient Literary Sources." *Journal of the Rocky Mountain Medieval Renaissance Association* 7 (1986): 1-15.

642. **Pankiewicz, Ryszard.** "The Value of Gold in Relation to Goods in the Late Roman Empire." *Eos* 73 (1983): 171-182.

643. *The Roman Imperial Coinage VI: From Diocletian's Reform (A. D. 294) to the Death of Maximinus (A. D. 313).* By C. H. V. Sutherland. London: Spink and Son, 1967.   The coinage is fitted into its political and economic contexts: a happy example of the use of coins to enhance knowledge of a time in history for which the primary

sources are less than satisfactory. V. R. Desbourough, *Journal of Roman Studies* 58 (1968): 278-279 (+); A. S. Robertson, *Classical Review* 19 (1969): 351-353 (+).

644. *The Roman Imperial Coinage VII: Constantine and Licinius (A. D. 313-337).* By Patrick Bruun. London: Spink and Son, 1966.

645. *The Roman Imperial Coinage VIII: The Family of Constantine I (A. D. 337-364).* By J. P. C. Kent. London: Spink and Son, 1981.

646. Shelton, K. J. "Usurper's Coins: The Case of Magnentius." *Byzantinische Forschungen* 8 (1982): 211-235.

647. Sperber, Daniel. "Denarii and Aurei in the Time of Diocletian." *Journal of Roman Studies* 56 (1966): 190-195. There has been scholarly debate over the reliability of the text of the Edict of Diocletian where it says that there were 50,000 denarii to the aurei. Sperber says the text is accurate and shows why.

648. Stewart, B. H. I. H. "A Doubted London Coin of Constantine I." *Numismatic Chronicle* 26 (1986): 224-225.

649. Sutherland, C. H. V. "Denarius and Sestertius in Diocletian's Coinage Reform." *Journal of Roman Studies* 51 (1961): 94-97.

650. Sutherland, C. H. V. "Diocletian's Reform of the Coinage: A Chronological Note." *Journal of Roman Studies* 45 (1955): 116-118. The reform was done in stages in a lengthy process from around 286 to 294.

651. Tomlin, R. S. O. "Fairy Gold: Monetary History in the Augustan History." In *Imperial Revenue, Expenditure and Monetary Policy in the Fourth Century A. D.*, pp. 255-279. Edited by C. E. King. Oxford: British Archaeological Reports, 1980. Don't believe much of anything you read in the *Historia Augusta,* including monetary references.

652. **West, Louis C.** "The Coinage of Diocletian and the Edict on Prices." In *Studies in Roman Economic and Social History,* pp. 291-302. Edited by Paul R. Coleman-Norton. Princeton, N. J.: Princeton University Press, 1951; Freeport, N. Y.: Books for Libraries Press, 1969. West relates the coinage reform of Diocletian to the Edict on Prices (A. D. 301) to help find the answers to questions on the actual value of Roman money at that time.

653. **Whittaker, J. M.** "Coins and Christian Symbolism." *The Numismatic Circular* 87 (January 1979): 3-4. Whittaker is concerned mostly with fourth century coin issues, some of which used Christian symbolism during and after the time of Constantine the Great.

654. **Woloch, G. Michael.** "Indications of Imperial Status on Roman Coins, A. D. 337-383." *Numismatic Chronicle* 6 (1966): 171-178. The question of status was of endless interest to the Romans, who probably discussed the coin images that Woloch uses with as much interest as we do today.

VI. Economy, Technology, Science, and Medicine

This chapter includes taxation.

655. **Alic, Margaret.** "Women and Technology in Ancient Alexandria: Maria and Hypatia." *Women's Studies International Quarterly* 4 (1981): 305-312. Alic sees a "slight renaissance" in the scientific life of Alexandria in the fourth century. Hypatia was an important person in both Alexandrian science and politics in the later fourth century, until her death at the hands of fanatical monks in 415. Alic also has out a book: *Hypatia's Heritage: A History of Women in Science from Antiquity Through the Nineteenth Century* (Boston: Beacon Press, 1986).

656. **Anderson, Perry.** *Passages From Antiquity to Feudalism.* London: New Left Books, 1974. Economic determinism (tempered by political considerations) with a Marxist flavor applied to the later empire. The reviews indicated below will help considerably in putting Anderson's thoughts into perspective in the context of current developments, especially of a Marxist orientation, in economic historical writing. M. Hechter, *American Journal of Sociology* 82 (1977): 1057-1074 (+-); J. Marino, *Journal of Modern History* 51 (1979): 99-107 (+-).

657. **Bagnall, R. S.** "Agricultural Productivity and Taxation in Later Roman Egypt." *Transactions of the American Philological Association* 115 (1985): 289-308. Tax rates on land were low in fourth century Egypt, says Bagnall, but they were inflexibly applied, and when the irrigation system

collapsed in the Arsinoite Nome, there was great difficulty paying the bill.

658. **Bagnall, Roger S.** "Bullion Purchases and Landholding in the Fourth Century." *Chronique d'Egypte* 52 (1977): 322-336.

659. **Bagnall, Roger S.** *Currency and Inflation in Fourth Century Egypt.* Chico, CA: Scholars Press, 1985. "The principal aim of this book is to define more precisely the changes of price levels as they are seen in the papyri, that is, quoted in the accounting units in use in the period" (p. 2). Bagnall sees a direct link between price level changes and monetary changes. In other words, people using currency were quick to determine the precious metal content of new issues and adjusted prices accordingly. Bagnall discusses the nature and limited effect of inflation in the ancient economy. Very technical.

660. **Baldwin, Barry**. "Beyond the House Call: Doctors in Early Byzantine History and Politics." *Dumbarton Oaks Papers* 38 (1984): 15-19. Includes some fourth century doctors who were in high politics.

661. **Barnish, S. J. B.** "Pigs, Plebeians and Potentates: Rome's Economic Hinterland c. 350-600 A. D." *Papers of the British School in Rome* 55 (1987): 157-185.

662. **Bernardi, Aurelio**. "The Economic Problems of the Roman Empire at the Time of Its Decline." *Studia et Documenta Historiae et Juris* 31 (1965): 110-170. In the fourth century the empire was economically prosperous but was overtaxed by a government whose corrupt bureaucracy prevented a great deal of the money from arriving at the public treasury. An agrarian economy trying to support a huge government establishment was a source of tension in the fourth century and of disaster in the fifth when military attacks and increased barbarian pressure combined to disrupt the entire system.

663. **Bowman, Alan K.** "The Economy of Egypt in the Earlier Fourth Century A. D." In *Imperial Revenue, Expenditure and Monetary Policy in the Fourth Century A. D.*, pp. 23-40. Edited by C. E. King. Oxford: B. A. R., 1980. Using papyri evidence, Bowman concludes that the tax burden was not outrageous, that the agricultural economy was still very much in the hands of small landowners, and that fluctuations in prices have more to do with actual market conditions of the moment than with large scale inflation.

664. **Bowman, Alan K.** "Landholding in the Hermopolite Nome in the Fourth Century A. D." *Journal of Roman Studies* 75 (1985): 137-163. Bowman stresses the danger of forcing limited evidence to prove generalizations about landholding patterns in Egypt in the later empire. The land registers of the Hermopolite district at least do little to support traditional notions of the growth of larger and larger estates at the expense of the small landowner in a fourth century Egypt of declining prosperity. Reading the conditions of the sixth century (for which there is also a small amount of data) back into the fourth "requires a tremendous leap of the imagination."

665. *The Cambridge Economic History of Europe.* 8 vols. London and New York: Cambridge University Press, 1941- . Vol I: *The Agrarian Life of the Middle Ages.* 2nd ed. 1966. Vol. II: *Trade and Industry in the Middle Ages.* 2nd ed. 1987. Some chapters are of great value on the later empire. Example: F. W. Walbank, "Trade and Industry Under the Later Roman Empire in the West," in Vol. II.

666. **Caputo, G. and Goodchild, R.** "Diocletian's Price-Edict at Ptolemais (Cyrenaica)." *Journal of Roman Studies* 45 (1955): 106-115.

667. **Crawford, M. H. and Reynolds, Joyce.** "The Publication of the Prices Edict: A New Inscription from Aezani." *Journal of Roman Studies* 65 (1975): 160-163. The edict of a local governor was appended to Diocletian's price edict. Translation and discussion.

668. **Den Hengst, D.** "Ammianus Marcellinus on Astronomy (*Res Gestae* 20.3)." *Mnemosyne* 39 (1986): Den Hengst reconsiders some interpretations of this part of Ammianus by Joachim Szidat.

669. **Downey, Glanville.** "The Economic Crisis at Antioch under Julian the Apostate." In *Studies in Roman Economic and Social History in Honor of Alan Chester Johnson*, pp. 312-321. Edited by P. R. Coleman-Norton. Princeton, N. J.: Princeton University Press, 1951.

670. **Ericsson, Christoffer H.** *Navis Oneraria. The Cargo Carrier of Late Antiquity.* Acta Academiae Aboensis, Ser. A, Vol. 63, Nr. 3. Abo, Finland: Abo Akademii, 1984. The title is a bit misleading, since ships back to archaic Greece are considered. B. Kreutz, *American Journal of Archaeology* 90 (1986): 256-257 (+); *Classical World* 79 (1986): 412.

671. **Erim, Kenan T. and Reynolds, Joyce.** "The Aphrodisias Copy of Diocletian's Edict on Maximum Prices." *Journal of Roman Studies* 63 (1973): 99-110.

672. **Erim, Kenan and Reynolds, Joyce.** "The Copy of Diocletian's Edict on Maximum Prices from Aphrodisias in Caria." *Journal of Roman Studies* 60 (1970): 120-141.

673. **Frank, Richard I.** "Ammianus on Roman Taxation." *American Journal of Philology* 93 (1972): 69-86. First there is a helpful outline of the late Roman tax system; then Ammianus is shown as an excellent source for understanding the working of the tax system and how evading it became a large factor in the weakening of the state.

674. **Garnsey, Peter and Whittaker, C. R., eds.** *Trade and Famine in Classical Antiquity.* Cambridge Philological Society Suppl. Vol. 8. Cambridge Philological Society, 1983. The last paper in this anthology is relevant to the fourth century. From the review by N. R. E. Fisher, *Greece and Rome* 31 (1984): 213: "Whittaker offers striking hypotheses about the economic roles of the Empire's frontiers in the last

centuries of the Empire, in particular pointing to the crucial, finally decisive, part played by competition for the basic food resources."

675. Gill, Linda L. "The Financial Administration of the Later Roman Empire with Specific References to Roman Britain." M. A. thesis, Duquesne University, 1975.

676. Goffart, Walter. *'Caput' and 'Colonate': Towards a History of Late Roman Taxation.* Toronto: University of Toronto Press, 1974. The late Roman tax system is now remembered as unfair and oppressive, but in fact it was designed, primarily by Diocletian, to be rational, fair, and free from abuses. Explaining the new system in detail is difficult both because it changed over time and because the evidence is less than satisfactory. Goffart offers an impressive structure of explanation on what some scholars consider a shaky foundation of evidence. The effort to come to grips with the Roman tax structure will go on. R. P. Duncan-Jones, *Journal of Roman Studies* 67 (1977): 202-204 (-); R. E. Mitchell, *American Historical Review* 75 (1976): 831-832 (+).

677. Gray, William D. "The Roman Depression and Our Own." *Classical Journal* 29 (1934): 243-256. Gray sees unhappy parallels between the later Roman empire and America in the 1930s.

678. Gunderson, G. "Economic Change and the Demise of the Roman Empire." *Explorations in Economic History* 13 (1976): 43-68. Rising incomes, increased land productivity, new lands brought under cultivation, increasing population - all this and more in the fourth century Roman empire? Yes, very likely, says Gunderson. And he is talking about places like northern Gaul, not some safe province in Asia. And now hear this on late Roman taxation, which we have all always believed to be the Great Curse of the late Roman economy: "True, the Roman government grew progressively more expensive to maintain but that taxation was merely the other side of the services the system provided: defense; justice; roads; utilities; public welfare programs; and an enormous free market within which goods, services, resources, and ideas moved freely" (p. 60). And a little later: "One can make a plausible case that Roman taxation, rather than pushing and punishing the economy, was constantly being adapted to catch up with changes which had already occurred in the economic structure" (p. 60). And so on: all jaw-dropping stuff for students and scholars raised on doom and gloom in fourth century Rome. Then there is his theory of the fall: "voluntary decentralization" (p. 67). A very stimulating read.

679. **Hendy, Michael F.** *Studies in the Byzantine Monetary Economy, c. 300-1450.* Cambridge: University Press, 1985. There is important information here on the relations of the state and the economy in the fourth century, and specifically on state monetary policy as developed from the time of Diocletian. Hendy has an essential premise that the coinage system was designed by the state to serve its own needs and was not directed towards the civilian population, which functioned under the umbrella of the state's economic power, but was to some extent living in an economic world of its own. F. Millar, *Journal of Roman Studies* 78 (1988): 198-202 (++-) ("The essential question put before us by H.'s book is how the massive and complex late Roman-Byzantine state managed to live off a relatively undeveloped pre-industrial economy").

680. **Iluk, J.** "The Export of Gold from the Roman Empire to Barbarian Countries from the 4th to the 6th Centuries." *Munsterische Beitrage zur Antiken Handelsgeschichte* IV, I (1985): 79-102.

681. **Jones, A. H. M.** "Over-taxation and the Decline of the Roman Empire." *Antiquity* 33 (1959): 39-43. Although he later withdrew from a reliance on internal weaknesses of the Roman state as an explanation of its decline and fall, Jones here makes a case for the unfortunate consequences of high taxes.

682. **Jones, A. H. M.** *The Roman Economy: Studies in Ancient Economic and Administrative History.* Edited by P. A.

Brunt. Oxford: Blackwell; Totowa, N. J.: Rowman and Littlefield, 1974. This is a useful supplement to Jones' *Later Roman Empire* (37). It contains some unique material, but in fact almost all the chapters are reprints of articles already published. Not all the material has to do with the late Roman economy, but a great deal of it relates in some fashion to late Roman conditions. P. J. Cuff, *English Historical Review* 91 (1976): 169 (+); *Economist* 252 (September 14, 1974): 131-132 (+).

683. **Jonge, Pieter de.** "Scarcity of Corn and Cornprices in Ammianus Marcellinus." *Mnemosyne* 1 (1948): 238-245. More on Julian's unsuccessful effort to moderate corn prices in Antioch in 362. The sources, Ammianus, Julian, Libanius, and Socrates, are weighed and compared. Apart from bad crops, there was another factor, generally ignored but at least mentioned by Socrates, exacerbating the situation: the huge concentration of troops in Antioch, waiting for the Persian campaign. They took a heavy toll on the food supply.

684. **Keay, Simon J.** *Late Roman Amphorae in the Western Mediterranean: A Typology and Economic Study: The Catalan Evidence.* 2 vols. British Archaeological Reports, 1984.

685. **Lewis, Archibold R.** *The Northern Seas: Shipping and Commerce in Northern Europe A.D. 300-1100.* Princeton, N. J.: Princeton University Press, 1958. See Chapter I, "Northern Europe in the 4th Century." Lewis stresses that Rome was a Mediterranean empire whose interests in northern Europe were primarily defensive. Nevertheless, the Roman world had other important interests in northern Europe, and the imperial government saw to these vigorously until late in the fourth century. Lewis tells the story of the economy, of relations with the barbarians, of trade, of threats to the system in general which began to take on serious proportions after the battle of Adrianople in 378.

686. **Liebeschutz, W.** "Money Economy and Taxation in Kind in Syria in the Fourth Century A. D." *Rheinisches Museum* 104 (1961): 242-256.

687. **Lindberg, David C.** "Science and the Early Church." *Isis* 74 (December 1983): 509-530. The fourth century is the background for much of this discussion, by way of Basil of Caesarea and Augustine. Lindberg's conclusion is that although the study of science or natural philosophy was at most of secondary importance to Christians, it would be inaccurate to think that the Church ignored or killed science. The Church fathers found some aspects of Greek natural science useful, and encouraged man's rational capacities, but in support of Christianity of course.

688. **MacMullen, Ramsay.** "Diocletian's Price Edict and the *castrensis modius.*" *Aegyptus* 41 (1961): 3-5. MacMullen refers in his title to the economic edict of 301, an effort to stabilize prices, and to the "camp measure," which became a standard measure for many items in the fourth century. He reviews fourth century evidence to show "first, that the effect of the edict of Diocletian was by no means transitory, and second, that the force behind it was the army, active in surveying work, and the chief consumer of the empire" (p.5).

689. **MacMullen, Ramsay.** "Manufactures for the State in the Later Roman Empire." Ph. D. dissertation, Harvard University, 1957.

690. **MacMullen, Ramsay.** "Tax-Pressure in the Roman Empire." *Latomus* 46 (1987): 737-754. MacMullen investigates taxes and tax collecting in the Roman world from Augustus to the fifth century. In the later empire, it was not that taxes were overall so much worse than before, but rather that corruption was so much worse, deriving in part from a larger bureaucracy which required its cut, legal and illegal, before the emperor ever got his.

691. **Miller, Timothy S.** *The Birth of the Hospital in the Byzantine Empire.* Baltimore: Johns Hopkins University Press, 1985. "The decades of the fourth century . . . witnessed the birth of the hospital" (p. 68). Miller devotes an interesting

chapter to the social and religious influences that came to bear on this development, especially the Arian movement.

692. **Nutton, Vivian.** "From Galen to Alexander: Aspects of Medicine and Medical Practice in Late Antiquity." *Dumbarton Oaks Papers* 38 (1984): 1-14. Nutton finds medicine in a more dynamic condition than we usually read about for the later empire. There is a fair amount of fourth century material.

693. **Percival, John.** "Seigneurial Aspects of Late Roman Estate Management." *English Historical Review* 84 (1969): 449-473. Percival reviews very cautiously the signs that late Roman villa estates were turning into medieval manors. He believes in the link without expecting the entire Roman world to show the same pattern of change. Also, the evidence is scanty and treacherous and requires great restraint in interpretation.

694. **Sambursky, Samuel.** *The Physical World of Late Antiquity.* London: Routledge and Kegan Paul, 1962. Limited to Greek authors as sources, Sambursky reviews concepts of space and time, matter, mechanics, concepts of action, physics, and astronomy. W. H. Stahl, *Latomus* 23 (1964): 412-413 (+).

695. **Scarborough, John.** "Gnosticism, Drugs and Alchemy in Late Roman Egypt." *Pharmacy in History* 13 (1971): 151-157. The "alchemical-drug tradition" of the ancient world was by the fourth century permanently wrapped in "mystical confusion," which stunted any real growth in chemistry beyond some important but isolated technical advances.

696. **Simms, D. L.** "Water-driven Saws, Ausonius, and the Authenticity of the Mosella." *Technology and Culture* 24 (1983): 635-643. Arguing against Lynn White Jr., Simms accepts the authenticity of Ausonius' most famous poem, dating from around 370, and with it the accuracy of the reference to a stone-sawing mill. There is a brief addendum to this article in *Technology and Culture* 26 (1985): 275-276 with some

technical considerations as to how the waterwheel operated the saw.

697. Sperber, Daniel. *Roman Palestine 200-400. The Land. Crisis and Change in Agrarian Society as Reflected in Rabbinic Sources.* Ramat-Gan: Bar-Ilan University, 1978. Sperber presents a Palestine in agricultural decline in the third and fourth centuries, with a modest recovery in the late fourth. R. P. Duncan-Jones, *Classical Review* 30 (1980): 98-100 (+-).

698. Szilagyi, Janos. "Prices and Wages in the Western Provinces of the Roman Empire." *Acta Antiqua Academiae Scientiarum Hungaricae* 11 (1963): 325-389. A great deal of this extensive material has to do with the early empire, but a fair amount goes into the time of Diocletian. Some of the information, or at least the way it is presented, must be regarded with caution or even suspicion. The evidence cannot sustain some of the conclusions, especially the comparisons over long periods of time. Nevertheless, there are lots of interesting data here for the economic historian.

699. Tengstrom, Emin. *Bread for the People: Studies of the Corn Supply of Rome during the Late Empire.* Stockholm: Svenska Instituteti Rom, 1974. Tengstrom covers the period 350-400, and analyzes the system from the growth of the corn in Africa to its distribution as bread in Rome. G. E. Rickman, *Gnomon* 50 (1978): 88-90 (+-).

700. Thomas, J. David. "Epigraphai and Indictions in the Reign of Diocletian." *Bulletin of the American Society of Papyrologists* 15 (1978): 133-145. Thomas sorts out the vocabulary and stages of introducing new tax systems in Egypt.

701. Vanags, Patsy. "Taxation and Survival in the Late Fourth Century: The Anonymous' Programme of Economic Reforms." In *De Rebus Bellicis,* pp. 47-57. Edited by M. W. C. Hassall and R. I. Ireland. Oxford: British Archaeological Reports, 1979. Taxes were a burden in the late empire, but were not exactly putting everyone out of business. There were forces at work to reduce taxes, and many emperors did so. It was also in the interests of the central government to protect small freeholders from ruin, and efforts were made to do so. Indeed, the reform movement of the later fourth century "suggests a climate of optimism where bold solutions to problems were attempted" (p. 54).

702. White, K. D. "Harvesting, Palladius, and Technology in the Later Roman Empire." In *De Rebus Bellicis,* pp. 39-45. Edited by M. W. C. Hassall and R. I. Ireland. Oxford: British Archaeological Reports, 1979. Technology was not at a standstill in the late western Roman empire. But in general economic conditions did not require great innovations of technique either.

703. Whittaker, C. R. "Agri Deserti." In *Studies in Roman Property*, pp. 137-165. Edited by M. I. Finley. Cambridge: University Press, 1976. There has been a long debate among scholars as to the extent of agricultural decline in the late Roman period. Whittaker doubts that there was a general decline, saying that we have relied too much on literary sources which exaggerated the problem for polemical purposes. Whittaker's conclusion: "Unless one can sustain the proposition of a manpower crisis or of a downturn in the forces of production, implying new and less efficient agricultural methods or combinations of labour - neither of which is possible, in my opinion - agricultural production must have remained relatively static (p. 164)"

704. Whittaker, C. R. "Inflation and the Economy in the Fourth Century A. D." In *Imperial Revenue, Expenditure and Monetary Policy in the Fourth Century A. D.*, pp. 1-22. Edited by C. E. King. Oxford: British Archaeological Reports, 1980. In a provocative essay, Whittaker finds, among other things, that inflation was "unimportant" in the late Roman economy, that official tax rates were "not particularly oppressive," and that the fiscal problems of the central government, especially in the later fourth century, had to do with the policy of letting rich landlords collect taxes from their tenants. In essence, the emperors lost control of taxation to local magnates who kept much of the wealth for themselves.

705. Wickham, Chris. "Marx, Sherlock Holmes, and Late Roman Commerce [rev art.]." *The Journal of Roman Studies* 78 (1988): 183-193. For those who want a taste of what is going on in scholarly Italian circles, especially Marxist circles, regarding the late Roman economic system. Wickham discusses all this in the context of a review of a large and important anthology of Italian studies of late Roman society, then moves along to his own views which stress the importance of the state in giving the commerce of the Roman world the breadth and vitality which it still continued to display in the fourth, and, to some extent, in the fifth centuries.

706. Wickham, Chris. "The Other Transition: From the Ancient World to Feudalism." *Past and Present* #103 (May 1984): 3-36. Wickham considers the collapse of the ancient world in Marxist economic terms. The tax-based ancient economy was swept away with the fall of the central Roman government; the replacement was a state in which the army was land-based and the great landowners were largely independent of a central government. Central taxation became largely irrelevant and gradually lapsed. But the feudal world was not a creation of the German successor states. Both the ancient and feudal systems existed side by side in the late Roman world. They did not live in harmony, but they did exist together for a long time. The fourth century was the high point of this tense relationship.

707. Wikander, Orjan. *Exploitation of Water-Power or Technological Stagnation? A Reappraisal of the Productive Forces in the Roman Empire.* Lund: C. W. K. Gleerup, 1984. Concentrating on water-mills as an example, Wikander shows that the Roman empire, even in its later phases, is unfairly stigmatized as technologically stagnant. The Roman world was not surging towards an industrial revolution, but its inhabitants were building modestly on their technological inheritance.

VII. Society and Art

Includes population studies, social relations, fashion, customs, food, travel, sports, women, and all things of an artistic nature including architecture.

708. **Adams, Jeremy D**. *The "Populus" of Augustine and Jerome: A Study in the Patristic Sense of Community.* New Haven: Yale University Press, 1971. Fourth century ideas and attitudes on the "people," as social and political groupings, culled from the writings of Augustine and Jerome. F. E. Cranz, *Speculum* 48 (1973): 724-727 (+-).

709. **Alexander, S. Spain.** "Studies in Constantinian Church Architecture." *Rivista di archeologia cristiana* 47 (1971): 281-230 and 49 (1973): 33-44.

710. **Alfoldi, Andras**. "Some Portraits of Julianus Apostata." *American Journal of Archaeology* 66 (1962): 403-405. A number of interesting pieces are discussed and illustrated.

711. **Armstrong, Gregory T**. "Constantine's Churches." *Gesta* 6 (January 1967): 1-9. A catalog of the many churches the first Christian emperor built, including the maybes and doubtfuls.

712. **Auerbach, Erich**. "The Arrest of Peter Valvomeres." In *Mimesis: The Representation of Reality in Western Literature,* pp. 50-76. Princeton, N. J.: Princeton University Press, 1953; reprint ed., New York: Doubleday and Co., Inc., 1957. Ammianus' description of an incident in the streets of Rome becomes the occasion for an essay on the "darkening of

the atmosphere of life" (p. 46) in the later empire. In comparing Ammianus with a roughly analagous incident in Tacitus, Auerbach laments "how much stronger the magical and the sensory has become at the expense of the human and the objectively rational" (p. 46).

713. Bagnall, Roger S. "The Camel, the Wagon and the Donkey in Later Roman Egypt." *Bulletin of the American Society of Papyrologists* 22 (no. 1-4, 1985): 1-6.

714. Bagnall, Roger S. "Church, State and Divorce in Late Roman Egypt." In *Florilegium Columbianum: Essays in Honor of Paul Oskar Kristeller*, pp. 41-61. Edited by Karl-Ludwig Selig and Robert Somerville. New York: Italica Press, 1987. Local divorce traditions counted for much more than either Christian or imperial legislation in Egypt, says Bagnall. Also, he argues that the effect of Christianity on imperial marriage legislation in this period was very limited; classical traditions still counted for much more. Bagnall is very firm on this point: "the imperial legislation of the fourth and fifth centuries is not 'Christian' legislation, and the empire was not a 'Christian' empire, no matter how often it is called one" (p. 45).

715. Bagnall, Roger S. "The Population of Theadelphia in the Fourth Century." *Bulletin de la Societe d'archeologie copte* 24 (1982): 35-57. Some detailed prosopographical work reveals the population and its trends in an agricultural village of Egypt in the first quarter of the fourth century.

716. Bagnani, G. "Misopogon: The Beard Hater." *Classical News and Views* 12 (1968): 73-79. A humorous review of the rise and fall and rise and fall of the beard, with some emphasis on the fourth century.

717. Berenson, Bernard. *The Arch of Constantine, or, The Decline of Form.* New York: Macmillan, 1954. The subtitle says everything. Berenson had no use for anything that failed the test of classical standards. P. Zucker, *Journal of Aesthetics and Art Criticism* 13 (1955): 539 (+-).

Society and Art

718. Bianchi Bandinelli, Ranuccio. *Rome, the Late Empire: Roman Art, A. D. 200-400.* Translated from the French by Peter Green. London: Thames and Hudson; New York: G. Braziller, 1971. The variety, richness, color, and imagination of late Roman art are truly impressive. Of course fourth century art is different from second century art; but immediately to assume decadence is to miss a wonderful experience of appreciation and enjoyment. Bianchi's book helps give that wonderful experience. S. Harcourt-Smith, *History Today* 21 (October 1971): 750-751 (+).

719. Bird, H. W. "Aurelius Victor on Women and Sexual Morality." *Classical Journal* 58 (no.1, 1982): 44-48. Victor "plainly appreciated how much Rome had suffered throughout the imperial period because of the excesses of imperial reprobates or the malign influence of dissolute consorts and counsellors. It is hardly surprising, then, that he concluded that such people should have no place in the affairs of state" (p. 48).

720. Bird, H. W. "A Reconstruction of the Life and Career of S. Aurelius Victor." *Classical Journal* 70 (1975): 49-54. Victor is a good example of a man of humble circumstances going high in the fourth century civil administration, first because he had a good education, and second because he came in contact with the right people, including emperors. Bird pulls the source material together to create a coherent biography.

721. Blasquez, J. M. "The Rejection and Assimilation of Roman Culture in Hispania during the Fourth and Fifth Centuries." *Classical Folia* 32 (1978): 217-242. In large parts of the Spanish peninsula Roman culture sat lightly on the shoulders of the provincials, unlike Roman taxes. Indigenous cultures survived in many areas. Of course there were Spanish Romans, and many of them, and these people directed Spanish society. Roman culture was a powerful dynamic in Spain, carrying with it the prestige of being associated with a world empire. But this was a matter of indifference to much of the Spanish population, who adopted the parts of Roman culture that seemed immediately useful, and jettisoned the rest. Many were not displeased when the opportunity arose to be rid of Roman administration and taxes. Within the limited evidence, Blasquez sorts out a complex story.

722. Blockley, R. C. "Roman-Barbarian Marriages in the Later Empire." *Florilegium* 4 (1982): 63-79. "In sum: although the data are not extensive, they do seem to indicate that, amongst the upper classes at least, marriages between Romans and barbarians were not rejected in the late Empire" (p. 73).

723. Boak, Arthur E. R. *Manpower Shortage and the Fall of the Roman Empire in the West.* Ann Arbor: University of Michigan Press, 1955. This is THE work to consult for those who believe in population decline in the late empire period. In the absence of conclusive statistics, we may expect the debate on population trends to go on and on. M. I. Finley, *Journal of Roman Studies* 48 (1958): 156-164 (-).

724. Boak, Arthur E. R. and Youtie, H. C. *The Archive of Aurelius Isidorus.* Ann Arbor: University of Michigan Press, 1960. The papers of a fourth century Egyptian land entrepreneur.

725. Bonfante, Larissa Warren. "Emperor, God and Man in the IV Century: Julian the Apostate and Ammianus Marcellinus." *La Parola del Passato* 19 (1964): 401-427. Through the writings of Julian and Ammianus, Bonfante shows us the world of the fourth century as it saw itself, through its gods, its emperors, its armies, its art. Bonfante finds that Christians and pagans were very close in the fundamentals of the cultural climate of the age.

726. Bonney, Robert. "A New Friend for Symmachus?" *Historia* 24 (1975): 357-374. In an elaborate discussion Bonney finds it possible to assign receipt of many anonymous letters of Symmachus to specific persons and to reassign other letters.

727. Brenk, Beat. "The Imperial Heritage of Early Christian Art." In *Age of Spirituality: A Symposium,* pp. 39-52. Edited by Kurt Weitzmann. New York: Metropolitan Museum of Art, in Association with Princeton University Press, 1980. Christian art took on very imperial overtones in the fourth century. Brenk tells the story in a heavily and beautifully illustrated article.

728. Brennan, Brian. "Athanasius' *Vita Antonii.* A Sociological Interpretation." *Vigiliae Christianae* 39 (1985): 209-227. A sociologist takes on the fourth century. Brennan's aim is "to examine Athanasius' literary portrayal of Antony the hermit in terms of the broader fourth-century context in which it was written using the Weberian sociological model of the charismatic figure and of the routinization of charisma" (p. 209). After this remark, the sociological jargon is kept to a minimum, and the "multi-faceted" *Life of Antony* emerges as a remarkable response to and commentary on political and religious issues of the mid-fourth century.

729. Brilliant, R. "Temporal Aspects in Late Roman Art." *L'Arte* #10 (1970): 65-87. Through specific pieces, such as sarcophagi and triumphal arches, the author ruminates on "the changing quality of Roman attitudes about time" in late antiquity. Christian art figures prominently in the discussion.

730. Brown, Peter. "Art and Society in Late Antiquity." In *Age of Spirituality: A Symposium,* pp. 17-27. Edited by Kurt Weitzmann. New York: Metropolitan Museum of Art, in Association with Princeton University Press, 1980. Brown analyzes the roots and the vitality of public and private art in the late empire, whether secular or religious. It is a very upbeat story, of a world still full of cities, great wealth, a growing population (at least in the east), and grandiose building projects. Most usefully, Brown takes fourth century art out from under the shadow of classical standards and lets it stand on its own merits.

731. Brown, Peter. "Late Antiquity." In *A History of Private Life.* Vol. I: *From Pagan Rome to Byzantium,* pp. 237-

311. Edited by Paul Veyne. Cambridge, Mass.: Harvard University Press, 1987. Through changing sexual mores, changing styles of social expression and displays of wealth, and the movement of public community life from the forum to the church (or sometimes to the desert), Brown charts the glacial movement of the Roman world from a classical to a Christian culture. The rise of the celibate clergy and the progress of monasticism signified the ever-widening gap between life in the church and life in the world - i.e., the world of classical life. The great period of tension and transition was the fourth century, but Brown's analysis comprehends the period from Marcus Aurelius to Justinian. The usual rich intellectual feast one would expect from Brown. C. Edwards, *Journal of Roman Studies* 78 (1988): 224-225 (+).

732. Brown, Peter. "Sorcery, Demons and the Rise of Christianity." In *Witchcraft Confessions and Accusations,* pp. 17-45. Edited by M. Douglas. Tavistock Publications Ltd., 1970. Reprinted in his *Religion and Society in the Age of Saint Augustine,* pp. 119-146. New York: Harper and Row, 1972. Brown relates the increase in sorcery charges in the mid-fourth century to social tensions in the governing class of the empire, which was undergoing change.

733. Cameron, Alan. "Earthquake 400." *Chiron* 17 (1987): 343-360. Cameron pronounces himself satisfied that the earthquake of 400 really did take place in 400. In demonstrating this, he presents the really interesting features of the article: how the large Gothic colony in Constantinople in the late fourth century influenced the sartorial customs of the city, how they worshipped; sailing conditions for private travelers; interesting asides about John Chrysostom and Synesius of Cyrene; etc.

734. Cameron, Alan. "A Note on Ivory Carving in Fourth Century Constantinople." *American Journal of Archaeology* 86 (1982): 126-129. Reprinted in his *Literature and Society in the Early Byzantine World,* Chap. XVII. London: Variorum Reprints, 1985. A number of beautiful ivory diptychs survive from the late empire. Cameron explores some questions concerning not only where these art treasures were made, but their relevance to the aristocracies of east and west.

735. **Cameron, Alan.** "Polynomy in the Late Roman Aristocracy: The Case of Petronius Probus." *Journal of Roman Studies* 75 (1985): 164-182. Fourth century nomenclature is discussed, and the implications for prosopography and other historical studies.

736. **Cameron, Alan.** "The Roman Friends of Ammianus." *Journal of Roman Studies* 54 (1964): 15-28. Cameron doubts that Ammianus Marcellinus was an intimate of the Roman aristocracy, as has sometimes been claimed.

737. **Ceran, W.** "Stagnation or Fluctuation in Early Byzantine Society?" *Byzantino-Slavica* 31 (1971): 192-203. Further proof, with much help from Chrysostom and data from Antioch, of the dynamic and prosperous conditions of the fourth century empire, and of the significant level of social fluidity - at least in the east.

738. **Chadwick, Henry.** "The Relativity of Moral Codes: Rome and Persia in Late Antiquity." In *Early Christian Literature and the Classical Intellectual Tradition*, pp. 135-153. Edited by William R. Schoedel and Robert L. Wilken. Paris: Editions Beauchesne, 1979. Diocletian's edict against the Manichees and the edict against incest in 295 are the centerpieces for a discussion of Roman intolerance of Persian mores.

739. **Clark, Elizabeth A.** *Ascetic Piety and Women's Faith: Essays on Late Ancient Christianity.* Studies in Women and Religion, 20. Lewiston, N. Y.: Edwin Mellon Press, 1986. In this anthology of thirteen essays written between 1977 and 1985, Clark explores the relationship of women to the changing Roman mores of the fourth and fifth centuries. A major theme is the new and in some senses liberating careers women could experience as part of the ascetic movement in Christianity, a movement denounced by some women. In any event, women, like Roman armies, barbarian tribes, and social climbers, were

on the move as never before. Clark is well founded in the sources, and offers a challenging report for the student of later Roman life.

740. Conant, Kenneth J. "The Original Buildings at the Holy Sepulchre in Jerusalem." *Speculum* 31 (1956): 1-48. Conant describes in detail the "pagan magnificence" of the buildings that Constantine and his family donated to the site of Jesus' burial. Impressive illustrations.

741. Couasnon, C. *The Church of the Holy Sepulchre in Jerusalem.* Translated by J.-P. B. and Claude Ross. London: Oxford University Press for the British Academy, 1974. The church's story from the fourth century to current restoration projects. Excellent illustrations of the fourth century complex of buildings.

742. Crowfoot, John W. *Early Churches in Palestine.* British Academy Schweich Lecture. London: Published for the British Academy by H. Milford, Oxford University Press, 1941.

743. D'Arms, John H. *Romans on the Bay of Naples: A Social and Cultural Study of the Villas and Their Owners from 150 B. C. to A. D. 400.* Cambridge, Mass.: Harvard University Press, 1970.

744. Davies, J. G. "Eusebius' Description of the Martyrium at Jerusalem." *American Journal of Archaeology* 61 (1957): 171-173. After reviewing Eusebius and other material, Davies concludes that the "Constantinian Martyrium . . . consisted of a rectangular building, having the exceptional number of five aisles, with a circular chapel at its west end above the place where the Cross was discovered" (p. 173). Includes illustrations.

745. Dembinska, Maria. "Diet: A Comparison of Food Consumption between Some Eastern and Western Monasteries in the Fourth-Twelfth Centuries." *Byzantion* 55 (1985): 431-462.

746. **Dorigo, Wladimiro.** *Late Roman Painting: A Study of Pictorial Records, 30 BC-AD 500.* Translated by James Cleugh and John Warrington. New York: Praeger, 1971. Despite the subtitle, most of the book has to do with the fourth century. Heavily and beautifully illustrated. M. A. R. Colledge, *Greece and Rome* 19 (1972): 107 (-); D. J. Smith, *American Journal of Archaeology* 76 (1972): 347-348 (+-); P. Q., *History Today* 21 (1971): 599 (+-).

747. **Downey, Glanville.** "Constantine's Churches at Antioch, Tyre, and Jerusalem. Notes on Architectural Terms." *Melanges Universite Saint Joseph* 38 (1962): 191-196.

748. **Downey, Glanville.** "The Olympic Games of Antioch in the Fourth Century A. D." *Transactions of the American Philological Association* 70 (1939): 428-438.

749. **Drinkwater, John F.** "Peasants and Bagaudae in Roman Gaul." *Classical Views* 3 (1984): 349-371. In a provocative article, Drinkwater reminds us that peasants were not all poor, and in his view the peasants of Gaul generally were reasonably well off. He hypothesizes that the Bagaudae rebellions of the late third century resulted not from the oppression of peasants by the nobility, but from unique conditions of government withdrawal and social chaos which opened "a great mixture of emotions and motives" among some types of peasants and army deserters and such like, who fought the restoration of traditional government and social order under Diocletian.

750. **Dynes, W.** "The First Christian Palace-Church Types." *Marsyas* 11 (1962-64): 1ff.

751. **Engemann, Josef.** "Christianization of Late Antique Art." In *The 17th International Byzantine Congress: Major Papers,* pp. 83-115. Dumbarton Oaks/Georgetown University, Washington, D. C., August 3-8, 1986. New Rochelle, N. Y.: A. D. Caratzas, 1986. Engemann discusses many specific pieces of late antique art to show that Christianity did not develop its

own art but fed from the mainstream of Roman art, which was adapted to Christian themes. In a very concrete and illuminating point, Engemann reminds us that "during late antiquity the same workshops frequently worked for Christians and non-Christians alike" (p. 89).

752. **Farid, Farouk.** "Paniskos: Christian or Pagan?" *Museum Philologum Londiniense* 2 (1977): 109-117. Farid reviews the correspondence of one Paniskos, an Egyptian from the time of Diocletian, and finds that the religious expressions in the letters say more about the scribes who were hired to write them than about Paniskos, who was illiterate.

753. **Forsyth, George H., Jr.** "The Transept of Old St. Peter's at Rome." In *Late Classical and Mediaeval Studies in Honor of Albert Mathias Friend, Jr.*, pp. 56-70. Edited by Kurt Weitzmann. Princeton, N. J.: Princeton University Press, 1955. Forsyth concludes that the design of the fourth century St. Peter's "can best be understood as an original development intended to satisfy the twofold purpose of a pilgrimage church and of a triumphal monument" (p. 70). The triumph, of course, was that of Constantine and Christ his ally.

754. **Frazer, Alfred K.** "Four Late Antique Rotundas: Aspects of Fourth Century Architectural Style in Rome." Ph. D. dissertation, New York University, 1964. The four rotundas: the Mausoleum of Romulus in Via Appia Antica, the "Heroon Romuli," or "Templum Divi Romuli," in Via Sacra, Minerva Medica, and the *caldarium* of the Terme del Bacucci near Viterbo. Volume I is text; Volume II, illustrations.

755. **Frazer, Alfred.** "A Graphic Reconstruction of Old St. Peter's." M. A. thesis, Institute of Fine Arts, New York University, [?]. By old St. Peter's is meant the basilica in Rome built in the early fourth century.

756. **Frazer, M.** "The Iconography of the Emperor Maxentius' Buildings in Via Appia." *Art Bulletin* 48 (1966): 385-392.

Society and Art

757. **Frend, W. H. C.** "The Revival of Berber Art." *Antiquity* 16 (1942): 342-352. Reprinted in his *Town and Country in the Early Christian Centuries*, Ch. XX. London: Variorum Reprints, 1980. The revival of native art in a large part of Roman Africa in the 4th century is set against the economic, religious, and political background of the time.

758. **Gangwere, Blanche.** *Music History from the Late Roman Through the Gothic Periods, 313-1425: A Documented Chronology.* Westport, Conn.: Greenwood Press, 1986. G. L. Mayer, *American Reference Books Annual* 18 (1987): 481 (+).

759. **Grabar, Andre.** *The Beginnings of Christian Art, 200-395.* Translated by S. Gilbert and J. Emmons. London: Thames and Hudson, 1967.

760. **Gregory, Timothy E.** "Urban Violence in Late Antiquity." In *Aspects of Graeco-Roman Urbanism,* pp. 138-161. Edited by Ronald T. Marchese. BAR International Series, 188. Oxford: British Archaeological Reports, 1983. Covering A. D. 300-600, Gregory finds that urban riots were rarely concerned with political issues, "despite the supposed oppression that characterized the period" (p. 145). Certainly there was no thought of overthrowing the social structure or the Roman state. Often religious issues or controversies relating to the games of the hippodrome sparked trouble. In the absence of adequate city police forces, events often got out of control. When things did not cool down in a reasonable period, or when the central authority felt threatened, the army intervened, usually with bloody results. Gregory adduces many specific cases of urban troubles, carefully described and analyzed.

761. **Grigg, Robert.** "Inconsistency and Lassitude: The Shield Emblems of the *Notitia Dignitatum*." *Journal of Roman Studies* 73 (1983): 132-141. Grigg finds that "the shield emblems of the Notitia Dignitatum were largely ad hoc fabrications" (p. 132).

762. Grigg, Robert. "Portrait Bearing Codicils in the Illustrations of the *Notitia Dignitatum*?" *Journal of Roman Studies* 69 (1979): 107-124. We are warned "not to expect more from the extant illustrations than a general idea of the appearance of late Roman insignia."

763. Hanfmann, George M. "The Continuity of Classical Art: Culture, Myth, and Faith." In *Age of Spirituality: A Symposium*, pp. 75-99. In late antiquity, classical art was transformed into Christian art. A lot of classical baggage was carried along with this transformation, but the themes and high classical poses and style of pagan art were pretty well dropped. Heavily illustrated.

764. Harries, Jill. "'Treasure in Heaven': Property and Inheritance Among Senators of Late Rome." In *Marriage and Property*, pp. 54-70. Edited by Elizabeth Craik. Aberdeen: University Press, 1984. Harries looks at the conflict between traditional ways of handling property and the attitudes of the aristocratic ascetics who were popping up with alarming regularity in the households of the great Roman families of the late fourth century.

765. Harrison, Evelyn B. "The Constantinian Portrait." *Dumbarton Oaks Papers* 21 (1967): 81-96. The art of portraiture was "restless" in the early fourth century, says Harrison. The result was impressive variety. Excellent illustrations.

766. Hayes, J. W. *Late Roman Pottery*. London: British School at Rome, 1972.

767. Henig, M. E. "Late Antique Book Illustration and the Gallic Prefecture." In *De Rebus Bellicis*, pp. 17-28. Edited by M. W. C. Hassall and R. I. Ireland. Oxford: British Archaeological Reports, 1979. Henig finds evidence for a fourth century culture in Gaul and Britain displaying "a sophistication equal to that of Antioch or Alexandria or Milan" (p. 210).

768. Hickey, Anne E. "Women of the Senatorial Aristocracy of Late Rome as Christian Monastics. A Sociological and Cultural Analysis of Motivation." Ph. D. dissertation, Vanderbilt University, 1983. To some extent, the ancient ideals of the virtuous Roman woman met in the monastic ideology of the late fourth century. In the language of the sociologists, Hickey analyzes this development.

769. Hopkins, Keith. "Elite Mobility in the Roman Empire." *Past and Present* #32 (1965): 12-26. There was much mobility into the Roman aristocracy. Hopkins generalizes over the entire history of the empire, including a good deal of material relating to the fourth century.

770. Hopkins, M. K. "Social Mobility in the Later Roman Empire: The Evidence of Ausonius." *Classical Quarterly* 11 (1961): 239-249. Hopkins offers evidence that fourth century society was not a caste system, regardless of laws reflecting an occasional government hope that it could become so. "The society of the fourth century may have been stable. It was not static" (p. 239).

771. Hunt, E. D. *Holy Land Pilgrimage in the Later Roman Empire AD 312-460.* Oxford: Clarendon Press, 1982. From the time of Constantine, the tourist industry of the Roman world was re-oriented to Jerusalem and other sites in Palestine. Hunt studies this development in all its aspects and phases. Averil Cameron, *American Historical Review* 89 (1984): 106 (+); H. Drake, *Catholic Historical Review* 71 (1985): 452 (+).

772. Jonas, R. "A Newly Discovered Portrait of the Emperor Julian." *American Journal of Archaeology* 50 (1946): 277-282. Jonas discusses a marble head purchased in Jerusalem in 1942. Through a consideration of fourth century literature, coins and sculpture, Jonas concludes that the piece is Julian. Illustrated.

773. Jones, A. H. M. "The Caste System in the Later Roman Empire." *Eirene* 8 (1970): 79-96. "In this paper I shall endeavor to prove that in practice status and occupation were to a large extent hereditary under the principate, and that the later emperors did little more than give legal sanction to a system which was . . . beginning to break down." Jones also shows that the caste system was "by no means all-embracing, and in practice was not rigorously enforced" (p. 79).

774. Jones, A. H. M. "Census Records of the Later Roman Empire." *Journal of Roman Studies* 43 (1953): 49-64. Jones takes a look at late third or early fourth century census records from western Asia Minor to find statistical information "on the distribution of landed property, on the density of the agricultural population, and on the proportion of slave to free labor" (p. 49).

775. Keenan, James G. "On Law and Society in Late Roman Egypt." *Zeitschrift fur Papyrologie und Epigraphik* 17 (1975): 237-250. Keenan advances evidence to show that even in late Roman Egypt, social fluidity was a regular feature despite imperial laws that tried to regulate where men lived and what they did. Where things were static, they were often so by custom rather than by law.

776. Keenan, Mary E. *The Life and Times of Saint Augustine as Revealed in His Letters.* Washington, D. C.: Catholic University Press, 1935. North African life in the late fourth and early fifth centuries. Keenan is largely concerned with economic, social, political, and religious life; but there are as well interesting and unexpected little features, such as remarks on climate, musical instruments, and travel.

777. Kelly, M. J. *Life and Times as Revealed in the Writings of St. Jerome Exclusive of His Letters.* Washington, D. C.: Catholic University Press, 1944.

778. Kent, J. P. C. and Painter, K. S., eds. *The Wealth of the Roman World A. D. 300-700.* London: British Museum Publications, 1977. This is a beautifully illustrated catalog of a gold and silver exhibition at the British Museum, with helpful narrative by Kent and Painter. A wonderful browse through the artistic use of the two precious metals in late antiquity, from cups to coins. J. Beckwith, *Antiquaries Journal* 58P (Winter 1978): 187-188 (+).

779. **Kitzinger, Ernst**. "A Marble Relief of the Theodosian Period." *Dumbarton Oaks Papers* 14 (1960): 17-42. Kitzinger discusses a beautiful marble relief with a Christian theme in the context of the "classicizing taste" of the imperial court in the East in the late fourth century. Illustrated.

780. **Kitzinger, Ernst**. "The Threshold of the Holy Shrine: Observations on Floor Mosaics at Antioch and Bethlehem." In *KYRIAKON: Festschrift Johannes Quasten*, pp. 639-647. Edited by Patrick Granfield and Josef A. Jungmann. 2 vols. Munster: Aschendorff, 1970. Fourth century mosaics and their symbols.

781. **Kleinbauer, W**. "Toward a Dating of San Lorenzo in Milan." *Arte Lombarda* 13 (1968): 1ff. Masonry techniques as indicators of chronology in fourth century Milan construction.

782. **Korsunski, A. R**. "The Church and the Slavery Problem in the 4th Century." In *Miscellanea Historiae Ecclesiasticae, VI: Congres de Varsovie (25 Juin-1er Juillet 1978). Section I: Les Transformations dans la Societe Chretienne au IVe Siecle*, pp. 95-110. Bibliotheque de la Revue d'Histoire Ecclesiastique, 67. Bruxelles: Editions Nauwelaerts, 1983. Korsunski finds the church working both sides of the street on slavery: on the one side, Christianity proclaimed the equality of slaves and masters before God and in the church; on the other, the church sanctioned slavery as part of the order of things and preached consideration by masters and cooperation by slaves. Master and slave could pray together, but they were also expected to stay together - as master and slave.

783. **Krautheimer, Richard**. "The Beginnings of Early Christian Architecture." *The Review of Religions* 3 (1938-1939): 127-148. Constantine figures prominently in the

adoption of the public basilica as a prototype for Christian church buildings.

784. Krautheimer, Richard. "The Constantinian Basilica." *Dumbarton Oaks Papers* 21 (1967): 115-140. Krautheimer discusses the development of the fourth century basilica, encompassing religious and secular functions. Illustrated.

785. Krautheimer, Richard. *Early Christian and Byzantine Architecture.* 4th ed. New York: Viking Penguin, 1986. Includes a good section on the fourth century. Illustrated. Other editions are 1965, 1975, and 1979.

786. Krautheimer, Richard. "Success and Failure in Late Antique Church Planning." In *Age of Spirituality: A Symposium,* pp. 121-139. Edited by Kurt Weitzmann. New York: Metropolitan Museum of Art in Association with Princeton University Press, 1980. Krautheimer studies "the transfer to church buildings of elements and concepts rooted in the realm of Late Antique villa and palace planning" (p. 138). This was not always done successfully, as the author demonstrates through the church of St. Stefano Rotondo in Rome, which is described as a "beautiful freak" (p. 138), and. to him, "the most fascinating church in Rome" (p. 124).

787. LaBranche, Carol L. "Roma Nobilis: The Public Architecture of Rome, 330-476." Ph. D. dissertation, Northwestern University, 1968. All construction within the Aurelian walls is included, except things devoted exclusively to private, Christian or funereal use. The material is arranged in an index, plus a chronological commentary. Construction is related to changing social circumstances.

788. Lavin, Irving. "The Ceiling Frescoes in Trier and Illusionism in Constantinian Painting." *Dumbarton Oaks Papers* 21 (1967): 97-113. Important and beautiful frescoes from Trier dating c. 320 are the basis of Lavin's discussion of a renaissance of art in the early fourth century. Extensive illustrations.

789. **Lehmann, Karl.** "Sta. Costanza." *The Art Bulletin* 37 (1955): 193-196. A jewel of early fourth century architecture in Rome, generally associated with the Christianized Constantinian family because it was constructed on Imperial property and later became a mausoleum for two of Constantine's daughters, the church of Sta. Costanza is upon detailed investigation revealed by Lehmann as having been built originally as a pagan mausoleum.

790. **Lewis, S.** "Function and Symbolic Form in the Basilica Apostolorum." *Journal of the Society of Architectural Historians* 28 (1969): 83ff.

791. **Lewis, S.** "Problems of Architectural Style and the Ambrosian Liturgy in Late Fourth-Century Milan." In *Hortus Imaginum*, pp. 11ff. Edited by R. Enggass and M. Stokstad. Lawrence, Kansas, 1974.

792. **Lewis, S.** "San Lorenzo Revisited: A Theodosian Palace Church at Milan." *Journal of the Society of Architectural Historians* 32 (1973): 197ff.

793. **L'Orange, H. P.** *Art Forms and Civic Life in the Late Roman Empire.* Princeton, N. J.: Princeton University Press, 1965. Art mirrors social change. The author applies this dictum to the third century and beyond, and sees the chaos of the time before Diocletian and the new order of the fourth century reflected in art and architecture. Translated from the Norwegian edition of 1958. Richly illustrated in both this edition, and the complementary edition of 1985, *The Roman Empire: Art Forms and Civic Life.* R. A. Pack, *American Journal of Philology* 89 (1968): 121-122 (+).

794. **Lyman, Richard B., Jr.** "Barbarism and Religion: Late Roman and Early Medieval Childhood." In *The History of Childhood*, pp. 75-100. Edited by Lloyd de Mause. New York: Psychhistory Press, 1974. Lyman considers the period 200 to 800, but in fact finds himself mostly restricted to the late Roman period. The point of the essay is mostly to suggest

sources that can be used to do a proper history of childhood for the period.

795. MacCormack, Sabine G. *Art and Ceremony in Late Antiquity.* Transformation of the Classical Heritage, 1. Berkeley: University of California Press, 1981. The ceremonies of *adventus* (arrival), *consecratio* (death and heavenly assumption of the emperor), and accession: these are the three imperial events around which MacCormack organizes her involved but useful contemplation of the changing patterns of thought and life in the late empire, based on literary and artistic responses to the three ceremonies. G. M. Woloch, *Classical Journal* 80 (1985): 366-368 (++-); E. D. Hunt, *Classical Review* 33 (1983): 83-86 (+); T. E. Gregory, *American Historical Review* 87 (1982): 1373-1374 (++-); K. J. Shelton, *Classical Philology* 79 (1984): 259-264 (+--); J. Trilling, *Times Literary Supplement* (August 13, 1982): 884 (+-).

796. MacDonald, William L. *Early Christian and Byzantine Architecture.* New York: G. Braziller, 1962. Heavily Illustrated.

797. MacMullen, Ramsay. *Enemies of the Roman Order: Treason, Unrest, and Alienation in the Empire.* Cambridge, Mass.: Harvard University Press, 1967. During all of its long history the Roman state had its malcontents, and many of them. No one will ever be able to deny this after reading MacMullen's richly documented book. There is a good deal of valuable information on the late empire period. It will give the reader a better perspective to remember that MacMullen is not always clear about who was an enemy and who was merely different, and who wanted some changes but not wholesale revolution. O. Murray, *Journal of Roman Studies* 59 (1969): 261-265 (+-); P. A. Brunt, *English Historical Review* 84 (1969): 139-140 (--+); W. O. Moeller, *American Journal of Archaeology* 72 (1968): 87 (+-).

798. MacMullen, Ramsay. "Late Roman Slavery." *Historia* 36 (1987): 359-382. After a region by region survey of the later empire, MacMullen concludes that slavery, although highly visible in the cities and in Italy, was not so extensive in most parts of the empire as we might have supposed, and overall was of small consequence to the fundamental economic underpinnings of the state.

799. MacMullen, Ramsay. "Social History in Astrology." *Ancient History* 2 (1971): 105-116. MacMullen takes the writings of a fourth century astrologer and compares them with earlier writings to indicate changes in the social composition and dynamics of the later Roman empire. Perhaps the most startling change is in the importance of the central government in comparison with an earlier age when municipal government loomed in men's minds: "Nothing similar to Firmicus' emphasis on the style, size, and ubiquity of the central government can be found among earlier writers in the astrological tradition" (p. 115). MacMullen takes a moment at the end to remind us that non-traditional and perhaps slightly unorthodox primary sources such as this can counteract the distortions of more regular sources: "From literary writers, we learn only of an upperclass world that never heard of beggary; from the legislators in the law codes, we learn of a static world, fixing every man in an inherited home and condition. But clients resorted to Firmicus Maternus for a truer picture of the fourth-century empire" (p. 116).

800. MacMullen, Ramsay. "Social Mobility and the Theodosian Code." *Journal of Roman Studies* 54 (1964): 49-53. There was plenty of social mobility in the later empire, despite legal restrictions. Says MacMullen: "The *Code* certainly reveals what the emperors intended, but it should be used with great caution by anyone seeking to describe the realities of the time."

801. MacMullen, Ramsay. "Some Pictures in Ammianus Marcellinus." *Art Bulletin* 46 (1964): 435-455. MacMullen's article is not for those who will persist in seeing the later Roman empire as a depressing place, dark, dull, sorrowful, poor, divided by classes of people without common culture, common sympathies. In fact, says MacMullen, there was a unity of culture, a very theatrical culture, among the peoples of the empire, who from top to bottom of the social ladder embraced the Renaissance-like ambiance of the life of the age: colorful, costumed, jewelled, posed, noisy, exaggerated, ordered into rich pageants in which all had their parts and knew their lines. MacMullen culls Ammianus primarily, but many others too, for his information. There is at least one modern miniature parallel, actually derived in its theatrical aspects from the later empire, which may give the contemporary student a sense of the flavor of fourth century social ~~pression: a papal investiture.

802. Mango, Cyril. "The Development of Constantinople as an Urban Centre." In *The 17th International Byzantine Congress: Major Papers*, pp. 117-136. Dumbarton Oaks/Georgetown University, Washington, D. C., August 3-8, 1986. New Rochelle, N. Y.: A. D. Caratzas, 1986. Mango is heavily concerned with the fourth and early fifth centuries in this interesting look at the growth of the new imperial capital. We always hear what a wonderful site Byzantium was for a great city. Mango, very helpfully, takes the opportunity to show why it was not an ideal site in some respects, why it had been rejected (if ever considered) as an imperial capital before Constantine, and how Constantine took a "considerable risk" in trying the site, which of course in the end was a great success, thanks not only to some natural advantages but as well to "quite extraordinary exertions" by other fourth century emperors.

803. Mango, Cyril. "A Late Roman Inn in Eastern Turkey." *Oxford Journal of Archaeology* 5 (1986): 223-231.

804. Martindale, J. R. "Public Disorders in the Late Roman Empire, Their Causes and Character." B. Litt. thesis, Oxford University, 1961.

805. Matthews, John F. "Continuity in a Roman Family: The Rufii Festi of Volsinii." *Historia* 16 (1967): 484-509. Reprinted in his *Political Life and Culture in Late Roman Society*, Ch. VI. London: Variorum Reprints, 1985. Matthews takes a prominent Roman family and traces its

Society and Art 171

activities through the religious and political changes of the fourth and fifth centuries.

806. **Merriman, Joseph F.** "Aristocratic and Imperial Patronage of the Decorative Arts in Rome and Constantinople, A. D. 337-395: The Role of Sculpture, Painting, Mosaics, and the Minor Arts in the Fourth Century." Ph. D. dissertation, University of Illinois at Urbana-Champaign, 1975. Merriman stresses the basic cultural unity of the fourth century despite religious conflicts. The rich patrons of Old and New Rome participated in a certain rivalry, in which both teams displayed their wealth and the culture of their city through the decorative arts. The emperors participated in patronage in both cities, in such a way as to encourage local loyalties to the regime, but also to display their devotion to Greco-Roman civilization (with a Christian twist perhaps).

807. **Milburn, Robert L. P.** *Early Christian Art and Architecture.* Berkeley: University of California, 1988.

808. **Millar, Fergus.** "Condemnation to Hard Labour in the Roman Empire, from the Julio-Claudians to Constantine." *Papers of the British School at Rome* 52 (1984): 124-147.

809. **Murphy, Francis X.** "Melania the Elder, a Biographical Note." *Traditio* 5 (1947): 59-78. Melania the Elder was a fourth century Roman lady of wealth and distinction who gave up the traditional life of an aristocrat and found a virtual career in the church, where her independent spirit, talents, and wealth could all be put to use. She is an excellent example of the social fluidity of the fourth century for women as well as men, a phenomenon that gave the government such a headache. The rich as well as the poor were finding new roles in life, very often in the Christian church.

810. **Newbold, R. F.** "Boundaries and Bodies in Late Antiquity." *Arethusa* 12 (1979): 93-114. In an interesting exercise, Newbold compares early Roman with later Roman writers to find "that the circumstances of say, A. D. 340-420, created a general predisposition or tendency towards boundary

concern" (p. 107). Often this was expressed in terms of the human body. Newbold uses some rich examples, especially from Ammianus and Jerome.

811. Newbold, R. F. "Centre, Periphery, and Eye in the Late Roman Empire." *Florilegium* 3 (1981): 72-103. In a very involved article Newbold tries to analyze the expressions of tension in late Roman society deriving from the increased centralization, organization, and domination of the government, which while not entirely unwelcome in the presence of the difficult times represented by rapid political and cultural changes, nonetheless grated against the desire to be free, spontaneous, unconstrained, individualistic. Newbold's application of a kind of uptown psychoanalysis to the later Roman empire may not be to everyone's taste, but there are helpful insights awaiting the persistent reader.

812. Norman, A. F. "Gradations in Later Municipal Society." *Journal of Roman Studies* 48 (1958): 79-85. Norman discusses social stratification in the East in the fourth century, mostly through the eyes of the famous sophist of Antioch, Libanius.

813. Pack, Roger A. "Ammianus Marcellinus and the Curia of Antioch." *Classical Philology* 48 (1953): 80-85. Pack offers some more source material to be thrown "into the orbit of conjecture" on Ammianus' relation to the curial class in Antioch.

814. Pack, Roger A. "The Roman Digressions of Ammianus." *Transactions of the American Philological Association* 84 (1953): 181-189. Pack discusses Ammianus' satirical review of society in the city of Rome in the late fourth century.

815. Pack, Roger A. "Studies in Libanius and Antiochene Society under Theodosius." Ph. D. dissertation, University of Michigan, 1935.

816. **Painter, K. S.** "A Fourth Century Christian Silver Treasure Found at Water Newton." *Rivista di Archeologia Cristiana* 51 (1975): 333-345.

817. **Painter, K. S.** "The Mildenhall Treasure: A Reconsideration." *British Museum Quarterly* 37 (1973): 154-180.

818. **Painter, K. S.** *The Mildenhall Treasure: Roman Silver from East Anglia.* London: British Museum Publications, 1977.

819. **Painter, K. S.** *The Water Newton Early Christian Silver.* London: British Museum, 1977.

820. **Pond, Margret S.** "The Arch of Galerius: A Sculptural Record of the Age of the Tetrarchies." Ph. D. dissertation, University of Michigan, 1970.

821. **Pond Rothman, Margret S.** "The Panel of the Emperors Enthroned on the Arch of Galerius." *Byzantine Studies/ Etudes Byzantines* 2:1 (1975): 19-40.

822. **Pond Rothman, Margret S.** "The Thematic Organization of the Panel Reliefs on the Arch of Galerius." *American Journal of Archaeology* 81 (1977): 427-454. A thorough and illustrated discussion of the arch, built around 300 as part of the palace complex in Salonika, and still standing.

823. **Poulter, Andrew G.** "Roman Towns and the Problem of Late Roman Urbanism: The Case of the Lower Danube." *Hephaistos* (Hamburg) 5-6 (1983-1984): 109-132. Poulter raises questions on changes between Balkan towns in the later versus the earlier Roman period, and compares the later Balkan developments with urban developments at the same time in the western provinces.

824. **Riegl, Alois.** *Late Roman Art Industry.* Translated from the original Viennese edition with foreword and annotations

by R. Winkes. Archaeologica, 36. Rome: G. Bretschneider, 1985.

825. **Ross, Marvin C.** "Two Gem Carvings of the Fourth Century A. D." *American Journal of Archaeology* 61 (1957): 173-174. Miniature portraits of the Constantinian family. Includes illustrations.

826. **Rouselle, Aline.** *Porneia: On Desire and the Body in Late Antiquity.* Translated by Felicia Pheasant. New York: Basil Blackwell, 1988. Rouselle works with "the idea of tracing the way in which physcial beauty . . . , which was so important to the Greeks . . . , became such an intolerable obstacle to the accomplishment of God's will" (p. 1). The third and fourth centuries were a watershed in this transition of attitudes towards the body, its relation to other bodies, its social and political context. The material that Rouselle adduces to develop her theme will be of great interest and instruction to the student of the fourth century trying to come to grips with the phenomena of abstinence and of monasticism which flowered in the later part of the century.

827. **Ruether, Rosemary.** "Mothers of the Church: Ascetic Women in the Late Patristic Age." In *Women of Spirit: Female Leadership in the Jewish and Christian Traditions,* pp. 71-98. Edited by Rosemary Reuther and Eleanor McLaughlin. New York: Simon and Schuster, 1979. Asceticism as a liberating force for women in the fourth and fifth centuries.

828. **Ruggini, Lellia Cracco.** "Intolerance: Equal and Less Equal in the Roman World." *Classical Philology* 82 (1987): 187-205. Roman attitudes towards women, barbarians, Christians and Jews. A considerable part of the essay has to do with the fourth century, when attitudes were in a state of flux.

829. **Russell, Josiah C.** *The Control of Late Ancient and Medieval Population.* Philadelphia: American Philosophical Society, 1985. Covers the first through the fifteenth centuries. Various demographic features discussed, based on

the usual inadequate evidence. Z. Razi, *American Historical Review* 91 (1986): 369-370 (-).

830. Russell, Josiah C. *Late Ancient and Medieval Population.* Transactions of the American Philosophical Society, new ser., v.48, pt. 3. Philadelphia: The Society, 1958. We enter here the slippery science of population trends based upon scanty and usually indirect evidence. Russell is decent enough to give us lots of precautions. R. A. Newhall, *American Historical Society* 64 (1959): 345-346 (+); I. B. Taeuber, *American Journal of Sociology* 64 (1958-1959: 644 (+); S. L. Thrupp, *Speculum* 34 (1959): 509 (-).

831. St. Clair, Archer. "The Apotheosis Diptych." *Art Bulletin* 46 (1964): 205-211. This fifth century piece in the British Museum is Julian ascending into heaven. St. Clair supports the idea advanced by Klaus Wessel that it dates specifically to 431, the one hundredth anniversary of Julian's birth.

832. Shaw, Brent D. "The Family in Late Antiquity: The Experience of Augustine." *Past and Present* #115 (May 1987): 3-51. The fourth century part of Augustine's life is scrutinized to learn about the concept of family and the relationship of family members to each other in late Roman society. In his first footnote, Shaw lists as "forthcoming" another study entitled, "The Concept of Family in the Later Roman Empire: *Familia* and *Domus.*"

833. Shaw, Brent D. "Latin Funerary Epigraphy and Family Life in the Later Roman Empire." *Historia* 33 (1984): 457-497. Using tombstone inscriptions Shaw considers the general pattern of family life in the western empire after 300. He finds that the nuclear family was still at the heart of the social system, as it had been for centuries.

834. Sivan, Hagith S. "Who Was Egeria? Piety and Pilgrimage in the Age of Gratian." *Harvard Theological Review* 81 (1988): 59-72. Under Sivan, Egeria loses her traditional identity as a Spanish nun or aristocrat: "She is best perceived as a layperson, a member of a group of pious and devout women who decided to follow aristocratic precedents of pilgrimage to the East. Her undeniable affluence would point to a social class such as an urban bourgeoisie, for only urban wealth based on trade can plausibly account for what appears to be her contacts spread over the empire like a commercial network. Egeria serves as an example of the intensity of urban Christianity as well as of the spread of aristocratic fashions to other classes of society in late antiquity" (p. 72). Sivan speculates that Egeria was from a city along the Rhone, probably Arles.

835. Smith, D. J. "Three Fourth-Century Schools of Mosiac in Roman Britain." In *La Mosaique greco-romaine,* pp. 95-116. Colloque international organisee a Paris par G. Picard et H. Stern . . . , 1963. Paris, 1965.

836. Sperber, Daniel. "Patronage in Amoraic Palestine (c. 220-400): Causes and Effects." *Journal of the Economic and Social History of the Orient* 14 (1971): 227-252. Sperber advances Palestinian Rabbinic evidence to show the growth of large estates and the patronage system in the fourth century, and simultaneously the "rapidly diminishing area of land under Jewish ownership, and the rapidly dwindling numbers of Jews owning land" (p.252).

837. Stapleford, R. "Constantinian Politics and the Atrium Church." In *Art and Architecture in the Service of Politics,* pp. 2-18. Edited by H. A. Millon. Cambridge, Mass., 1979. "The Constantinian atrium in the final analysis must be seen to be an unexpected and eccentric choice, deriving from the iconography not of religious architecture but of imperial semipublic domestic architecture" (p. 17).

838. Thompson, E. A. "Ammianus Marcellinus and the Romans." *Greece and Rome* 11 (1941-1942): 130-134. Ammianus, whose active and sometimes dangerous military career on behalf of the Roman empire is sympathetically sketched, was shocked by the self-indulgent and narrow lifestyles of the rich and famous in the city of Rome, where he lived his last years. Thompson discusses the reasons behind this reaction to life in the imperial city.

839. Toynbee, J. M. C. "A New Roman Mosaic Pavement Found in Dorset." *Journal of Roman Studies* 54 (1964): 7-14. Fourth century pieces. Colored and black and white illustrations.

840. Toynbee, J. M. C. "Roma and Constantinopolis in Late Antique Art from 312 to 365." *Journal of Roman Studies* 37 (1947): 135-144. "The aim of this paper has been to trace the historical sequence and development of Roma and Constantinopolis types in the art of the middle decades of the fourth century" (p. 144). Illustrated.

841. Toynbee, J. M. C. "Roma and Constantinopolis in Late Antique Art from 365-Justin II." In *Studies Presented to David M. Robinson,* pp. 261-277. Edited by George E. Mylonas. Saint Louis: Washington University, 1953.

842. Van Dam, Raymond. *Leadership and Community in Late Antique Gaul.* Berkeley: University of California Press, 1985. The imperial presence, the local aristocrats, the Christian bishops, the Bagaudae, Priscillianism, Martin of Tours: all these and more of the traditionally discussed leading types of fourth century Gaul (and later) are reviewed in new and interesting ways. The Bagaudae, for instance, rather than seen as peasant bandits, are identified as men rallying together around local leaders for defense. S. Benko, *American Historical Review* 91 (1986): 367-368 (+); J. Harries, *Journal of Roman Studies* 76 (1986): 290-291 (+).

843. Van Sickle, C. E. "The Public Works of Africa in the Reign of Diocletian." *Classical Philology* 25 (1930): 173-179. Van Sickle reviews the building or re-building activities of the age of Diocletian to show that there was still wealth and a sense of civic pride in the cities, and that the central government encouraged and participated in useful projects such as road construction and the restoration of public buildings. The evidence in Africa suggests a Diocletian interested in the restoration of Roman civilization after the chaotic events of the third century, rather than the extravagent and selfish tyrant portrayed by Lactantius.

844. **Vickers, Michael.** "The Hippodrome at Thessaloniki." *Journal of Roman Studies* 62 (1972): 25-32. An investigation of the site of the infamous slaughter of thousands in 390 upon orders of the emperor Theodosius.

845. **Vickers, Michael.** "Observations on the Octagon at Thessaloniki." *Journal of Roman Studies* 63 (1973): 111-120. Part of an early fourth century imperial palace is discussed. Illustrated.

846. **Ward-Perkins, John B.** "Constantine and the Origins of the Christian Basilica." *Papers of the British School at Rome* 22 (1954): 69-90. After an interesting survey of the pagan origins of the basilica, Ward-Perkins goes on to find the immediate inspiration for the fourth century Christian basilica, so many of them sponsored by Constantine, in the "ceremonial halls of contemporary Court life " (p. 87). This would not of course rule out the less direct influence of earlier public basilicas, whose architectural style was more sympathetic to the requirements of Christian services than pagan temples.

847. **Ward-Perkins, J. Bryan.** *From Classical Antiquity to the Middle Ages: Urban Public Building in Northern and Central Italy AD 300-850.* New York: Oxford University Press, 1984. Private money largely dried up after 300 for the building and repair of public buildings. This money went for other purposes. The government, whether local or central, stepped in to fill the gap. And much private money still went for churches. In the fourth century the great monuments of antiquity were largely preserved in one way or another. From there the story becomes sadder and sadder as conditions deteriorated and needs changed in the society of Italy. Ward-Perkins documents the unhappy tale. K. McCulloch, *History Today* 35 (December 1985): 55-57 (+).

848. Weitzmann, Kurt, ed. *Age of Spirituality: Late Antique and Early Christian Art, Third to Seventh Century.* Catalog of the exhibition at the Metropolitan Museum of Art, November 19, 1977-February 12, 1978. Princeton, N. J.: Princeton University Press, 1980. Includes introductory essays, as well as the excellent illustrations of the exhibition pieces. See also the related volume of essays edited by Weitzmann entitled *Age of Spirituality: A Symposium.* R. M. Grant, *Journal of Religion* 61 (1981): 125-126 (+).

849. Weitzmann, Kurt. "Book Illustration of the Fourth Century. Tradition and Innovation." In *Akten des VII. Internationalen Kongresses fur Christliche Archaologie* (Trier, 1965), pp. 257-281. Vatican: Pontificio Instituto de Archeologia Cristiana, 1969.

850. Wightman, Edith. "Peasants and Potentates in Roman Gaul." *American Journal of Ancient History* 3 (1978): 97-128. Wightman surveys the whole history of Gaul, lingering on the late Roman period, to argue "that there is a strong unbroken thread between Gaul of the late Iron Age and the early Middle Ages, and that modified continuity rather than radical transformation is the key-note of agrarian society, and particularly of the relationship between peasants and potentates" (p. 117).

851. Wild, J. P. "Fourth Century Underwear with Special Reference to the *Toracomachus*." In *De Rebus Bellicis,* pp. 105-110. Edited by M. W. C. Hassall and R. I. Ireland. Oxford: British Archaeological Reports, 1979. The discussion reviews mostly military clothing. There is a reminder of one of the most irritating problems of ancient life: lice.

852. Wilson-Kastner, Patricia. "Egeria: Account of Her Pilgrimage." In *A Lost Tradition: Women Writers of the Early Church*, pp. 71-135. Edited by Patricia Wilson-Kastner. Washington, D. C.: University Press of America, 1981. Wilson-Kastner provides an interesting essay on Egeria and her travels, followed by a translation of Egeria's journal. She

describes the translation as a compromise between a very literal rendering and a free translation.

853. Wolff, Hans J. "Doctrinal Trends in Postclassical Roman Marriage Laws." *Zeitschrift der Savigny-Stiftung fuer Rechtsgeschichte, Romanistische Abteilung* 67 (1950): 261-319. This essay is heavy going, but for those who wish to get a sense of the direction of thought in late Roman times regarding marriage and divorce, it is important. Specifically, Wolff offers a good deal of information concerning the influence of Christianity on classical theoretical approaches to marriage and divorce. In the course of the essay, Wolff has occasion to advance and pass judgment on the views of modern European scholars. His conclusion: "The institution of marriage thus emerges as one of those which in the postclassical period were subject to deep external changes due to outside influences, but which never lost their true Roman character as far as their doctrinal foundations were concerned" (p. 319).

VIII. Foreign Affairs and Barbarians

Includes barbarians living inside and outside the empire.

854. **Abbott, Donald R.** "Germanic Attitudes Toward the Roman Empire." M. A. thesis, San Diego State University, 1978. "The thesis concludes that the Germans who served the Empire in the fourth century sought many things Roman: citizenship, military commands, and social recognition. They were almost all loyal. Rather than condemning them as unsuccessful predecessors of the destroyers of Rome, we should recognize them as very successful Roman soldiers, officers and statesmen" (p. 96)

855. **Alonso-Nunez, J. M.** "Roman Knowledge of Scandinavia in the Imperial Period." *Oxford Journal of Archaeology* 7 (1988): 47-64. From the summary: "This paper aims to provide a framework of literary evidence as a basis for study of the relations between the Roman Empire and Scandinavia from an archaeological point of view. It covers from Augustus to the end of the fourth century."

856. **Bachrach, B. S.** *A History of the Alans in the West: From Their First Appearance in the Sources of Classical Antiquity Through the Early Middle Ages.* Minnesota Monographs in the Humanities, 7. Minneapolis: University of Minneapolis Press, 1973. The Alans ended up in Africa with the Vandals, but in the fourth century they were in the steppes east of the Don. Ammianus Marcellinus wrote of them. E. A. Thompson, *Journal of Roman Studies* 65 (1975): 205 (+).

857. **Banchich, Thomas M.** "An Identification in the Suda: Eunapius on the Huns." *Classical Philology* 83 (1988): 53.

858. **Barnes, Timothy D.** "Constantine and the Christians of Persia." *Journal of Roman Studies* 75 (1985): 126-136. Barnes adduces seldom used source material to show that at the time of his death Constantine was preparing to invade Persia to liberate the Christians there, who expected him to be successful. Constantine's successor Constantius II had little luck in the Persian wars, and all Persian Christians got was persecution by Shapur, their king.

859. **Bartholomew, Philip.** "Fourth-Century Saxons." *Britannia* 15 (1984): 169-185. There is no evidence for Saxon invasions of Britain in the fourth century, and the expression "Saxon shore" may refer to where Saxons first settled rather than where they invaded.

860. **Baynes, Norman H.** "Rome and Armenia in the Fourth Century." *English Historical Review* 25 (1910): 625-643. Reprinted in his *Byzantine Studies and Other Essays*, pp. 186-208. London: Athlone Press, 1955; Westport, Conn.: Greenwood Press, 1974. Baynes here looks at "the chronology and the historical value of the work of Faustus of Byzantium," and attempts "to estimate his contribution to our knowledge of Roman history in the fourth century" (p. 186 BSOE). Baynes finds Faustus very helpful in illuminating Roman problems on the eastern frontier and in corroborating much of the material in Ammianus.

861. **Bichir, G.** *Archaeology and History of the Carpi from the Second to the Fourth Century A. D.* Rev. ed. Translated by N. Hampartumian. British Archaeological Reports, suppl. ser., 16. Oxford: B. A. R., 1976.

862. **Blockley, Roger C.** "The Division of Armenia between the Romans and the Persians at the End of the Fourth Century A. D." *Historia* 36 (1878): 222-234. Blockley sees a prolonged process in the division of Armenia, lasting from 363 to well into the fifth century, and involving the participation of the Armenian leaders themselves. A watershed event was a treaty of 387 by which two kings were permitted

in Armenia, one loyal to the Romans and another loyal to the Persians. The complexity of Armenian politics and the usual difficulties with the primary sources make Blockley's task of disentanglement trying indeed, but the resulting thesis offers at least the hope of approaching resolution to a perennial issue in late Roman studies.

863. **Blockley, Roger C.** "The Romano-Persian Peace Treaties of AD 299 and 363." *Florilegium* 6 (1984): 28-49. In 299, the Romans had the advantage; in 363, the Persians did. Nevertheless, there was a tacit understanding that neither party could totally predominate, and Blockley sees the treaties as "instruments in this developing search for accommodation . . ." (p. 38). Blockley also sees here the beginnnings of "byzantine" diplomacy.

864. **Blockley, Roger C.** "Subsidies and Diplomacy: Rome and Persia in Late Antiquity." *Phoenix* 39 (1985): 62-74. There is some fourth century material here; most of it, however, relates to the fifth and sixth centuries.

865. **Brady, Caroline.** *The Legends of Ermanaric.* Berkeley: University of California Press, 1943. This Ermanaric was in fact a great Gothic king of the mid-fourth century who in the 370s unsuccessfully faced the challenge of the Huns to his territories. There is an account in Ammianus, another in Jordanes. Brady discusses the extraordinary legends which in later centuries grew up among the Nordic and Germanic peoples about this king.

866. **Brennan, Peter.** "Diocletian and the Goths." *Phoenix* 38 (1984): 142-146. In the context of a discussion of whether Diocletian ever assumed the title Gothicus, Brennan discovers that relations with the Gothic authorities were generally very good in Diocletian's time.

867. **Bullough, Vern L.** "The Roman Empire vs. Persia, 362-502: A Study of Successful Deterrence." *Journal of Conflict Resolution* 7 (1963): 55-63. How the Persians and the Romans avoided total war with each other, knowing that

they could not destroy each other, and that each had barbarian enemies requiring constant vigilance.

868. Burns, Thomas S. "The Barbarians and the *Scriptores Historiae Augustae*." In *Studies in Latin Literature and Roman History*, pp. 521-540. Vol I. Edited by Carl Deroux. Brussels: Latomus, 1979.

869. Burns, Thomas S. "The Germans and Roman Frontier Policy (ca. A. D. 350-378)." *Acta Archaeologica* [Arkeoloski Vestnik. Ljubljana, Academie slovene] 32 (1981): 390-404. Constantius II and his successors understood what they were facing across the Rhine and Danube; hence the great fortifications programs and the brutal campaigns against barbarian tribes. But the barbarians "responded to increasing Roman pressure by increased cohesion." The better organized and more co-operative tribes had their day at Adrianople, which ended the Roman policy of defense through raids and promiscuous slaughter.

870. Burns, Thomas S. *A History of the Ostrogoths*. Bloomington: Indiana University Press, 1984. J. H. W. G. Liebeschuetz, *Classical Review* 36 (1986): 158-159 (+-); B. S. Bachrach, *Speculum* 62 (1987): 112-115 (-).

871. Burns, Thomas S. *The Ostrogoths: Kingship and Society*. Wiesbaden: Franz Steiner, 1980. Ostrogothic society from the third to the sixth centuries. C. Morton, *Speculum* 56 (1981): 924-925 (+).

872. Daly, Lawrence J. "The Mandarin and the Barbarian: The Response of Themistius to the Gothic Challenge." *Historia* 21 (1972): 351-379. Themistius belonged to what we would now call the pacifist camp. But he had his reasons, and he seriously sought a program that would accommodate the barbarian tribes to a place in the Roman world, with the emperor as the revered leader of all. It was a noble vision to plan an end to all the expensive wars which cost so much to Romans and barbarians generation after generation. In the wake of Adrianople in 378, the question of settling the problems between Goths and Romans took on a particular urgency, and in this setting the Themistian plan took on its greatest appeal. Daly traces the whole story.

873. **Diesner, Hans-Joachim.** *The Great Migration: The Movement of Peoples Across Europe, AD 300-700.* Translated by C. S. V. Salt and B. A. Hons. Leipzig: Edition Leipzig, 1978. This is a very fine coffee table book whose illustrations are more to be commended than some of the broad generalizations of the text on the fourth century.

874. **Geary, Patrick J.** *Before France and Germany: The Creation and Transformation of the Merovingian World.* New York: Oxford University Press, 1988. See Chapters I and II for a useful survey of the barbarian tribes as a part of the Roman world over a period of centuries, with an emphasis on the late empire period when a definition of the barbarian place in the Roman world was especially insistent. The overwhelming importance of Rome in the making of the barbarian world is a constant theme: "The Germanic world was perhaps the greatest and most enduring creation of Roman political and military genius. That this offspring came in time to replace its creator should not obscure that fact that it owed its very existence to Roman initiative, to the patient efforts of centuries of Roman emperors, generals, soldiers, landlords, slave traders, and simple merchants to mold the (to Roman eyes) chaos of barbarian reality into forms of political, social, and economic activity which they could understand and, perhaps, control" (p. vi).

875. **Goffart, Walter.** *Barbarians and Romans, A. D. 418-584: The Techniques of Accommodation.* Princeton, N. J.: Princeton University Press, 1980. Goffart's book, having to do with his thesis that barbarian settlers were given rights to collect taxes rather than given land directly, deals mostly with events well beyond the fourth century; however, there is a fascinating first chapter which explores the initiative of the Roman government (and the reasons for the initiative) in bringing barbarian groups within the orbit of Roman life, politically and militarily. "When set in a fourth-century

perspective, what we call the Fall of the Western Empire was an imaginative experiment that got a little out of hand" (p. 35). W. E. Kaegi, *American Historical Review* 87 (1982): 432 (+-); E. James, *Speculum* 57 (1982): 885-886 (+).

876. Gray, E. W. "The Roman Eastern Limes from Constantine to Justinian - Perspectives and Problems." *Proceedings of the African Classical Association* 12 (1973): 24-40. The eastern frontier with Persia was remarkably stable during the later empire. Gray considers the many forces inside and outside both empires which combined to make this so.

877. Heather, P. J. "The Anti-Scythian Tirade of Synesius' *De Regno*." *Phoenix* 42 (1988): 152-172. "The anti-Scythian passages of *De Regno* may . . . contain some reference to Tribigild [a Gothic commander stationed in Asia Minor], but their main thrust is to argue that Alaric's Goths should be expelled from their privileged position within the East Roman state" (p. 154). Synesius was attached to a hardline political faction in Constantinople for whose Gothic policy he was a spokesman. Their concern, however, was not all Gothic groups, but largely the semi-independent ones given autonomous status by Theodosius in 382. This faction prevailed in Constantinople and in 401 Alaric moved his people west into Italy to try his luck there in finding a home and position for his people in the western Roman world.

878. Heather, Peter. "The Crossing of the Danube and the Gothic Conversion." *Greek, Roman, and Byzantine Studies* 27 (1986): 289-318. "It will be argued here that the primary accounts found in Socrates, Sozomen, and Eunapius can be reconciled with the secondary ones of Jordanes, Theodoret, and Orosius to suggest a Gothic conversion in 376. Further, combined with Ammianus, they strongly indicate that Christianity initially affected only elements of one Gothic group, the Tervingi, and was part of the agreement by which Valens allowed them to cross the Danube and enter the Empire in 376" (p. 289).

879. **Hewsen, R. H.** "The Successors of Tiridates the Great: A Constribution to the History of Armenia in the Fourth Century." *Revue des Etudes Armeniennes* 13 (1978-1979): 99-126.

880. **Hind, J. G. F.** "Who Betrayed Britain to the Barbarians in A. D. 367?" *Northern History* 19 (1983): 1-7.

881. **Ladner, Gerhart B.** "On Roman Attitudes Toward Barbarians in Late Antiquity." *Viator* 7 (1976): 1-26. Ambivalence is finally the only term to describe Roman attitudes toward the barbarians, who were at once attractive and repellent, useful and dangerous, to Romans and the Roman state. The one consistent thing is that the Romans wanted to treat barbarians always on Roman terms: in whatever way the barbarians were to have a part in the Roman world (and there was a general acceptance that they had a part to play), the Romans would by natural superiority make the principal arrangements and expect barbarian co-operation or acquiescence. Never was it thought that barbarians could run the show. Even the barbarians did not often presume to think this, though they were often successful at forcing the Romans to re-think the relationship. Ladner emphasizes the fourth century, when the Germanophobe and Germanophile factions kept the characteristic ambivalence of the Roman state at its height.

882. **Levi, Annalina C.** *Barbarians on Roman Imperial Coins and Sculpture.* Numismatic Notes and Monographs, 123. New York: American Numismatic Society, 1952. Interesting survey of coin types from Augustus through the fourth century which show barbarians. The relation of coin motifs to contemporary sculpture is considered. Good illustrations.

883. **MacMullen, Ramsay.** "Barbarian Enclaves in the Northern Roman Empire." *l'Antiquite Classique* 32 (1963): 552-561. The author provides a select catalog of barbarian groupings permitted to live in the empire, where they were to settle down, be useful (as farmers or soldiers), and pay taxes. MacMullen cites fourth century examples, but many before that

too. Such settlements were a traditional feature of Roman policy, long before the great Visigoth settlement after Adrianople; but the ones after the time of, say, Gallienus did present problems of assimilation. The cultural absorption of large coherent groups was difficult. Beyond that, MacMullen also sees that Roman cultural superiority was considerably diminished anyway in the northern provinces.

884. Maenchen-Helfen, Otto J. *The World of the Huns: Studies in Their History and Culture.* Edited by Max Knight. Berkeley: University of California Press, 1973. The full power of the Huns was impressed upon the Romans in the fifth century, but they were known in the late fourth, when Ammianus described them. Maenchen-Helfen gives the fullest account available, with not a little incidental information on the Romans and other barbarians in the late fourth century and beyond. D. Fishwick, *American Historical Review* 80 (1975): 390-391 (+); W. H. McNeill, *Church History* 43 (1974): 269 (+); W. Trousdale, *Speculum* 51 (1976): 763-766 (+).

885. Mann, J. C. "The Northern Frontier After A. D. 369." *Glasgow Archaeological Journal* 3 (1974): 34-42. In fact this is a useful summary of Rome's relations with the peoples of Scotland during the imperial period, with an emphasis on the fourth century.

886. Millar, Fergus. "Emperors, Frontiers, and Foreign Relations, 31 B. C. to A. D. 378." *Britannia* 13 (1982): 1-23. The limitations in the ancient world for gathering useful intelligence in a timely fashion about foreign lands and peoples is discussed. Some examples from the fourth century are helpful in trying to understand events. In the 360s, the Goths were not taken seriously as a great force, and nothing was known of the Huns. The Persians were considered the important danger. No doubt in general the Romans were light years ahead of others in knowing their enemies, and especially in the strategy of playing them off against one another. Still, they knew too little to be able accurately to anticipate from whence might come their greatest danger in the 370s.

887. **Okamura, Lawrence.** "*Allemannia Devicta:* Roman-German Conflicts from Caracalla to the First Tetrarchy (A. D. 213-305)." 2 vols. Ph. D. dissertation, University of Michigan at Ann Arbor, 1984.

888. **Richmond, Ian A.** "Roman and Native in the Fourth Century A. D. and After." In *Roman and Native in Northern Britain*, pp. 112-130. Edited by I. A. Richmond. Edinburgh and London: Nelson, 1958.   Richmond narrates Britains problems with barbarians. There is of course an emphasis on military events.

889. **Rubin, Zeev.** "The Conversion of the Visigoths to Christianity." *Museum Helveticum* 38 (1981): 34-54. This piece is an effort to restore the traditional dating of the conversion of the Visigoths to Christianity in the 370s, in response to E. A. Thompson's (891) effort to move the date up to the 380s or 390s.

890. **Shahid, Irfan.** *Byzantium and the Arabs in the Fourth Century.* Washington, D. C.: Dumbarton Oaks, 1984. It is unlikely that there will be a more exhaustive study in English of the relations of Arabs and Romans in the fourth century. Shahid takes the view that the Romans conferred a federate status upon Christianized Arab tribes early in the fourth century. The traditional view is that federate status came much later in the century. There is a complementary volume called *Rome and the Arabs: A Prologomenon to the Study of Byzantium and the Arabs,* which came out in the same year. For a thorough discussion of both, see G. W. Bowersock, "Byzantium and the Arabs," *Classical Review* 36 (1986): 111-117.

891. **Thompson, E. A.** "The Date of the Conversion of the Visigoths." *Journal of Ecclesiastical History* 7 (1956): 1-11. Thompson proposes that the Visigoths were converted to Christianity between 382 and 395, when they were already permanently settled in the Roman empire, rather than before, which is the more common view, for an example of which see Rubin (889).

892. Thompson, E. A. *The Early Germans.* Oxford: Clarendon Press, 1965.   Chapter 4, "Early Germanic Warfare," is especially good at sizing up the disadvantages that the Germans faced when conducting war against the empire. There are many references to late empire incidents.

893. Thompson, E. A. "The Passio S. Sabae and Early Visigothic Society." *Historia* 4 (1955): 331-338.   Thompson looks at the *Passio*, which commemorates the life of Saint Sabas who was martyred in Gothia in 372, as a source of information on the structure of Visigothic social organization in the middle of the fourth century.

894. Thompson, E. A. "The Visigoths from Fritigern to Euric." *Historia* 12 (1963): 105-126.   Reprinted in his *Romans and Barbarians: The Decline of the Western Empire*, pp. 38-57. Madison: University of Wisconsin, 1982.   Although most of the article concerns events of the fifth century, the first pages from 376 to the death of Theodosius in 395 and the election of Alaric as the leader of the Visigoths in the same year, are helpful towards an understanding of the profound dilemma facing the barbarians after their victory at Adrianople in 378. In the late fourth century they were neither strong enough as a military force or as a society to bring down or absorb the Roman empire, nor were they weak enough to be defeated and absorbed by the Romans. And the Goths, or at least their leaders, were not at all sure what they wanted from the Roman state anyway. There are some enlightening paragraphs on the phenomenon of Gothic "deserters" to the Roman cause. They were ready to be Romans, but on top of being rejected by the barbarians they were not entirely accepted among the Romans, who mostly used them to fight brigands and other barbarians.

895. Thompson, E. A. *The Visigoths in the Time of Ulfila.* Oxford: Clarendon Press, 1966.   In this important work, to a large extent a compilation of earlier studies, Thompson considers the changes that Visigothic society underwent in the fourth century, and how Christianity made its most successful inroads late in the century when that society was most fragmented and when the Goths were firmly in the orbit of Roman cultural influence. J. M. Wallace-Hadrill, *English Historical Review* 83 (1968): 146-147 (+-); P. R. L. Brown, *History* 54 (1969): 79-80 (+).

896. Todd, Malcolm. *The Everyday Life of the Barbarians: Goths, Franks and Vandals.* London: Batsford, 1972. Reprint ed., 1980, entitled *The Barbarians: Goths, Franks and Vandals.* Strong use of archaeology as well literary sources on the German tribes. Todd covers a lot of time in a generalized way, but there is a good deal that is relevant to the fourth century. *Times Literary Supplement* (May 7, 1973): 506 (-); *Irish Historical Studies* 18 (1972-1973): 640; *Kirkus Reviews* 41 (March 1, 1973): 263.

897. Tomlin, Roger. "The Date of the 'Barbarian Conspiracy.'" *Britannia* 5 (1974): 303-309. Tomlin reconstructs the chronology of events relating to the barbarian invasion of Britain in 367, and the successful response of the Roman government under Valentinian I.

898. Vasiliev, Alexander A. *The Goths in the Crimea.* Cambridge, Mass.: Medieval Academy of America, 1936. Vasiliev takes the story, or rather the stories since there can be no continuous narrative in the absence of source material for most of the time, to the end of the fifteenth century. There is some fourth century material about these peripheral Goths who were separated from the main body of Goths during the troubles with the Huns in the fourth and fifth centuries. E. H. Minns, *English Historical Review* 52 (1937): 687-690 (+); W, Miller, *History* 22 (1937): 255-256 (+).

899. Wiedemann, T. E. J. "Between Men and Beasts: Barbarians in Ammianus Marcellinus." In *Past Perspectives: Studies in Greek and Roman Historical Writing*, pp. 189-201. Papers presented at a conference in Leeds, 6-8 April 1983. Edited by I. S. Moxon, J. D. Smart, and A. J. Woodman. New York: Cambridge University Press, 1986. Ammianus followed ancient stereotypes in describing barbarians, but he did not mean to give literal descriptions, nor was he trying for serious ethnography. Indeed, he was not slow to use animal metaphors in describing Romans too. Apparently his standard was to apply stock phrases of the ancient world in describing barbarians to anyone or any group, whether German tribes or Roman Senators, who fell below the standards of civilized behavior.

900. Wolfram, Herwig. "Athanaric the Visigoth: Monarchy or Judgeship. A Study in Comparative History." *Journal of Medieval History* 1 (1975): 259-278. In the complex effort to disentangle issues of Gothic constitutional arrangements, Wolfram dispenses a pot pourri of interesting information about fourth century Gothia.

901. Wolfram, Herwig. "Gothic History and Historical Ethnography." *Journal of Medieval History* 7 (1981): 309-319. In an effort to sweep away historical misconceptions, Wolfram uses the approach of historical ethnography ("because it belongs to the domain of historians who work with the historical methods of source criticism and comparison" (p. 317)) to understand the nature and characteristics of the Gothic tribes in late antiquity.

902. Wolfram, Herwig. *History of the Goths.* Translated by Thomas J. Dunlap. Berkeley: University of California Press, 1987. This is THE book for the modern student to consult on the Goths. Wolfram emphasizes, and wisely, the extent to which we see the barbarian tribes as the Romans did, and, more importantly, the extent to which the Goths themselves depended upon the Romans to give them an identification and a place in history. We see them through a mirror darkly, a Roman mirror (which was often the mirror through which they saw themselves, especially as they became involved in Roman affairs), and we can never see them face to face. Nevertheless, Wolfram advances, compares, and weighs all sorts and conditions of evidence to give us a balanced portrait. The fourth century, a critical time in the relations of Romans and Goths, is heavily covered. There is much wisdom on Adrianople and its consequences. Sometimes Wolfram is a complex read, perhaps reflecting the attempt to be so thorough, but persistence will pay off handsomely.

IX. Religion and Philosophy

Includes the religions and philosophies of the Roman world, generally and specifically. Christianity, however, is included here only to the extent of its relations with the other religions and philosophies. For the rest of the story on the Christian movement, see "Christianity," and "Church and State." In Roman eyes, the Jews were often seen as a religious community or nation, rather than as an ethnic block like the Goths, so all aspects of the Jewish experience are filed here. This section also includes magic and the occult generally.

903. **Adler, M.** "The Emperor Julian and the Jews." *Jewish Quarterly Review* 5 (1893): 591-651.

904. **Alfoldi, Andras.** *A Festival of Isis under the Christian Emperors of the Fourth Century.* Budapest: Institute of Numismatics and Archaeology of the Pazmany University, 1937. Alfoldi first discusses late Roman coinage with pagan and especially Egyptian pagan references; then he follows with a look at the political importance of the Isis cult among the pagan nobles of Rome at the end of the fourth century. T. A. Brady, *Journal of Roman Studies* 28 (1938): 88-90 (+).

905. **Allberry, C. R. C.,** ed. *A Manichaean Psalm Book.* Part II. Stuttgart: W. Kohlhammer, 1938. Text and English translation on opposite pages.

906. **Armstrong, A. Hilary.** *Expectations of Immortality in Late Antiquity.* Milwaukee: Marquette University Press, 1987. Armstrong goes into what he rightly calls a "very misty area": the extent to which belief in after-life affected

Religion and Philosophy 195

performance and attitudes in this life in the later Roman empire.

907. Armstrong, A. Hilary. "Man in the Cosmos: A Study of Some Differences between Pagan Neoplatonism and Christianity." In *Romanitas et Christianitas: Studies in Honor of Jan Wazink*, pp. 5-13. Edited by William den Boer, etc. Amsterdam: North Holland Publishing Co., 1973. A remarkably succinct and illuminating discussion of profound differences between the outlook of the Neoplatonists (represented here by Plotinus) and Christianity (especially the post-Nicene variety), centering on a feature of Christianity which Plotinus disliked very much: extreme anthropocentrism.

908. Armstrong, A. Hilary. "The Way and the Ways. Religious Tolerance and Intolerance in the Fourth Century." *Vigiliae Christianae* 38 (1984): 1-17. Reprinted in *"To See Ourselves as Others See Us": Christians, Jews, "Others" in Late Antiquity*, pp. 357-372. Edited by J. Neusner and E. S. Frerichs. Chico, Ca.: Scholars Press, 1985. Armstrong reviews the fourth century to show that intolerance and proscription were not the inevitable results of religious squabbling, and that there were many Christians who had no interest in persecuting non-believers or heretics. Nevertheless, at the end of the century the final choice was made, and the Theodosian policy of intolerant state religion echoed through the history of Christian Europe, one of the less palatable legacies of the fourth century.

909. Askwith, Dora. "The Toleration and Persecution of the Jews in the Roman Empire." Ph. D. dissertation, Columbia University, 1915.

910. Bachrach, Bernard S. "The Jewish Community of the Later Roman Empire as Seen in the *Codex Theodosianus*." In *"To See Ourselves as Others See Us": Christians, Jews, "Others" in Late Antiquity*, pp. 399-421. Chico, Ca.: Scholars Press, 1985. Despite hostile rhetoric, the Roman government of the fourth and fifth centuries in fact respected the traditional rights and privileges on the Jews within the empire. Bachrach says this had more to do with a healthy respect for the Jews "as an aggressive, well organized, wealthy, and powerful minority" (p. 408) than with Roman respect for traditional policy. After an interesting review of incidents involving government relations with the Jews, Bachrach concludes that "an anti-Jewish policy was not pursued . . . because the imperial government had a sound understanding of political realities. It saw the potential cost, in terms of social dislocation, economic decline, and military conflict, that the Jewish *gens* could impose if it were attacked" (p. 421).

911. Barb, A. A. "The Survival of Magic Arts." In *The Conflict Between Christianity and Paganism in the Fourth Century,* pp. 100-125. Edited by A. Momigliano. New York: Oxford University Press, 1963. In the magic arts of the fourth century, Barb smells "the syncretistic, rotting refuse-heap of the dead and dying religions of the whole ancient world . . . " (p. 104).

912. Barnes, Timothy D. "Constantine's Prohibition of Pagan Sacrifice." *American Journal of Philology* 105 (Spring 1984): 69-72. In a little controversy with H. A. Drake, Barnes reaffirms his position that Constantine prohibited pagan sacrifices.

913. Barnes, Timothy D. "A Correspondent of Iamblichus." *Greek, Roman and Byzantine Studies* 19 (1978): 99-106. Barnes reconsiders some letters written to the philosopher Iamblichus, and concludes they were written between 314 and 319 by a correspondent associated with the court of Licinius. Barnes discusses the information that the letters reveal about the philosopher and events of the time.

914. Barnes, Timothy D. "Porphyry *Against the Christians:* Date and Attribution of the Fragments." *Journal of Theological Studies* 24 (1973): 414-424. Is there a link between Porphyry's anti-Christian tract and Diocletian's persecution of the Christians? Maybe, if the tract was published in the appropriate time-frame, and Barnes thinks it was.

915. Bell, Harold I., ed. *Jews and Christians in Egypt: The Jewish Troubles in Alexandria and the Athanasian Controversy.* London, 1924; Westport, Conn.: Greenwood Press, 1972. Translations with commentary of important documents from the sands of Egypt: letters relating to the Meletian schism which started during the persecutions by Diocletian, and relating to asceticism in the middle of the fourth century.

916. Bloch, Herbert. "A New Document of the Last Pagan Revival in the West, A. D. 393-394." *Harvard Theological Review* 38 (1945): 199-244. An inscription dating to 393, during the time of the usurper Eugenius, commemorating the restoration of a pagan temple of Hercules in Ostia, is the impetus for an important discussion of the fortunes and misfortunes of the effort by senatorial leaders to restore or at least salvage some part of the power and dignity of the ancient cults.

917. Bloch, Herbert. "The Pagan Revival in the West at the End of the Fourth Century." In *The Conflict between Paganism and Christianity*, pp. 193-218. Edited by Arnaldo Momigliano. New York: Oxford University Press, 1963. Bloch discusses the hopes and realities of the pagan cause, led by the aristocrats of Rome. In the end, the gods gave way to the Christian movement, but one activity of cultured pagan senators was of inestimable value and did survive: their conscious effort to preserve and protect Latin literature.

918. Bonner, Campbell. "Witchcraft in the Lecture-Room of Libanius." *Transactions of the American Philological Society* 63 (1932): 34-44. There was witchcraft in late fourth century Antioch. Bonner advances the evidence. From there he leaps to the excessive conclusion that "the fourth century was darkened by the most degrading of superstitions in a manner that can only be compared to . . . the later Middle Ages" (p. 44). The ancient world in fact was always riddled with what we might call superstition, and it is unlikely that things were much worse in the fourth century than earlier.

919. Bonner, G. "The Extinction of Paganism and the Church Historian." *Journal of Ecclesiastical History* 35 (1984): 339-357. There were not just Christians and pagans in the fourth century, says Bonner. There were also pagan Christians (who were within the church but carried a lot of pagan baggage with them), and semi-Christians (not members but sympathizers), and these groups tipped the balance in the inevitable triumph of the church, which took on some very pagan characteristics in this evolutionary process.

920. Brown, Peter. "The Diffusion of Manichaeism in the Late Roman Empire." *Journal of Roman Studies* 59 (1969): 92-103. Reprinted in his *Religion and Society in the Age of Saint Augustine*, pp. 94-118. New York: Harper and Row, 1972. Manichaeism was a missionary religion whose diffusion in the Roman state was arrested by the end of the fourth century. Its association with Persia was unhelpful, but not fatal. The times were against it. "To study Manichaeism is to study the fate of a missionary religion in a world of shrinking horizons," says Brown. He amplifies the point in an authoritative and convincing way.

921. Brown, Peter. *Religion and Society in the Age of Augustine*. New York: Harper and Row, 1972. The relevant essays are analyzed individually. The introductory essay, the only one written expressly for this collection, gives us an important reminder: " . . . nothing is quite what it appears in the Later Roman Empire" (p. 11). This is part of the great and unending attraction of the age. Just when we think we have come to grips with the fourth century, it offers a new pose, a new prospect, another irony, another reminder that the hugeness of the empire and the vastness of its experience insure that there will always be something new to learn about it. Peter Brown is generally to be recommended as a guide to help sort out the complexities of the late Roman experience. D. F. Wright, *Journal of Roman Studies* 65 (1975): 204 (+); G.

Bonner, *Journal of Ecclesiastical History* 24 (1973): 406-407 (+-).

922. Brown, Peter. "The Rise and Function of the Holy Man in Late Antiquity." *Journal of Roman Studies* 61 (1971): 80-101. This is one of the most famous essays on a religious and social development in the later empire, and is destined for life everlasting as a footnote reference in scholarly works, where it is usually described as a landmark. Brown mostly concentrates on Syria from the fourth to the sixth centuries, tracing the increasing importance of ascetic holy men living outside society as religious powers mediating between heaven and earth and as political powers mediating economic and social problems between government and the people and between social groups and between individuals.

923. Bundy, D. "Christians and Pagans in Northern Mesopotamia During the Fourth Century: Literary Sources." In *Twelfth Annual Byzantine Studies Conference Abstracts*, p. 34. Bryn Mawr, Pennsylvania, 1986.

924. Burkitt, F. C. *The Religion of the Manichees.* Cambridge: University Press, 1925.

925. The Cambridge History of Later Greek and Early Medieval Philosophy. Edited by A. H. Armstrong. Cambridge: University Press, 1967.

926. Cameron, Alan. "The Date of Iamblichus' Birth." *Hermes* 96 (1968): 374-376. Reprinted in his *Literature and Society in the Early Byzantine World*, Chap. XII. London: Variorum Reprints, 1985. Cameron narrows the philosopher's first earthly appearance down to 245-50.

927. Cameron, Alan. *The Last Pagans of Rome.* Forthcoming.

928. Cameron, Alan. "Paganism and Literature in Late Fourth-Century Rome." In *Christianisme et formes litteraires de l'antiquite tardive en Occident*, pp. 1-40. Fondation Hardt.

Entretiens sur l'antiquite classique, 23. Vandoeuvres-Geneva: Fondation Hardt, 1977. Cameron finds that late Roman paganism lacked vitality and mostly looked backwards, and thus contrasts unfavorably with the dynamic, experimental Christians, whose intellectual leaders were unafraid to shake up old literary forms and create new ones. Although paganism was not without some vigor, its strength came from the east, not from Rome.

929. Center for Hermeneutical Studies in Hellenistic and Modern Culture. *The Philosopher and Society in Late Antiquity*: Protocol of the Thirty-Fourth Colloquy, 3 December 1978. Berkeley, Ca: The Center, 1980.

930. Chambers, Henry E. "*Exempla virtutis* in Themistius and the Latin Panegyrists." Ph. D. dissertation, Indiana University, 1968. Themistius' aim was to promote the traditional virtues of kingship, which would mean the survival of many pagan ideals too. The Gallic orators, on the other hand, used the panegyric to promote immediate and local interests.

931. Cohen, J. "Roman Imperial Policy towards the Jews from Constantine until the End of the Palestinian Patriarchate." *Byzantine Studies* 3 (1976): 1-29.

932. Courcelle, P. "Anti-Christian Arguments and Christian Platonism: From Arnobius to Ambrose." In *The Conflict between Paganism and Christianity in the Fourth Century,* pp. 151-192. Edited by A. Momigliano. New York: Oxford University Press, 1963. Arnobius at the beginning of the fourth century and Ambrose at the end of it are consulted to discover the kinds of debate between Christians and pagans, and the growing extent to which Platonism had suffused the thinking of Christian intellectuals by the time of Ambrose.

933. Cox, Patricia. *Biography in Late Antiquity: The Quest for the Holy Man.* The Transformation of the Classical Heritage, 5. Berkeley: University of California Press, 1983. In the words of M. Sage, Cox "attempts to trace the interplay of biographical forms and the concept of the holy man, which provides the foundation for the use of biography as a vehicle for creative mythologizing and for developing an ideal in which history was distorted, if not actually lost." M. Sage, *American Historical Review* 90 (1985): 394-395 (+-).

934. Croke, Brian. "The Era of Porphyry's Anti-Christian Polemic." *Journal of Religious History* 14 (1984): 1-14. A counter-argument to Barnes' proposal (914) that Porphyry's *Against the Christians* was written in the time of Diocletian. Croke restores it to the traditional date c. 271/2.

935. Croke, Brain and Harries, Jill. *Religious Conflict in Fourth-Century Rome: A Documentary Study.* Sydney: Sydney University Press; Beaverton, OR: International Scholarly Book Services, 1982. Ninety-four documents of original sources in English, many translated for the first time. The collection focuses on the city of Rome, and around the efforts in 384 to persuade the Christian emperor to restore the Altar of Victory to the Senate house and the revival of pagan ceremonies in 394 during the time of the usurper Eugenius. But there are selections from throughout the fourth century, all, however, from the Latin world only. R. Sherk, *History: Review of New Books* 11 (April 1983): 140 (+).

936. Crown, A. D. "Samaritan Religion in the Fourth Century A. D." *Nederlands Theologisch Tijdschrift* 41 (1987): 29-47.

937. Daly, Lawrence J. "Themistius' Plea for Religious Tolerance." *Greek, Roman and Byzantine Studies* 12 (1971): 65-79. The fourth century Christian emperors were also technically head of the state cults. It was a doomed arrangement, but for three-quarters of a century it persisted. Themistius' solution to the contradiction was to secularize the emperor's religious role, in part by interpreting state ritual as an expression of support for the general culture of the empire, common to both pagans and Christians. Emperors were to support the diversity of belief in the empire, while preserving and living the common culture of all inherited from antiquity. Religious toleration was the key to unity in the Roman world of the time. The emperor was therefore in his official capacity to be a leader of culture and a philosopher, but not a theologian. Themistius was an influential and respected educator, with good connections at court, and a number of emperors tried to live in the spirit of his message, with some measure of success. In the end, a rising tide of religious fanaticism ruined the prospect of religious diversity and toleration in the empire; but, far from being a total failure, the influence of moderates like Themistius gave some measure of stability to religious developments in the fourth century.

938. Daly, Lawrence J. "Themistius' Refusal of a Magistracy (Or. 34, cc. xiii-xv)." *Byzantion* 53 (1983): 164-212.   Daly gives a very detailed analysis of some aspects of the public and political life of the philosopher Themistius.

939. Dodds, E. R. *Pagan and Christian in an Age of Anxiety: Some Aspects of Religious Experience from Marcus Aurelius to Constantine.* Cambridge: University Press, 1965. Mostly the third century comes under review. But this sets the stage for the triumph of Christianity in the fourth, which is discussed. The anxiety or nervousness of the educated classes over the traditional style of life and the subsequent search for new ways of thought and living offer an explanation for the rise of Christianity which has not won universal acceptance in the scholarly world. Nevertheless, the wealth of Dodds' learning has won general acknowledgment. See Robert C. Smith and John Lounibos, eds., *Pagans and Christian Anxiety: A Response to E. R. Dodds* (Lanham, MD.: University Press of America, 1984) for ten related studies (not, however, favorably reviewed by R. J. Lane Fox, *Journal of Roman Studies* 76 (1986), 304-305).   M. H. Shepherd, *American Journal of Philology* 88 (1967): 110-112.

940. Downey, Glanville. "Allusions to Christianity in Themistius' Orations." *Texte und Untersuchungen* 80 (Studia Patristica 5) (1960): 480-488. Berlin: Akademie-Verlag, 1962. "If Julian attacked Christianity, and Libanius ignored it, Themistius set himself to compete with it by endeavoring to show that . . . pagan philosophy offered all the good things that were to be found in Christianity. Instead of arguing against the Christian teaching, he sought to imply that the pagan way of life was in fact superior to the new Christian doctrine" (p. 481).

941. Downey, Glanville. "Julian and Justinian and the Unity of Faith and Culture." *Church History* 28 (1959): 339-349. " . . . Julian's attacking the Christian system on a comprehensive basis and attempting to replace it with a comprehensive classical system shows how important, to his mind, was the wholeness of faith and culture, whether the faith be pagan or Christian" (p. 343). This was not Julian's attitude alone. It was Justinian's belief too, only by then Christianity was the favored faith which would restore the world to ancient glories.

942. Downey, Glanville. "Julian the Apostate at Antioch." *Church History* 8 (1939): 303-315. More on Julian's effort to restore Hellenism as the premier philosophy of life for the empire, from the perspective of Julian's stay at Antioch from June 362 to March 363. Downey takes a lot of time with the *Misopogon,* Julian's satire on the Antiochenes, stressing that we must remember always to read the sources in the context of the times if they are truly to be useful to us.

943. Downey, Glanville. "*Philanthropia* in Religion and Statecraft in the Fourth Century after Christ." *Historia* 4 (1955): 199-208. The fourth century is remembered as a brutal time when the law codes indicated torture as a norm of juridical procedure and regimentation was the general theme of society. In fact the fourth century was an era of fluid and changing relations in society. The government was hard pressed to keep track of these trends, and in frustration often issued brutal decrees beyond its ability to enforce wholesale. In fact there was much thought about how men and governments could more agreeably get along with each other and with the supernatural forces that were so prominent in the lives of all Romans. The old Greek concept of philanthropia, concerning the love of the gods for men, and the love of men for each other, breathed new life in the fourth century as a vehicle for pagans and Christians to discover how men could bring peace and

harmony to their lives through humanitarian resolve. Downey adduces plenty of pagan and Christian examples to show the use of the concept touching upon a number of practical contemporary questions: How should the emperor behave towards his subjects? How should the barbarians be treated? And so on. The matter of the barbarians is particularly interesting. There was a strong intellectual faction at court, led by Themistius, pressing for a more rational way of managing the barbarian tribes than constant head-bashing, which seemed never to still them for long. The success of this faction is seen in the policy of Theodosius, who was encouraged and persuaded to see himself as emperor of the world, with the barbarians as his subjects who could be taught the ways of civilized behavior through the example of a loving emperor who disciplined them but also cared for them and brought them under his protection and into his service.

944. **Downey, Glanville.** "Themistius and the Defense of Hellenism in the Fourth Century." *Harvard Theological Review* 50 (1957): 259-274. Themistius, as a famous pagan teacher and orator with good connections at the Christian imperial court, promoted the principles of Hellenism without attacking Christianity. He carefully developed the many themes of Hellenism that were not incongruous with Christianity. He never lost an opportunity through his orations to fit Christian emperors into the general mold of good Greek kings. His diplomatic approach to the new imperial religion was more helpful to the reputation and survival of Hellenism than the approach of Libanius, who ignored Christianity, or Julian, who fought it.

945. **Ehrhardt, Arnold.** "Constantine, Rome, and the Rabbis." *Bulletin of the John Rylands Library* 42 (1959-1960): 288-312. A piece of source material, the *Actus Sylvestri*, after a popular medieval career, is advanced again, with many cautions, as having contributions to make to our knowledge of Constantine. Ehrhardt focuses on a section that reveals fourth century attitudes towards the Jews.

946. **Ferguson, John and Green, Miranda.** "Constantine, Sun-Symbols and the Labarum." *Durham University Journal* 80 (1987): 9-17. "The contention of this paper is . . . that in Constantine there was a fusion between Sol Invictus and Christ, and that he never threw off the power of the Sun in embracing Christ" (p. 17).

947. **Finamore, John F.** *Iamblichus and the Theory of the Vehicle of the Soul.* American Classical Studies, 14. Chico, Ca.: Scholars Press, 1985. For those who want a strong dose of later Neoplatonism, so influential in the fourth century. A. Sheppard, *Classical Review* 37 (1987): 104-105 (+).

948. **Fowden, Garth.** "Between Pagans and Christians [rev. art.]." *Journal of Roman Studies* 78 (1988): 173-182. In the context of an important review of Robin Lane Fox's *Pagans and Christians* (972), Fowden offers some useful observations of his own on the relations of pagans and Christians in late antiquity, which he sees as more intertwined than he thinks Lane Fox does. Fowden has interesting observations on Constantine's role in advancing Christianity, on the uncertainties about which religious attitudes would emerge victorious from the tense pluralism of the fourth century, on the "mobile world" of late antiquity where a religion that could travel would do better than a religion tied to a place. Very stimulating.

949. **Fowden, Garth.** *The Egyptian Hermes: A Historical Approach to the Late Pagan Mind.* New York: Cambridge University Press, 1986. Through an investigation of the Greek-Egyptian composite god Hermes Trimegistus and the philosophical texts resulting from the cult, Fowden seeks out the religious world of "the literate but not especially learned pagan" (p. xiii) of the late Roman world. There is much of value on late Roman Egypt and its place in the thought world of those times. S. Brown, *Choice* 25 (September 1987): 110 (+).

950. **Fowden, Garth.** "The Pagan Holy Man in Late Antique Society." *Journal of Hellenic Studies* 102 (1982): 33-59. There were lots of holy men in late antiquity. We now

remember the Christian ones, but there was an ample supply of pagan ones too, who nevertheless had much less popular appeal than their Christian equivalents. They tended to be what we might today call intellectual snobs. They had worked for years to acquire the philosophical knowledge that made them holy, and they were not about to admit people to their rarified society on a prayer or a few acts of charity. They tended to be urban, and not much interested in the poor or even the average person. Fowden gives the full story.

951. Fowden, Garth. "Pagan Philosophers in Late Antique Society." Ph. D. dissertation, Oxford University, 1979. Fowden focuses on Iamblichus and his followers.

952. Fowden, Garth. "The Platonist Philosopher and His Circle in Late Antiquity." *Philosophia* (Athens) 7 (1977): 359-383. Fowden has a look at the way Neoplatonist intellectual circles worked in late antiquity, and the atmosphere in which the intellectuals and holy men of paganism worked, including the relationship with Christianity. For the fourth century, Fowden concentrates on the philosopher Iamblichus and Aedesius.

953. Frend, W. H. C. "The Gnostic-Manichaean Tradition in Roman North Africa." *Journal of Ecclesiastical History* 4 (1953): 13-26.

954. Frend, W. H. C. "Prelude to the Great Persecution: The Propaganda War." *Journal of Ecclesiastical History* 38 (1987): 1-18. As in so many ideological confrontations, there was a long propaganda war before there was an opening of hostilities between Christians and pagans under Diocletian. It is easy now to look back and see Christianity's triumph; but the outcome was not so clear at the time, and the older, more traditional pagan forces had cause for optimism. As Frend says, "The case against Christianity . . . was formidable" (p. 13). Moreover, many of the Illyrian military emperors of the late third century were very conservative and disliked Christianity, which meant active government support for the older state cults. In Churchill's words, it is better to jaw-jaw than to war-war. Frend gives a well-crafted look at the interesting and useful intellectual interaction of pagans and Christians before the blood of the martyrs flowed in the streets of Diocletian's tidy new empire.

955. **Frend, W. H. C.** "Religion and Social Change in the Late Roman Empire." *The Cambridge Journal*, Vol. II, no. 8 (Cambridge, 1949): 487-496. Reprinted in *Religion Popular and Unpopular in the Early Christian Centuries*, Ch. XI. London: Variorum Reprints, 1976. Frend takes the fourth century as his laboratory and shows the relation of heresies and schisms and movements to social and political and general cultural considerations.

956. **Frend, W. H. C.** "Religion in Roman Britain in the Fourth Century." *Journal of the British Archaeological Association* 3 (1955): 1-18. Paganism, especially of the Celtic variety, but also mystery cults, flourished in fourth century Britain. Christianity was certainly there too, but "remained an official and somewhat extraneous worship" (p. 7), and made little impact outside the cities. Frend develops these themes taking into account library and archaeological evidence, and relates the British scene to the general Roman world.

957. **Gardner, Alice.** *Julian: Philosopher and Emperor and the Last Struggle of Paganism against Christianity.* New York: G. P. Putnam's Sons, 1895; reprint ed., New York: AMS Press, 1978. A bit dated, still a good general read.

958. **Geffcken, Johannes.** *The Last Days of Greco-Roman Paganism.* Europe in the Middle Ages, 8. Translated by Sabine MacCormack. New York: North Holland Publishing Co., 1978.

959. **Goodenough, Erwin R.** "The Religious Aspirations." In *The Age of Diocletian: A Symposium*, pp. 37-48. Moderated by Sterling A. Callisen. New York: Metropolitan Museum of Art, 1953. This excellent piece presents the case for the divine monarchy of the fourth century in a sympathetic way, and gives succinct and illuminating paragraphs on the religious developments of the time. A person wishing to comprehend the

relation of religion and state, and to gain a sense of the problem that Christianity posed (before it and the state were reconciled) might do well to memorize this passage: "In all state of the ancient world the state organization was primarily what we would call a church, in the sense that its purpose was to bring divine order on earth and to offer collective worship" (p. 38).

960. Gough, Michael R. E. "A Bath Inscription from Osrhoene."*Journal of Hellenic Studies* 74 (1954): 179-180. This is a pagan inscription that Gough dates to 361-363 and relates to the pagan renewal under Julian.

961. Grant, Robert M. "Porphyry among the Early Christians." In *Romanitas et Christianitas: Studies in Honor of Jan Waszink,* pp. 181-187. Edited by William den Boer, etc. Amsterdam: North Holland Publishing Co., 1973. Porphyry was at first sympathetic towards some aspects of Christianity, and Christians liked his early work. Only later was the name Porphyry dreaded because of the power of his arguments in *Against the Christians.*

962. Grant, Robert M. "The Religion of Maximin Daia." In *Studies in Judaism in Late Antiquity.* Vol 12: *Christianity, Judaism and Other Greco-Roman Cults, Studies for Morton Smith at Sixty,* Part 4, pp. 143-166. Edited by Jacob Neusner. Leiden: E. J. Brill, 1975. Maximin was a devoted pagan who vigorously worked to rejuvenate the state religion while as often as politically possible suppressing the Christians, who he thought were ruining the world.

963. Gregory, Timothy E. "The Survival of Paganism in Christian Greece: A Critical Essay." *American Journal of Philology* 107 (1986): 229-242. Gregory shows how to some extent Christian practice was new wine in old bottles. Gregory speaks of syncretism, accommodation, and certain parallel developments among Mediterranean religions generally in late antiquity, which made it possible for many aspects of paganism to survive even within the church.

964. **Grissom, F.** "Chrysostom and the Jews: Studies in Jewish-Christian Relations in Fourth-Century Antioch." Ph. D. dissertation, Southern Baptist Theological Seminary, 1978.

965. **Hayman, A. P.** "The Image of the Jew in the Syriac Anti-Jewish Polemical Literature." In *"To See Ourselves as Others See Us": Christians, Jews, "Others" in Late Antiquity*, pp. 423-441. Edited by J. Nuesner and E. S. Frerichs. Chico, Ca.: Scholars Press, 1985.   Hayman has two points to make about the perception of Jews among gentiles in late antiquity: first, the average Syriac writers "show no awareness that contemporary Jews are any different from biblical Israelites"; and, second, "that ordinary Syrian Christians . . . could . . . not distinguish clearly between Judaism and Christianity" (p. 440). What is more, the average Christian was more tolerant of the Jews in his midst than the Christian intellectuals and leaders were.

966. **Jones, A. H. M.** "The Social Background of the Struggle between Paganism and Christianity." In *The Conflict between Paganism and Christianity in the Fourth Century*, pp. 17-37. Edited by Arnaldo Momigliano. Oxford: Clarendon Press, 1963.   With artful and elegant simplicity, Jones presents a masterful sketch of the empire's social framework in the fourth century.   Jones allows the importance of government patronage in the growth of fourth century Christianity, but he finds a greater impetus in the social changes of the age, which propelled into political power people from the middle or lower classes who were more open than traditional leaders and aristocrats to the new religious experience.

967. **Jones, A. H. M**. "Were Ancient Heresies National or Social Movements in Disguise?" *Journal of Theological Studies* 10 (1959): 280-297.   No and no again. They were religious expressions, just as they claimed to be, and they had no political aims. There were regional forces, of course, and these had an influence; but there was never a hidden agenda involving the dismantling of the Roman state.

968. King, Noel Q. "*Compelle intrare* and the Plea of the Pagans." *The Modern Churchman* 4 (no.2, January 1961): 111-115. The Theodosian Code and Augustine make the case for religious coercion; Themistius and Libanius make the case for toleration. This is largely a fourth century debate, when both views had strong adherents.

969. King, Noel Q. "The Pagan Resurgence of 393: Some Contemporary Sources." *Studia Patristica (Texte und Untersuchungen* 79; Berlin 1961) 4: 472-477. After considering the sources, King concludes that the pagan "revolt" of 393 had behind it a religious motivation that was "active and lively but not fanatically anti-Christian" (p. 477), and was more interested in ancient literature than in the gods per se.

970. Kirschner, Robert. "The Vocation of Holiness in Late Antiquity." *Vigiliae Christianae* 38 (1984): 105-124. Holy men were all the rage in late antiquity. Kirschner analyzes three types: pagan philosophers, ascetic Christians, wise rabbis. Through his discussion of these three ways to be holy, Kirschner gives expression to three important thought-patterns of the late empire - pagan, Christian, Jewish -, whose differences were exacerbated rather than harmonized after the Christian triumph of the late fourth century. Nevertheless, all types of holy men had a fundamental mission: "the assertion of mastery over the unintelligible" (p. 120). This required "intimacy with the divine" (p. 120).

971. Klinck, Arthur W. "The Paganism of Julian: Its Development, Character and Influence on His Religious Policy." Ph. D. dissertation, University of Nebraska, 1935.

972. Lane Fox, Robin. *Pagans and Christians.* New York: Knopf, 1987. Lane Fox shows that third and fourth century paganism and Christianity are best studied together on their common turf if either is to be properly understood, even though he tends to see both as separate worlds. This large book is especially good at communicating the message that pagan culture and cults too were flourishing in the later empire, and that the triumph of Christianity was never guaranteed, although its prospects for domination were given a quantum leap by the unexpected conversion of Constantine in the first part of the fourth century. In the Roman world there was nothing quite like imperial patronage to give a cause a boost. In the Greek Orthodox Church Constantine is an official saint. Rightly so. Amen. M. Beard, *Times Literary Supplement* (February 20, 1987): 179 (++-); P. R. L. Brown, *New York Review of Books* 34 (March 12, 1987): 24-27 (++-); R. M. Grant, *Church History* 56 (1987): 379-381 (+-); G. Fowden, *Journal of Roman Studies* 78 (1988): 173-182 (+-).

973. Leadbeater, L. W. "Aspects of the Philosophical Priesthood in Iamblichus' *De Mysterii.*" *Classical Bulletin* 47 (1971): 89-72.

974. Levine, Lee I., ed. *The Synagogue in Late Antiquity.* Philadelphia: The American School of Oriental Research, 1987.

975. Levine, Philip. "The Continuity and Preservation of the Latin Tradition." In *The Transformation of the Roman World*, pp. 206-231. Edited by Lynn White, Jr. Berkeley: University of California Press, 1966. This interesting essay stresses how the "pagan religious crisis of the fourth century and its aftermath . . . contributed considerably to the preservation and revitalization of the Latin tradition" (p. 224).

976. Lewy, Hans. *Chaldaean Oracles and Theurgy: Mysticism, Magic and Platonism in the Later Roman Empire.* Paris: Etudes Augustiniennes, 1978.

977. Liebeschuetz, J. H. W. G. *Continuity and Change in Roman Religion.* New York: Oxford University Press, 1979. The last part of the book is the interesting one for the student of the fourth century, especially regarding the general religious orientation towards monotheism and the efforts of Christian apologists such as Lactantius and Arnobius to couch their arguments in language that would find a sympathetic ear in the pagan world. R. Seager, *Times Literary Supplement* (January 11, 1980): 44 (+); F. Millar, *English Historical Review* 95 (1980): 840-841 (+-).

978. Lieu, Samuel N. C. *Manichaeism in the Later Roman Empire and Medieval China: A Historical Survey.* Manchester: University Press, 1985. An authoritative reminder in 369 pages that Manichaeism was much more of a worldwide religion, perhaps much more able to be a worldwide religion, than the Christianity of the fourth century could hope to be. In the fourth century, Manichaeism had a strong but tenuous reach into the Roman state, but Christianity, which after all was home grown, stole the prize. R. A. Markus, *Journal of Roman Studies* 76 (1986): 305-306 (+); G. G. Stroumsa, *Classical Review* 37 (1987): 95-97 (+).

979. Lieu, Samuel N. C. "Some Themes in Later Roman Anti-Manichaean Polemics: I." *Bulletin of the John Rylands University Library* 68 (1986): 434-472.

980. Linder, Amnon, ed. *Jews in Roman Legislation.* Detroit: Wayne State University Press, 1987. Includes all the legal texts in Greek or Latin, plus an English translation, plus commentary, covering the second to the sixth centuries.

981. MacCormack, Sabine. "Roma, Constantinopolis, the Emperor, and His Genius." *Classical Quarterly* 25 (1975): 131-150. "The purpose of the present paper is to examine one way in which divine being or divine existence was expressed in the Ancient World, and to see how in late antiquity the expression of some aspects of divine existence was abandoned, while others survived" (p. 131). MacCormack adduces a great deal of interesting information about the tendency towards pairing in ancient thinking about divine things: the emperor paired with his genius or the spirit of Rome, cities and their divine protectors, and so on. She discusses ways in which Christianity both embraced and rejected the old pairing motif.

982. MacMullen, Ramsay. "Constantine and the Miraculous." *Greek, Roman, and Byzantine Studies* 9 (1968): 81-96. MacMullen discusses the grasp that supernatural forces, good and bad, had over the minds of men in the time of

Constantine. This was not a new feature of the Roman world, but MacMullen sees it as more powerful and shrill than ever: "But as the darkness of irrationality thickened over the declining centuries of the Roman empire, superstition blacked out the clearer lights of religion, wizards masqueraded as philosophers, and the fears of the masses took hold on those who passed for educated and enlightened" (p. 92).

983. MacMullen, Ramsay. *Paganism in the Roman Empire.* New Haven: Yale University Press, 1981. Particularly good in giving a sense of the richness and diversity of paganism, and how Christianity related to it all. Some fourth century material. G. J. D. Aalders H. Wzn., *Mnemosyne* 37 (1985): 249-251 (+).

984. Malley, William J. *Hellenism and Christianity: The Conflict between Hellenic and Christian Wisdom in the Contra Galilaeos of Julian the Apostate and the Contra Julianum of St. Cyril of Alexandria.* Analecta Gregoriana 210. Rome: Universita Gregoriana, 1978.

985. Matthews, John F. "Symmachus and the Oriental Cults." *Journal of Roman Studies* 63 (1973): 175-195. Reprinted in his *Political Life and Culture in Late Roman Society*, Ch. VIII. London: Variorum Reprints, 1985. It has been a commonplace that Symmachus had little or no interest in the Oriental cults, as distinguished from many of his prominent aristocratic contemporaries. Matthews reviews the evidence and comes away unconvinced of that conclusion. He warns against the "dangers of premature inference" (p. 190), an expression that should be engraved on the minds and hearts of all who research the past. Building on his reading of the evidence, Matthews forms the larger related conclusion that it is an unsafe view that "the pagan revival of the late fourth century was inspired by the Oriental cults rather than the Roman state religion . . . " (p. 195).

986. Mattingly, Harold. "The Later Paganism." *Harvard Theological Review* 35 (1942): 171-179. Paganism was changing too in the later empire, and in some respects these changes facilitated the movement towards Christianity, which won in the end but not entirely on its own merits or before a subtle and permanent absorption of many Greco-Roman values and points of view. The entire religious direction of the ancient world was undergoing a metamorphosis whose final form was not clear until very late in the fourth century.

987.   Miller, James. *Measures of Wisdom: The Cosmic Dance in Classical and Christian Antiquity.* Toronto: University of Toronto Press, 1986.   The stars and the planets were of interest to the ancients, as they are to us. An image that became highly developed in Platonic Greece to encompass the universe and the relation and movement of all its parts was the dance, the cosmic dance. This image filtered into the thought processes of late antique men, whether they were Neoplatonists of some sort or Christians of some sort.   Miller works at length with three persons to discuss the uses of the image of the dance in that great transitional period of the fourth century: the philosopher Calcidius (Miller infers that he is fourth century), the emperor Julian, and the Christian Gregory Nazianzus. Others, such as Constantine, Eusebius of Caesarea, and Synesius of Cyrene, make appearances too.   Though difficult (perhaps because we prefer to see the fourth century in our own terms), this book offers a unique opportunity to approach the cosmology (or cosmologies) of the fourth century in contemporary terms.

988.   Momigliano, Arnaldo, ed. *The Conflict between Paganism and Christianity in the Fourth Century.* Oxford: Clarendon Press, 1963.   These eight essays, originally lectures, have been very well received in the scholarly community; they are all annotated individually in this bibliography.   A. H. Armstrong, *Journal of Roman Studies* 54 (1964): 207 ("In general the main value of the book lies in the fact that it is a series of precise studies of particular questions, and by its attention to detail brings out something of the complexity of the relations between Christian and pagans in this period.")

989. **Momigliano, Arnaldo.** "Pagan and Christian Historiography in the Fourth Century A. D." In *The Conflict between Paganism and Christianity in the Fourth Century*, pp. 79-99. Edited by Arnaldo Momigliano. New York: Oxford University Press, 1963. Reprinted in *Essays in Ancient and Modern Historiography*, pp. 107-126. Edited by Arnaldo Momigliano. Oxford: Blackwell, 1977. Between pagan and Christian historiography there developed a chasm in the fourth century which was never subsequently bridged. "To put it briefly, the Christians invented ecclesiastical history and the biography of the saints, but did not try to christianize ordinary political history . . . . A reinterpretation of ordinary military, political, or diplomatic history in Christian terms was neither achieved nor even attempted" (p. 88). The pagans, for their part, continued the historiographical traditions of the classical past to a greater or lesser extent, and did not attempt to encompass Christianity. In this pattern of historiographical bifurcation is a reflection of the schizophrenia of the age.

990. **Momigliano, Arnaldo.** "Popular Religious Beliefs and the Late Roman Historians." *Studies in Church History* 8 (1971): 1-18. Reprinted in his *Essays in Ancient and Modern Historiography*, pp. 141-159. Oxford: Blackwell, 1977. A new feature entered classical historiography in the late Roman period: religion became an integral part of historical writing complementing (and in the case of church historians, replacing) the traditional interest in politics and military events. Everyone, of high status or low, was swept up in the same wave of religious developments, and Momigliano discourages the use of the word popular when considering religious beliefs of the age.

991. **Muller, Hendrik.** *Christians and Pagans from Constantine to Augustine.* 2 vols. Part I: *The Religious Policies of the Roman Emperors.* Part II: *The Spiritual Conflict.* Pretoria: Union Booksellers, 1946. This well-organized work is on the whole a very balanced, eloquent, and informed treatment of the religious transformation of the fourth century. Muller does incline to see the triumph of Christianity as "inevitable," but he is not dogmatic about this, and gives full

scope to the tenacity of the pagan resistance generally, the slow metamorphosis of the religious terrain, and the subtle impact of pagan culture which in some respects made Christianity over again during the fourth century: so that in its rituals, political philosophy, a fair amount of theology, holidays, protocol, titles, and so on, Christianity came rather closer in many ways to the great pagan cults that it rejected than to the messages of Jesus and Paul which it presumed to embrace.

992. Nathanson, Barbara G. "The Fourth Century Jewish 'Revolt' During the Reign of Gallus." Ph. D. dissertation, Duke University, 1981.

993. Nathanson, Barbara G. "Jews, Christians, and the Gallus Revolt in Fourth-Century Palestine." *Biblical Archaeologist* 49 (1986): 26-36. What was the condition of Jewry in fourth century Palestine? Although the Roman government maintained a tolerant (with reservations) attitude, there were problems: "The data do . . . suggest that the first generation of Christian rule was a period of strong, popular and ecclesiastical, anti-Jewish sentiment and an era of increasing insecurity and dislocation for the Jewish communities of Palestine" (p. 34).

994. Negri, Gaetano. *Julian the Apostate.* Translated by Duchess Litta-Visconti-Arese. 2 vols. London: T. Fisher Unwin; New York: Charles Scribners' Sons, 1905. The emphasis of this work is on the spiritual world of the fourth century. Specifically Negri is concerned with Christianity, and Julian is seen as a puritanistic Hellenist reacting to a Christianty corrupt with success. F. A. Christie, *American Historical Review* 11 (1906): 631-633 (++-).

995. Neusner, Jacob. *Judaism and Christianity in the Age of Constantine: History, Messiah, Israel, and the Initial Confrontation.* Chicago: University of Chicago Press, 1987. With so much in common, Judaism and Christianity had a basis for discussion. But from that point everything deteriorated into inimical conclusions. In the fourth century the Jewish sages began to take Christianity seriously as a rival, and Christian leaders were anxious to separate themselves from the Jews. Neusner sets the stage and follows the discussions in each camp. G. T. Armstrong, *Church History* 57 (1988): 520-522 (+).

996. Nuesner, Jacob. "Stable Symbols in a Shifting Society: The Delusion of the Monolithic Gentile in Documents of Late Fourth-Century Judaism." *History of Religions* 25 (1985): 163-175. Reprinted in *"To See Ourselves as Others See Us": Christians, Jews, "Others" in Late Antiquity*, pp. 373-396. Edited by J. Nuesner and C. S. Frerichs. Chico, Ca.: Scholars Press, 1985. To the Jews, Christianty was another kind of paganism. In the fourth century they still held to this concept.

997. Neusner, Jacob and Frerichs, Ernest S., eds. *"To See Ourselves as Others See Us": Christians, Jews, "Others" in Late Antiquity.* Chico, Ca.: Scholars Press, 1985. The relevant essays are treated individually elsewhere.

998. Nilsson, Martin P. "Pagan Divine Service in Late Antiquity." *Harvard Theological Review* 38 (1945): 63-71. "The similarity between pagan and Christian divine service is greater than is generally thought" (p. 69), and Nilsson draws up the comparisons.

999. O'Donnell, James J. "The Career of Virius Nicomachus Flavianus." *Phoenix* 32 (1978): 129-143. O'Donnell concludes: "Thus an important phase in modern accounts of the supposedly heated struggle between dying 'paganism' and rising Christianity disappears when the evidence is examined closely; in Virius Nichomachus Flavianus we are left with a single rather foolish figure prophesying victory for a usurper who never had a chance. Whatever went on in those years, it can no longer be claimed that anything like the 'last pagan revival' long imagined in the events of 392-394 has any basis in the documents on which we depend" (p. 143).

1000. O'Donnell, James A. "The Demise of Paganism." *Traditio* 35 (1979): 45-88. "Christianity triumphed, but paganism survived" (p. 83). Paganism as the worship of the ancient gods was definitely on the way out in the late fourth century, but paganism as "a tolerant, even careless attitude toward worship in general" was very persistent indeed. O'Donnell documents this persistence.

1001. O'Donnell, James A. "Paganus." *Classical Folia* 31 (1977): 163-169. Use of the word "pagan" *paganus* as we understand it came into common use in the middle of the fourth century.

1002. O'Leary, DeL. "The Destruction of Temples in Egypt." *Bulletin de la Societe d'Archeologie Copte* 4 (1938): 51-57.

1003. Pack, Roger A. "Notes on the *Caesars* of Julian." *Transactions of the American Philological Association* 77 (1946): 151-157. More than satire, Julian's *Caesars* is a serious work, another vehicle for expressing the philosophical and religious views of the last pagan emperor.

1004. Parkes, James. "Jews and Christians in the Constantinian Empire." *Studies in Church History* 1 (1962; published 1964): 69-79. In the pagan world reaction to the Jews was mixed: in the Christian world it was hostile. The fourth century empire set the stage and conditions for the future of the Jews in the Christian world: "According to Eusebius, there was not a single decent or righteous Jewish character in the whole of history" (p. 73). With an attitude like that leading the way and with the hardening attitude of the Church generally to those beyond its communion, the Jews were in for an increasingly rough time.

1005. Phillips, C. R. "Magic and Politics in the Fourth Century: Parameters of Groupings." *Studia Patristica* 18,1: 65-70. Phillips asks us to take the magic of the past on its own terms and in the context of contemporary social dynamics "without introducing the confusions of contemporary religious and scientific systems" (p. 67).

1006. Rike, R. L. *Apex Omnium: Religion in the Res Gestae of Ammianus.* Transformation of the Classical Heritage, 15. Berkeley: University of California Press, 1987. Ammianus is presented as an enthusiastic pagan who in his hierarchical view of religion was willing to give Christianity the status of *religio licita,* but did not think it a sufficiently matured, experienced cult to assist in the protection of the empire and the spread of civilization.

1007. Rist, John M. "Pseudo-Ammonius and the Soul/Body Problem in Some Platonic Texts of Late Antiquity." *American Journal of Philology* 109 (1988): 402-415. Rist ruminates on philosophical trends in discussing the relation of body and soul in Neoplatonic and Christian circles.

1008. Robinson, Dwight N. "An Analysis of the Pagan Revival of the Late Fourth Century, with Especial Reference to Symmachus." *Transactions of the American Philological Association* 46 (1915): 87-101. Robinson analyzes "the main tendencies of pagan thought and practice" leading to the fourth century revival. There was little harmony or focus except through an opposition to Christianity. The movement was Roman and aristocratic in leadership, some being devoted to Oriental cults, others, like Symmachus, believers in the traditional Roman gods and rituals.

1009. Rokeah, David. *Jews, Pagans and Christians in Conflict.* Jerusalem: Magnes Press, 1982. Taking the period from the second to the fifth centuries, with an emphasis on the fourth, Rokeah considers the ways in which religious beliefs and practices defined the nature of relations among Jews, pagans, and Christians, and their relations with the Roman state. Rokeah sees a situation in late antiquity where pagans and Christians were very hotly engaged in polemic, while their relations with the Jews were milder, involving disputes but not a campaign of conversion or destruction. In fact, says Rokeah, the relatively neutral Jews provided much of the intellectual format of the conflict between Christians and pagans but were otherwise mostly outside the struggle.

1010. Sallustius. *Concerning the Gods and the Universe.* Edited and translated by A. D. Nock. Cambridge: University Press, 1926. The emperor Julian commissioned this work as a guide for teachers to show them the proper way to teach the revived paganism which the emperor felt would help save the Roman world from a barbarism worse than the Germans: Christianity.

1011. Sambursky, S. and Pines, S. *The Concept of Time in Late Neoplatonism.* Texts with translation, introduction and notes. Jerusalem: The Israel Academy of Sciences and Humanities, 1971.

1012. Save-Soderbergh, T. "Some Remarks on Coptic Manichaean Poetry." In *Coptic Studies in Honor of Walter Ewing Crum.* Boston: Byzantine Institute, 1950.

1013. Seaver, James E. "The Jews in the Roman Empire from Constantine to Theodosius II." Ph. D. dissertation, Cornell University, 1946.

1014. Seaver, James. *Persecution of the Jews in the Roman Empire, 300-438.* Lawrence: University of Kansas Publications, 1952. To sum up: Jews were not nice to Christians in the fourth century, but Christians were downright nasty to Jews, and with the growing preponderance of numbers and influence in the government, set the tone and approach to anti-Jewish feeling which flourished in medieval Europe. Seaver gives a fair amount of space to the anti-Jewish mutterings of sanctified personalities such as John Chrysostom, Ambrose, Jerome, and Augustine. All in all, one of the unhealthiest legacies of the fourth century was government and church sponsored anti-semitism. C. Jenkins, *English Historical Review* 68 (1953): 122 (+-); R. Markus, *Speculum* 29 (1954): 318-319 (+).

1015. Sheridan, James J. "The Altar of Victory - Paganism's Last Battle." *l'Antiquite Classique* 35 (1966): 186-206.   In the last half of the fourth century, the fate of the altar of Victory, which had been in the Senate house since the time of Augustus, became a symbol of the struggle between pagan and Christian predominance in the Roman state. The best remembered part of the drama came during the confrontation of Ambrose and Symmachus in the 380s, but Sheridan covers the whole story from Constantius II to Honorius.

1016. Sihler, E. G. *From Augustus to Augustine: Essays and Studies Dealing with the Contact and Conflict of Classic Paganism and Christianity.* Cambridge: At the University Press, 1923.   The following chapters are useful on the fourth century: VI. "Neoplatonism and Christianity"; VII. "In the Era of Diocletian"; VIII. "The Emperor Julian and His Religion"; IX. "The Old Believers in Rome and the Dusk of the Gods"; X. "The Earlier Stages of Augustine." Sihler is anti-pagan and pro-Christian, which colors his treatment.   F. Christie, *American Historical Review* 29 (1923): 318-319 (+-).

1017. Simon, Marcel. *Verus Israel: A Study of the Relations between Christians and Jews in the Roman Empire (AD 135-425).* Translated from the French by H. McKeating. Oxford: University Press, 1986.   First published in Paris in 1948, this important work successfully contends that Judaism, far from withdrawing into itself after the destruction of the temple, remained active and successful in the Roman world, competing often successfully with Christianity for influence and even growth until the combined weight of imperial protection and support and a doctrine that was more agreeable to the Roman and Greek climate of thought gave Christianity the edge in the fourth century. Increasingly persecuted as the century progressed, the Jews finally did find themselves forced to retreat from full participation in the world around them in a way that anticipated the ghettos of later times.   A. J. Avery-Peck, *Choice* 24 (September 1986): 148 (+); *Classical World* 80 (1987): 448.

1018. Smith, John Holland. *The Death of Classical Paganism.* New York: Scribner's, 1976. Paraphrasing a famous expression by Andre Piganiol ("La civilisation remaine n'est pas morte de sa belle mort. Elle a ete assassinee."), Smith takes this attitude on the contest between ancient gods and Christianity: "The gods did not die of old age. The Christians assassinated them" (p. 6). In Smith's view, therefore, the fourth century was a sad tale of Christian fanaticism which brought intolerance and chaos to the civilized world. A good antidote to pro-Christian points of view. R. M. Grant, *Christian Century* 94 (November 23, 1977): 1096 (+-).

1019. Stertz, Stephen A. "Themistius: A Hellenic Philosopher-Statesman in the Christian Roman Empire." *Classical Journal* 71 (April-May 1976): 349-358. Themistius was the Great Mediator of the fourth century. His "watchwords were adaptation and moderation" (p. 350). Not an original thinker, Themistius was nevertheless very well versed in the great philosophical traditions of the ancients, and he was very well received in the Christian court of the later fourth century emperors. His goal was to preserve classical culture, and he would do it through Christians if he had to. He would even quote scripture to hold the attention of his Christian audience at court while educating them in the principles of Hellenic philosophy. Themistius intended to have his culture saved if not his gods, and Stertz sees a large measure of success in this effort.

1020. Trombley, F. R. "Greek Paganism and Christianity in Late Antiquity: Some Continuities in Cultural Forms." In *The 17th International Byzantine Congress: Abstracts of Short Papers*, pp. 361-362. Washington, D. C., August 3-8, 1986, Dumbarton Oaks/Georgetown University. Baltimore: U. S. National Committee for Byzantine Studies, 1986.

1021. Vanderspoel, John. "Iamblichus at Daphne." *Greek, Roman and Byzantine Studies* 29 (1988): 83-86. Vanderspoel sorts through the bits and pieces of evidence to learn a little more about the philosopher Iamblichus.

1022. **Vanderspoel, John.** "Themistios and the Origin of Iamblichos." *Hermes* 116 (1988): 125-128. Eunapius says Iamblichus the philosopher was born in one place. Themistius, and some other evidence, convince Vanderspoel that Iamblichus was born in another place, which may be where Eunapius really meant anyway.

1023. **Visotzky, Burton L.** "Hillel, Hieronymous and Praetaxtatus." *Journal of the Ancient Near Eastern Society of Columbia University* 16-17 (1984-1985): 217-224. The setting is the late fourth century. Visotzky works through the persons of Jerome (and a little bit of Augustine), the great Roman pagan senator Praetaxtatus (and a little bit of Symmachus), and some fourth century legends about Hillel, the first century Jewish sage, to give us a feeling for Christian, pagan, and Jewish responses to the religious patterns of the age, overshadowed by the triumph of Christianity.

1024. **Wallis, R. T.** *Neoplatonism.* New York: Scribner's, 1972. Here is Neoplatonism for the layman. As the predominant philosophical school of the fourth century, Neoplatonism must have a moment or two in the serious student's schedule of readings, and the Wallis book is a good start. *Classical World* 67 (February 1974): 246; *Times Literary Supplement* (July 28, 1972): 896 (+).

1025. **Weitzmann, Kurt, ed.** *Age of Spirituality: A Symposium.* New York: Metropolitan Museum of Art, in Association with Princeton University Press, 1980. Nine papers, plus an introduction by Weitzmann, prompted by the 1978 exhibit at the Metropolitan Museum entitled, "The Age of Spirituality," encompassing late antiquity generally with a strong emphasis on the fourth century. Papers most relevant to the fourth century are individually analyzed. B. McGinn, *Journal of Religion* 64 (1984): 117-118 (+).

1026. **Wilken, Robert L.** *The Christians as the Romans Saw Them.* New Haven: Yale University Press, 1984. This is the best effort to date showing the reactions of pagans to the rise of Christianity. To an impressive extent Christian theology and thought in general were a reaction to pagan criticism. For the student of the fourth century the section on Julian will be the most useful. W. H. C. Frend, *Classical Review* 37 (1987): 124 (+).

1027. Wilken, Robert L. "Pagan Criticism of Christianity: Greek Religion and Christian Faith." In *Early Christian Literature and the Classical Intellectual Tradition: In Honorem Robert M. Grant*, pp. 117-134. Edited by William R. Schoedel and Robert L. Wilken. Paris: Editions Beauchesne, 1979. Wilken rejuvenates the tantalizing prospect that Porphyry was "asked by the emperor to prepare a defense of the traditional religion and to provide a philosophical basis for the repression of Christianity" (p. 118). The result, says Wilken, was the *Philosophy from Oracles* (often thought to have been written in Porphyry's youth), which was an indirect attack on fourth century Christianity by way of a positive portrait of the traditional religious dispensation of the Roman world, which could encompass Jesus in the divine hierarchy leading to the One True God by making him a divine man or great sage.

1028. Witt, Rex E. "Iamblichus as a Forerunner of Julian." In *De Jamblique a Proclus,* pp. 35-67. Entretiens sur l'antiquite classique, 21. Geneva: Fondation Hardt, 1975.

X. Christianity

As a movement, way of life, way of thought. Includes relations of sects within the Christian world; but for formal relations with the Roman state, see "Church and State." For relations with other religions, see "Religion and Philosophy." This chapter includes Christian literature.

1029. Adkin, Neil. "A Problem in the Early Church: Noise During Sermon and Lesson." *Mnemosyne* 38 (1985): 161-163. Apparently fourth century churches were noisy places, even during services, full of chattering and loud devotions. Adkin has gathered the evidence.

1030. Andel, G. K. van. *The Christian Concept of History in the Chronicle of Sulpicius Severus.* Amsterdam: Adolf M. Hakkert, 1976. Andel gives an interesting study of the late fourth century ascetic Severus, whose *Chronicle* was written "to open the eyes and ears of his contemporaries to the life and doctrine of the last truly prophetic or apostolic figures [Hilary of Poitiers and Martin of Tours] in the Church. He did so with an eye to the imminent coming of Antichrist and the horrors which would accompany it" (p. 139).

1031. Applebaum, S. "A Note on Ambrosius Aurelianus." *Britannia* 14 (1983): 245-246. Several British place names, such as Amesbury, may derive from Ambrose.

1032. Arianism: Historical and Theological Reassessments. Papers from the Ninth International Conference on Patristic Studies, September 5-10, 1983, Oxford, England. Philadelphia Patristic Foundation, 1985.

1033. Arnobius of Sicca. *The Case Against the Pagans.* Translated and annotated by G. E. McCracken. 2 vols. Westminster, Md.: Newman Press, 1949. Arnobius, writing in the time of Diocletian, represents the fanatical sledgehammer approach to non-Christians, a feature not entirely out of fashion even in our own enlightened times.

1034. Athanasius. *The Life of Antony and the Letter to Marcellinus.* Translated by Robert C. Gregg. New York: Paulist Press, 1980. One of the most influential books ever written, a fourth century classic.

1035. Athanasius. *On the Incarnation.* Translated by a religious of C. S. M. V. Centenary Press, 1944; reprint ed., Cambridge: University Press; Crestwood, N. Y.: St. Vladimir's Orthodox Theological Seminary, 1982. A good example, in a good translation, of the power that Athanasius' writings had in his own time. Delightful introduction by C. S. Lewis.

1036. Barnard, Leslie W. "The Antecedents of Arius." *Vigiliae Christianae* (1970); 72-88.

1037. Barnard, Leslie W. "Athanasius and the Meletian Schism in Egypt." *Journal of Egyptian Archaeology* 59 (1973): 181-189.

1038. Barnard, Leslie W. "The Date of S. Athanasius' Vita Antonii." *Vigiliae Christianae* 28 (1974): 169-175.

1039. Barnard, Leslie W. "Marcellus of Ancyra and the Eusebians." *Greek Orthodox Theological Review* 25 (Spring 1980): 63-76. Who's orthodox and who isn't in the 340s, starring the bishop of Rome, the bishop of Ancyra, Athanasius, other famous church personalities, a few emperors, and the Council of Serdica.

1040. Barnard, Leslie W. "Pope Julius, Marcellus of Ancyra and the Council of Serdica - a Reconsideration." *Recherche de Theologie Ancienne et Medievale* 38 (1971): 69-79. "It was one of the tragedies of the fourth century that the division between East and West hardened so rapidly in the six years between 337 and 343" (p. 78). Barnard refers to the Christian church during the maturation of the Arian controversy, yet another of the doctrinal disputes that expressed both the vigor of theological thought and the unlimited opportunities for misunderstanding between the Latin west and the Greek east.

1041. Barnes, Timothy D. "Angel of Light or Mystic Initiate? The Problem of the *Life of Antony*." *Journal of Theological Studies* 37 (1986): 353-368. Barnes argues that the fourth century *Life of Antony* was not written by Athanasius, as is now commonly believed, but was written in Coptic by a close associate of Antony. The Coptic edition was lost but a Syriac translation survives. The surviving Greek edition was a reworking of the original Coptic version, and was modified to suit the tastes of urban Christians in the Roman world, far from the deserts of Egypt.

1042. Barnes, Timothy D. "The Beginnings of Donatism." *Journal of Theological Studies* 25 (April 1975): 13-22. Donatism, an African schism that troubled both church and state throughout the fourth century, has for us very murky beginnings. The surviving sources are, as usual, inadequate; but they are also on many points slanted and misleading, which is worse. Barnes discusses the sources, the chronology of events, and some specific problems.

1043. Barnes, Timothy D. "The Composition of Eusebius' Onomasticon." *Journal of Theological Studies* 26 (1975): 412-415. Barnes dates this gazetteer of Biblical place-names to before A. D. 300.

1044. Barnes, Timothy D. "The Editions of Eusebius' *Ecclesiastical History*." *Greek, Roman and Byzantine Studies* 21 (1980): 191-201. Barnes settles on a first edition ca. 295, a second ca. 313/14, a third ca. 315, and a fourth in 325. Getting right with the dates for the *Ecclesiastical History* is fundamental for understanding a number of political and other developments in the first quarter of the fourth century; hence the continuing efforts of scholars like Barnes to sort it all out.

1045. Barnes, Timothy D. "The Emperor Constantine's Good Friday Sermon." *Journal of Theological Studies* 27 (1976): 414-423. About the authenticity of Constantine's speech, called "To the Assembly of the Saints (*Oratio ad Sanctos*)," there has been no end of controversy. Barnes seeks to demonstrate that it was indeed Constantine's own speech, delivered in Serdica on Good Friday, 12 April 317.

1046. Barnes, Timothy D. "Lactantius and Constantine." *Journal of Roman Studies* 63 (1973): 29-46. Barnes reworks some early fourth century chronology to show that Lactantius' *De Mortibus Persecutorum* was not a piece of propaganda for Constantine. Naturally Lactantius was in favor of Christian emperors, or at least sympathizing emperors; but he exercised independence of judgment nevertheless. Barnes dates the death of Diocletian to 311 or 313, the first war between Constantine and Licinius to 316/17, and the *De Mortibus* to 314 or early 315.

1047. Barnes, Timothy D. "Panegyric, History and Hagiography in Eusebius' Life of Constantine." [forthcoming as of early 1988].

1048. Barnes, Timothy D. "Some Inconsistencies in Eusebius." *Journal of Theological Studies* 35 (1984): 470-475. Barnes defends his thesis (1044) regarding the editions and versions of Eusebius' *Ecclesiastical History* and *Martyrs of Palestine* against R. M. Grant, who in his *Eusebius as Church Historian* (1133) proposes that the *EH* underwent more revisions than Barnes allows.

1049. Barnes, Timothy D. "Two Speeches by Eusebius." *Greek, Roman and Byzantine Studies* 18 (1977): 341-345. The famous "Tricennial Oration" is really two speeches. Barnes shows why there are two, describes the purpose of each, and dates each one, while explaining how confusion arose on the matter.

1050. Basil of Caesarea: Christian, Humanist, Ascetic. A Sixteen-Hundredth Anniversary Symposium. Part One: Vita, Opera, Doctrina; Part Two: The Tradition. Edited by Paul J. Fedwick. Toronto: Pontifical Institute of Mediaeval Studies, 1981. This two volume set of papers should fit the requirements of those who want a good dose of recent studies of this important fourth century religious leader and the context of his life. C. Kannengiesser, *Catholic Historical Review* 70 (1984): 114-116 (+).

1051. Baur, Chrysostomus. *John Chrysostom and His Time.* 2 vols. Translated from the German ed. of 1929-30 by Sr. M. Gonzaga. London: Sands and Co. Ltd., 1959. This work might safely be characterized as the traditional Catholic point of view on the fourth century. On the fall of the Arians: ". . . the sudden emergence of Theodosius meant for the Arians the unexpected but well deserved end of their dominance. . . . It was a blessing for Christianity and Christian culture that this poison plant finally disappeared from the world" (p. 128). Naturally Chrysostom is treated very well. A valuable study if the reader is able to remember that the perspective of the author is narrow. Large bibliography.

1052. Baynes, Norman H. "Alexandria and Constantinople: A Study in Ecclesiastical Diplomacy." In his *Byzantine Studies and Other Essays*, pp. 97-115. New York: John DeGraff, 1955. Which city would lead Christianity in the eastern empire? The question became important when Constantinople became the capital. Alexandria had the advantage of strong, independent bishops, far from the imperial court; but a determined emperor could bring it to heel. And Constantinople had what we might call the momentum of events on its side. Baynes narrates the titanic struggle, ending at the Council of Chalcedon.

1053. Baynes, Norman H. "An Athanasian Forgery?" In his *Byzantine Studies and Other Essays*, pp. 282-287. London: Athlone Press, 1955; Westport, Conn.: Greenwood Press, 1974. Baynes contends with Otto Seeck about the authenticity of a critical piece of primary source material for the events of Athanasius' life.

1054. Baynes, Norman H. "Athanasiana." *Journal of Egyptian Archaeology* 11 (1925): 61-65.

1055. Beaver, Robert P. "The Donatist Circumcellions." *Church History* 4 (1935): 123-133. Although moderate Donatists sometimes disowned them, the militant Circumcellions were a necessity to the survival of the Donatist schism in Africa in the fourth century. Beaver tells their colorful story, labelling them "remarkable bands of nomadic terrorists, recruited at haphazard from the dregs of the population, from the discontented of every native race and province, fugitive slaves, ruined farmers, oppressed colons, outlawed criminals, social failures, excommunicated Catholics, and purely religious fanatics" (p. 125)

1056. Beaver, Robert P. "The Rise of Monasticism in the Church of Africa." *Church History* 6 (1937): 350-372. Monasticism was introduced into Africa by Augustine when he returned home in the 380s. Augustine largely dominated its development, with some success, but the Arian Vandals destroyed the institution entirely after the 430s.

1057. Bell, H. I. "Athanasius: A Chapter in Church History." *Congregational Quarterly* #2 (1925): 158-176. Generally a helpful introduction to Athanasius and the controversy over Arianism. Bell is very much an admirer of Athanasius, described as "virile, confident, alive, fronting the dawn, the light of the coming generation, the builder of a new order" (p. 176).

1058. Booth, Alan D. "The Chronology of Jerome's Early Years." *Phoenix* 35 (1981): 237-259.   Interesting biographical information on Jerome and his friends and other contemporaries in the fourth century.

1059. Booth, Alan D. "The Date of Jerome's Birth." *Phoenix* 33 (1979): 346-353.   After a thorough review of the evidence, Booth decides on the latter half of 347 or the beginning of 348.

1060. Bregman, Jay A. *Synesius of Cyrene: Philosopher-Bishop.* The Transformation of the Classical Heritage, 2. Berkeley: University of California Press, 1982. The elusive Synesius is presented here as very much the fourth century philosopher who never really wanted to be a Christian, much less a bishop, but decided he could manage both if the church would accommodate his philosophical principles and inquiries. P. Henry, *American Historical Review* 88 (1983): 369-370 (+).

1061. Brock, Sebastian. "Christians in the Sasanid Empire: A Case of Divided Loyalties." In his *Syriac Perspectives on Late Antiquity*, Ch. VI. London: Variorum Reprints, 1984. Christianity never became a state religion in Persia, as it did in the fourth century Roman state. But it was an important movement there too. Brock outlines the Christian experience in Persia, so different from developments going on simultaneously across the border in Roman territory.

1062. Brock, Sebastian. "Early Syrian Asceticism." *Numen* 20 (1973): 1-19. Reprinted in his *Syrian Perspectives on Late Antiquity*, Ch. I. London: Variorum Reprints, 1984. Brock shows "the indigenous character of Syriac asceticism" (p. 3) in the fourth century, relating it to Christian developments in the area long before Christianity became identified with Greek or Roman culture.

1063. Brown, Peter. "Aspects of the Christianization of the Roman Aristocracy." *Journal of Roman Studies* 51 (1961): 1-11. Reprinted in his *Religion and Society in the Age of Saint Augustine,* pp. 161-182. New York: Harper and Row, 1972. Brown explores the less dramatic, more persistent features that brought about the general conversion of the Roman aristocracy to Christianity in the late fourth century and early fifth centuries, with a minimum of bad feeling and a continuity of culture and prestige.

1064. Brown, Peter. *Augustine of Hippo: A Biography.* Berkeley: University of California Press, 1967. Brown presents a flesh and blood Augustine. Theology and philosophy are well in the background, when they appear at all. This is the real Augustine, functioning in the setting of the late Roman empire, and one can see the contrasts between the fourth century empire and the fifth century empire in the long life of this one individual. In the words of M. D. Knowles' review: "Augustine's boyhood was passed in the warm autumn of Roman provincial life; his last years in its November." B. Tierney, *American Historical Review* 74 (1968): 126 (+); M. D. Knowles, *English Historical Review* 84 (1969): 338-339 (+-).

1065. Brown, Peter. *The Body and Society: Men, Women and Sexual Renunciation in the Early Church.* New York: Columbia University Press, 1988. Brown carefully explores the growth of sexual renunciation in the church, noting the views of asceticism which prevailed in pagan society and Judaism, and contrasting these with the views of Christians. How to bring the human body under control: this was the question of concern behind sexual mores in the Roman world. For the pagans, the body was to be brought into a permanent and stable procreational setting for the sake of the community, the city; for the Christians, the body had another function, which was to be used - or, better perhaps, cast off - in the search for God. This view, or something like it in the service of a higher philosophy, was not a complete stranger to paganism; but it took on a particular intensity and a larger presence in the Christian world. Brown lingers on the fourth century, the "golden century," as he calls it, when the ascetic ideal, inherited from the young church, really blossomed into a compelling and growing aspect of service to the church, although it was variously explained and used from region to region, and was often heavily resisted in a world still moored to classical standards of behavior. The increasing appeal of the church and its ascetic dimension to the leading elements of western Roman society is nicely contrasted against the backdrop of increasing political disintegration in the late fourth century empire. W. H. C. Frend, *New York Review of Books* 36 (February 2, 1989): 39-41 (+); H. Chadwick, *Times*

Literary Supplement #4473 (December 23, 1988): 1411-1412 (+).

1066. Brown, Peter. "Christianity and Local Culture in Roman North Africa." *Journal of Roman Studies* 58 (1968): 85-95. Reprinted in his *Religion and Society in the Age of Saint Augustine,* pp. 279-300. New York: Harper and Row, 1972. "This, I would suggest, was the cultural function of the rise of Christianity in Late Roman Africa: far from fostering native tradition, it widened the franchise of the Latin language" (p. 92). Christianity, ironically, became the great vehicle for the further spread of Latin culture in the fourth century, as the army had been in, say, the first century.

1067. Brown, Peter. *The Cult of the Saints: Its Rise and Function in Latin Christianity.* Chicago: University of Chicago Press, 1980. The power structure of the late fourth century and beyond began to include the departed saints of the Christian church whose supernatural power and intercession between heaven and earth had an inherent appeal to all classes of people. The problem of who was to have control of the approaches to this power - i.e., the great aristocratic families or the bishops of the entire congregation - was one of the important issues of the age. The bishops won. J. Sumption, *Times Literary Supplement* (May 1, 1981): 479 (+-); B. W. Scholz, *American Historical Review* 86 (1981): 1080-1081 (+).

1068. Burn, Andrew E. *The Council of Nicaea.* New York: MacMillan, 1925.

1069. Callam, Daniel. "Clerical Continence in the Fourth Century: Three Papal Decretals." *Theological Studies* 41 (1980): 3-50. Callam works within the context of fourth century views of the relationship between continence and ritual observance to understand the bishop of Rome's legislation in the late fourth century. The Jovinians and the Priscillians receive appropriate attention.

1070. Cameron, Alan. "Palladas and Christian Polemic." *Journal of Roman Studies* 55 (1965): 17-30. Reprinted in his

Literature and Society in the Early Byzantine World, Ch. IV. London: Variorum Reprints, 1985. "It is the purpose of this paper to show (a) that there is no reason for supposing that Palladas had any knowledge of the Bible or indeed any knowledge of Christian teaching at all, but (b) that he was nevertheless familiar with the catch-phrases and cliches of Christian apologetic, and that the realization of this is the key to some of his most enigmatic poems" (p. 17).

1071. Cameron, Averil. "Eusebius of Caesarea and the Rethinking of History." In *Tria Corda: Scritti in Onore de Arnaldo Momigliano*, pp. 71-88. Edited by E. Gabba. Como: Edizioni New Press, 1983. Let's stop picking on Eusebius when he fudges things a little, and changes his tune from time to time, says Cameron. After all, he was not writing scientific history as we know it: he was writing as a "committed believer" in the Christian movement and its mission. The spectacular career of Constantine gave Eusebius cause to do a considerable amount of rethinking as the years went along and it increasingly appeared that Constantine was a special feature in the design of Providence to unite Christianity and the Roman empire in a holy alliance.

1072. Cameron, Averil. "New and Old in Christian Literature." In *The 17th International Byzantine Congress: Major Papers*, pp. 46-58. Dumbarton Oaks/Georgetown University, Washington, D. C., August 3-8, 1986. New Rochelle, N. Y.: A. D. Caratzas, 1986. Cameron sees "the development of Christian writing as a powerful and innovative factor" in promoting Christianity, and argues that "most of the Christian literary genres favoured by the Byzantines in later periods arose in the context of the social and economic conditions of the later Roman empire" (p. 45). The author stresses that Christianity and its literature did not develop in a separate environment: its literature worked in the same ring with pagan literature.

1073. Cardman, Francine. "The Rhetoric of the Holy Places: Palestine in the Fourth Century." *Papers presented at the Eighth International Conference on Patristic Studies,*

Oxford, September 3-8, 1979. Alas, this piece was not printed in the published papers of the conference, *Gnosis and Gnosticism* (Brill, 1981).

1074. Carter, Robert E. "The Chronology of Saint John Chrysostom's Early Life." *Tradition* 18 (1962): 357-364.

1075. Casey, Stephen. "Lactantius' Reaction to Pagan Philosophy." *Classica et Mediaevalia* 32 (1971-80): 203-219. Lactantius is "more lenient with pagan philosophy than most other Christian writers," and is very sympathetic towards certain philosophers. Nevertheless, he is mostly concerned to promote Christianity, and he uses and abuses philosophy as it suits his polemical needs.

1076. Chadwick, Henry. *Augustine*. New York: Oxford University Press, 1986. Very helpful on the development of Augustine's thought in the formative years of the fourth century.

1077. Chadwick, Henry. "Conversion in Constantine the Great." In *Studies in Church History.* Vol. 15: *Religious Motivation*, pp. 1-13. Edited by Derek Baker. Oxford: Basil Blackwell, 1978.

1078. Chadwick, Henry. "Faith and Order at the Council of Nicaea: A Note on the Background of the Sixth Canon." *Harvard Theological Review* 53 (1960): 171-195.

1079. Chadwick, Henry. "The Fall of Eustathius of Antioch." *Journal of Theological Studies* 49 (1948): 27-35.

1080. Chadwick, Henry. "Ossius of Cordova and the Presidency of the Council of Antioch, 325." *Journal of Theological Studies* 9 (October 1958): 292-304.

1081. Chadwick, Henry. *Priscillian of Avila: The Occult and the Charismatic in the Early Church.* Oxford: Clarendon Press, 1976. Chadwick looks at the confluence of events in late fourth century Spanish and Gallic Christianity, far from the centers of Christian thought in Rome and the east, which led to the execution of Priscillian, the first heretic to die at the hands of a Christian emperor. E. R. Hardy, *Church History* 46 (1977): 105-106 (+).

1082. Chadwick, Owen. *John Cassian, a Study in Primitive Monasticism.* 2nd ed. Cambridge: University Press, 1950; 1968. Cassian's creative period of monastic development in the west was in the fifth century of barbarian invasions; but he had done his homework in Egypt in the late fourth century, and it was this brand of fourth century monasticism that he introduced to Gaul with modifications. Like Synesius and Augustine, Cassion was a fourth century person facing the challenge of fifth century realities, rather in the way that nineteenth century Victorian gentlemen had to face the realities of twentieth century warfare In 1914-1918.

1083. Chesnut, Glenn F. "Fate, Fortune, Free Will and Nature in Eusebius of Caesarea." *Church History* 42 (1973): 165-182.

1084. Chesnut, Glenn F. *The First Christian Historians: Eusebius, Socrates, Sozomen, Theodoret, and Evagrius.* Paris: Editions Beauchesne, 1977. The works of Eusebius, Socrates, Sozomen and Theodoret encompass the fourth century. The latter three lived well beyond the fourth century, and their distance influenced their perspective, but they must be consulted. Chesnut offers an analysis of the thought-world in which these Christian historians operated. R. H. Storch, *Catholic Historical Review* 70 (1984): 102-103 (+).

1085. Chicoteau, M. *The Journey to Martyrdom of Saints Felix and Regula Circa 300 A. D.: A Study of Sources and Significance.* Studies on Early Christian Art, Archaeology and Liturgy. Brisbane: Watson Ferguson, 1984.

1086. Chitty, Dervas James. *The Desert a City: An Introduction to the History of Egyptian and Palestinian Monasticism under the Christian Empire.* Crestwood, N. Y.: St. Vladimir's Seminary Press, 1966.

1087. Clark, Elizabeth A. *Jerome, Chrysostom, and Friends: Essays and Translations.* Studies in Women and Religion, 2. New York: E. Mellon Press, 1979. "As a whole, the book illustrates the thesis that there was with patristic Christianity an elevation of status for celibate women, but not for married ones" (p. vi). Clark includes some first-ever-in-English translations of some writings of Chrysostom which generally bear on the theme of the book.

1088. Clarke, W. K. Lowther. *St. Basil the Great: A Study in Monasticism.* New York: Macmillan Co., 1913.

1089. Coleman-Norton, P. R. "St. Chrysostom and Greek Philosophers." *Classical Philology* 25 (1930): 305-317. Chrysostom had a "low opinion" of Greek philosophy and philosophers. Coleman-Norton adduces the evidence for this from Chrysostom's voluminous writings.

1090. Crawford, W. S. *Synesius the Hellene.* London: Rivingtons, 1901.

1091. Croke, Brian. "The Originality of Eusebius' Chronicle." *American Journal of Philology* 103 (1982): 195-200. Croke says there was no real precedent for the complex kind of world-wide chronological comparison which was the fundamental feature of Eusebius' *Chronicle*. It was innovative, just as Eusebius had said.

1092. Cross, F. L. "The Council of Antioch in 325 A. D." *Church Quarterly Review* 128 (1939): 49-76.

1093. Cross, F. L. *The Study of St. Athanasius.* An Inaugural Lecture Delivered Before the University of Oxford on 1 December 1944. Oxford: Clarendon Press, 1945. Good review and further discussion of Athanasius by N. H. Baynes, *Journal of Roman Studies* 35 (1945): 121-122.

1094. Dechow, Jon F. *Dogma and Mysticism in Early Christianity: Epiphanius of Cyprus and the Legacy of Origen.*

Patristic Monograph Series, 13. Macon, Ga.: Mercer University Press, 1988. This is most useful for those who want to get a sense of the intellectual and practical efforts, increasingly with government support, of the dogmatic Christian right wing to destroy pluralistic thought within the Christian movement in the late fourth century. For an orthodox thinker like the bishop Epiphanius, informed and encouraged by the rather narrow-minded and often fanatical monks of the eastern empire, the goal was to promote Nicene orthodoxy against all comers, from the contemporary Arius to the long dead Origen, whose often misinterpreted works were scathingly condemned. The mysticism of the age, in part an inheritance from Origen, was condemned too. In a Christian context, Dechow presents a chapter in the story of the triumph of orthodoxy; but in the larger, Roman context, Dechow's valuable work may be seen as a sad instance of the rise and ultimate success of a fanaticism of religious belief that helped transform the Roman spiritual world from the tolerant ambience of classical times to the narrow thought-world of medieval times.

1095. De Mendieta, E. Amand. "The Official Attitude of Basil of Caesarea as a Christian Bishop towards Greek Philosophy and Science." In *Studies in Church History.* Vol. 13: *The Orthodox Churches and the West,* pp. 25-49. Edited by Derek Baker. Oxford: Basil Blackwell, 1976. Officially, Basil condemned Greek philosophy and science; privately he had a more relaxed view. After all, he had studied in Athens. Such paradoxical attitudes were characteristic of many fourth century bishops.

1096. De Ste. Croix, Geoffrey E. M. "Early Christian Attitudes to Property and Slavery." In *Studies in Church History.* Vol. 12: *Church Society and Politics,* pp. 1-38. Oxford: Basil Blackwell, 1975. ". . . it was precisely the exclusive concentration of the early christians upon the personal relations between man and man, or man and God, and their complete indifference, as christians, to the institutions of the world in which they lived, that prevented christianity from ever having much effect for good upon the relations between man and man" (p. 36).

1097. Dietrich, B. C. "The Triumph of Barbarism and Religion: The Early Christians in the Roman World." *Acta Classica* 18 (1975): 71-84.   "The sad but inescapable conclusion seems to be that in human affairs only violent self-assertion is crowned with success, and the Christian Church was no exception" (p. 84).

1098. Donaldson, Christopher. *Martin of Tours.* London: Routledge and Kegan Paul, 1980.   A vigorous biography of one of the most interesting and influential holy men of the fourth century western empire. A section on daily life in the Roman army may seem a surprising entry, but Martin was a soldier for many years before becoming a saint. Donaldson is not a scholar of the period, so there is room for criticism of his knowledge of many aspects of the fourth century.   His contrast of empire and church may raise eyebrows among Romanophiles: "The unity of the empire was reasonably apparent, but was a superficial and brittle creation, with no deep significance, and was often maintained by means of secret police and informers; the unity of the church was something that, in spite of internal disagreements, went deep and provided its members with a sense of belonging to a worldwide institution with ever-spreading frontiers far beyond the bounds of the empire" (p. 15).   G. F. Chesnut, *Church History* 50 (1981): 362-363 (+); J. Richards, *History* 65 (1980): 458 (+); J. McClure, *Times Literary Supplement* (September 26, 1980): 1069 (-).

1099. Downey, Glanville. "The Perspective of the Early Church Historians." *Greek, Roman and Byzantine Studies* 6 (1965): 57-70.   Socrates, Sozomen and Evagrius are discussed. The first two are important to the fourth century, about which they wrote in their church histories.

1100. Drake, H. A. "Athanasius' First Exile." *Greek, Roman and Byzantine Studies* 27 (1986): 193-204.   Drake reviews the events of 335 pertaining to the Council of Tyre, the activities of Athanasius, and the continuing efforts of Constantine to bring unity and peace to the Christian church.

1101. Drake, H. A. "Eusebius on the True Cross." *Journal of Ecclesiastical History* 36 (1985): 1-22. With Eusebius and recent archaeological data at hand Drake discusses the discovery of the Holy Sepulchre and the Cross during the time of Constantine.

1102. Drake, H. A. *In Praise of Constantine: A Historical Study and New Translation of Eusebius' Tricennial Orations.* Berkeley: University of California Press, 1976. The oration, "In Praise of Constantine," is in fact two orations: one is the original, "In Praise of Constantine," the other is "On the Holy Sepulchre." Drake also has the interesting view that the "In Praise" was phrased carefully to appeal to the large number of pagans who would have been in the audience. Eusebius diplomatically used theological expressions common to Christians and pagans alike. This point is reinforced by Drake's helpful translation of the original Greek. E. D. Hunt, *Classical Review* 29 (1979): 27-28 (+); J. Eadie, *American Historical Review* 82 (1977): 931-932 (+); G. C. Stead, *Journal of Ecclesiastical History* 29 (1978): 94-95 (+).

1103. Drake, H. A. "Suggestions of Date in Constantine's *Orations to the Saints.*" *American Journal of Philology* 106 (1985): 335-349. Drake reviews the relevant literature on this famous oration, but concludes that it is beyond precise dating. Eusebius took it as an example of the mature thought of the emperor, thus placing it later rather than earlier in the reign.

1104. Drake, H. A. "What Eusebius Knew: The Genesis of the *Vita Constantini.*" *Classical Philology* 83 (1988): 20-38. Drake suggests that Eusebius had access to more information about Constantine than is generally believed in current scholarly circles; but his use of that information was selective and reveals a tendency to promote his own agenda, which was in essence to show a Constantine more inflexibly in favor of the new religion than in fact was the case. Constantine favored religious unity through compromise and flexibility, a feature that does not come through in Eusebius, at least not intentionally.

1105. Dudden, Frederick Homes. *The Life and Times of St. Ambrose.* 2 vols. New York: Oxford University Press, 1935; Wilmington, Del.: International Academic Pub., 1979. Essential. It is best, however, to keep in mind the observation of Norman Baynes: "Dr. Homes Dudden's picture of St Ambrose could easily be transferred to a stained-glass window" (*Byzantine Studies and Other Essays*, p. 354).

1106. Elm, Susannah K. "The Organization and Institutions of Female Asceticism in Fourth-Century Cappadocia and Egypt." Ph. D. dissertation, Oxford University Press, 1987.

1107. Ettlinger, Gerard H. "Some Historical Evidence for the Date of St. John Chrysostom's Birth in the Treatise 'ad viduam iuniorem.' " *Traditio* 16 (1960): 373-380.

1108. Eunomius. *The Extant Works.* Translated with commentary by Richard Paul Vaggione. Oxford Early Christian Texts. Oxford: Clarendon Press, 1987. The late fourth century Arian philosopher-theologian Eunomius' surviving works are translated and scrutinized. Vaggione provides a substantial introduction for those who wish to follow the intellectual trends of later Arianism, sometimes called neo-Arianism. F. W. Norris, *Church History* 58 (1989): 85-86 (+).

1109. *The Fathers Speak: St. Basil the Great, St. Gregory Nazianzus, St. Gregory of Nyssa.* Edited and translated by Georges Barrios. Crestwood, N. Y.: St. Vladimir's Seminary Press, 1986. The fourth century Cappadocian fathers are revealed through excerpts from over 150 of their letters, translated into idiomatic English, plus commentary. A. Tripolitis, *Church History* 58 (1989): 138-139 (+).

1110. Fedwick, Paul Jonathan, ed. *Basil of Caesarea, Christian, Humanist, Ascetic: A Sixteen-Hundredth Anniversay Symposium.* Toronto: Pontifical Institute of Mediaeval Studies, 1981.

1111. Fedwick, Paul Jonathan. *The Church and the Charisma of Leadership in Basil of Caesarea.* Toronto: Pontifical Institute of Mediaeval Studies, 1978.

1112. Fisher, Arthur L. "Lactantius' Ideas Relating Christian Truth and Society." *Journal of the History of Ideas* 43 (1982): 355-377. Fisher "traces and analyzes some of Lactantius' ideas in an attempt to see some contours of what was thinkable for a converted intellectual layman between perhaps 303 and 310" (p. 357).

1113. Foakes-Jackson, Frederick J. *Eusebius Pamphili: A Study of the Man and His Writings.* Cambridge: W. Heffer and Sons, Ltd., 1933.

1114. Frend, W. H. C. "Athanasius as an Egyptian Christian Leader in the Fourth Century." *New College Bulletin* 8 (1974): 20-37. Reprinted in his *Religion Popular and Unpopular in the Early Christian Centuries,* Ch. XVI. London: Variorum Reprints, 1976. Frend gives a full description and analysis of the extraordinary Athanasius, who as bishop of Alexandria took on all, from small time heretics and schismatics to emperors, in defense of orthodox Christianity.

1115. Frend, W. H. C. "Circumcellions and Monks." *Journal of Theological Studies* 20 (1969): 542-549.

1116. Frend, W. H. C. *The Donatist Church: A Movement of Protest in Roman North Africa.* Oxford: Clarendon Press, 1952. Donatism was a particularly troublesome movement in the fourth and early fifth centuries. It was largely religious but encompassed many types of protest. Frend knows the source material and uses archaeology as well to recreate a complex and troubling issue both for the Roman state and the church. J. P. Christopher, *Catholic Historical Review* 39

(1953): 308-309 (+); A. Pincherle, *Journal of Roman Studies* 44 (1954): 138-139 (+); J. M. Wallace-Hadrill, *History* 39 (1954): 102-103 (+).

1117. Frend, W. H. C. "Ecclesia Britannica: Prelude or Dead End?" *Journal of Ecclesiastical History* 30 (1979): 129-144. Reprinted in his *Town and Country in the Early Christian Centuries,* Ch. XII. London: Variorum Reprints, 1980. Christianity in Britain lacked popular support and suffered a severe eclipse when the island was separated from the influence of the better established churches of Gaul. "Christianity in fourth-century Britain presents a series of disjointed cameos. The literary evidence suggests a poor and rather undeveloped Church, following the lead of more experienced continental Churches but contributing little itself " (p. 136).

1118. Frend, W. H. C. *Martyrdom and Presecution in the Early Church: A Study of a Conflict from the Maccabees to Donatus.* New York: New York University Press, 1967. Frend sees a trend in the west where martyrdom gained in popularity, blossoming in Donatism, and in the east where martyrdom lost its appeal, giving way to monasticism. The fourth century was, in its usual way, the crossroads in this historical shift. G. Downey, *American Historical Review* 73 (1968): 784-785 (+); L. Feldman, *Classical Journal* 65 (1970): 186-188 (+-); *Times Literary Supplement* (March 3, 1966): 175 (+-).

1119. Frend, W. H. C. "The Organisation of the Donatist and Catholic Churches in the North African Countryside." In *Settimani de Studio del Centro Italiano de Studi sull' Alto Medioevo,* pp. 601-637. V. 28. Spoleto, 1982.

1120. Frend, W. H. C. "Paulinus of Nola and the Last Century of the Western Empire." *Journal of Roman Studies* 59 (1969): 1-11. Reprinted in his *Town and Country in the Early Christian Centuries,* Ch. XIV. London: Variorum Reprints, 1980. In the fourth century half of his life, Paulinus was an aristocrat pursuing a public career; in the fifth, he was a priest without concern for the fate of the Roman state: "He represents the dramatic shift that seems to have taken place in the west after the death of Theodosius I in January 395, from the predominance in public affairs of literary men like Symmachus and Ausonius, moulded in the classics, to men of intense and sombre religiosity that characterized a Count Marcellinus or Augustine himself" (p. 7).

1121. Frend, W. H. C. *Religion, Popular and Unpopular in the Early Christian Centuries.* London: Variorum Reprints, 1976. Reprints of articles done between 1942 and 1975. The relevant ones are individually analyzed.

1122. Frend, W. H. C. *The Rise of Christianity.* Philadelphia: Fortress Press, 1984. The student of the fourth century will especially wish to consult the sections entitled "Christianity and the Roman Empire," and "From Constantine to Chalcedon," of this monumental work. Frend tends to be oriented toward western rather than eastern Christianity, and there is an emphasis on the Jewish factor over the Hellenistic factor in coloring Christianity. The great diversity and even disunity of Christianity is a constant theme. As a kind of summary of his themes, Frend has an article in *The American Scholar* 54 (Summer 1985), 397-402, entitled "The Rise of Christianity," which might be good to read before tackling the book. There is also his *The Early Church* (1965; 1981) to consider. E. D. Hunt, *Journal of Roman Studies* 76 (1986): 301-302 ("displaying a comprehensiveness and degree of detail which arouses nothing but admiration"); E. TeSelle, *Christian Century* 102 (1985): 330-331 (+-); S. H. Griffith, *Journal of Religion* 66 (1986): 431-436 (+-); P. Garnsey, *Times Literary Supplement* (April 5, 1983): 380- (+-).

1123. Frend, W. H. C. *Saints and Sinners in the Early Church: Differing and Conflicting Traditions in the First Six Centuries.* Wilmington, Del.: Michael Glazier, 1985. Frend looks at who was in and who was out as the church moved along the uncertain road of self-definition. Frend looks at the fourth century outsiders sympathetically. The chapters on Donatism are outstanding. H. Chadwick, *Times Literary Supplement* (November 8, 1985): 1271 (+).

1124. Frend, W. H. C. "Town and Countryside in Early Christianity." In *The Church in Town and Countryside*, pp. 25-42. Edited by Derek Baker. Oxford: Blackwell, 1979. Frend takes us on a voyage back to A. D. 350, and like a good tour guide points to various changes taking places in the empire, and invites us to consider why Christianity was developing in different ways here and there in the Roman world. Then he takes us back to the beginnings of Christianity and explains the origins of features that were maturing in the fourth century.

1125. Frend, W. H. C. "The Two Worlds of Paulinus of Nola." In *Latin Literature of the Fourth Century*, pp. 100-132. Edited by J. W. Binns. Boston: Routledge and Kegan Paul, 1974. Reprinted in his *Religion Popular and Unpopular in the Early Christian Centuries*, Ch. XV. London: Variorum Reprints, 1976. A wholesale abandonment of secular life and responsibilities seems to have become trendy among wealthy and well-educated persons in the late fourth century. These people's talents went to religious devotions and contemplations rather than to the state. The effects were unhelpful when the Roman state needed all the help it could get. Frend gives a full analysis of Paulinus of Nola, a rich and powerful nobleman with government service behind him who stunned contemporaries by abandoning all for religion.

1126. Frend, W. H. C. and Clancy, K. "When Did the Donatist Schism Begin?" *Journal of Theological Studies* 28 (April 1977): 104-109. Frend reviews the evidence and the arguments, and concludes that although there can be no "absolute certainty," it would be better for now to leave the Donatist schism as having started in 311-312 rather than 307, as is sometimes proposed.

1127. Frend, W. H. C. "The Winning of the Countryside." *Journal of Ecclesiastical History* 18 (1967): 1-14. Reprinted in his *Town and Country in the Early Christian Centuries*, Ch. II. London: Variorum Reprints, 1980. It was no easy business to convert the stubborn and traditional country people to the new religion, and progress was not uniform in the huge Roman empire. The fourth century was critical, when monks and holy men really started to turn the tide.

1128. Geoghegan, A. T. *The Attitude Towards Labor in Early Christianity and Ancient Culture.* Studies in Christian Antiquity, VI. Washington, D. C.: Catholic University Press of America, 1945. The latter part of the book (originally the author's dissertation) deals with the Christian attitude towards labor, which was considered a tool of discipline as well as a productive effort, in both east and west. As was so often the case in fourth century Christianity, the monastic movement was in the forefront, formulating an approach to labor helpful towards Christian goals of discipline, charity, and spiritual development.

1129. Gilliard, Frank D. "Senatorial Bishops in the Fourth Century." *Harvard Theological Review* 77 (1984): 152-175. "I propose to argue here that when the identification of fourth-century bishops with imperial senators is cross-examined, it seldom carries conviction, and that the episcopal lists of the fourth century contain surprisingly few names from senatorial families" (p. 154). Where did they come from? They were middle and upper middle class types: " . . . if you scratch a bishop you will most likely find a *curialis* " (p. 155).

1130. Gilliard, Frank D. "The Social Origins of Bishops in the Fourth Century." Ph. D. dissertation, University of California, Berkeley, 1966. Most bishops were from the middle class, and this drain of talent into the church was a loss to the state, which was now competing for middle class talent.

1131. Gould, Graham. "Pachomios of Tabennesi. and the Foundation of an Independent Monastic Community." In *Studies in Church History.* Vol. 23: *Voluntary Religion*, pp. 15-24. Edited by W. J. Shiels and Diana Wood. Oxford: Basil Blackwell, 1986.

1132. Grant, Robert M. "The Case Against Eusebius, or, Did the Father of Church History Write History?" *Studia Patristica* 12 (1975): 413-421.   Did Eusebius write history? No, says Grant, at least not by any standard of historical honesty and comprehension that we know. He fudged chronology; he was "crudely moralistic," and glossed over the failures of his heroes; he doctored events to suit the times in which he wrote; and so on. Grant summarizes: "The *Church History* of Eusebius can be viewed . . . as his survival kit. It was written so that he could survive not only as subject of the emperor but as a Christian bishop in a time of great trouble" (p. 421).

1133. Grant, Robert M. *Eusebius as a Church Historian.* Oxford: Clarendon Press, 1980.   Through the *Historia Ecclesiastica* Grant analyzes the kind of historian Eusebius was and how he related to historiography as it was generally perceived in the Roman world of the time.   E. M. Yamauchi, *American Historical Review*   86 (1981): 1079 (+-); T. A. Kopecek, *Journal of Religion*   64 (1984): 115-116 (+).

1134.   Grant, Robert M.   "Religion and Politics at the Council of Nicaea." Inaugural lecture of Carl Darling Buck Professor in the University of Chicago, 1973.

1135. Green, M. R. "The Supporters of the Antipope Ursinus." *Journal of Theological Studies* 22 (1971): 531-538. Green reviews the violence and controversy surrounding the election of a new pope in A. D. 366, and reveals how imperial pressures and theological controversies had practical results in the factionalism that enveloped local ecclesiastical elections.

1136. Greenslade, S. L. "Heresy and Schism in the Later Roman Empire." In *Studies in Church History.* Vol. 9: *Schism, Heresy and Religious Protest*, pp. 1-20. Edited by Derek Baker. Cambridge: University Press, 1972.

1137. Greenslade, S. L. "The Illyrian Churches and the Vicariate of Thessalonica, 378-95." *Journal of Theological Studies*   46 (1945): 17-30.   The complex civil and ecclesiastical developments in Illyricum, a strategically critical area caught between east and west, are given full airing. The source material is critically reviewed.

1138. Greer, R. A. "The Antiochene Christology of Diodore of Tarsus." *Journal of Theological Studies* 17 (1966): 327-341. Diodore was a prominent monastic and clergyman of the second half of the fourth century, very much involved in the disputes and well known among the great personalities of the age, from emperors to clerics.

1139. Gregg, Robert C., ed. *Arianism: Historical and Theological Reassessments.* Papers from the Ninth International Conference on Patristic Studies. September 5-10, Oxford, England. Cambridge, Mass.: Philadelphia Patristic Foundation, 1985.

1140. Gregg, Robert C. *Consolation Philosophy: Greek and Christian Paideia in Basil and the Two Gregories.* Patristic Monograph Series 3. Cambridge, Mass.: Philadelphia Patristic Foundation, 1975. These fourth century Cappadocian bishops wrote eloquent consolation letters and funeral orations which Gregg analyzes, finding a large continuity with pagan prototypes. T. A. Kopecek, *Church History* 46 (1977): 104-105 (+).

1141. Gregg, Robert C. and Groh, Dennis E. "The Centrality of Soteriology in Early Arianism." *Anglican Theological Review* 59 (1977): 260-278. For an expansion of the Gregg/Groh position, see their book *Early Arianism* (1142).

1142. Gregg, Robert C. and Groh, Dennis E. *Early Arianism: A View of Salvation.* Philadelphia: Fortress Press, 1981. A refreshing and compelling treatment of the first stages of Arianism, revolving around the authors' clearly enunciated thesis: "We contend that early Arianism is most intelligible when viewed as a scheme of salvation. Soteriological concerns dominate the texts and inform every major aspect of the controversy. At the center of the Arian soteriology was a redeemer, obedient to his Creator's will, whose life of virtue modeled perfect creaturehood and hence the path of salvation for all Christians" (p. x). J. T. Lienhard, *Religious Studies Review* 8 (October 1982): 331-337 (+); E. Ferguson, *Church History* 52 (1983): 201 (++-).

1143. **Gregory, Timothy E.** "Novatianism: A Rigorist Sect in the Christian Roman Empire." *Byzantine Studies* 2 (1975): 1-18. The Novationists, an orthodox but aloof set of rigorists, prospered in the fourth century but declined suddenly in the fifth. Gregory analyzes the sect in prosperity and in decline.

1144. **Gregory, Timothy E.** "Zosimus 5.23 and the People of Constantinople." *Byzantion* 43 (1973): 61-83. John Chrysostom, the monks, and the people of Constantinople.

1145. **Gwatkin, Henry M.** *Studies of Arianism: Chiefly Referring to the Character and Chronology of the Reaction Which Followed the Council of Nicaea.* 2nd ed. Cambridge: Deighton Bell and Co., 1900; reprint ed., New York: AMS Press, 1978. This classic on Arianism in the fourth century is still considered standard fare. Gwatkin, in the 1882 preface, called his study "a review of the forces at work in the different stages of the controversy, traced out with special regard to the sequence of events and to their connexion with the social characteristics and political history of the Empire." Scholars still find it indispensable, but it is not without pitfalls. It is out of date in some areas, and Gwatkin is in the end strongly anti-Arian. He has strong views in other directions too. Calling pagans "heathens" may merely reflect the style of his time, but his reference to "the selfish cowardice of the monastic life" (p. 235) should alert the reader to beware. Regarding Arianism, Gwatkin concludes that "It went too far for heathenism, not far enough for Christianity" (p. 273).

1146. **Hagendahl, Harald.** *Latin Fathers and the Classics: A Study on the Apologists, Jerome, and Other Christian Writers.* Goteborg, Sweden: Elanders Boktryckeri Aktiebolag, 1958. Hagendahl first considers the relationship of Arnobius,

Lactantius, and others, to earlier writers and philosophers, especially Lucretius; then he devotes the larger part of the book to Jerome, in whom the struggle between Christian faith and the classics was more acute than in most educated Christians of the time. Cicero, Horace, Virgil: these were his favorites, and fluctuating between "aversion and adhesion to the classics Jerome never succeeded in getting over the internal conflict or in reaching a stable equilibrium" (p. 92). Hagendahl at great length documents the struggle, a very fourth century phenomenon for many Christian intellectuals.

1147. **Hall, Stuart G.** "The Sects under Constantine." In *Studies in Church History*. Vol. 23: *Voluntary Religion*, pp. 1-13. Edited by W. J. Shiels and Diana Wood. Oxford: Basil Blackwell, 1986.

1148. **Hanson, R. P. C.** "The Date and Authorship of Pseudo-Anthimus' *de Sancte Ecclesia*." *Proceedings of the Royal Irish Academy* 83 (1983): 251-254. Internal evidence is adduced to show that the short theological piece known as *de Sancta Ecclesia* is an anti-Arian tract dating from the late fourth century, c. 370, and originated in Antioch.

1149. **Hanson, R. P. C.** "The Doctrine of the Trinity Achieved in 381." *Scottish Journal of Theology* 36 (1983): 41-57. How the fourth century orthodox Christian thinkers finally put the Arians and what we might call hellenizing Christians intellectually in their place: outside the Christian fellowship. In this sense 381 is a milestone in the evolution of the Christian Roman world.

1150. **Hanson, R. P. C.** "The ORATIO AD SANCTOS Attributed to the Emperor Constantine and the Oracle at Daphne." *Journal of Theological Studies* 24 (1973): 505-511. Using internal and external evidence, Hanson advances the argument that Constantine could not possibly have written the *Oratio ad Sanctos,* and that it comes from the period 362 to 382.

1151. **Hardy, Edward R., Jr.** *Christian Egypt: Church and People; Christianity and Nationalism in the Patriarchate of Alexandria.* New York: Oxford University Press, 1952.

1152. **Hardy, Edward R., Jr.** "National Elements in the Career of St. Athanasius." *Church History* 2 (1933): 187-196. An effort to see nationalism and Christianity walking hand in hand in fourth century Egypt, encouraged by Athanasius. But, as the author admits, nationalism is a subject that the sources "do not consciously treat and must be a matter of interpretation rather than merely of quotation of evidence" (p. 187). Reader beware.

1153. **Haugaard, William P.** "Arius: Twice a Heretic?" *Church History* 29 (1960): 251-263. After reading this article one can only sympathize with Constantine's call for an end to quarreling among Christians over trifles. Of course the issues at stake were not trifles; but they must ever seem so to the modern layman first confronting them.

1154. **Hess, Hamilton.** *The Canons of the Council of Sardica, A. D. 343: A Landmark in the Early Development of Canon Law.* New York: Oxford University Press, 1958.

1155. **Hill, C.** "Classical and Christian Traditions in Some Writings of Saint Ambrose of Milan." Ph. D. dissertation, Oxford University, 1979.

1156. *Holy Women of the Syrian Orient.* Translated by Sebastion Brock and Susan Harvey. The Transformation of the Classical Heritage, 13. Berkeley: University of California Press, 1987. Fifteen hagiographies on holy women, translated from Syriac. The texts date from the fourth to seventh centuries.

1157. **Honigmann, E.** "The Original Lists of the Members of the Council of Nicaea, the Robber-Synod and the Council of Chalcedon." *Byzantion* 16 (1942-43): 20-80.

1158. Hubbell, Harry M. "Chrysostom and Rhetoric." *Classical Philology* 19 (1924): 261-276. In the fourth century the pagan art of rhetoric "gains full control of preaching, and then the victory is sudden and decisive" (p. 262). Hubbell examines the extent to which this is true in one of the greatest preachers of the time, John Chrysostom.

1159. Hunt, E. D. "Christians and Christianity in Ammianus Marcellinus." *Classical Quarterly* 35 (1985): 186-200. Hunt sees Ammianus as not being particularly troubled by Christianity per se. What he disliked was religion out of control. For him, "the business of government and empire could not successfully be dictated by religious conviction" (p. 200). The neutrality of government in religious matters was the best policy, and this was the feature of Valentinian's regime that Ammianus especially liked.

1160. Hunt, E. D. "From Dalmatia to the Holy Land: Jerome and the World of Late Antiquity." [Review of J. N. D. Kelly. *Jerome: His Life and Controversies*] *Journal of Roman Studies* 67 (1977): 166-171. In the context of a review of Kelly, Hunt encourages seeing Jerome "not only as a father of the church but as a man of his times" (p. 171). Jerome was all over the Roman world during his life, and seemed especially attracted to centers of power, such as Trier and Constantinople and Rome. His involvement in fourth century Roman society deserves more study. Hunt offers some preliminary directions.

1161. Hunt, E. D. "Palladius of Helenopolis: A Party and Its Supporters in the Church of the Late Fourth Century." *Journal of Theological Studies* 24 (1973): 456-480. An interesting story of how the tensions and disagreements of the western religious settlements in Jerusalem and Bethlehem were carried through the Roman world by people like Palladius who were associated for a time with one or other camp.

1162. Hunt, E. D. "St. Silvia of Aquataine: The Role of a Theodosian Pilgrim in the Society of East and West." *Journal of Theological Studies* 23 (1972): 351-373. "I have tried to suggest, from the example of Silvia, how the early Christian pilgrim, in taking the decisive step of journeying to the Holy Land, destined himself for a major role in the life of the church, not only at the scene of the holy places but no less in the community to which he returned" (p. 373).

1163. **Hunter, David G.** "Borrowings from Libanius in the *Comparatio Regis et Monachi* of St. John Chrysostom." *Journal of Theological Studies* 39 (1988): 525-531. The young John Chrysostom, around 378, struck against his former teacher Libanius and defended Christianity and the monks in one of his earliest essays.

1164. **Hunter, David G.** "Resistance to the Virginal Ideal in Late-Fourth-Century Rome: The Case of Jovinian." *Theological Studies* 48 (1987): 45-64. Aseticism, although gaining popularity in the later fourth century, was nevertheless not universally embraced as a better way of life. In fact, there was a reaction against the movement, and Jovinian was one monk associated prominently with this reaction. But Hunter qualifies Jovinian's position. He argues "that Jovinian is best understood not as an opponent of Christian virginity or asceticism per se, but rather as an opponent of Manicheism and of what he saw as Manichean tendencies among the Christian ascetics at Rome" (p. 46).

1165. **Huskinson, Janet.** *Concordia Apostolorum: Christian Propaganda at Rome in the Fourth and Fifth Centuries: A Study in Early Christian Iconography and Iconology.* Oxford: British Archaeological Reports, 1982. Huskinson gives a full analysis of the context in which Saints Paul and Peter were treated as equals in importance in the Roman church during the last half of the fourth century. E. D. Hunt, *Journal of Roman Studies* 74 (1984): 229-231 (+-).

1166. *In Honor of St. Basil the Great 379.* Still River, Mass.: St. Bede's Publications, 1979. Ten essays on the famous fourth century Cappadocian.

1167. Ison, David J. "The Constantinian Oration to the Saints - Authorship and Background." Ph. D. dissertation, University of London, 1985.

1168. Ison, David J. " [PAIS THEOU] in the Age of Constantine." *Journal of Theological Studies* 38 (1987): 412-419. Ison investigates an uncommon but apparently acceptable liturgical way in Greek of describing the relationship of Christ to God in the context of Constantine's *Oratio to the Saints*, where the style is used "as a bridge in the discussion between Christianity and paganism, and as an analogy for the divine Father/Son relationship drawn from imperial terminology for the emperor and his sons" (p. 419).

1169. Jalland, Trevor G. *The Church and the Papacy: A Historical Study.* New York: Morehouse-Gorham, 1944. Of the eight lectures included, two are of interest: IV. The Papacy and the Constantinian Autocracy; V. The Papacy and the Later Roman Empire. In long and dignified periods, the author weaves an informed and generously documented narrative of the ambitions and growth of authority of the bishop of Rome in the fourth century.

1170. John Chrysostom. *Discourses Against Judaizing Christians.* Edited by Paul Harkins. The Fathers of the Church, 68. Washington, D. C., 1979. See Robert Wilken, *John Chrysostom and the Jews* (1285), for the context of these late fourth century sources of anti-semitism.

1171. Jones, A. H. M. "St. John Chrysostom's Parentage and Education." *Harvard Theological Review* 46 (1953): 171-173. Jones sorts through the evidence to learn that Chrysostom was from a good but not rich Antiochene family, and that he was educated in rhetoric with the goal of preparation for a career in high imperial civil service.

1172. Judge, E. A. "The Earliest Use of Monachos for 'Monk' (P. Coll. Youtie 77) and the Origins of Monasticism." *Jahrbuch fur Antike und Christentum* 20 (1977): 72-89.

1173. Kannengiesser, Charles. "The Athanasian Decade 1974-1984: A Bibliographical Report." *Theological Studies* 46 (1985): 524-541.

1174. Kannengiesser, Charles. *Holy Scripture and Hellenistic Hermeneutics in Alexandrian Christology: The Arian Crisis.* Berkeley, Ca.: Center for Hermeneutical Studies in Hellenistic and Modern Culture, 1982.

1175. Kelly, J. F. "The Gallic Resistance to Eastern Asceticism." *Studia Patristica* 17, pt. 2 (1982): 506-510. Kelly sees the Priscillian connection as a factor that helped give asceticism generally a bad press in some circles in late fourth century Gaul.

1176. Kelly, J. N. D. *Jerome: His Life, Writings, and Controversies.* New York: Harper and Row, 1976. Lucid and well-documented, the best biography currently available in English. E. D. Hunt, *Journal of Roman Studies* 67 (1977): 166-171 (+-).

1177. Kelly, J. N. D. "The Nicene Creed: A Turning Point." *Scottish Journal of Theology* 36 (1983): 29-39. The matured Nicene Creed formulated at the First Council of Constantinople in October 381 represented the final stages of the effort to tighten up permissible theological concepts in Christian thinking. Although Kelly does not say so explicitly, the finalized creed may be seen as a symbol that the rather free thinking fourth century was coming to a close, and that the Arian bridge to the pagan intelligentsia (not to mention the barbarians) was soon to be no more.

1178. Kidd, Beresford J. *A History of the Church to A. D. 461.* Vol. 2: *A. D. 313-408.* Oxford: Clarendon Press, 1922; reprint ed., New York: AMS Press, 1976. Volume One cannot be overlooked entirely, including as it does the time of Diocletian and the early Constantine; but the bulk of the fourth century material is in the second volume. Kidd expects readers to have a copy of his *Documents Illustrative of the History of the Church* at their sides. It is sometimes difficult to see the forest for the trees in Kidd; but there is no denying the value of the bulky references to primary as well as secondary material, nor can anyone belittle the strong effort to be impartial when treating the great controversies of the early church. Also helpful is the effort to set events in their political and social context. A. Gardner, *English Historical Review* 38 (1923): 95-96 (+-); C. Jenkins, *History* 7 (1923): 291-293 (+-).

1179. Kidd, Beresford J. *The Roman Primacy to A. D. 461.* New York: Macmillan Co., 1936. A good deal of the material here pertains to the fourth century, especially the time of pope Damasus (366-384), at time when the bishops of Rome were beginning to look for something more than just "primacy of honor." C. C. Richardson, *Church History* 6 (1937): 385-386 (+).

1180. Kirkpatrick, H. B. "The Church History of Philostorgius: A Dissertation on the Significance of a Eunomian Historian." M. A. thesis, University of Manchester, 1968. Although only surviving in fragments, Philostorgius' history is important to us as a view of fourth century Christian developments from the Arian perspective.

1181. Kopecek, Thomas A. *A History of Neo-Arianism.* 2 vols. Patristic Monograph Series, 8. Cambridge, Mass.: Philadelphia Patristic Foundation; Winchendon, Mass.: Distributed by Greeno, Hadden, 1979. Kopecek tells the story of Arianism in its mature and most ambitious and successful stage: the second half of the fourth century, when Aetius and Eunomius were the driving intellectual forces behind the movement, and the emperors Constantius II and Valens were the driving political forces. Kopecek concentrates on neo-Arianism as an intellectual movement, causing no end of debate as Christianity was forced to come to grips with a more precise definition of its theology, not only for itself but to distinguish it from the non-Christian philosophical trends of the day. Imperial intervention was a regular feature in the process of defining orthodoxy in Christianity, and in the end was decisive under Theodosius I and his sons in defeating Arianism as a theoretical and practical force in the Christian communities of the empire. J. T. Lienhard, *Religious Studies Review* 8 (1982): 330-337 (+).

1182. **Kopecek, Thomas A.** "The Social Class of the Cappadocian Fathers." *Church History* 42 (1973): 453-466. The famous fourth century church leaders from Cappadocia were upper middle class types, members of good curial families.

1183. **Kopecek, Thomas A.** "Social/historical Studies in the Cappadocian Fathers." Ph. D. dissertation, Brown University, 1972.

1184. **Labriolle, Pierre de.** *Life and Times of St. Ambrose.* Translated by Herbert Wilson. St. Louis: B. Herder Book Co., 1928.

1185. **Ladner, Gerhart B.** *The Idea of Reform: Its Impact on Christian Thought and Action in the Age of the Fathers.* Cambridge: Harvard University Press, 1959. Reform or renewal in the late empire was mostly a concept of personal rather than institutional improvement within the church. Ladner weaves a complex story, but that is the essence of it. H. G. J. Beck, *American Historical Review* 66 (1961): 427-428 (+); R. M. Grant, *Speculum* 36 (1961): 140-142 (+).

1186. **Ladner, Gerhart B.** "The Philosophical Anthropology of Saint Gregory of Nyssa." *Dumbarton Oaks Papers* 12 (1958): 61-94.

1187. **Laeuchli, Samuel.** *Power and Sexuality: The Emergence of Canon Law at the Synod of Elvira.* Philadelphia: Temple University, 1972. Laeuchli probes the canons from the Council of Elvira (A.D. 309, the author thinks) to learn how the church was beginning to respond to its new, more positive relationship with the Roman state under Christian emperors, and how it was growing into a new role as a significant force in worldly affairs. The struggle between the worldly and the other worldly is centered on sexuality, to the regulation of which half the canons are devoted.

1188. Lawler, Thomas C. "Jerome's First Letter to Damasus." In *KYRIAKON: Festschrift Johannes Quasten*, pp. 548-552. Vol. 2. Edited by Patrick Granfield and Josef A. Jungmann. Munster Westfalen: Verlag Aschendorff, 1970. At the height of the divisiveness surrounding the Arian heresy, the young Jerome wrote the bishop of Rome in 376, asking for guidance on the use of Greek theological terms in reference to the Trinity. The letter is of interest for evidence as to the perceived primacy of the Roman bishop, even in the time of Ambrose of Milan.

1189. Lawlor, Hugh J. *Eusebiana: Essays on the Ecclesiastical History of Eusebius, Bishop of Caesarea.* Oxford: Clarendon Press, 1912: reprint ed., Amsterdam: Philo Press, 1973.

1190. Liebeschuetz, J. H. W. "Problems Arising from the Conversion of Syria." In *Church in Town and Countryside*, pp. 17-24. Edited by Derek Baker. Oxford: Blackwell, 1979. Liebeschuetz raises questions that suggest the importance of government patronage, economic change, and monks in the spread of Syrian Christianity in the fourth and fifth centuries.

1191. Liebeschuetz, J. H. W. "Why Did Synesius Become Bishop of Ptolemais?" *Byzantion* 56 (1986): 180-195. In a sense, Synesius stepped right from his fourth century world of contemplative philosophy and the leisured life of the cultured nobility into the fifth century life of the late Roman bishop. Synesius would not have put it this way, but he knew the change would be dramatic. He was reluctant to make it, says the author, partly because he did not want to give up his old way of life, and partly because he thought himself unworthy and untrained for the office of bishop.

1192. Lienhard, Joseph T. *Paulinus of Nola and Early Western Monasticism, with a Study of the Chronology of His Works and an Annotated Bibliography, 1879-1976.* Theophaneia, 28. Cologne: Hanstein, 1977.

1193. **Lienhard, Joseph T.** "Recent Studies in Arianism." *Religious Studies Review* 8 (October 1982): 330-337. In a review of nine recent studies, Lienhard conveniently summarizes the latest thinking on Arianism.

1194. **Lietzmann, Hans.** *A History of the Early Church.* Vol. 3: *From Constantine to Julian;* Vol. 4: *The Era of the Church Fathers.* New York: Scribner, 1952.

1195. ***The Lives of the Desert Fathers: The Historia Monachorum in Aegypto.*** Translated by Norman Rusell. Kalamazoo, Michigan: Cistercian Publications, 1981. First English translation of *Historia Monachorum*, written in the late fourth century in Greek. R. T. Meyer, *Catholic Historical Review* 70 (1984): 106-107 (+).

1196. **Louth, Andrew.** "St Athanasius and the Greek *Life of Antony*." *Journal of Theological Studies* 39 (1988): 504-509. Louth modifies an argument of T. D. Barnes about the authorship of the *Life of Antony*, and concludes that Athanasius did in fact write the Greek version.

1197. **Lovejoy, A. O.** "The Communism of Saint Ambrose." *Journal of the History of Ideas* 3 (1942): 458-468. Lovejoy quotes at length from the writings of Ambrose to show that in him the fourth century had a strong proponent of communism. But little came of it, and Ambrose was partly the reason. Like any good bishop, he was more interested in saving souls for the life hereafter, than in being a revolutionary for the earthly economy.

1198. **Luibheid, Colm.** "The Alleged Second Session of the Council of Nicaea." *Journal of Ecclesiastical History* 34 (1983): 165-174. Luibheid reviews the evidence and comes away unconvinced that there was a second council.

1199. **Luibheid, Colm.** *The Council of Nicaea.* Galway: Halway University Press, 1982. There is a general focus on the development of Arianism in and out of the context of Nicaean politics.

1200. Luibheid, Colm. ed. *The Essential Eusebius.* New York: New American Library, 1966. Selections from the bishop of Caesaraea's works. Luibheid's introduction has a noteworthy discussion of Arianism.

1201. Luibheid, Colm. *Eusebius of Caesarea and the Arian Crisis.* Dublin: Irish Academic Press, 1981. Was Eusebius an Arian? After a complex, careful, measured consideration of all the evidence, Luibheid concludes that "one may justly say that he worked far beyond the level of the crude Arianism so often and so unjustly ascribed to him" (p. 125).

1202. MacMullen, Ramsay. *Christianizing the Roman Empire A. D. 100-400.* New Haven: Yale University Press, 1984. MacMullen reviews the motives and manner of conversion, which changed when Christianity became a state religion in the early fourth century. State sponsorship, later combined with persecution, replaced the earlier emphasis on miracles as incentives for conversion. J. O'Brien, *Classical Journal* 82 (1987): 162-163 (+); R. P. C. Hanson, *Classical Review* 35 (1985): 335-337 (-); H. A. Drake, *Classical Philology* 82 (1987): 81-85 (+).

1203. MacMullen, Ramsay. "What Influence Did Christianity Make?" *Historia* 35 (1986): 322-343. Covering the hundred years after 312, MacMullen decides that both pagans and Christians were moving along in the same direction regarding styles of morality, and that the only area where Christianity imposed a distinct and noticeable difference was in the matter of sexual conduct, most especially celibacy.

1204. Markus, R. A. *Christianity in the Roman World.* London: Thames and Hudson, 1974. Beginning with Chapter Five, Markus deals with the problems and adjustments of Christianity in the fourth century Roman world. J. S. Preus, *American Historical Review* 82 (1977): 1223-1224 (+).

1205. Marrow, H. I. "Synesius of Cyrene and Alexandrian Neoplatonism." In *The Conflict Between Paganism and*

Christianity, pp. 126-150. Edited by Arnaldo Momigliano. New York: Oxford University Press, 1963. For Synesius, as for many other cultured gentlemen, the obstacle to embracing Christianity was not paganism but Hellenistic philosophy, representing a way of life and inquiry dear to them. Synesius helped lay the groundwork for the Christianized Neoplatonism which helped make Christianity acceptable to the highly cultivated.

1206. **Maxwell, C. M.** "Chrysostom"s Homilies Against the Jews: An English Translation." Ph. D. dissertation, University of Chicago, 1967.

1207. **Meijering, E. P.** "Athanasius on the Father as the Origin of the Son." *Nederlands Archief voor Kerkgeschiedenis* 55 (1974): 1-14.

1208. **Meijering, E. P.** *Orthodoxy and Platonism in Athanasius: Synthesis or Antithesis?* Leiden: E. J. Brill, 1968.

1209. **Miethe, Terry L., compiler.** *Augustinian Bibliography 1970-1980: With Essays on the Fundamentals of Augustinian Scholarship.* Westport, Conn.: Greenwood Press, 1982.

1210. **Momigliano, Arnaldo D.** "The Life of Saint Macrina by Gregory of Nyssa." In his *On Pagans, Jews, and Christians*, pp. 206-221. Middleton, Conn.: Wesleyan University Press, 1987. Momigliano works with the source material generated by an aristocratic mid-fourth century Cappadocian family to learn more about styles of Christian biography, about the social dynamics of aristocratically controlled monasteries, and about aristocratic women in the Christian movement.

1211. **Monceaux, Paul.** *St. Jerome: The Early Years.* Translated by F. J. Sheed. London: Sheed and Ward, 1933.

1212. Munz, P. "John Cassian." *Journal of Ecclesiastical History* 11 (1960): 1-22.   An interesting account of the thought-world of the famous fourth century Egyptian monk who put his thoughts into action in fifth century Gaul. Cassian is a good example of a type really coming into the limelight in the later fourth century: the monastic ascetic whose goal is freedom from the world and all its imperfections. But the inspiration now is from the Christian subculture rather than the philosophical schools.

1213. Murphy, Francis X., ed. *A Monument to Saint Jerome: Essays on Some Aspects of His Life, Works and Influence.* New York: Sheed and Ward, 1952.   Includes an introductory biography of Jerome by the editor, who also contributed a chapter, "St. Jerome as an Historian." The others are: F. Cavallera, "The Personality of St. Jerome"; L. N. Hartmann, "St. Jerome as an Exegete"; G. Bardy, "St. Jerome and Greek Thought"; E. P. Burke, "St. Jerome as a Spiritual Director"; J.-R. Palanque, "St. Jerome and the Barbarians"; E. A. Quain, "St. Jerome as a Humanist"; M. L. W. Laistner, "The Study of St. Jerome in the Early Middle Ages"; and P. W. Skehan, "St. Jerome and the Canon of the Holy Scriptures."   A. D. Nock, *American Historical Review* 58 (1953): 592-593 (+).

1214. Murphy, Francis X. *Rufinus of Aquileia (345-411): His Life and Works.* Washington, D. C.: Catholic University Press, 1945.   Rufinus was an important fourth century intellectual and ascetic best remembered now as a friend and then bitter enemy of Jerome. But, as Murphy says, "Rufinus is much more important for the part he played in the promotion of western monasticism, in the development of church history, and in the preservation of the works of Origen . . . " (p.vii). Murphy gives a reasonably balanced portrait of Rufinus and his place in the intellectual life of the age, against an interesting backdrop of great cities and great events in the Roman state.   C. Je., *English Historical Review* 62 (1947): 116 (+).

1215. **Murray, Robert.** *Symbols of Church and Kingdom: A Study in the Early Syriac Tradition.* New York: Cambridge University Press, 1975. Beyond the Christianity of educated prelates, babbling away in Greek and Latin about abstract theological problems, there was another Christianity: that of the millions who were outside classical culture. Murray is concerned to bring alive Syriac Christianity through the poet monks of the late empire. It is a different thought world, full of Semitic thought patterns and images, difficult then as now for the Graeco-Roman mentality to appreciate. But it was a cultural force and a religious outlook of significance and influence, and Murray reveals it to us through some prominent fourth century poets. P. Brown, *New York Review of Books* 23 (April 15, 1976): 14-18 (+).

1216. **Neumann, C. W.** *The Virgin Mary in the Works of Saint Ambrose.* Paradosis 17. Fribourg-en-Suisse: University Press, 1962.

1217. **Norman, A. F.** "The Life of Libanius." Ph. D. dissertation, University College, Hull, 1956.

1218. **Nyman, J. R.** "The Synod of Antioch (324-5) and the Council of Nicaea." *Studia Patristica* 4 (Berlin, 1961): 483-489.

1219. **Ogilvie, R. M.** *The Library of Lactantius.* New York: Oxford University Press, 1978. Lactantius knew less of pagan, especially Greek, literature than we might expect; and most of what he did know was not from the original works, but from anthologies and commentaries.

1220. **O'Meara, John J.** *The Young Augustine: An Introduction to the Confessions of St. Augustine.* New York: Longman, 1980. A 1954 edition was subtitled *The Growth of St. Augustine's Mind up to His Conversion.* This is Augustine up to about 387. As biography, the O'Meara study is useful; as an introduction to the *Confessions* it is more useful; as an effort to separate the fourth century Augustine from the fifth century saint, it is most useful. E. Henry, *Times Educational Supplement* (March 6, 1981): 28 (+-).

1221. Pachomian Koinonia. Vol. I: *The Life of Saint Pachomius and His Disciples.* Vol. II: *Pachomian Chronicle and Rules.* Vol. III: *Instructions, Letters, and Other Writings of Saint Pachomius and His Disciples.* Translated with an introduction by Armand Veilleux. Kalamazoo, Mich.: Cistercian Publications, 1980-1982. Almost all the fourth century source material on Pachomius and his movement will be found in translation in these volumes. M. Slusser, *Catholic Historical Review* 70 (1984): 105-106.

1222. Paredi, Angelo. *St. Ambrose: His Life and Times.* Translated by M. J. Costelloe. Notre Dame, Ind.: University of Notre Dame Press, 1964. First published in Italian in 1961, this is a sympathetic portrait of Ambrose. There is a helpful focus on the city of Milan, an imperial center in the fourth century. M. R. P. McGuire, *Catholic Historical Review* 47 (1961): 359-360 (+).

1223. Paulinus Mediolanensis. *Vita Sancti Ambrosii, mediolanensis episcopi, a Paulino euis notario ad beatum Augustinum conscripta*; a revised text, and commentary, with an introduction and translation by Sister Mary Simplicia Kaniecka. Washington, D. C.: Catholic University Press of America, 1928. A contemporary biography of Ambrose, bishop of Milan.

1224. Phillips, L. T. *The Subordinate Temporal, Causal, and Adversative Clausea in the Works of St. Ambrose.* CUA Patristic Studies, XLIX. Washington, D. C.: Catholic University Press, 1937.

1225. Pickman, Edward M. *The Mind of Latin Christendom.* New York: Oxford University Press, 1937. Against the backdrop of a failing worldly empire, which is usefully discussed, Pickman considers the intellectual development of the period 373 to 496, with an inevitable emphasis on theology and of course Augustine. Although this is largely a fifth century story, there is enough earlier material to make this a very desirable read for the student of the fourth century. M. Helm, *Church History* 6 (1937): 276-277 (+); F. J. E. Raby, *History* 24 (1939): 64-65 (+); F. S. Lear, *Speculum* 13 (1938): 253-254 (+).

1226. **Pollard, T. E.** "The Exegesis of Scripture in the Arian Controversy." *Bulletin of the John Rylands Library* (1959): 414-429.

1227. **Pollard, T. E.** "Logos and Son in Origen, Arius and Athanasius." *Studia Patristica* 2 (Berlin, 1957): 282-287.

1228. **Pollard, T. E.** "The Origins of Arianism." *Journal of Theological Studies* 9 (1958): 103-111.

1229. **Quasten, Johannes.** *Patrology.* Vol. III: *The Golden Age of Greek Patristic Literature from the Council of Nicaea to the Council of Chalcedon.* Westminster: Newman Press, 1960. A good survey of Christian authors of the eastern empire, and the controversies that motivated most of the writings. H. G. J. Beck, *Catholic Historical Review* 47 (1961): 360-361 (+).

1230. **Ramsey, Boniface.** "Almsgiving in the Latin Church: The Late Fourth and Early Fifth Centuries." *Theological Studies* 43 (1982): 226-259. Ramsey considers the views of contemporary Christian writers to conclude that late Roman almsgiving was encouraged both for the atonement of sin and to put the giver into the feeling of a special relationship with Christ, who had himself been associated with the interests of the poor.

1231. **Ricciotti, Giuseppe.** *The Age of Martyrs: Christianity from Diocletian to Constantine.* Translated by Anthony Bull. Milwaukee: Bruce Publishing Co., [1959].

1232. **Roberts, M.** *Biblical Epic and Rhetorical Paraphrase on Late Antiquity.* ARCA: Classical and Medieval Texts, Papers and Monographs, 16. Liverpool: F. Cairns, 1985.

1233. Robinson, James M., ed. *The Nag Hammadi Library.* New York: Harper and Row, 1978. Translation with commentary of the famous Christian Gnostic texts which informed some strands of the monastic life in fourth century Egypt. For more, see the interesting pamphlet by Robinson, *The Nag Hammadi Codices* (1977), which has maps, photographs, and the story of the codices: dates, discovery, etc.

1234. Roots, Peter A. "The *De Opificio Dei:* The Workmanship of God and Lactantius." *Classical Quarterly* 37 (1987): 466-486. Before he was the Christian Cicero, Lactantius was a highly regarded pagan rhetorician. Roots studies the *De Opificio Dei* as an example of Diocletian era rhetoric rather than as the work of a Christian apologist.

1235. Rousseau, Philip. *Ascetics, Authority and the Church in the Age of Jerome and Cassian.* New York: Oxford University Press, 1978. Rousseau traces the growth of the public power of the monks in the fourth century. The ascetic trend had a great vogue, from its origins in the eastern empire to its gradual appeal in the west, among all classes. Gradually it began to attract talented persons who worked to promote their style of Christian living and to participate in the direction of the worldly society around them. They had considerable success despite great opposition both in pagan and in Christian circles. In an interpretative rather than narrative fashion, Rousseau presents this controversial social development. E. D. Hunt, *Journal of Roman Studies* 71 (1981): 196-197 (+); R. M. Grant, *American Historical Review* 84 (1979): 723-724 (+-); G. Constable, *Speculum* 54 (1979: 625-626 (+-).

1236. Rousseau, Philip. *Pachomius: The Making of a Community in Fourth Century Egypt.* The Transformation of the Classical Heritage, 6. Berkeley: University of California Press, 1985. Rousseau gives an informed study of Pachomian monasticism in the context of fourth century Egyptian life. S. N. C. Lieu, *Journal of Roman Studies* 77 (1987): 216-218 (+-).

1237. **Ruether, Rosemary R.** *Gregory of Nazianzus: Rhetor and Philosopher.* New York: Oxford University Press, 1969. Gregory, like most educated Christian leaders of the fourth century, was caught up in the internal tensions of pagan as well as Christian cultural trends. There was a tension between the rhetoricians and the philosophers of the age, especially regarding the extent to which the intellectual should actively participate in the society around him. Gregory inclined towards the quiet contemplative life encouraged by the philosophers; but of course as a Christian bishop he had to give up this hope. Ruether unfolds the story of Gregory's attitudes towards rhetoric and philosophy, and incidentally sheds much light on the intellectual tensions of the age generally, whether Christian or pagan. R. J. Murray, *Classical Journal* 67 (1971): 188-189 (+); H. Dressler, *Catholic Historical Review* 57 (1971-72): 464-466 (+-).

1238. **Salisbury, Joyce E.** "'The Bond of a Common Mind': A Study of Collective Salvation from Cyprian to Augustine." *Journal of Religious History* 13 (1985): 235-247. Salisbury investigates the concept of collective salvation, by which a group rather than individuals determined the salvation of a congregation. This notion, much opposed by Augustine, had a long life in Africa, especially amoung fourth century Donatists.

1239. **Salisbury, Joyce E.** "The Latin Doctors of the Church on Sexuality." *Journal of Medieval History* 12 (1986): 279-289. Jerome, Ambrose and Augustine on sex. For Jerome and Ambrose it was bad, bad, bad; for Augustine it was good or bad, depending on circumstances. In any event, sex represented carnal and worldly things, away from which these fourth century Christian leaders were trying to lead their flocks, in order to be purely spiritual.

1240. **Sellars, Robert V.** *Eustathius of Antioch and His Place in the Early History of Christian Doctrine.* Cambridge: University Press, 1928. "The primary object of this study is to try and reveal the position of Eustathius, Bishop of Antioch, in the Syrian tradition in the history of dogma" (p. 1).

Sellars also reveals much about the wild and furious ecclesiastical politics of the Constantinian church induced by the Arian movement before, during, and after the Council of Nicaea, where the orthodox Eustathius had a prominent role.

1241. Sevcenko, Ihor. "A Shadow Outline of Virtue: The Classical Heritage of Greek Christian Literature (Second to Seventh Century)." In *Age of Spirituality : A Symposium*, pp. 53-73. Edited by Kurt Weitzmann. New York: Metropolitan Museum of Art, in association with Princeton University Press, 1980. Sevcenko follows the absorption of classical thought and styles of writing into Christian culture over a period of five centuries, but with a strong fourth century emphasis.

1242. Shepherd, Massey H., Jr. "The Liturgical Reform of Damasus I." In *KYRIAKON: Festschrift Johannes Questen*, pp. 847-863. Edited by Patrick Granfield and Josef A. Jungmann. 2 vols. Munster: Aschendorff, 1970. Damasus, as bishop of Rome, 366-384, played a large role in setting the tone and standard of Roman ritual and government in the church. From the mid- and later fourth century comes much of the style of the Roman church, still familiar today in everything from architecture to liturgy.

1243. Skarsaume, O. "A Neglected Detail in the Creed of Nicaea." *Vigiliae Christianae* 41 (1986): 34-54. "The creed of Nicaea is not a piece of Western theology forced upon the Eastern Church by Ossius and Constantine. It is a product of the Alexander party, probably in close cooperation with Ossius, and - to quote Kelly - 'the emperor had been won over to be their mouthpiece.'"

1244. Smith, Macklin. *Prudentius' Psychomachia: A Reexamination.* Princeton, N. J.: Princeton University Press, 1976. Smith sees the *Psychomachia* as a heroic poem glorifying the great Christian struggle and victory over paganism in the late fourth century. And Prudentius was not above using Virgil to promote Christianity: Virgil's style is used to advantage in showing the falsity of pagan values which Virgil cherished. J. D. Campbell, *Library Journal* 101 (April

15, 1976) : 1021 (+-); J. J. O'Donnell, *American Journal of Philology* 99 (1978): 257-260   (+-).

1245. **Snee, Rochelle E.** "Gregory Nazianzen's Constantinopolitan Career, A. D. 379-381." Ph. D. dissertation, University of Washington, 1981. In the wake of the political failure of Arianism after the death of Valens in 378, the Nicenes or orthodox Christians seized their moment. But their own party was not free from dissension. Gregory was caught up in the mess. Here is yet another story of the sort that inspired Ammianus Marcellinus to observe that the Christians were more intolerant of each other than of any religious community in the Roman state.

1246. **Snee, Rochelle E.** "Valens' Recall of the Nicene Exiles and the Anti-Arian Propaganda." *Greek, Roman and Byzantine Studies* 26 (1985): 395-419.   By the fifth century, anti-Arian propaganda may have effected the transfer of responsibility for the recall of the exiles from the Arian Valens to the Nicene Gratian. In his translation of Eusebius' *Chronicle,* Jerome attributed the recall to Valens in the spring of 378.

1247.   **Soby Christensen, Arne.** *Lactantius the Historian: An Analysis of the De Mortibus Persecutorum.* Copenhagen: Museum Tuscalanum, 1980.   Christensen labors to show that the *De Mortibus Persecutorum* was not written as Constantinian propaganda; instead, it expresses the personal point of view of the author on the great events and meanings surrounding the Great Persecution. The DMP was discovered in 1679, and has been shaking a lot of research cages since then. Christensen helps set the tone and standard for future discussion.

1248. **Springer, Sr. M. T.** *Nature-Imagery in the Works of Saint Ambrose.* Washington, D. C.: Catholic University Press, 1931.

1249.   **Stancliffe, Clare.** *St. Martin and His Hagiographer: History and Miracle in Sulpicius Severus.*

Oxford: Clarendon Press, 1983. Martin and Sulpicius Severus were a fourth century team made in heaven: the former became a saint and the latter became his expert propagandist. Stancliffe gives a careful analysis of this development and its setting in Gaul. I. N. Wood, *Journal of Roman Studies* 75 (1985): 267-268 (+).

1250. Stead, G. C. "'Eusebius' and the Council of Nicaea." *Journal of Theological Studies* 24 (April 1973): 85-100. The theology of Eusebius of Caesarea and Eusebius of Nicomedia, and the part each played at Nicaea.

1251. Stead, G. C. "The Platonism of Arius." *Journal of Theological Studies* 15 (April 1964): 16-31. Stead measures the extent to which Platonism, as it had filtered into Christian thinking, influenced the theological position of Arius.

1252. Stead, G. C. "The Significance of the *Homoousios*." In *Studia Patristica*, pp. 397-412. Vol. III, pt. 1. Texte und Untersuchungen, 78. Edited by F. L. Cross. Berlin: Akademie-Verlag, 1961. Fourth century Trinitarian theology, especially as Athanasius understood it.

1253. Steeger, William P. "Arian Influence Upon the Emperor Julian and the Pagan-Christian Struggle." M. A. thesis, University of Louisville, 1972. "This investigation has attempted to demonstrate that the proposed Arian influence upon the Emperor Julian is not as clearly evidenced as so often supposed. Further, the influence upon the Apostate is not a distinctive development of Arian doctrine but simply the form of Christianity Julian grew to hate from childhood. It is highly probable that other forms of Christianity wielded with the same force and permitted that same abuse of privilege, as the Arianism of Constantius, would have influenced the Apostate in a similar manner. In addition this investigation fails to uncover any clues to the proposition that Arian Christianity was more conducive to pagan revival or barbarian acceptance than Athanasian orthodoxy" (p. 76).

1254. Stertz, Stephen A. "Christianity in the *Historia Augusta.*" *Latomus* 36 (1977): 694-715. "Like many of his pagan contemporaries, he [the author of the HA] tried not to think of it and, when thought could not be avoided, treated it [Christianity] with ironical resignation" (p. 715).

1255. Stevenson, James. "Aspects of the Relations between Lactantius and the Classics." *Studia Patristica* (Texte und Untersuchungen 79; Berlin, 1961) 4: 497-503. Stevenson shows Lactantius' disappointment that ancient education emphasized style at the expense of truth, and that classical philosophy had failed through its inability to find divine truth. But Lactantius responded only to very old and Latin classical authors, like Cicero, and was not really very up on contemporary trends in philosophy (neo-Platonism) or religion, except to go out of his way to condemn Jupitor and Hercules who were enjoying a contemporary popularity because of imperial patronage. Even these two he saw through classical eyes rather than fourth century eyes.

1256. Stevenson, James, ed. *Creeds, Councils and Controversies: Documents Illustrative of the History of the Church, AD 337-461.* London: SPCK, 1972.

1257. Stevenson, James. "Life and Literary Activity of Lactantius." *Studia Patristica* (Texte und Untersuchungen 63; Berlin 1957) 1, pt.1: 661-677. Stevenson critiques the sources, and summarizes what can be known of Lactantius' life and his literary activities.

1258. Stevenson, James, ed. *A New Eusebius: Documents Illustrative of the History of the Church to A. D. 337.* London: SPCK, 1957; reprint ed., 1983. Stevenson based his collection on B. J. Kidd's *Documents Illustrative of the History of the Church* (1920; 1933).

1259. Stevenson, James. *Studies in Eusebius.* Cambridge: University Press, 1929. Although very dated in some respects, this nevertheless remains a useful study of

Eusebius, his life, his work, his involvement in the great issues of his time.

1260. Storch, Rudolph H. "The 'Eusebian Constantine.'" *Church History* 40 (1971): 145-155. Storch explains the image of Constantine that emerges from the *Vita Constantini* through four of its important themes: "(1) all success and benefit derive from the favor of the divinity; (2) only the pious receive divine favor; (3) the most important indication of divine favor for a pious ruler is military victory; and (4) with the victory secured, divine favor will produce peace and unity for the realm" (p. 146). Of course, Constantine came out favorably on all these tests, at least in his own eyes and those of his biographer.

1261. Stringer, Daniel. "The Political Theology of Eusebius Pamphylix, Bishop of Caesarea." *Patristic and Byzantine Review* 1 (1982): 137-151.

1262. Strunk, Oliver. "St. Gregory Nazianzus and the Proper Hymns for Easter." In *Late Classical and Mediaeval Studies in Honor of Albert Mathias Friend, Jr.*, pp. 88-95. Edited by Kurt Weitzmann. Princeton, N. J.: Princeton University Press, 1955. Strunk finds evidence of actual tunes used in the sixth century and perhaps earlier.

1263. *The Study of Liturgy*. Edited by C. Jones, G. Wainwright, and E. J. Yarnold. London: Oxford University Press, 1978. There are contained in this anthology some interesting studies of the rituals of the Christian church in the fourth century.

1264. Swift, Lewis J. "Arnobius and Lactantius: Two Views of the Pagan Poets." *Transactions of the American Philological Association* 96 (1965): 439-448. Using their approaches to poetic myth as a guide, Swift highlights the unyielding attitude of the apologist Arnobius towards paganism versus the more understanding approach of his student Lactantius.

1265. Swift, Lewis J. "Lactantius and the Golden Age." *American Journal of Philology* 89 (1968): 144-156. Swift looks at the "ambivalent attitude of Christian Latin authors toward pagan literature" through one example: "Lactantius' treatment of the Golden Age in his *Divinae Institutiones* provides some insight into the Christian's appreciation of his own pagan literary background, and the limitations imposed on that appreciation by his newly found faith" (p. 144).

1266. Taylor, Justin. "St. Basil the Great and Pope Damasus I." *Downside Review* 91 (1973): 186-203, 262-274. Taylor reviews the complex politics of Christian leaders in the 370s. The main part of the story has to do with Basil's efforts to get the orthodox Western church lined up with him in the struggle in the East against the Arian church, which had the support of the emperor Valens.

1267. Telfer, W. "The Author's Purpose in the Vita Constantini." *Studia Patristica* (Texte und Untersuchungen 63; Berlin 1957) 1 (i): 157-167. Telfer believes that the *Vita Constantini* was written by Eusebius (as most scholars do now), and that it was being worked on after Constantine's death as an interpretive guide to recent events and as a guide for Christians as they prepared to live in the new Christian empire in the post-Constantinian period.

1268. Theodoretus. *A History of the Monks of Syria.* Translated and edited by R. M. Price. Cistercian Studies Series, 88. Kalamazoo: Cistercian Publications, 1985.

1269. Thomas, Charles. *Christianity in Roman Britain to A. D. 500.* Berkeley: University of California Press, 1981. This is the most thorough contemporary discussion of the topic available. Plenty of fourth century material.

1270. Thompson, E. A. "Christianity and the Northern Barbarians." In *The Conflict between Paganism and Christianity in the Fourth Century*, pp. 56-78. Edited by Arnaldo Momigliano. New York: Oxford University Press, 1963. Christianity filtered into barbarian lands casually through

Roman prisoners of war, returning converted soldiers, and merchants; but these channels had a small effect in general, and the church made little effort to make conversions beyond the boundaries of the fourth century empire. It was not until the fifth century, when barbarian tribes were living in Christianized Roman territory, that large-scale conversions occurred.

1271. Tsirpanlis, Constantine N. "The Origenistic Controversy in the Historians of the Fourth, Fifth and Sixth Centuries." *Patristic and Byzantine Review* 4 (1985): 85-89.

1272. Turner, C. H. "The Lausiac History of Palladius." *Journal of Theological Studies* 6 (1904-5): 321-355. Turner discusses the primary source material for fourth century monasticism, then turns to Palladius, whose well-informed history of monasticism, written for an official named Palladius who had requested it, is of great importance for illuminating one of the permanently significant religious movements originating in the fourth century. Turner's article is helpful for a consideration of the problems of text transmission, corruption, abridgment, combination, translation, and so on.

1273. Vanderspoel, J. "Claudian, Christ and the Cult of the Saints." *Classical Quarterly* 36 (1986): 244-255. Claudian was anti-Christian in some matters. Even poets took part in the struggle between paganism and Christianity at the end of the fourth century: Claudian versus Prudentius. Claudian thought that Christians relied too much on miracles and saints for victories over the Goths.

1274. Vigna, G. "The Influence of Epideictic Rhetoric on Eusebius of Caesarea's Political Theology." Ph. D. dissertation, Northwestern University, 1980.

1275. Voobus, Arthur. "The Origin of Monasticism in Mesopotamia." *Church History* 20 (December 1951): 27-37. Voobus locates the beginnings of Syrian monasticism in the time of Diocletian, and discovers its roots in the monasticism of

Manichaeism in Mesopotamia, rather than in the deserts of Egypt.

1276. **Wallace-Hadrill, D. S.** *Eusebius of Caesarea.* Westminster, Md.: Canterbury Press, 1961. Wallace-Hadrill offers a helpful and balanced summary of a half a century of scholarly activity on Eusebius in all aspects: biography, philosophy, theology, history, and so on. E. G. Weltin, *Catholic Historical Review* 48 (1962): 216-218 (+).

1277. **Wallace-Hadrill, D. S.** "The Work of Eusebius of Caesarea in the Light of Recent Rsearch." In *Politische Geschichte: Provinzen und Randvolker: Syrien, Palastina, Arabien.* Aufstieg und Niedergang der Romischen Welt, 2. Edited by Hildegard Temporini and Wolfgang Haase. Berlin: W. de Gruyter, 1977.

1278. **Walsh, William J.** "The Image of the Church in Lactantius' *De Mortibus Persecutorum.*" In *KYRIAKON: Festschrift Johannes Quasten,* pp. 521-526. Vol. 2. Edited by Patrick Granfield and Josef A. Jungmann. Munster Westfalen: Verlag Aschendorff, 1970. Walsh probes Lactantius and finds an interesting perspective on the church, the perspective of an early fourth century western (by origin) layman, who gives a snapshot of an educated man's view of the church just after Diocletian and just before the full impact of Constantine's policies which transformed it forever.

1279. **Warmington, B. H.** "Did Athanasius Write History?" In *The Inheritance of Historiography 350-900,* pp. 7-16. Edited by Christopher Holdsworth and T. P. Wiseman. Exeter, U. K.: University of Exeter, 1986. No. He wrote "instant history." "His so-called historical works . . . were all polemical works and testify to a need to present his case immediately and forcefully to as wide a readership as possible" (p. 13).

1280. **Way, Agnes C.** *The Language and Style of the Letters of St. Basil.* Washington, D. C.: Catholic University Press of America, 1927.

1281. Weltin, E. G. *Athens and Jerusalem: An Interpretive Essay on Christianity and Classical Culture.* Atlanta, Ga.: Scholars Press, 1987. Covering the first 450 years A. D., Weltin looks at the development of a "new intellectual synthesis" (p. 2) resulting from centuries of interaction between Christian thinkers and their classical environment and inheritance. The fourth century was a crucial phase in the synthesis, and receives appropriate attention. This is not an easy read for the layman, but Weltin does give enough background material on the various philosophies and religious attitudes of antiquity to enable a beginner to follow things with some hope of grasping a complex development over a long period of time.

1282. Wiesen, D. S. *St. Jerome as a Satirist: A Study in Christian Latin Thought and Letters.* Ithica, N. Y.: Cornell University Press, 1964. Jerome is the perfect example of church fathers of the fourth century who were always borrowing from their pagan educations to find the right turn of phrase in their writings. Indeed, there was not much else they could do in the circumstances. Contemporaries were more impressed by a demonstration of vast knowledge of classical writers than they were by original expressions. The church fathers were always pushing the classical authors out the front door while bringing them back in again through the back door. Jerome's fourth century: the age of paradox. F. X. Murphy, *Speculum* 42 (1967): 211-213 (+).

1283. Wiles, Maurice. "In Defence of Arius." *Journal of Theological Studies* 13 (1962): 339-347. Here is something hard to get: a sympathetic portrayal of Arius and his teachings. Nevertheless, Wiles does not find Arianism a satisfactory approach to the Christian message.

1284. Wiles, Maurice. "The Nature of the Early Debate about Christ's Human Soul." *Journal of Ecclesiastical History* 16 (October 1965): 139-151. Another theological problem debated and resolved into orthodoxy in the fourth century.

1285. **Wilken, Robert L.** *John Chrysostom and the Jews: Rhetoric and Reality in the Late Fourth Century.* Berkeley: University of California Press, 1983. Wilken sets the context for the anti-Semitic ramblings of John Chrysostom. In the middle of the fourth century Antioch and indeed throughout the empire, Christianity was only one of many competing religions, and it was the new kid on the block, with the usual insecurities. The efforts of Julian to unseat Christianity and to favor the Jews was especially alarming. In this situation anti-Jewish propaganda takes on new dimensions, interestingly revealed by Wilken. J. Seaver, *American Historical Review* 89 (1984): 1059-1060 (+).

1286. **Williams, R.** "Arius and the Melitian Schism: The Codex Veronensis LX." *Journal of Theological Studies* 37 (1986): 35-52. This is not the Arius of Arianism, although there has been confusion since the late fourth century.

1287. **Williams, Rowan.** *Arius: Heresy and Tradition.* London: Darton, Longman and Todd, 1987. "This book has attempted to view Arius without the distorting glass of Athanasian polemic . . ." Arius in fact responded to "the fourth-century crisis" of self-identity in a church entering the mainstream of intellectual and political life in the Roman state, and thus inaugurated "a debate about the kinds of continuity possible and necessary in the Church's language" (p. 234), and the search for how the church should "become intellectually self-aware and . . . move from a 'theology of repetition' to something more exploratory and constructive" (p. 235). R. A. Markus, *Times Literary Supplement* (May 6, 1988): 510 (+).

1288. **Williams, R. D.** "The Logic of Arianism." *Journal of Theological Studies* 34 (1983): 56-81. This is a heavier dose of fourth century theology than most of us may care to tackle. But Williams has a very good phrase which defines a great deal of what the church was about in that period: Arius "stirred an intellectually careless Church into a ferment of conceptual reconstruction . . . " (p.81).

1289. Wolfson, H. A. "Philosophical Implications of Arianism and Apollinarianism." *Dumbarton Oaks Papers* 12 (1958): 3-28. In the fourth century, the thought processes of Aristotle and Plato were still very much in evidence among Christians trying to resolve theological problems. The theological issues of the time may not be much to our taste, but one can appreciate the high and sophisticated level of debate that was still possible in that age, when educated Christians had one foot firmly planted in a rich and ancient culture still fully available to them.

1290. Yarbrough, Anne. "Christianization in the Fourth Century: The Example of Roman Women." *Church History* 45 (1976): 149-165. In Rome, there were the respectable aristocratic Christian women who were the bridges their families quietly crossed from paganism into Christianity, carrying with them a lot of traditional Roman cultural baggage. Then there was a group of aristocratic women who were of a more fanatical spirit, who practised a Christian asceticism and withdrawal which may have been praised by Jerome, since the movement served his purposes, but which was not well received generally. It is this fringe group that Yarbrough explains.

1291. Young, Frances M. *From Nicaea to Chalcedon: A Guide to the Literature and Its Background.* Philadelphia: Fortress Press, 1983. This helpful book is for those with a smattering of knowledge of the Christian theological development and its literary expression in the fourth and fifth centuries, and who wants to begin to pull it all together into some kind of coherence. It is also a good reference for those students of the fourth century who need to freshen up a bit on specific persons and debates, from Eusebius to Synesius. Young includes a good bibliography. E. TeSelle, *Church History* 53 (1984): 381-382 (+-); C. Kannengiesser, *Catholic Historical Review* 71 (1985): 455 (+-).

1292. Young, Frances M. "The God of the Greeks and the Nature of Religious Language." In *Early Christian Literature and the Classical Intellectual Tradition: In Honorem Robert M.*

Grant, pp. 45-74. Edited by William R. Schoedel and Robert L. Wilken. Paris: Editions Beauchesne, 1979. An interesting essay about fourth century God-talk, starring Gregory Nazianzen (representing a "patristic theological concensus") in the context of the struggle against Arianism. This stratum of Christian discussion was suffused with ancient Greek philosophy, as Young clearly shows.

XI. Church and State

Includes state-sponsored persecutions.

1293. Alfoldi, Andras. *The Conversion of Constantine and Pagan Rome.* Translated by Harold Mattingly. New York: Oxford University Press, 1948; 1969. The hardening of attitudes between the Christian Constantine and the resolutely pagan Senate led to the new capital of Constantinople and exacerbated the division between old and new in the Roman empire. Strong use of numismatic material. H. St. L. B. Moss, *Journal of Roman Studies* 39 (1949): 167-169 (+-); F. Cramer, *Speculum* 28 (1953): 128 (+-).

1294. Alfoldi, Andreas. "The Initials of Christ on the Helmet of Constantine." In *Studies in Roman Economic and Social History in Honor of Allan Chester Johnson,* pp. 303-311. Edited by P. R. Coleman-Norton. Princeton, N. J.: Princeton University Press, 1951. Proof through coins that a Christian monogram was used at the Battle of the Milvian Bridge in 312, just as the historical sources say. Heavily illustrated.

1295. Alfoldi, Andras. "The Helmet of Constantine with the Christian Monogram." *Journal of Roman Studies* 22 (1932): 9-23. With the use of coins, Alfoldi (translated by Glanville Downey) tells the story of Constantine's Christianized helmet.

1296. Alonso-Nunez, J. M. "The Emperor Julian's *Misopogon* and the Conflict between Christianity and Paganism." *Ancient Society* 10 (1979): 311-324. After a review of the pagan and Christian sources for events in Antioch in A. D. 363, of modern treatments of the period, and of the *Misopogon* itself, Alonso-Nunez decides in favor of economic causes for the trouble between Antioch and its emperor, rather than religious ones.

1297.   Ambrose. *Sancti Ambrosii Liber de Consolatione Valentiniana*. Text with a Translation, Introduction, and Commentary by Thomas A. Kelly. Washington, D. C.: Catholic University Press, 1940.   Valentinian II is the subject of Ambrose's consolation of the surviving family.

1298.   Ambrose. *Sancti Ambrosii Oratio de Obitu Theodosii*. Text, Translation, Introduction and Commentary by Sister Mary Dolorosa Mannix. Washington, D. C.: Catholic University, 1925.   An important piece of source material relating to the death of the emperor Theodosius I in 395.

1299.   Anastos, Milton V. "The Edict of Milan (313): A Defense of Its Traditional Authorship and Designation." *Revue des Etudes Byzantines* (Melanges Venance Grumel, II) 35 (1967): 13-41.

1300.   Armstrong, Gregory T. "Church and State Relations: The Changes Wrought by Constantine." *Journal of Bible and Religion* 32 (1964): 1-7.   This is a clear and well organized summary of the change of fortunes for both church and state when Constantine took the initiative and catapulted Christianity into the most prestigious religious society in the empire and wedded it to the imperial governmental structure.

1301.   Armstrong, Gregory T. "Imperial Church Building and Church-State Relations, A. D. 313-363." *Church History* 36 (1967): 3-17.   All emperors worth their salt were great builders.   Had the construction of many state-sponsored basilicas anything to do with state policy towards Christianity? Yes, says Armstrong. The building projects were to give both practical and symbolic effect to the plan of the family of Constantine to make their religion a mainstay of the empire, with civil as well as spiritual duties. Julian was no different, though his religion was Hellenism. "These emperors [Constantine and Julian] all attempted to shore up the collapsing structure of society with the monuments of a universal ideology" (p. 19). For all the emperors, faith and culture and the state's prosperity were intermingled in a way almost unintelligible to a modern student.

1302. Baker, George P. *Constantine the Great and the Christian Revolution.* New York: Dodd, Mead and Co., 1930; New York: Barnes and Noble, 1967.   The psychological treatments are perhaps a bit suspect, but Baker is a good read, full of helpful background material.   H. M., *Journal of Roman Studies* 22 (1932): 244 (+); *Christian Century* 48 (February 4, 1931): 176 (+).

1303. Barnard, Leslie W. "Athanasius and the Roman State." *Latomus* 36 (1977): 422-437.   "His [Athanasius'] ideal was probably cooperation between Church and State with the bishops having freedom to decide Church matters in their own gatherings and the Emperor having the right to maintain the peace of the Church and to defend its faith" (p. 437).

1304. Barnard, Leslie W. "Church-State Relations, A. D. 313-337." *Journal of Church and State* 24 (Spring 1982): 337-355.   "Church-state relations between 313 and 337 present a checkered picture. The bishops of the church were unprepared for the risks involved in Christianity's becoming a *religio licita*. Moreover, Constantine himself had no fixed plan for dealing with the church, beyond a vague aspiration for unity, and his actions, at times, verge on total bewilderment. The bishops, especially in the East, were not so much doctrinal as political and personal opponents of Athanasius and his Western supporters.   Only later would the doctrinal differences, which lay below the surface, come to play a major role in the relation of East and West and in the relation of both to the state" (p. 355).

1305. Barnard, Leslie W. "The Emperor Constans and the Christian Church." *Rivista Storica dell' Antichita* 11 (1981): 205-214.   Constans, son of Constantine the Great, was an orthodox Christian whose support for Athanasius and the western church was important in the 340s.

1306. Barnes, Timothy D. *Constantine and Eusebius.* Cambridge, Mass.: Harvard University Press, 1981. In this important work we get the view that Constantine was a fanatical Christian who made his cult the "official religion" (pp. 97, 224) of the empire and who intended that it should replace all other cults. The treatment of Eusebius is full of helpful insights. Barnes is impatient with the on-the-one-hand-but-on-the-other-hand brand of history: he wants to get to the heart of the matter. This leads to conclusions that modest evidence can have difficulty sustaining. Still, Barnes is wonderfully well informed and gives essential reading on Diocletian, Constantine, and Eusebius. H. A. Drake, *American Journal of Philology* 103 (Winter 1982): 462-466 (+-); Averil Cameron, *Journal of Roman Studies* 73 (1983): 184-190; R. M. Grant, *Catholic Historical Review* 70 (1984): 100-101 (+); W. E. Kaegi, *American Historical Review* 87 (1982): 1372 (+); K. McCulloch, *History Today* 32 (July 1982): 54-55 (+).

1307. Barnes, Timothy D. "Emperor and Bishops, A. D. 324-344: Some Problems." *American Journal of Ancient History* 3 (Spring 1978): 53-75. The primary source material is sifted for information on Constantine and the Council of Nicaea, councils at Antioch and Nicomedia, Athanasius, Constantius II, the early bishops of Constantinople, the council of Serdica, Constans, and related persons and matters. Barnes stresses the utmost caution in using the ecclesiastical historians of the fifth century as guides to fourth century events.

1308. Barnes, Timothy D. "Sossianus Hierocles and the Antecedents of the 'Great Persecution.'" *Harvard Studies in Classical Philology* 80 (1976): 245-252. A seldom read tract of Eusebius, *Contra Hieroclem*, in conjunction with other primary source material, is pressed for information on the events and personalities leading to the persecution of the Christians in the age of Diocletian.

1309. Baus, Karl et al. *The Imperial Church from Constantine to the Early Middle Ages.* Translated by Anselm

Biggs. *History of the Church*, v.2. New York: Seabury Press, 1980. Karl Baus wrote the first three parts of this excellent study, and it is these three which encompass the fourth century. Part One concerns the development of the church in the context of the empire and imperial religious policy; Part Two reviews the theological controversies of the fourth and fifth centuries; Part Three looks at the inner life of the church - missionaries, liturgy, organization, clergy, monasticism, etc. - in the fourth and fifth centuries.

1310. Baynes, Norman H. *Constantine the Great and the Christian Church.* 2nd ed. New York: Oxford University Press, for the British Academy, 1972. First published in 1931, and based on the Raleigh Lecture on History (British Academy), 1929, this work by Baynes still holds its own in the academic world. It remains the touchstone for twentieth century discussion, at least in the English-speaking world, of Constantine and his relation to the new religion.

1311. Baynes, Norman H. "Eusebius and the Christian Empire." *Annuaire de l'Institut de Philologie et d'Histoire Orientales (Melanges Bidez)* 2 (1934): 13-18. Reprinted in his *Byzantine Studies and Other Essays*, pp. 168-172. London: Athlone Press, 1955. Eusebius found it easy and irresistible to move the Christian God and Constantine into the orbit of a relationship defined by Hellenistic political philosophy and theology, an orbit from which neither God nor the Roman emperor was ever entirely freed in the thinking of men thereafter. The basis of the Eusebian political philosophy of the Roman empire "is to be found in the conception of the imperial government as a terrestrial copy of the rule of God in Heaven" (p. 168).

1312. Baynes, Norman H. "Two Notes on the Great Persecution." *Classical Quarterly* 18 (1924): 189-193. Baynes discusses the Fourth Edict of persecution from the time of Diocletian. He considers the sources and reconstructs the chronology of political events informing the issuance and enforcement of the edict in 304 and 305. Then Baynes discusses political and religious developments of 312-313 with Eusebius at hand.

1313. Birley, A. R. "Magnus Maximus and the Persecution of Heresy." *Bulletin of the John Rylands University Library* 66 (Autumn 1983): 13-43. The emperor Magnus Maximus was a major player in the death of Priscillian, the Spanish heretic who troubled segments of the western church. Birley explores events and motives.

1314. Blake, Robert P. "Studies in the Religious Policy of Constantine and His Successors." Ph. D. dissertation, Harvard University, 1916.

1315. Bowersock, G. W. "From Emperor to Bishop: The Self-Conscious Transformation of Political Power in the Fourth Century A. D." *Classical Philology* 81 (1986): 298-307. To go from the time of Constantine the Great to the time of Theodosius the Great is to move from a world where the emperor commanded the church to a world where the church commanded the emperor. Constantine could think of himself as a bishop as well as pontifex maximus, without a ripple of protest anywhere: Christians were glad to have an imperial patron and pagans saw an emperor directing religious affairs as all the old pagan emperors had done too. But Theodosius was neither a bishop nor a pontifex maximus, and it was impossible to be either if he wished to please the matured, orthodox, narrow-minded, powerful church, which he did. Bowersock has deftly crafted the story of this political metamorphosis, and has identified the problems that the new system posed for the future.

1316. Boyd, William K. *The Ecclesiastical Edicts of the Theodosian Code.* New York: Columbia University Press, 1905; reprint ed., New York: AMS, 1969. Based on the Theodosian Code, Boyd reviews fourth and fifth century ecclesiastical developments, specifically: the conflict between paganism and Christianity, heresy and the church, relations of church and society, church courts, and the influence of the Code in early medieval times. It is Boyd's view that the church was "a disintegrating factor in Roman civilization" (p. 9).

1317. Brown, Peter. "Religious Dissent in the Later Roman Empire: The Case of North Africa." *History* 46 (1961): 83-101. Reprinted in his *Religion and Society in the Age of Saint Augustine*, pp. 237-259. New York: Harper and Row, 1972. Local issues may have contributed to religious dissent in the Roman state, but the real issue in the fourth century had usually to do with varying views of the relations of church and state and the place of religion in society.

1318. Cadoux, C. John. *The Early Christian Attitude to War.* London: Headly Bros., 1919; New York: Seaburg Press, [1982].

1319. Carter, B. H. A. "A Study of Imperial Religious Policies from the Accession of Jovian to the Death of Theodosius I." Ph. D. dissertation, Princeton Unviersity, 1956.

1320. Christensen, Torben. "The So-Called Edict of Milan." *Classica et Mediaevalia* 35 (1984): 129-175. The manuscript traditions of the text of the Edict of Milan are harmonized, and an historical context is provided involving the political maneuvers of Constantine, Licinius and Maximin in 313.

1321. Coleman, C. B. *Constantine the Great and Christianity. Three Phases: The Historical, the Legendary, and the Spurious.* Columbia University Studies in History, Economics and Public Law, Vol. 60, No. 1. New York: Columbia University, 1914.

1322. Coleman-Norton, P. R., ed. *Roman State and Christian Church: A Collection of Legal Documents to A. D. 535.* 3 vols. Naperville, Ill.: Alex R. Allenson, 1966. This is a priceless translation with annotations of 652 legal documents relating to the church and the Roman empire. These are all secular documents, emanating from the state. The western

Church and State

empire is covered to 476. G. Downey, *American Journal of Philology* 89 (1968): 351-356 (+).

1323. Cranz, F. E. "Kingdom and Polity in Eusebius of Caesarea." *Harvard Theological Review* 45 (January 1952): 47-66. In Eusebius' thought the Roman state and the Christian church were destined to blend and fuse, representing yet another stage in the great pilgrimage of man to the heavenly kingdom, of which the Roman state under Constantine was becoming more and more a reflection. Cranz tells the story, and to assist in clarification he compares Eusebius with Augustine (and others), who has a very different view of the place of the Roman state in relation to the kingdom (or city) of God.

1324. De Clerq, Victor. *Ossius of Cordova: A Contribution to the History of the Constantinian Period.* Studies in Christian Antiquity, no. 13. Washington, D. C.: Catholic University of America Press, 1954.

1325. De Ste. Croix, Geoffrey E. M. "Aspects of the 'Great' Persecution." *Harvard Theological Review* 47 (1954): 75-113. De Ste. Croix reviews the edicts of persecution, the nature and effects of the first edict, the types of enforcement in east and west of the first and fourth edicts, the administration of the fourth edict, and then adds appendices of useful political and other information about the Roman world in the first decades of the fourth century.

1326. Doerries, Hermann. *Constantine and Religious Liberty.* Translated by Roland Bainton. New Haven: Yale University Press, 1960. Constantine subscribed to religious liberty as a matter of personal belief, not political opportunism, says Doerries. *Christian Century* 78 (July 19, 1961): 879 (+); *Catholic Historical Review* 47 (1961): 211.

1327. Doerries, Hermann. *Constantine the Great.* Translated by Roland H. Bainton. New York: Harper and Row, 1972. Almost unrestrained admiration for Constantine and the Christian church of his day. R. A. Markus, *History* 58 (1973): 250-251 (+-).

1328. Drake, H. A. "Semper Victor Eris: Evidence for the Policy and Belief of Constantine I Contained in Eusebius' Tricennial Oration." Ph. D. dissertation, University of Wisconsin, 1970. Conclusions: Constantine by stages became a sincere Christian, and his goal was to integrate the church into the empire. He wanted to build bridges to monotheistic pagans, and to emphasize similarities, at least in his official capacity as emperor of all Romans.

1329. Duncan-Jones, R. "An African Saint and His Interrogator." *Journal of Theological Studies* 25 (1974): 106-110. The saint is Felix, the interrogator is Magnilianus, and the emperor is Diocletian. At issue in the article is the town in which the interrogation took place.

1330. Dvornik, Francis. *Early Christian and Byzantine Political Philosophy: Origins and Background.* 2 vols. Washington, D. C.: Dumbarton Oaks, 1966. Scholarly odyssey from the Sumerians to Justinian, showing the basis, development and maturation of the political philosophy which guided Christian emperors from the time of Constantine to the end of the Byzantine state. P. Alexander, *American Historical Review* 73 (1967-68): 777-779 (+); P. Charanis, *Speculum* 44 (1969): 459-460 (+).

1331. Eadie, John W., comp. *The Conversion of Constantine.* Huntington, N. Y.: R. E. Krieger, 1977. The subject of Constantine's relation to Christianity has elicited a large literary response from twentieth century historians. Eadie has compiled an anthology especially helpful for the translated European literature included. On Constantine as a political pragmatist there are selections from Henri Gregoire and Jean-Jacques Hatt; also a nineteenth century selection from Jacob Burkhardt. On Constantine as a pagan syncretist there are Andre Piganiol and Jacques Moreau. On Constantine as a Christian there are Norman Baynes, J.-R. Palanque, Andreas Alfoldi, Patrick Bruun, Ramsay MacMullen, and A. H.

M. Jones. Finally there is a synthesis by Joseph Vogt. Eadie has appended a useful bibliography.

1332. Elliott, Thomas G. "The Tax Exemptions Granted to Clerics by Constantine and Constantius II." *Phoenix* 32 (1978): 326-336.   Elliott reviews each law having to do with clerical exemptions. He reports that the basic policy of both emperors was consistent, and that many of the laws that have been interpreted as changes were really just efforts to plug loopholes or discourage abuses.

1333. Fowden, G. "Bishops and Temples in the East Roman Empire A. D. 320-435." *Journal of Theological Studies* 29 (1978): 53-78.   Fowden offers an "examination of the manner in which the Church collaborated with the civil authorities in the attack on the pagan temples and cults . . . " (p.53). Even at the end of the fourth century the government was still rather restrained in its actual treatment of temples and cults (perhaps because so many pagans were still in the government), but there was a lot of winking as bishops and monks became more belligerent and used violence against pagan practices and properties.

1334. Frazer, Charles A. "Late Roman and Byzantine Legislation on the Monastic Life from the Fourth to the Eighth Centuries." *Church History* 51 (1982): 263-279.   In the fourth century monks were quickly swept into the vortex of Roman life, perhaps often against their will, and into the political activities of emperors and bishops. Frazer gives about four pages of material on fourth century legislation.

1335. French, Dorothea R. "Christian Emperors and Pagan Spectacles: The Secularization of the 'Ludi' A. D. 382-525." Ph. D. dissertation, University of California, Berkeley, 1985.   French has a look at how state games and other entertainments were separated from their close association with the old pagan cults.

1336. Frend, W. H. C. "Constantine's Settlement with the Church and Its Legacy." *Modern Church* 6 (1962): 32-46.

Frend's conclusions may not be to everyone's tastes, but the real substance of the article is in the helpful analysis of the meaning of Christianity to Constantine and the reactions of the Christian churches to a Christian Caesar.

1337. Frend, W. H. C. "The Failure of the Persecutions." *Past and Present* 16 (1959): 10-30. Reprinted in his *Town and Country in the Early Christian Centuries*, Ch. X. London: Variorum Reprints, 1980. Frend compares the Decian persecution with the one under Diocletian, and discusses the growing strengths of Christianity which enabled it to prevail against the persecutors, despite close calls. One strength especially stressed is the rapid spread of Christianity into the countryside of some populous and important provinces, changing Christianity from a merely urban religion into a "universal and popular one."

1338. Frend, W. H. C. "A Note on the Great Persecution in the West." *Studies in Chruch History* 2 (1965): 141-148. Reprinted in his *Religion Popular and Unpopular in the Early Christian Centuries*, Ch. VI. London: Variorum Reprints, 1976. Frend identifies factors, such as the different values placed on handing over scripture versus making sacrifices, which gave the Diocletianic persecution contrasting manifestations in east and west.

1339. Frend, W. H. C. "The Roman Empire in the Eyes of the Western Schismatics During the 4th Century." *Miscellanea Historiae Ecclesiasticae*, pp. 9-22. Stockholm, 1960; Louvain, 1961. Reprinted in his *Religion Popular and Unpopular in the Early Christian Centuries*, Ch. X. London: Variorum Reprints, 1976. With the conversion of Constantine it became very easy for Christians to see the Roman state as a complement to the church, and a support for the Christian mission. It became easy but it did not become universal. Many groups of Christians, for one reason or another, would not cozy up to the emperor or the state. Many were uncertain how to see the Roman state in their lives. Frend tells the story.

1340. **Geanakoplos, D. J.** "Church Building and 'Caesaropapism', A. D. 312-565." *Greek, Roman and Byzantine Studies* 7 (1966): 167-186.

1341. **Gillman, I.** "Some Reflections on Constantine's 'Apostolic' Consciousness." *Texte und Untersuchungen zur Geschichte der Altchristlichen Literatur* 79 (1961): 422-428.

1342. **Greenslade, Stanley L.** *Church and State from Constantine to Theodosius.* Toronto: Ryerson Press, 1953; reprint ed., Westport, Conn.: Greenwood Press, 1981. In this brief work, originating from three lectures, Greenslade recounts the see-saw relationship of church and state in the fourth century regarding power and influence in each other's affairs, culminating in the dualist relationship that was starting to be enunciated by Ambrose and others at the end of the century. T. MacVicar, *Catholic Historical Review* 41 (1955): 29-30 (+-).

1343. **Harnack, Adolf.** *Militia Christi: The Christian Religion and the Military in the First Three Centuries.* Translated and introduced by David M. Gracie. Philadelphia: Fortress Press, 1981. First published in 1905, Harnack's little book is a classic formulation of the hawkish point of view, showing that Christian soldiers serving Rome were not a problem for the church.

1344. **Harries, Jill.** "Church and State in the *Notitia Galliarum*." *Journal of Roman Studies* 68 (1978): 26-43. The *Notitia Galliarum*, dating from the late fourth century, is a list of the seventeen provinces of Gaul with their important cities originally drawn up in the time of the usurper Magnus Maximus, who ruled 383-388 and who did some provincial reorganizing. Later, bishops requisitioned the list for ecclesiastical administrative purposes, but it was clearly secular in origin, says Harries.

1345. **Helgeland, John.** "Christians and the Roman Army A. D. 173-337." *Church History* 43 (1974): 149-163; 200. There is not much evidence for early church pacifism, says

Helgeland. Christians had problems with Roman gods in the army rather than with the Roman army.

1346. Hornus, J. M. *It is Not Lawful for Me to Fight. Early Christian Attitudes Towards War, Violence, and the State.* Rev. ed. Translated by A. Kreider and O. Coburn. Scottsdale, Pa.: Herald Press, 1980.

1347. Huttman, Maude A. *The Establishment of Christianity and the Proscription of Paganism.* New York: Columbia University, 1914. Includes the text in translation of all laws touching on the subject, as well as a narrative events. There is a lengthy discussion of the schools of thought on the Edict of Milan. Based on her dissertation done at Columbia.

1348. Isichei, Elizabeth A. *Political Thinking and Social Experience: Some Christian Interpretations of the Roman Empire from Tertullian to Salvian.* University of Canterbury Publications, 6. Christchurch, N. Z.: University of Canterbury, 1964. Includes Tertullian, Eusebius, Lactantius, Augustine, Orosius, Salvian. G. Bonner, *Journal of Ecclesiastical History* 17 (1966): 107-108 (+-).

1349. Jones, A. H. M. *Constantine and the Conversion of Europe.* London: English Universities Press, 1948; New York: Macmillan Co., 1949. A lucid and valuable piece on Constantine as a sincere convert to Christianity, as he understood it. His ambition, assurance, strength, and determination made him the ideal ally for a minority religion not averse to an opportunity to dominate the world. J. H. S. B., *English Historical Review* 64 (1949): 385-386 (+); M. L. W. Laistner, *American Journal of Archaeology* 53 (1949): 422 (+-).

1350. Kee, Alistair. *Constantine Versus Christ.* London: S. C. M. Press, 1982. Constantine was not a real Christian, and Christianity was corrupted by its association with the imperial court. K. McCulloch, *History Today* 32 (July 1982): 55 (-).

1351. **Keresztes, Paul.** *Constantine, a Great Christian Monarch and Apostle.* Amsterdam: J. C. Gieben, 1981. Panegyric passing for history. Although some faults are acknowledged, Constantine still emerges the Great Hero of the church. R. B. Eno, *Catholic Historical Review* 70 (1984): 99-100 (-).

1352. **Keresztes, Paul.** "From the Great Persecution to the Peace of Galerius." *Vigiliae Christianae* 37 (1983): 379-399. Keresztes takes a close look at the events and personalities of the first decade of the fourth century, when the persecution of the Christians, after so many decades of tolerance, again became the order of the day.

1353. **Keresztes, Paul.** "Patristic and Historical Evidence for Constantine's Christianity." *Latomus* 42 (1983): 84-94. Constantine was "a genuine Christian monarch and a true apostle" (p. 94).

1354. **Kesich, V.** "Empire-Church Relations and the Third Temptation." *Studia Patristica (Texte und Untersuchungen* 79; Berlin 1961) 4: 465-471. For those without Bible studies, the third temptation refers to Christ's rejection of the kingdom's of the world which were offered to him on the mountain top by Satan. Early Christian writers read into this event a rejection, perhaps not of an active kind but still an ultimate rejection, of the Roman empire. In the fourth century, when the state was the church's ally, this attitude would no longer do. Kesich uses Eusebius to show a new attitude to the third temptation which dissociates it from Rome.

1355. **King, Noel Q.** *The Emperor Theodosius and the Establishment of Christianity.* Philadelphia: Westminster Press, 1961. A very helpful narrative and analysis, based soundly on the sources, of the final triumph of Christianity in the Roman state. H. Kreilkamp, *Catholic Historical Review* 49 (1963): 399-400 (+); E. R. Hardy, *Church History* 31 (1962): 361 (+); P. Brown, *History* 49 (1964): 202-203 (+-).

1356. King, Noel Q. "The Theodosian Code as a Source for the Religious Policies of the First Byzantine Emperors." *Nottingham Mediaeval Studies* 6 (1962): 12-17. The Code is a minefield of trouble for innocent scholars. King shows a healthy reserve and identifies a number of no-no's when probing the Code. Here is a useful dictum from the article: "If one asks an ancient source a question out of keeping with its nature, one gets the wrong answer or no answer at all" (p. 15). There is a great deal of helpful information about religious policies of some emperors, but even then "the Code as a source lets us hear but a whisper of their voice and to know but the outskirts of their ways of thought" (p. 17).

1357. Knipfing, John R. "The Edict of Galerius (311 A.D.) Re examined." *Revue Belge de Philologie et d'Histoire* 1 (1922): 693-705. Knipfing explains the origin and meaning of the edict, which he considers significant. Both the Latin and an English translation of the edict are included.

1358. Knipfing, John R. "Religious Tolerance During the Early Part of the Reign of Constantine the Great (306-313)." *Catholic Historical Review* 4 (1925): 483-503. Detailed discussion of the Edict of Galerius (A.D. 311) and the Edict of Milan (A.D. 313), the latter called "the Constitution of Licinius" by Knipfing.

1359. Kopecek, Thomas A. "The Cappadocian Fathers and Civic Patriotism." *Church History* 43 (1974): 293-303. The Cappadocian fathers, being of the curial class, showed concern for the fortunes of their native cities. Their efforts and views foreshadowed the time when bishops and clerical authorities would virtually assume the governing and representing of the cities of the empire. Kopecek adduces an interesting example of the local effects of splitting up a province, in the time of Valens, and the criticism it could draw from vested interests.

1360. Labriolle, Pierre de, Bardy, G., and Palanque, J.-R. *The Church in the Christian Roman Empire.* New York: Macmillan, 1953. Originally published in French in 1947 as Volume 3 of *Histoire de l'Eglise*, edited by A. Fliche and

V. Martin, and titled *De la Paix Constantinienne a la Mort de Theodose.*

1361. MacMullen, Ramsay. "The Meaning of A. D. 312: The Difficulty of Converting the Empire." In *The 17th International Byzantine Congress: Major Papers,* pp. 1-15. Dumbarton Oaks/Georgetown University, Washington, D. C., August 3-8, 1986. New Rochelle, N. Y.: A. D. Caratzas, 1986. Paganism had plenty of life left in the fourth century; the conversion of Constantine did not at first have much effect on anyone, including Constantine whose head was filled with (and never entirely emptied of) the old ways of doing things; Christianity was a minority religion throughout the fourth century, and the best perspective is to accept pluralism as the fundamental religious fact of the period; and Christianity and paganism could exist at many levels of expression without much inherent conflict, especially because so much of paganism had to do with ritual expression (which could often not only be tolerated but even adopted by Christians) rather than correct belief. These are the points MacMullen has us ponder as he takes us back to a world of thought from which our own developed, but which is now so hard to recapture on its own terms.

1362. McGuire, Martin R. P. "A New Study on the Political Role of St. Ambrose." *Catholic Historical Review* 22 (1936-37): 304-318. In a lengthy review of J.-R. Palanque's *Saint Ambrose et l'Empire Romain,* McGuire addresses a number of important issues not only on Ambrose but on the late fourth century generally.

1363. Mellon, Doss B. "Theodosius and the Conversion of the Roman Pagan Aristocracy." M. A. thesis, Gonzaga University, Spokane, Washington, 1984.

1364. Michaels-Mudd, Mary. "The Arian Policy of Constantius II and Its Impact on Church-State Relations in the Fourth-Century Roman Empire." *Byzantine Studies* 6 (1979): 95-111. Constantius is presented as an Arian who wanted uniformity of belief in the church and went to unprecedented lengths to impose the will of the imperial office upon ecclesiastical matters. His Arian and heavy-handed policy came to full flower when his anti-Arian brothers and co-rulers were dead.

1365. Mitchell, Stephen. "Maximinus and the Christians in A. D. 312: A New Latin Inscription." *Journal of Roman Studies* 78 (1988): 105-124. After a review of the new Latin inscription from Asia Minor (known in Greek through Eusebius), a review of all the legislation towards the Christians, favorable and unfavorable, from 303 to 313, and a review of Maximinus' emperorship and his strong religious views, Mitchell invites us to see the inscription of 312 in the context of Maximinus' effort to encourage local anti-Christian sentiment through tax relief to co-operative cities. The actual inscription, engraved in a language unintelligible to most people in the east, was "emphatically a symbolic gesture, not a literal attempt to communicate imperial law" (p. 124).

1366. Momigliano, Arnaldo. "Christianity and the Decline of the Roman Empire." In *The Conflict Between Paganism and Christianity in the Fourth Century,* pp. 1-16. Edited by Arnaldo Momigliano. New York: Oxford University Press, 1963. Momigliano restores and updates the thesis that the church helped undermine the empire, in part by absorbing a great deal of talent that would have been most useful in the service of the state. The fourth century is seen as the critical period in this development.

1367. Momigliano, Arnaldo. "The Disadvantages of Monotheism for a Universal State." *Classical Philology* 81 (1986): 285-297. In his usual lucid way, Momigliano adduces evidence and arguments to show "that the pagans never managed . . . to produce a consistent case for the interdependence between polytheism and political pluralism in the Roman Empire" (p. 296). But the Christians developed, especially in the fourth century, a strong case for the part of the unified Roman state in bringing all people to the one true God. The success of the Christian point of view was fatal for a pluralistic society. The Christians captured the Roman empire, but the price for driving out pluralism and enforcing uniformity was heavy: "The pagans and the heretics, not to speak of the Jews, lost interest in the Roman State" (p. 297).

1368. **Morino, Claudio.** *Church and State in the Teaching of St. Ambrose.* Translated by M. J. Costelloe. Washington, D. C.: Catholic University Press, 1969. Although a paean to Ambrose and the Catholic Church, this book will provide the careful reader with the historical position of Ambrose regarding church-state relations. The author also adduces many interpretations of Ambrose's positions by other writers. Even through this rose-colored treatment, Ambrose emerges for what he was: a competent, determined believer, who would stop at nothing to make the world Christian and who believed the Roman church should influence and direct the state in every matter of religion or even morality.

1369. **Morrison, Karl F.** *Rome and the City of God: An Essay on the Constitutional Relationships of Empire and Church in the Fourth Century.* Philadelphia: American Philosophical Society, 1964. In the fourth century church and state were still very separate institutions, with areas of common interest that underwent definition throughout the century. Christianity was not actually even the state religion until late in the century; and even then those who remembered Julian knew that things could change again quickly. In the fourth century we are still very far from the caesaropapism of the Byzantine state. Morrison conveys the story in rich detail, relying heavily on Athanasius, Augustine, and others, to get a sense of the independence which the Christians saw for themselves in relation to the state. A. H. M. Jones, *English Historical Review* 80 (1965): 811-812 (-).

1370. **Nordberg, Henric.** *Athanasius and the Emperor.* Societas Scientiarum Fennica, Commentationes Humanasum Litterarum, 30, 3. Helsinki, 1963.

1371. **Ocker, C.** "Unius arbitrio mundum regi necesse est. Lactantius' Concern for the Preservation of Roman Society."

Vigiliae Christianae 40 (1986): 348-364. In Lactantius' view, the survival of the empire and of the Roman way of life depended on the triumph of Christianity, an event happily confirmed through the career of Constantine.

1372. Odahl, Charles. "The Celestial Sign on Constantine's Shield at the Battle of the Milvian Bridge." *Journal of the Rocky Mountain Medieval and Renaissance Association* 2 (January 1981): 15-28. Odahl works through the evidence to ascertain the exact symbol used on Constantine's banners at the Milvian Bridge: the Christogram - i.e., the Chi-Rho.

1373. Odahl, Charles M. "Constantine and the Militarization of Christianity: A Contribution to the Study of Christian Attitudes toward War and Military Service." Ph. D. dissertation, University of California at San Diego, 1976. Odahl argues the case that the pacifism of the early church and its leaders was undermined during the time of Constantine and after. Once the church became an imperial church it had also to become a militant church, in order to preserve its great victory over the evil powers of the world. Odahl stresses the pacifism of the early church to a point beyond acceptance by some scholars today.

1374. Pagels, Elaine. "The Politics of Paradise." *New York Review of Books* 35 (May 12, 1988): 28-37. In the fourth century a great issue undergirded arguments over free will versus the will in bondage as extrapolated from extreme views of original sin. That issue was whether the church should be voluntary and egalitarian or coercive and hierarchical, using the state for practical support in keeping man's sinful nature in line with the goal of reaching salvation. The debate was won in the fifth century, when the Augustinian view prevailed, with centuries of unhappy consequences for individuals and groups who espoused a different view of life from the state church. The richness and often the profundity of the debate speak well for the intellectual ambience of the fourth century; but there also emerges the narrow, dogmatic, and fanatical streak which broke the bounds of restraint, captured the imperial court at the end of the fourth century, and in conjunction with the victory of the anti-free will faction, imposed the restricted parameters of thought so powerful in later centuries. Pagels outlines the debate in the fourth century and the results in the fifth. For more on the history of Christianity's intellectual move from free will to bondage in sin and all of its practical ramifications, see Pagel's book, *Adam, Eve and the Serpent* (1988), from which the essay here is taken.

1375. Seston, W. "Constantine as a 'Bishop.'" *Journal of Roman Studies* 37 (1947): 127-131. Seston says the theory of Constantine as "bishop of those outside the church" does not come from Eusebius, and that the *Vita Constantini* is a mixed bag, not all from the hand of Eusebius. The author of the Constantine-as-bishop part intended to give the emperors a place in relation to but still far from the center of ecclesiastical power.

1376. Setton, Kenneth M. *The Christian Attitude Towards the Emperor in the Fourth Century.* Columbia Studies in History, Economics, and Public Law, 482. New York: Columbia University Press, 1941. Reprint ed., New York: AMS Press, 1967. Setton puts on stage such fourth century luminaries as Eusebius, Athanasius, Ambrose, and John Chrysostom, as well as some minor figures, to discuss the meaning of the emperor and his functions to the increasingly powerful Christian movement. In the first half of the fourth century there tended to be an uncritical acceptance of the benefits of a Christian emperor; in the last half doubts developed, leading to serious thinking about the limits of imperial authority relating to the church. M. L. W. Laistner, *American Historical Review* 47 (1942): 405 (+-); G. Downey, *Church History* 11 (1942): 69-70 (+-).

1377. Setton, Kenneth M. "Christian Attitudes Towards the Emperor in the Fourth Century, Especially as Shown in Addresses to the Emperor." Ph. D. dissertation, Columbia University, 1941.

1378. Shepherd, Massey H., Jr. "Liturgical Expressions of the Constantinian Triumph." *Dumbarton Oaks Papers* 21 (1967): 59-78.   "The sanctification of the temporal order through the Christian renovation of the Empire, is the key to the liturgical innovations of Constantine" (p. 75). There was also need to counteract the pagan liturgies. Shepherd tells the story to the extent that we can know it from the fourth century sources.

1379. Snee, Rochelle. "Valens' Recall of the Nicene Exiles and Anti-Arian Propaganda." *Greek, Roman and Byzantine Studies* 26 (1985): 395-419.   An adequate study of the reign of Valens needs to be done. In the meantime Snee offers some views of the religious policy of this ill-fated emperor by looking at the events of 377-378, when Valens permitted exiled bishops to return and when he was preparing for his last and fatal military campaign in Thrace. There is a careful review of the primary source material, and how it has been used by other scholars.

1380. Storch, Rudolph H. "The Trophy and the Cross: Pagan and Christian Symbolism in the Fourth and Fifth Centuries." *Byzantion* 40 (1970): 105-118.   Storch gives the story of the struggle between the Roman trophy and the Christian cross as the great victory symbol of the Roman state. Storch finds the end of the story on a coin from the time of Theodosius II, just after the end of the fourth century: "Here . .
is Victoria now holding a long cross, as an emblem of the victorious Christian state, and not the *tropaeum* symbol of the military might of pagan Rome" (p. 117).

1381. Straub, Johannes. "Constantine as KOINOS EPISKOPOS: Tradition and Innovation in the Representation of the First Christian Emperor's Majesty." *Dumbarton Oaks Papers* 21 (1967): 37-55.   Both church and state were unprepared for the appearance of a Christian emperor. Both had to adapt to the new situation, and the emperor, Constantine, had to mediate. Constantine was a man of initiative and innovation, but he had political sense as well as a devotion to the new religion, and he worked within the political traditions of the empire. The fusion of the interests of the state and those of the church was manifested in interesting ways, explained by Straub with some tips from Eusebius.

1382. Telfer, W. "Constantine's Holy Land Plan." *Studia Patristica (Texte und Untersuchungen* 63; Berlin 1957) 1: 696-700. How Jerusalem and the Holy Land were to become the spiritual focus of the Roman world.

1383. Thompson, A. R. "Dio Chrysostom and the Roman Empire." M. A. thesis, Nottingham University, 1964.

1384. Ullmann, Walter. "The Constitutional Significance of Constantine the Great's Settlement." *Journal of Ecclesiastical History* 27 (1976): 1-16. Once the church became a legal public body, it became subject to the public law of the Roman state. Constantine worked on the basis that his intervention in the affairs of the church would be expected and accepted by the Christians in their new status as full participants in the burdens as well as the privileges of public recognition; and for the most part he was right. Constantine's main goal was to strengthen the Roman state, and he expected the Christians to do their part by bringing spiritual and intellectual renewal, as well as the strength of their organizational structure. His interventions in church affairs were directed to these ends, and were well within the prerogative of a Roman emperor as the office was understood at the time.

1385. Walsh, P. G. "Paulinus of Nola and the Conflict of Ideologies in the Fourth Century." In *KYRIAKON: Festschrift Johannes Questen,* pp. 565-571. Edited by Patrick Granfield and Josef A. Jungmann. 2 vols. Munster: Aschendorff, 1970. Walsh analyzes the attitude of Paulinus to the secular world, an attitude shared by many noteworthy contemporaries. Althougn not seeking the ruin of the Roman government or empire, Paulinus showed little enough concern for these. His attitude, which had the effect of withholding much needed talent from the state, can be summarized in a letter which Walsh quotes: "You cannot serve two masters, God and Mammon, Christ and

Caesar, even though Caesar himself is now keen to be Christ's servant" (p. 566).

1386. Williams, George H. "Christology and Church-State Relations in the Fourth Century." *Church History* 20 (September 1951): 3-33; (December 1951): 3-26. "It is the purpose of the present study to examine briefly some of the reasons for the initially uncritical submission of the Church to imperial supervision and then to show how the Arian controversy, which originally necessitated the summoning of the Council of Nicaea, became in the course of the fourth century the religio-political occasion for and in part the theological means of clarifying the proper relationship between the Church and the Christianized magistracy" (Sept., p. 5). This is a rich and important contribution to our understanding of the great appeal of Arianism, whose patterns of thought represented a more congenial basis for discussion with the pagan political and religious culture of the fourth century than did the orthodox Christian point of view.

1387. Woodward, E. L. *Christianity and Nationalism in the Later Roman Empire.* London: Longmans, Green and Co., 1916. Woodward presents the classic argument that nationalist desires were expressed in regional Christian developments, and made a contribution to the disintegration of the Roman state.

Appendix I: Final Entries

These last minute entries, mainly from 1989, are organized only by the author's name; so the entire set must be browsed for relevance to a specific topic.

1387.5. Arthur, Paul. "Some Observations on the Economy of Bruttium under the Later Roman Empire." *Journal of Roman Archaeology* 2 (1989): 133-142.

1388. Barnish, S. J. B. "A Note on the *Collatio Glebalis.*" *Historia* 38 (1989): 254-256. In the late fourth century, the nobility grumbled endlessly about this tax, which has perplexed historians because on the surface it looks modest. But Barnish takes a new view, pointing out how it could be seen as a "dangerous and humiliating nuisance" (p. 256).

1388.4. Bastien, P. "Imitations of Roman Bronze Coins A. D. 318-363." *American Numismatic Society. Museum Notes* 30 (1985): 143-177.

1388.5. Bradbury, Scott A. "Innovation and Reaction in the Age of Constantine and Julian." Ph. D. dissertation, University of California Berkeley, 1986. Bradbury looks at aspects of the Julian reaction to the Constantinian revolution, and considers the general reaction of conservatives like Julian to changes in the perceived traditional patterns of life in the Roman world.

1388.6. Burgess, R. W. "Consuls and Consular Dating in the Later Roman Empire [rev. art.]." *Phoenix* 43 (1989): 143-157.

1389. Davies, Roy W. *Service in the Roman Army.* New York: Columbia University Press, 1989. Although largely concerned with the early and high empire periods, some material from the later empire is adduced, and there is much quoting of Vegetius.

1389.5. Di Maio, Michael. "The Emperor Julian's Edicts of Religious Toleration." *Ancient World* 20 (1989): 99-109. Julian hoped to restore paganism to all its former glories, with the concomitant diminution of Christianity. Di Maio doubts that he could have succeeded even had his reign been a long one.

1389.6. Di Maio, Michael. "Smoke in the Wind: Zonaras' Use of Philostorgius, Zosimus, John of Antioch, and John of Rhodes in His Narrative on the Neo-Flavian Emperors." *Byzantion* 58 (1988): 236-237.

1389.7. Di Maio, Michael. "The Transfer of the Remains of the Emperor Julian from Tarsus to Constantinople." *Byzantion* 48 (1978): 43ff.

1389.8. Di Maio, Michael; Zeuge, Jorn; and Zotov, Natalia. "*Ambiguitas Constantiniana:* The *Calleste Signum Dei* of Constantine the Great." *Byzantion* 58 (1988): 350ff.

1390. Dunn, E. C. *The Gallican Saint's Life and the Late Roman Dramatic Tradition.* Washington, D. C.: Catholic University Press, 1989. Dunn investigates how the typical late Roman expressions of drama through mime and pantomine informed efforts to convey the lives of the saints to a largely illiterate society.

1390.1. Edmondson, J. C. "Mining in the Later Roman Empire and Beyond: Continuity or Disruption?" *Journal of Roman Studies* 79 (1989): 84-102.

1390.2. Elliott, Thomas G. "Constantine's Early Religious Development." *Journal of Religious History* 15 (1989): 283-291.

Appendix I: Final Entries

1390.2.1. Errington, R. Malcolm. "Constantine and the Pagans." *Greek, Roman, and Byzantine Studies* 29 (1988): 309-318.

1390.3. Evans-Grubb, Judith. "Abduction-Marriage in Antiquity: A Law of Constantine (*CTh* IX.24.1) and Its Social Context." *Journal of Roman Studies* 79 (1989): 59-84.

1390.4. Fowden, G. "Bishops and Temples in the Eastern Roman Empire A.D. 320-435." *Journal of Theological Studies* 29 (1978): 52-56.

1391. Greer, Rowan A. *The Fear of Freedom: A Study of Miracles in the Roman Imperial Church.* University Park: Pennsylvania State University Press, 1989. Rowan sees old notions of Christian free will sliding into the shadow of an emphasis on the sovereignty of God, the need of grace for salvation, and the authority of the church. The relative diminution of personal freedom was a trend consonant with the church's change from its early image to that of an imperial church, meshing with the interests of an authoritarian system of government. Augustine is seen as a pivotal figure in the transition.

1392. Guzman, Gregory. "Were the Barbarians a Negative or Positive Factor in Ancient and Medieval History?" *Historian* 50 (1988): 558-572.

1392.5. Hanson, R. P. C. "The Source and Significance of the Fourth Oratio Contra Arianos Attributed to Athanasius." *Vigiliae Christianae* 42 (1988): 257-266.

1393. Harries, Jill. "Towards a New Constantine?" *Ancient Society, Resources for Teachers* XV, pp. 71-83. North Ryde, N. S. W. Australia: Macquarie University; Macquarie Ancient History Association, 1985.

1393.5. Ivanovski, M. "The Grave of a Warrior from the Period of Licinius Found at Tarenes." *Archaeologiae Iugoslavica* 24 (Ljubljana 1987): 81-90.

1394. Jensen, R. C. "The Kourion Earthquake: Some Possible Literary Evidence." *Report of the Department of Antiquities, Cyprus*, pp. 307-311. Nicosia, Cyprus: Zavallis Press, 1985. If Ammianus Marcellinus (*Res Gestae* xxvi, 10, 15-19) discusses the Kourion earthquake, the date would have been July 21, 365.

1395. *Liber Pontificalis, to 715 A. D.* Translated and with an introduction. Liverpool, England: University of Liverpool, 1989.

1395.3. Long, Jacqueline. "A New Solidus of Julian Caesar." *American Numismatic Society. Museum Notes* 33 (1988): 111-118.

1395.5. Luibheid, C. "Antony and the Renunciation of Society." *Irish Theological Quarterly* 52 (1986): 304-314.

1395.6. MacMullen, Ramsay. "The Preacher's Audience (AD 350-400)." *Journal of Theological Studies* 40 (1989): 503-511.

1396. Malamud, Martha A. *A Poetics of Transformation: Prudentius and Classical Mythology.* Ithaca, N. Y.: Cornell Unviversity Press, 1989.

1396.5. Matthews, John. *The Roman Empire of Ammianus.* Baltimore: Johns Hopkins University Press, 1989.

1396.6. Mayerson, P. "Libanius and the Administration of Palestina." *Zeitschrift fuer Papyrologie und Epigraphik* 69 (1987): 251-260.

1397. Norwich, John J. *Byzantium: The Early Centuries.* New York: Knopf, 1989. From Constantine to Charlemagne's coronation as western emperor in 800. A good read, emphasizing personalities and events at the center of political life: Constantinople and the court. Constantine and Julian receive high billing. M. Angold, *Times Literary Supplement* #4478 (January 27, 1989): 83 (+).

1398. O'Meara, Dominic. *Pythagoras Revived: Mathematics and Philosophy in Late Antiquity.* New York: Oxford University Press, 1989.

1399. Palmer, Anne-Marie. *Prudentius on the Martyrs.* Oxford: Clarendon Press, 1989. The *Persitephanon* comes under investigation in the setting of the late fourth century culture and politics of a changing empire.

1399.5. Pitts, Lynn F. "Relations Between Rome and the German 'Kings' on the Middle Danube in the First to Fourth Centuries A. D." *Journal of Roman Studies* 79 (1989): 45-58.

1400. Roberts, Michael. *The Jeweled Style: Poetry and Poetics in Late Antiquity.* Ithaca, N. Y.: Cornell University Press, 1989. The styles of poetry in the fourth and fifth centuries are discussed in the context of the general culture of the age, including interesting comparisons to prose, dress, and art.

1401. Rodgers, Barbara S. "Constantine's Pagan Vision." *Byzantion* 50 (1980): 259-278. Constantine was a great one for having visions, or at least for having them attributed to him. Before his final commitment to the Christian cause, or in any event before his understanding of the exclusive claims of the Christian way of life, he was given a vision of Apollo, according to a panegyrist writing in 310. Rodgers discusses the political context, the association with the Roman past, especially Augustus, and the success of the panegyrist in bringing imperial aid to the city of Autun in Gaul.

1402. Rodgers, Barbara S. "The Metamorphosis of Constantine." *Classical Quarterly* 39 (1989): 233-246. Using the *Panegyrici Latini*, Rodgers surveys the "tension between form and function" as the Latin orators worked their magic within the rules of their art to portray Constantine over the years in a way that would satisfy both art and politics.

1402.5. Salzman, Michele R. "Reflections on Symmachus' Idea of Tradition." *Historia* 38 (1989): 348-364. "In the final analysis, although it may have been the circumstances which forced men such as Symmachus to adopt a dogmatic stand in defense of tradition, they also were able to define and valorize this idea. As a result, the idea of the past with its traditional pagan religious components crystallized and was made relevant to succeeding generations of Christian aristocrats" (p. 364).

1403. *The 17th International Byzantine Congress: Abstracts of Short Papers.* Washington, D. C., August 3-8, Dumbarton Oaks/Georgetown University. Baltimore: U. S. National Committee for Byzantine Studies, 1986.

1404. Simpson, Jane. "Women and Asceticism in the Fourth Century: A Question of Interpretation." *Journal of Religious History* 15 (1988): 38-60.

1404.5. Stead, C. "Athanasius' Earliest Written Work." *Journal of Theological Studies* 39 (1988): 76-91.

1404.6. Talley, T. J. "Constantine and Christmas." *Studia Liturgica* 17 (1987): 191-197.

1405. Vegetius. *Military Institutions of the Romans.* Edited by T. R. Phillips. London: Greenwood Press, 1985. Vegetius may have written in the late fourth century or well along into the fifth. Historians are still debating this point. In any event, Vegetius had a dream which only a Roman traditionalist, and there were still many of them in those times, both Christian and pagan, could have concocted: the solution to Rome's problems was to restore the army in every way to the army of Augustus or Trajan.

1406. Whitby, Michael. *The Chronicon Paschale: From the Conversion of Constantine to Herclius' Victory Over Persia, 311-628 A. D.* Liverpool, England: Liverpool University Press,

1987. There is also now his translation, *Chronicon Paschale, 284-628* (1989).

1407. Wiedemann, Thomas. *Adults and Children in the Roman Empire.* New Haven: Yale University Press, 1989. Wiedemann offers an important discussion of the contrasting ways in which children were treated and viewed in the early Roman empire versus the later period under the influence of the Christian church.

1408. Williams, Rowan, ed. *The Making of Orthodoxy: Essays in Honour of Henry Chadwick.* New York: Cambridge University Press, 1989.

Subject Index

Numbers refer to entry numbers not page numbers. Saints are listed by name: look under Augustine rather than Saint Augustine. But for churches named after saints look under the full title - e.g., St. Peter's. This index should be used in conjunction with the table of contents: the entries are already organized by broad subject categories; the index will permit more specific retrieval within the larger categories. The names of emperors are in capital letters. Latin expressions are in italics.

Abinnaeus 91, 111
Adoratio purpurae 85, 306
Adrianople, battle of 150, 183, 251, 343, 344, 345, 347, 410, 499, 570, 685, 869, 872, 894, 901
Africa 67, 100, 101, 332, 757, 843, 953, 1056, 1066, 1116, 1119, 1317, 1329
Agentes in rebus 302. See also Secret Service.
Agriculture 657, 703
Alans 856
Alchemy 695
Alexandria 915, 1052, 1151
Allectus 159
Almsgiving 1230
Altar of Victory 211, 1015
Ambrose 5, 932, 1031, 1105, 1155, 1184, 1197, 1216, 1222, 1223, 1224, 1248, 1297, 1298, 1362, 1368
Ammianus Marcellinus 77, 115, 160, 188, 282, 345, 346, 356, 357, 387, 394, 412, 414, 417, 427, 438, 449, 450, 453, 481, 485, 489, 499, 500, 502, 504, 517, 519, 520, 523, 528, 536, 539, 545, 546, 547, 548, 552, 553, 558, 559, 562, 564, 565, 575, 576, 577, 584, 589, 590, 596, 597, 598, 603, 668, 673, 683,

712, 725, 736, 801, 810, 813, 814, 838, 1006, 1159, 1394, 1396.5
Amphorae 684
Anthony the Hermit 728, 1034, 1041, 1196, 1395.5
Antioch 21, 22, 45, 138, 191, 669, 683, 737, 748, 812, 813, 815, 942, 1296
Apollinarianism 1289
Arabs 890
Arbogast 167, 484
Architecture 42, 569, 708-851 *inter alia*
Arius and Arianism 691, 1032, 1036, 1040, 1057, 1108, 1139, 1141, 1142, 1145, 1148, 1149, 1153, 1174, 1177, 1180, 1181, 1193, 1201, 1226, 1227, 1228, 1240, 1251, 1253, 1283, 1286, 1287, 1288, 1289, 1292, 1364, 1386
Armenia 860, 862, 879
Arnobius 932, 1033, 1146, 1264
Art 1, 11, 708-853 *inter alia*
Asceticism 739, 915, 1062, 1106, 1164, 1175, 1404
Astronomy 668
Astrology 102, 599, 799
Athanaric 900
Athanasius 5, 728, 1034, 1035, 1037, 1038, 1041, 1053, 1054, 1057, 1093, 1100, 1114, 1152, 1173, 1196, 1207, 1208, 1227, 1252, 1279, 1303, 1307, 1370, 1392.5, 1404.5
Athens 60
Augustine 687, 708, 776, 1056, 1064, 1076, 1209, 1220, 1323, 1391
Aurelius Victor 446, 447, 454, 549, 557, 568, 588, 601, 602, 719, 720
Ausonius 422, 443, 456, 458, 508, 529, 606, 609, 696, 770
Autun 241

Bagaudae 325, 749, 842
Barbarians 39, 43, 193, 854-901 *inter alia*, 1270, 1392, 1399.5
Basil, Bishop of Caesarea 326, 687, 1050, 1088, 1095, 1109, 1110, 1111, 1140, 1166, 1266, 1280
Basilicas (Christian) 784, 846

Beards 716
Book illustrations 767, 849
Books 572
Brigands 262
Britain 18, 28, 33, 43, 65, 118, 159, 174, 184, 202, 307,
    328, 336, 349, 353, 354, 367, 368, 373, 374, 383,
    385, 398, 411, 675, 835, 859, 880, 888, 897, 956,
    1031, 1117, 1269
Bruttium 1387.5
Bureaucracy 235, 285, 286, 337
Bureaucratese 238

Caesares 87, 227
Caesaropapism 1340
Calendars 57, 58
Cappadocia 222, 326, 1106
CARAUSIUS 159, 328, 335
CARINUS 113
Carpi 861
CARUS 113
Caste System 773, 800
Cavalry 351, 362, 399, 403
Census records 774
Ceremonial 795
Chamberlain (office) 178
Children 794, 1407
Christian church 782, 1029-1387 *inter alia*
Christianity 907, 1029-1387 *inter alia*, 1395.6
Christians 858
Christmas 1404.6
Church buildings 742, 747, 753, 781, 784, 785, 786, 789,
    790, 792, 1301, 1340
Church of the Holy Sepulchre 740, 741
Circumcellions 1055, 1115
Cities 260, 383
City land 49
Civil Service 210
Civil Wars 293, 294, 295, 331
Claudian (poet) 90, 105, 153, 228, 229, 443, 473, 483, 1273
Climate 776

Clothing customs 733, 851
Codex 572
Coinage 309, 311, 389, 613-654
Coins 143, 144, 146, 147, 156, 219, 254, 882, 1388.4, 1395.3
Comes Sacrarum Largitionum 218
Comites 384
Comites Orientis 176
Commendabiles 188
Communism 1197
Consistorium Domini 195
CONSTANS 92, 97, 340, 1305, 1307
CONSTANTINE I 82, 93, 109, 128, 141, 142, 146, 147, 148, 158, 172, 183, 185, 186, 197, 203, 217, 231, 234, 266, 274, 284, 293, 304, 316, 327, 329, 334, 342, 375, 388, 392, 401, 402, 405, 492, 604, 605, 711, 858, 912, 945, 946, 982, 1045, 1046, 1077, 1103, 1147, 1150, 1167, 1260, 1293, 1294, 1295, 1300, 1302, 1306, 1307, 1310, 1314, 1321, 1326, 1327, 1328, 1331, 1332, 1336, 1341, 1349, 1350, 1351, 1353, 1373, 1375, 1381, 1382, 1384, 1388.5, 1389.8, 1390.2, 1390.2.1, 1393, 1397, 1401, 1402, 1404.6
Constantinople 74, 110, 193, 223, 490, 734, 802, 840, 841, 981, 1052, 1144, 1245, 1293, 1397
CONSTANTINUS 96, 97, 340
CONSTANTIUS CHLORUS 184
CONSTANTIUS II 78, 96, 97, 103, 116, 117, 170, 177, 181, 207, 225, 265, 295, 301, 312, 336, 340, 369, 405, 489, 565, 1307, 1332, 1364
Consulares Syriae (Governors of Syria) 176
Consuls 86, 243, 1388.6
Corn 683, 699
Cornuti 342
Corruption 46, 237, 256, 263
Council of Antioch 1080, 1092, 1307
Council of Chalcedon 1052, 1157
Council of Elvira 1187
Council of Nicaea 498, 1068, 1078, 1134, 1157, 1198, 1199, 1218, 1250, 1307
Council of Serdica 1040, 1154

Index 315

Council of Tyre 1100
Count of the Privy Purse 264
Counterfeiting 196
Court ceremony 234
Crispus 82, 198, 289
Curial class 222, 1130
Cyrenaica 53, 365

Dacia 61
Damasus, Bishop of Rome 1179, 1188, 1242, 1266
Dance 987
De re militari 506
De rebus bellicis 390, 416, 424, 487, 488, 608, 701
Dexippus of Athens 451, 462
Diet 745
DIOCLETIAN 1, 5, 24, 47, 76, 109, 112, 113, 139, 204, 296, 297, 306, 317, 338, 339, 341, 348, 352, 361, 388, 392, 402, 404, 583, 587, 627, 629, 630, 650, 652, 667, 671, 672, 688, 700, 738, 843, 866, 1046, 1306, 1308
Diodore of Tarsus 1138
Diplomacy 244
Divorce 714, 853
Doctors (medical) 660
Donatism 67, 1042, 1055, 1116, 1119, 1126, 1238
Dress 235
Drugs 695
Duces 384

Earthquakes 32, 56, 59, 733, 1394
Economy 655-707 *inter alia,* 1387.5
Edict of Galerius 1357, 1358
Edict of Milan 1299, 1320, 1347, 1358
Education 175, 270, 413-612 *inter alia*
Egeria 496, 497, 834, 852
Egypt 123, 133, 319, 320, 321, 322, 323, 352, 357, 659, 663, 664, 695, 700, 713, 714, 715, 724, 752, 775, 915, 949, 1002, 1037, 1106, 1236
Emperor (office) 127, 130, 220, 240, 259, 261, 1315, 1376, 1377

Emperors, Roman 194, 232, 233, 314
Epiphanius of Cyprus 1094
Epitome de Caesaribus 439
EUGENIUS 89, 168, 247, 283, 484
Eumenius of Autun 241, 467
Eunapius of Sardes 160, 287, 419, 433, 434, 435, 436, 437, 451, 452, 459, 460, 462, 463, 469, 476, 503, 558, 570, 579, 857
Eunomius 1108
Eunuchs 205, 206
Eusebius, Bishop of Caesarea 333, 479, 485, 492, 494, 501, 522, 551, 561, 744, 1043, 1044, 1047, 1048, 1049, 1071, 1083, 1084, 1091, 1101, 1102, 1104, 1113, 1132, 1133, 1189, 1200, 1201, 1250, 1258, 1259, 1260, 1261, 1267, 1274, 1276, 1277, 1306, 1308, 1311, 1323, 1328, 1375
Eusebius of Nicomedia 1250
Eustathius of Antioch 1079, 1240
Eutropius 114, 444, 445, 454

Families 832, 833
Famine 674
Faustus of Byzantium 860
Festus (historian) 425, 454, 495, 566, 586
Foederati 397
Frescoes 788

GALERIUS 269, 820, 821, 822, 1352, 1357
GALLIENUS 109, 403
GALLUS 116, 126, 565, 992, 993
Gaul 70, 71, 72, 325, 349, 355, 383, 511, 678, 749, 842, 850, 1249, 1344, 1401
Gelasius of Cyzicus 498
Gibbon, Edward 11, 69
Gildo, Count of Africa 90, 279
Gnosticism 695
Gold 680
Goths 405, 518, 733, 854, 865, 866, 878, 889, 891, 893, 894, 895, 896, 898, 900, 901, 902
Governor (office) 258

Index

Grafitti 34
Grand Chamberlain 124
GRATIAN 92, 154, 455, 526, 565
Grave digs 1393.5
Greece 963
Gregory Nazianzus 427, 1109, 1140, 1237, 1245, 1262, 1292
Gregory of Nyssa 1109, 1140, 1186, 1210

Helena Augusta 216
Hellenism 81
Heresy 1136
Hermes 949
Hillel 1023
Himerius (teacher) 94
Historia Augusta 413, 420, 422, 423, 427, 428, 430, 431, 432, 441, 442, 448, 513, 516, 544, 550, 590, 591, 592, 593, 594, 607, 651, 868, 1254
Historiography (ancient) 426, 515, 543, 989, 990, 1084, 1133, 1271
Holy men 11, 922, 933, 950, 970
Horoscopes 554
Hospitals 691
Huns 884
Hypatia 655

Iamblicus (philosopher) 913, 926, 947, 951, 952, 973, 1021, 1022, 1028
Illyricum 1137
Images and Christianity 197
Immortality 906
Inflation 704
Influence peddling 192
Imperial properties 240
Isis 904
Italy 49, 52

Jerome 228, 434, 482, 708, 777, 810, 1023, 1058, 1059, 1087, 1146, 1160, 1176, 1188, 1211, 1213, 1282
Jerusalem 740, 741, 744, 747, 1382

Jews 136, 903-1028 *inter alia*
John Cassian 1082, 1212
John Chrysostom 531, 733, 737, 964, 1051, 1074, 1087, 1089, 1107, 1144, 1158, 1163, 1170, 1171, 1206, 1285
John Malalas 542
John of Antioch 489
Jordanes 89, 168, 524
JOVIAN 565
Jovinian 1164
Judicial punishments 236
JULIAN 5, 11, 21, 22, 63, 81, 83, 87, 97, 107, 108, 116, 119, 126, 128, 129, 131, 134, 136, 137, 157, 160, 172, 175, 177, 179, 191, 192, 199, 201, 213, 214, 215, 221, 230, 242, 267, 272, 275, 276, 278, 281, 291, 298, 324, 375, 376, 394, 441, 442, 478, 489, 565, 628, 669, 683, 710, 725, 772, 903, 941, 942, 957, 984, 994, 1003, 1253, 1296, 1388.5, 1389.5, 1389.7, 1395.3, 1397
JUSTINIAN 941

Kourion 32, 59, 1394

Labarum 946
Lactantius 5, 268, 269, 492, 530, 1046, 1075, 1112, 1146, 1219, 1234, 1247, 1255, 1257, 1264, 1265, 1278, 1371
Laeti 397
Lausiac History 464, 466
Law 1, 317, 980
Legal system 204
Libanius 21, 45, 272, 281, 394, 435, 533, 812, 815, 918, 1163, 1217, 1396.6
Lice 851
LICINIUS 284, 293, 1046, 1320
Limes 365, 370
Limitanei 370
Literature 1, 413-612 *inter alia*
Liturgy (church) 1263, 1378

Index

Macrobius 482, 538
Macsen, dream of 248
Magic 911, 976, 1005
Magister 122
Magister Officiorum 120, 124
MAGNENTIUS 295, 336, 646
MAGNUS MAXIMUS 18, 173, 248, 294, 307, 1313
Mamertinus (panegyrist) 119, 556
Manichaeans 139, 738, 905, 920, 924, 953, 978, 979, 1012
Manpower shortage 24
Manufacturing 689
Marcellus of Ancyra 1039, 1040
Marriage 722, 853, 1390.3
Martin of Tours 1098, 1249
Martyrs 501, 1118, 1231
Marxist thought and Rome 705, 706
Maternus Cynegius 249
Mathematics 1398
Mauretania 547
Mavia, Queen of the Saracens 132
MAXENTIUS 401, 756
MAXIMIAN 112, 268, 271, 305, 313, 341
MAXIMIN DAIA 318, 962, 1320
MAXIMINUS 1365
Maximus of Byzantium 600
Medicine 655-707 *inter alia*
Melania the Elder 809
Meletian Schism 915, 1037, 1286
Merobaudes 294
Milan 223, 226, 781, 1222
Mildenhall Treasure 817, 818
Military matters 28, 277, 342-412, 1098, 1389
Milvian Bridge, Battle of 140, 147, 342, 395, 401, 1294, 1372
Mime 1390
Mining 1390.1
Mints 146, 219, 310, 635
Miracles 982, 1391
Misopogon 191
Mithraism 5

Moesia 62, 350
Monasteries and monasticism 745, 768, 1056, 1086, 1128, 1131, 1210, 1233, 1236, 1272, 1275, 1334
Monetary policy 613-654, 679
Monks 570, 1115, 1144, 1172, 1195, 1235, 1268
Morality 738
Mosaics 780, 835, 839
Music 758, 776, 1262
Mysticism 976, 1094

Nag Hammadi texts 1233
Names, proper 735
Naples 743
Nationalism 1151, 1152, 1387
Neoplatonism 907, 947, 976, 1007, 1011, 1024, 1205, 1251
Nicene Creed 1177, 1243
Nicomachus Flavianus 999
Nisibis 378
Notitia Dignitatum 330, 349, 364, 409, 415, 465, 581, 761, 762
Notitia Galliarum 1344
Novatianism 1143
NUMERIAN 113

Olympic games 748
Olympiodorus of Thebes 452, 462
Optatian Porfyry 532
Oration to the Saints (Constantine) 208, 1150
Orcades (province) 202
Oribasius 88
Orosius 510, 560
Ossius of Cordova 1080, 1324

Pacatus 173
Pachomius 534, 1131, 1221, 1236
Pacificism 1345, 1373
Paganism 903-1028 *inter alia*, 1333, 1335, 1347, 1361, 1390.2.1
Palaces 47
Palestine 44, 56, 697, 742, 836, 993, 1073, 1396.6

Palladas 1070
Palladius 464, 563, 574, 702, 1272
Palladius of Helenopolis 1161
Panegyrics 270, 271, 280, 540, 541, 556, 573, 585, 604, 930, 1402
Pannonia 180
Pantomine 1390
Papacy 1135, 1169, 1179, 1395
Papyri (source material) 418
Paschale Chronicle 480 1406
Patricians 244
Patriotism, civic 1359
Patrocinium 75
Paulinus of Nola 163, 443, 509, 1120, 1125, 1192, 1385
Peasant revolts 325
Peasants 749
Peregrinatio Egeriae 486
Persecution (religious) 954, 1014, 1118, 1308, 1312, 1313, 1325, 1329, 1337, 1338, 1352
Persia 115, 375, 394, 738, 858, 862, 863, 864, 867, 876, 1061
Peter Valvomeres 712
Philanthropia 943
Philosophy 903-1028 *inter alia*, 1075, 1089, 1095, 1140, 1398
Philostorgius 172, 1180
Pilgrimages 771
Poetry 610, 1400
Political thought 149, 1330, 1348
Pontifex Maximus 154
Population studies 723, 829, 830
Porphyry 914, 934, 961, 1027
Portraiture (imperial images) 145
Pottery 766
Praepositus 282
Praetaxtatus 1023
Praetorian prefects 209
Primary sources 157
Priscillianism 1069, 1081, 1175, 1313
Privita 261

Probus, Sextus Petronius 256
Proconsuls 100, 101
Procopius (usurper) 84, 565
Procurator 282
Propaganda, Christian 1165
Prosopography 3, 38, 735
Provincial assemblies 224
Prudentius 95, 443, 512, 567, 1244, 1396, 1399

Quaestor 200

Reform movements 1185
Religion 903-1028 *inter alia*
Rhetoric 527, 1158
Riots 760
Roads 404
Roman empire (east versus west) 35, 74, 121, 135
Romanus, Count of Africa 332
Rome (city) 74, 92, 193, 223, 299, 303, 383, 406, 814, 840, 841, 981
Rotundas 754
Rufinus of Aquileia 105, 561, 1214
Rufinus (secular writer) 578

St. Costanza (church) 789
St. Peter's Basilica 753, 755
Sallustius 1010
Samaritans 936
San Lorenzo (church) 781, 792
Saws, water-driven 696
Saxons 859
Scandinavia 855
Schism 1136, 1339
Scholae Palatinae 189, 190
Science 655-707 *inter alia*
Scotland 885
Secret Service 177, 300, 302
Senate (Rome) 73, 79, 274
Senators and senatorial class 102, 253, 764, 1063, 1129, 1363

Sexual mores 1065, 1069, 1187, 1203, 1239
Ships 54, 670
Sirmium 50, 51, 389
Silvanus 125
Silvia of Aquataine 1162
Slavery 66, 782, 798, 1096
Society 708-853 *inter alia*, 1182, 1183
Socrates (church historian) 1084, 1099
Sol (god) 143
Sorcery 732
Sossianus Hierocles 1308
Souda 600
Sozomen 1084, 1099
Spain 41, 325, 721
Stilicho 155
Suffragium 169, 192
Sulpicius Severus 514, 1030, 1249
Sun-Symbols 946
Symbolism (Christian) 653
Symmachus 5, 106, 165, 166, 252, 257, 443, 484, 726, 985, 1008, 1402.5
Synesius of Cyrene 101, 163, 164, 595, 733, 877, 1060, 1090, 1191, 1205
Synod of Antioch 1218
Syria 686, 1062, 1190, 1215, 1268

Tacitus (historian) 453
Taxes 133, 219, 337, 657, 673, 676, 678, 681, 686, 690, 700, 701, 875, 1332, 1388
Teachers 455, 458
Technology 66, 655-707 *inter alia*
Temples 1333, 1390.4
Theater 1390
Themistius 134, 491, 492, 493, 872, 930, 937, 938, 940, 944, 1019, 1022
Theodoret 1084
Theodosian Code 147, 288, 800, 910, 1316, 1356
THEODOSIUS I 155, 173, 182, 212, 245, 246, 249, 279, 280, 290, 512, 815, 1298, 1355, 1363
Theodosius (count) 118, 252

Thessalonica 144, 844, 845, 1137
Thrace 61, 62, 350
Time (concept of) 729, 1011
Tourism 771
Tradition 1402.5
Travel 733, 776
Treason 797
Trier 72, 788

Underwear 851

VALENS 7, 326, 344, 445, 565, 566, 1246, 1379
Valentia (province) 174, 202
VALENTINIAN I 5, 7, 73, 332, 389, 565
VALENTINIAN II 1297
VALENTINIAN III 167
Vandals 518
Vegetius 347, 366, 506, 1389, 1405
Velleius Paterculus 77
Verona List 104, 152
Vicars 80
Victory celebrations 255, 308
Villa estates 693, 743
Visigoths. See Goths or Barbarians.
Vitruvius 569

Walls (town) 355, 383, 406
War (attitude towards) 1318, 1343, 1345, 1346, 1373
Waterwheel 696, 707
Witchcraft 918
Women 655, 719, 739, 768, 827, 828, 1106, 1156, 1210, 1290, 1404

York 354

Zonaras 171, 172, 489, 1389.6
Zosimus 160, 292, 394, 419, 503, 507, 510, 558, 570, 571, 582, 1144